FOREWORD TO THE ENGLISH EDITION

History is marked by moments when an in[dividual or a] nation must take great risks if it wishes [...] moments are not summoned, and in fact they [...] options: seize it or let it go. The consequences [of a] decision are not clear, and the people who must decide at the[se] moments take a great responsibility upon themselves.

During the period covered in this book, there were many such moments, as well as many people who had to make decisions. Most of these moments were correctly exploited, and most of the decisions were good ones. Today we know what the situation would have been had we decided otherwise. At that time, we only sensed it. It was impossible to calculate everything in advance.

We, Slovenians, had long been inculcated with the notion that we were as a nation historically insignificant. We started to outgrow this thinking, however, when in issue 57 of the magazine *Nova Revija* in 1987 the first complete and modern programme of national formulation appeared. In this way we were prepared for the storms raised by the Serbian attempt to bring Yugoslavia under a strongly centralised communist state, or to create a Greater Serbia.

At the critical moment we did not waver. We were prepared for sacrifices, and for this reason there were very few. If we had wavered, as others have done elsewhere, we would have paid in blood. We were also prepared to negotiate, and we stood by the agreements we made. This was the only example of its kind in the entire crisis across the territory of the former Yugoslavia.

Now, in May 1994, Slovenia is an independent and internationally recognised country. It is engaged primarily with the problems of transition, the changeover from the communist system to parliamentary democracy, and from centrally planned socialism to a free market economy. Yet today we can see that neo-communist forces have retained the majority power, and that for the most part they continue to rule, eventhough under a different guise, in much the same way as before. These forces are also recognisable in the story of Slovenia's emancipation. These forces were not exactly overjoyed at Slovenian independence, but they could not stop it. The democratic forces in Slovenia are currently in a similar position to that of 1989, except that Yugoslavia and the Yugoslav Army, which then protected the communist system in Slovenia, are now no-existant. For this reason democracy has every chance of becoming permanently rooted here, on the sunny side of the Alps.

Ljubljana, May 1994

Janez Janša

Janez Janša

THE MAKING OF THE SLOVENIAN STATE 1988–1992

THE COLLAPSE OF YUGOSLAVIA

Založba Mladinska knjiga
Ljubljana 1994
MLADINSKA KNJIGA PUBLISHING HOUSE

Table of contents

In the period discussed in this book there were days when death came dangerously close. Many members of the Territorial Defence (TO) and the police force selflessly risked their lives in defence of their homeland and the protection of their loved ones.

Jernej Molan, Franc Uršič, Peter Petrič, Edvard Peperko, Vinko Repnik, Stanko Strašek, Robert Hvalc, Bojan Štumberger and Željko Ernoič sacrificed their lives, and to them I dedicate this book.

INTRODUCTION

No country in the world came into existence in the same way as Slovenia. The initiative for creating the Slovenian state goes back centuries, and many achievements of the past which have contributed to Slovenian statehood remain obscure or have not been given the attention they deserve. It is not the intention of this book to redress such wrongs.

This book does not describe the process of the creation of a state, but focuses on the final stages of that process and on the concerted efforts and energy invested in this undertaking over the last few years, particularly in 1991. Nothing has been given to us for free, but still, the price we paid was relatively low. In no more than a year, the decision of the plebiscite – an independent and sovereign Slovenia – was adopted and implemented. This was achieved through a great deal of hard work, struggle and negotiation. And this is what this book attempts to address.

On 26 December 1990, the results of the plebiscite were made public: the Slovenians had opted for independence and sovereignty. Six months later Slovenia effectively took control of its own territory. Then followed the attack by the Yugoslav Army, successful resistance, the Brioni Declaration and finally the withdrawal of the Yugoslav Army from Slovenia on 26 October. Even before that date all Slovenian soldiers had been released from the Yugoslav Army. Slovenia introduced its own currency and on 23 December 1991 the parliament adopted a new, modern – and Slovenia's first independent – Constitution. On 15 January, Slovenia was finally recognised by the international community.

Events in the last few years were coming to a head. The year 1991 will be written into world and Slovenian history as a turning point: this was the year when Slovenia successfully defended itself. The last days of June 1991 were decisive not merely for the fate of Slovenia, but also for the course the Yugoslav crisis would take. Had Slovenia been brought to its knees, and had the Yugoslav Army taken control of the border crossings and the airport, it would have proved that the right of a nation to self-determination could easily be denied by force. In view of the pronounced disinclination of the European Community and the USA towards the independence of individual republics, the use of force would have been considered an internal affair for internationally recognised Yugoslavia, and there would have been no Brioni agreements, no conference in The Hague, and no discussions on international recognition. If the Yugoslav Army had had its way in Slovenian territory, Croatia would not have been able to resist it over a longer period of time, and Macedonia and Bosnia would probably not even have tried.

In this event we would have been at the mercy of Ante Marković and the Army, who would supervise the borders and thus exercise complete control over the flow of goods, imports, exports and transit, and Slovenia would inevitably have remained within Yugoslavia. We would have been footing a quarter of the federal budget, sending our recruits thousands of kilometres away and paying the debts of others. This scenario would most likely have come true had we not in that fateful hour offered resistance. Yugoslavia as a unified state would, of course, not have survived. The international community, however, would most probably apply the Soviet model of a union of sovereign states to solve the Yugoslav crisis. And in that case, Slovenia would certainly have been much worse off.

Little time has passed and the story has barely been brought to a close. All the main protagonists are (luckily) still alive and they can tell their own story, or at least add a chapter of their own. However, more time must pass, and in some instances I shall leave out the details and my personal opinion which may come in handy in future years, when the naming of this or that person will no longer bear on day-to-day politics. My notes and documents contain many explanations which essentially differ from the generally accepted views.

However, this does not change the general impression, and above all the final, positive outcome which was achieved at a small price. States are born in blood. Slovenia was not spared this. However, thanks to those mentioned and those whose names do not appear in this book, we managed to substitute most of the blood for the sweat that was required in year-long preparations to safeguard the decisions of the plebiscite, and take the risk of setting up our own military sovereignty and obtaining the bargaining skills that were needed before, during and after the war. For the first time in Slovenian history, the great majority of Slovenians were aware of the importance of that moment; we seized the opportunity and saw it through to the end.

To describe only the most significant moments in the ten-day war I would need at least ten times more space and time than is available. I shall therefore relate only those events which left an indelible impression in my mind. Perhaps they were not even the most significant events that took place on any specific day.

I hope that more detailed accounts of the battles at Medvedjek, Šentilj, Holmec, Krakovski Gozd, Rožna Dolina, Brnik, Trzin, Prilepi, Kog, Gornja Radgona, Ormož and others will be forthcoming from the principal actors and participants of those events, and that they will complete the picture of the war for Slovenia. The intensity of events and their monitoring from the operations room rendered them more general and political than one might have wished. The enclosed chronology of the most important events will, I hope, serve as a basis for more detailed accounts of the period discussed. I will gratefully acknowledge any comments and suggestions, especially those concerning the exact dates in the chronology of events, some of which, despite checking, may still not be correct. Any comments will certainly be taken into account in the second, revised edition.

I do not pretend that my version of events as they are related in this book corresponds exactly to the perception of events entertained by the great majority of readers. While the documents are objective, the descriptions and analyses are necessarily subjective and reflect the views of all of us who were directly involved. Above all, they reflect my point of view. The book is written for all those who would like to have an insider's view of recent events, but the final judgement on it will of course be passed by the reader.

Ljubljana, April 1992   *Janez Janša*

FOREWORD
TO THE SECOND EDITION

The second edition remains essentially unchanged. I have made some corrections to dates, names of people and places. I would like to thank all those who came forward with more accurate facts and descriptions.

The documentary part of the book contains some (3) new pages. We have added reproductions of several magazine articles, published just before the declaration of independence, by well-known Slovenian authors, attesting to their negative stance towards this historical act by Slovenians. The positions they take express the true opinion of their authors. They were not persecuted for their writings. No one even had the will or energy to polemicise with them in those hectic, complicated times.

The photocopies have been added to avoid any pretence of ignorance on the part of their authors, and I affirm the following: In the spring of 1991, just before the proclamation of independence and at a most critical time in our history, the critics of Moves considered it morally acceptable to denounce our modest defence preparations as a "road to fascism" or "death trade", while today, when the major threat is behind us, it is considered immoral to mention these authors in a book, immoral to quote their own words and immoral for this book to see the light of day.

The would-be advocates of freedom of thought fail the test as soon as they encounter valid arguments, however soft-spoken they may be. Their virulent criticism and political intervention has shown that this is something they cannot stand. This book makes them face their own words, aberrations and traumas, which they refuse to recognise as their own. They sound somehow foreign to them, because the events that have taken place between then and now have rendered them false. "It wasn't quite like that," they say, but fail to explain what it was like. It all became even more unpleasant for them when General Milan Aksentijević publicly admitted that some of the delegates of the left-wing parties in the Slovenian Assembly had suggested to him that the Yugoslav Army tanks take Slovenia in a rapid swoop.

Some proponents of this policy seek refuge in well-known formulas, claiming that they were "objectively" in the right since without their opposition the decisions Slovenia would have adopted would have been too radical.

The democratic process has played an important role in decision-making. In practice those who opposed the decisions which prevailed later and were proved effective, often contributed to good resolutions, because their opposition required that the solutions be further elaborated and substanti-

11

ated. This is undeniably true. However, even though we acknowledge the substantial significance of this irreplaceable instrument of democracy and the good intentions of many who took a wrong stand at a crucial moment, one must always ask oneself what would have happened had the opposition prevailed. What would have happened to Slovenia had we not offered resistance at that critical moment? Could we have resisted had we agreed to the logic and the position taken by the Liberal Democratic Party, contending that "demilitarisation is the only viable way to secure Slovenian sovereignty?" Had we not adopted defensive laws and a budget? What would have happened to us if we had agreed to "endless negotiations", while we were being shot at, which is what happened in Bosnia? If we had promptly returned to the Yugoslav Army the confiscated arms and seized warehouses, in keeping with the Brioni Declaration? If we had been divided in adopting or rejecting the Brioni agreement?

In normal human relationships it is customary to admit mistakes. In politics, unfortunately, things are often done differently. Less than a year ago, there were many banners bearing the slogan: "Independent Slovenia? – No, thank you!" But we have extricated ourselves from the bloody mess of the Yugoslav crisis so promptly and relatively inexpensively, so that today, when eight months later we can say that the value of the Slovenian tolar is ten times that of the Serbian dinar, they shout: "We stood up as one man!"

If feigning ignorance was dangerous before independence, it is outright ridiculous today. The author of this book will continue to counter, verbally and through other democratic political means, the many simplified schemes and redeeming ideas which may eventually take us back to the point of departure, to the Balkan cauldron of strife where innocent people pay with their blood and their lives for the naivety of their politicians. But we can proceed with a much greater optimism, born from the recent experience in which the Slovenian nation demonstrated that it can achieve historical goals through democratic means and that it can tolerate a high degree of contention from within, without jeopardizing its existence in crucial moments.

Janez Janša

1. ARREST AND IMPRISONMENT

I was jolted out of sleep by the shrill sound of the doorbell. It was dawn, 31 May 1988. The next moment I sank back to sleep and a second later found myself staring at the faces of unknown, dark figures of men who told me to get dressed and come with them. They bundled me into a Renault 18 and took me to Cankarjeva 10 in Ljubljana, the office of the Mikro Ada company. Then followed a search of the company's premises and of my home, yielding several documents, which were confiscated, ranging from published articles to a copy of a so-called "classified military document". I was taken to the police headquarters at Prešernova street for a brief interrogation and then I was locked up at the detaining centre on Povšetova street. I was given a cell without a bed or daylight. The prison staff were impersonal, except for the interrogator who, it turned out later, was one of the chiefs of state security, Miran Frumen. He tried the sugar-coated approach (tell us everything and everything will be fine). When I was taken to Povšetova, all my personal effects, my belt and shoelaces, were taken away. In a few hours I was released from the cell, given back all the items on the list and taken for interrogation at Prešernova street. When they realised that I was still unperturbed, they repeated the procedure, but in the reverse order. They put me through the same procedure three times to soften me up. Slowly it began to dawn on me what they were after. The confiscated sheets of the military document constituted for them undeniable proof of guilt and Miran Frumen initially told me that the officer who had given me the document had already been arrested and that as far as they were concerned the case was closed. If I refused to confess I would be handed over to the Army, which would certainly know how to deal with the likes of me. They were more interested in the company I kept, the people I knew from the editorial board of Nova Revija and they particularly wanted to know the name of the person who had given me the shorthand minutes of the discussion which Milan Kučan had had at the Presidency of the CK ZKJ (Central Committee of the League of Communists of Yugoslavia) containing discussions of arrests and military repression. Miran Frumen told me that the party minutes were a state secret and that the punishment for their misappropriation was even more severe than for the misappropriation of a military document. It was obvious that they could not understand how the minutes, which had been given to only a handful of high-ranking Slovenian functionaries, had come into my possession; this was the disturbing element in the whole scenario, because it threatened to implicate persons who had no wish to become involved.

After unsuccessful interrogations and trips from Prešernova to Povšetova I went through the routine "prison treatment", i.e. I was photographed wearing an identification number on my chest, thoroughly fingerprinted and had my teeth counted. On 1 June, the unmarked vehicle of the state security service with which I was driven from one place to another did not turn on towards Prešernova, but rather towards Metelkova street, where the headquarters of the then Ljubljana Army District were located. Only when I was taken past the guards to the building with grated windows did I realise that Metelkova street in the middle of Ljubljana also housed a military prison. The UDBA (Yugoslav secret police) agents greeted the KOS (counter-intelligence) agents as if they were old friends. I was taken to the military prosecutor, Živko Mazić, and the military examining magistrate, Milan Ranić. The former was particularly pleased to see me, wringing his hands with delight. We had first met in 1985 when I was indicted for publishing an article in the investigative weekly Mladina in which I proposed that compulsory military service be reduced.

Their pleasure was dampened when I stated that I had no intention of giving any statements without the presence of my lawyer and before viewing the indictment documents.

I was then handed over to a second lieutenant who spoke Slovenian and whose approach was rather more decent than the behaviour displayed by the officers of the state security service over the previous few days. My clothes were taken away and two military policemen took me to cell No. 21, where I spent the next two months.

* * *

The military high command in Belgrade was disturbed and uneasy about the reports they were getting from the security agencies in Slovenia, which relayed the critical writings on the Yugoslav National Army (YNA) and the attempts to introduce a multi-party system in this northern republic. The last straw was the articles published in Mladina on Mamula's villa and especially the one entitled "The Night of the Long Knives". The reports by the 2nd District of the General Headquarters (GHQ) of the YNA to Mamula fingered Janez Janša, and his narrow circle of adherents, as the author of all "attacks against the YNA" and even against the Federal Secretary for Civil Defence. The reports indicated that the Slovenian people did not support such activity, but that the Slovenian republican bodies were too lenient in stamping out such harmful acts. Mamula decided that this had to stop. The 2nd District of the General Staff entrusted the implementation of this action to Colonel Aleksander Vasiljević,[1] who had excelled in the beginning of the eighties in KOS operations against the Albanians in Kosovo.

---

[1] Aleksander Vasiljević is today Major-General of KOS of the YNA General Staff.

On 25 March 1988 a meeting of the Military Council took place in Belgrade. At this meeting the process of liberalisation in Slovenia was officially labelled as anti-revolutionary. At the same time, the commander of the Ljubljana Army District, Svetozar Višnjić, who is now enjoying peaceful retirement in Slovenia, was given the task of establishing contacts with corresponding republican levels and ensuring the cooperation of the Slovenian repression apparatus in the event that the military prosecutor instituted, on the basis of assessments by the Military Council, criminal proceedings against the authors of certain articles on the YNA, if imprisonment pending trial was ordered and if a protest march took place. Despite the reservations expressed by some of those present at the Planica meeting[2] Višnjić willingly agreed to such cooperation. Consultations followed between the heads of the then Republic Secretariat for Internal Affairs and LJAO (Ljubljana military district), or the 2nd District of the GHQ of the YNA, at various levels, with Slovenian participants, such as Tomaž Ertl, Secretary of Internal Affairs, Ivan Eržen, head of the state security service and Štefan Tepeš, his assistant, operative Miran Frumen and many others, and YNA representatives, Colonel Aleksander Vasiljević, and Lt-Colonels Boško Mutić and Emin Malkoć plus their associates.

The state security service was given the task of finding a way to arrest and try me. In view of the interest with which the state security service had followed my activities ever since 1982, when preparations began for the Conference on Security and Defence within the then ZSMS (The Socialist Youth League of Slovenia), the task was by no means difficult. Options were analysed; secret searches were performed, but above all, and without the knowledge of the courts, my telephone was bugged. I suddenly became surrounded by many enthusiastic "followers" whose enthusiasm, however, was transparent and most of them already had records as informers. Agents of the SDV (state security service) hit the jackpot on 27 April 1988 when they broke into the premises of Mikro Ada at Cankarjeva 10 and discovered a tape recording of the 72nd session of the CK ZKJ with conversations about two arrests and two pages of a military document which were later used as corpus delicti in the trial staged against the Four, namely Ivan Borštnar, David Tasić, Franci Zavrl and Janez Janša. Prominent Slovenian politicians were immediately and with immense pleasure notified of the results of this search, and on 28 April 1988 the Council for the Protection of the Constitutional Order at the Presidency of the Socialist Republic of Slovenia was officially notified.[3] There were two options for the initiation of formal

---

[2] The meeting at Planica on 27 March 1988 between Svetozar Višnjić, Stane Dolanc, Tomaž Ertl, Milan Kučan and Ivan Eržen. The meeting was convened by Tomaž Ertl, who did not dare aprove the proposals relayed to him by Višnjić after the session of the Military Council. Ertl thought that key Slovenian politicians should be informed. The group that met at Planica was kept informed of all the events to the end of the trial against the Four.

[3] The Council for the Protection of Constitutional Order, as a part of the one-party political system, dealt primarily with the protection of the monopoly of the ruling party and the positions of individual politicians. In addition to Andrej Marinc, member of the Presidency of

charges (the tape recording as a state secret and the pages of the military document as a military secret) and the pros and cons of the two were weighed. Disclosure of a state secret called for harsher punishment, but the trial would have to be held in a civilian court. It was therefore decided, to the great satisfaction of the Slovenian representatives, that the charges of disclosure of a military secret would be pressed before a court martial, which meant exclusion of both the public and a civilian lawyer.

Two weeks after the secret search had been carried out at Mikro Ada, a delegation of the editorial staff of Mladina met with Peter Bekeš, Sonja Lokar and Slavko Soršak of CK ZKS. On this occasion the editors were strongly advised against publishing my editorials written for Mladina, the reason being that the issues which I addressed were important, but that my "method was not right".

The activities of the editors of Mladina were "covered" externally: telephones were bugged and conversations in the editorial office were recorded, as was all written communication, and internally through state security operatives working as editors, like the editor-in-chief Robert Botteri. Thus the plotters of the arrests could quite simply include the editors of Mladina in their plan of vengeance at Mamula's express request. Robert Botteri was a direct link with Miran Frumen and the information which he provided was considered first class, together with the information gathered by technical means. This was the decisive factor which led to the choice of Miran Frumen as the officer in charge of the entire operation, because he was considered very promising in the state security circles. He had managed to infiltrate the very "nest of anti-state activities", i.e. the editorial office of the influential weekly Mladina.

The security agencies of the YNA monitored closely the activities of Second Lt Ivan Borštner, who did not hide his "pro-Slovenian" stance and publicly spoke out in defence of the articles published in Nova Revija, and promoted Mladina. When he quit the League of Communists of Yugoslavia, control was tightened. When enough information had been gathered, the state security service worked out an operative plan for the arrests and colonel Aleksander Vasiljević, who arrived in Ljubljana on 20 May with a team of assistants, and Živko Mazić with his co-workers[4] worked out a plan of "direct processing" of those detained and the course the criminal proceedings would take. In order to make it as convincing as possible, especially in the event that the public exhibited an unusual interest in the proceedings, the two agencies, KOS and UDBA exchanged useful information and worked jointly on preparing and extending the indictments to include cooperation with foreign intelligence services and "enemy" émigré elements.

---

the Socialist Republic of Slovenia, who was then its chairman, all the other members were the most trusted party functionaries at the republican level.

[4] The YNA founded a formal headquarters for the implementation of the entire operation which was composed of Colonel Aleksander Vasiljević, Colonel Boško Mutić, Lt-Colonel Emin Malkoć, Colonel Živko Mazić and examining magistrate of the court martial, Milorad Vukosav.

A starting point for the extension of the indictment was the visit Igor Bavčar and I paid to the Slovenian hotel owner Vinko Levstik in Gorizia.

On Monday, 30 May 1988, a meeting took place at the headquarters of the KOS IX Army in the barracks on Metelkova street. The last details concerning the arrest were outlined. The meeting was chaired by Colonel Aleksander Vasiljević and assistant to the head of state security of the RSNZ (Republic interior secretariat) Štefan Tepeš. After the meeting the centre of the state security service for Ljubljana-City formed a team of operatives,[5] who were supposed to carry out the arrests and searches, and the dates and times for specific tasks were set. On the same day the details of the operation were officially briefed to Andrej Marinc, president of the Council for the Protection of the Constitutional Order at the Presidency of the SRS, and unofficially all Slovenian politicians in key positions in Ljubljana and Belgrade were also briefed. Tomaž Ertl briefed the Federal Secretariat for Internal Affairs, by telephone and in writing. Two letters containing the details were dispatched to Belgrade as early as 31 May and 2 June 1988.

* * *

The arrest came as a huge shock for me. Even though I had been aware for a long time that the (then) authorities viewed with displeasure our political activities and initiatives for a new Constitution, freedom of speech and expression, our wish to print Kavčič's Diary and Memoirs, our criticism of the YNA and the League of Communists and, in the months before the arrest, our open support of the multi-party system, neither my friends nor I expected such a sharp reaction. We were certain that we were risking prosecution with every article we published, but not before a court martial, and not from behind prison walls, without legal representation.

The 2 by 3-metre solitary cell, which cut me off from the external world, was in such sharp contrast to the revival of the political and calendar spring, from which I was plucked so suddenly that in the first week of my incarceration my reactions were purely instinctive. I felt sick at the sight of food and in five days I lost seven kilos. The light in my cell was turned on constantly, and the heat, because of the location of the cell and high outside temperatures, was unbearable. There was a draft in my narrow cell from under the door to the grated window and I suffered from a nasty cold and an earache.

I began to write short notes the very first day, just facts, because it was impossible to hide paper in the small cell. I managed to save these notes behind the dust cover of the Criminal Code with its foreword by Dr Bavcon, and carry them out of prison. They help me to account for almost every hour spent in the cell and later at the trial. Because this book is concerned with other events, I will leave a detailed description of these hours to a later time,

---

[5] The members of the group were Miran Frumen, Dragan Isajlović, Zvonko Hrastar, Franci Pivk and several dependable criminalists who were all collaborators of the state security service. The operation was monitored and directed at close range by Peter Prebil, chief of the centre of the state security service for Ljubljana-City.

when, I hope, I will have more free time. It is difficult to find words to describe the feelings I felt during my spiritual and physical isolation in the cell. When, after the ordeal of the trial, I discussed these feelings with others, my descriptions were only understood by those with a similar experience. I talked to many who, unfortunately, had spent much more time in solitary confinement than I had. In the beginning of my third week of solitary confinement, and at the time of the harshest interrogations, I wrote a poem, which always brings back the actual emotions I felt at the time.

NIGHT OF THE WITCHES

Justice strolls around
in uniform
Counting the thoughts
and gauging the souls

The rows are aligned
they march
with trimmed hearts
and measured souls

They wash the brains of excavated thoughts
pour courage into the difference

the howling crowds block out the sun
the streets are dusty and the plaster peels off
the green shutters lie unhinged
a single hinge squeals achingly
the garden fence is trampled

Fear assumes a shapeless form
you get to know time
they put a pair of scales in your head
and shine a light from behind

They tie weights on the feet of the day
and you are not allowed
to look back

With a torn parachute
they throw you from the plane

Meanwhile someone
rolls a rug in the living room
and breaks a piggy bank

18

They put a candle in the pumpkin
and acted out the night of the witches

A crow crows in the sky
There are pits in the forest
filled with injustices

transported on trucks
and bulldozed over

There are more and more of them
This is a technical problem
says the judge
we need new trucks
We are a humane society
we hide the injustices
it is criminal to alarm the public

(Military Prison, Ljubljana, June 1988)

The military prosecutor Živko Mazić and the examining magistrate Milan Ranić behaved like two hunters who have just shot a precious trophy on safari. As three days passed and I continued to demand legal representation and to be told what the charges against me were, their patience began to wear thin. The matter was then taken over by Colonel Aleksander Vasiljević who had moved to Ljubljana for this very purpose. Together with Emin Malkoć they came and went as they liked. They tried every tactic in the book. What they were least interested in was the military document which was the reason for my arrest. They wanted to know similar things to Frumen and company, immediately following my arrest, i.e. the names of my collaborators, my "connections" with Slovenian politicians, the names of secret organisations, etc. They were very keen on finding out how I had come into possession of the tape of the session of the Central Committee of the League of Communists of Yugoslavia, at which arrests in Slovenia were discussed. They pretended they already knew everything. After two or three attempts Aleksander Vasiljević came to the prison one evening in quite a good mood. After a somewhat lengthy introduction and my reiterated assurances that it was not difficult to obtain the tape, because every journalist in Ljubljana already had it,[6] he betrayed the reason for his good mood. He said that a tape had also

---

[6] This, of course, was not true since the tape was ferreted out by Igor Bavčar using his connections at the RK SZDL (Republic Conference of the Socialist Alliance of Working People), where one day it was pilfered from the slightly intoxicated Jože Smole. I handed a copy of it to Franci Zavrl on the evening of 26 April. This provided the basis for the article "The night of the long knives", which provoked the confiscation of Mladina.

19

been found in the locker of Jožef Školč, who was at the time doing his military service at Vrhnika and that experts had confirmed that the copies matched. All I had to do was tell them who had given it to me, the rest was quite clear. Of course, the punishment for disclosure of a state secret was much more severe than for disclosure of a military secret and I could be saved from spending fifteen years in prison only by cooperating with them and telling them the name of the person who had given me the tape. KOS were certain that it was someone with influence in Slovenian politics who acted in this way against Yugoslavia and against the Army.

Jožef Školč later said that he had shown the tape to a major to convince him that arrests were in fact discussed in Belgrade. The Army's official position was that this was a fabrication by Mladina.

Because he was unsuccessful with the tape, Aleksander Vasiljević changed the topic of conversation to "enemy émigré elements". He began with the visit Bavčar and I paid to Vinko Levstik in Gorizia in connection with Kavčič's Diary and Memoirs. I categorically denied that I had ever known anyone called Levstik. I was forced to drink great amounts of coffee, which gave me splitting headaches and made me apathetic. I suspected that I was being drugged so I refused to drink coffee, giving cardiac arrhythmia as an excuse.

Because the state security had precise information on our visit to Gorizia, Aleksander Vasiljević was enraged by my stubborn denials. I don't know how the whole thing would have turned out had the Committee not stirred such great public reaction. Thanks to the public outcry, no "harder" options were used to elicit a confession from me.

Milan Ranić, the examining magistrate once again took the initiative. I finally decided to be represented by a military lawyer. I had hoped that with his assistance I could lay my hands on the laws and other regulations which I would need for my defence. I was in luck. The lawyer's name was Mihajlo Krpan and I did not choose him myself. He was the only lawyer around – the only military counsel still available, but he dealt in matters related to construction. The other two lawyers had already been assigned to "represent" Ivan Borštner and David Tasić. Soon after our first meeting he admitted to me that he was not at all versed in criminal law and that my case did not bode well. After a few more consultations I found out that he was a Croatian national and that he had himself been court-martialled because of his pro--Russian tendencies. He was far from being an extremist. He admitted that after each session with me he had to report to KOS. Gradually he managed to tell me, even though he was strictly forbidden to do so, what was going on outside the prison walls and so I learned of the activities of the Committee. I talked him into meeting with Igor Bavčar and Drago Demšar. I didn't trust him implicitly, nor did Bavčar and Demšar. I know now that we did him a great injustice. Despite the mistrust, Drago Demšar gave him the necessary professional advice related to the defence. His information meant more than food to me. His greatest achievement was to smuggle into prison, a few days before the court session began, an issue of Mladina. He removed the cover page and I camouflaged it between the cover pages of KiH, one of the few magazines allowed in the prison. But the next time he tried he was caught. In the visiting room, as he was trying to slip me clippings from Delo under the table, we were not careful enough and the camera which recorded the conversations through the mirror, recorded some suspicious moves. He could thank the fact that there were only a few days left before the start of the trial and that public opinion was enraged, for not being put behind bars himself. However, our conversations à deux ended. We had managed to communicate in codes, or with pieces of paper, while pretending to write an appeal to the indictment or hearing. From that time on at least one military policeman was present in the room.

Because of public pressure the Yugoslav army speeded up the main trial. Captain Milan Ranić quickly patched up the minutes from the interrogations and edited the dates, but in his hurry forgot to carry out the prima facie evidence procedure. When this came to light during the trial, the president of the court martial, Colonel Đuro Vlaisavljević recalled him from Serbia, where he had been sent on a "well-deserved vacation". This, however, had no effect whatsoever on the judgment, but it caused problems for the senate who had to substantiate the sentence.

In the two months I spent in military prison, I never met Ivan Borštner or David Tasić, even though our cells were quite close together. The isolation was complete. At the time, Lance-Corporal Roman Leljak was also in prison and a few days before the trial ended, he called out to me in a hushed voice during a walk in the prison yard that he was working on my case and that he would pay me a visit one day. He kept his promise, and he described the background, or his work in KOS in his book Sam proti njim (Alone against Them).

Owing to the relatively valuable information which Mihajlo Krpan[7] relayed to me in the second half of July about the events and protests in Slovenia, I was well-prepared for the trial. My sister also managed to pass a newspaper clipping into my hands during a heavily-guarded visit. I was thoroughly searched after each visit but I managed to smuggle it into my cell, where I read the list of the incredible number of organisations which had joined the Committee.

The only unpleasant piece of news which came from the outside while the trial was still going on, was one I did not believe at first. Before the arrest I was one of three candidates for president of the ZSMS. I decided to run for president mostly because it would give me the possibility to speak in public and less so because I wanted to be president. In opposition to the other two candidates I had prepared a very radical manifesto summed up in the slogan "Struggle for Power", which meant political competition with the

---

[7] Mihajlo Krpan died in 1991 in Ljubljana. While lying in the military hospital we tried in vain to secure his transfer to the UKC (University Medical Center). Regrettably the vicious disease was terminal.

ruling party. After the arrest I was certain that the ZSMS would be tactful enough to put the elections on hold while one of the candidates was in prison. I counted on my candidacy to provide me with at least some protection. The second day of the trial, my legal counsel Krpan told me that the ZSMS had held the elections and that Jožef Školč had been elected president. In his first interview with Mladina after his election the new president commented on his "great success":

ERVIN HLADNIK-MILHARČIČ: Your election is burdened with the heaviest political mortgage of the last forty years. Janez Janša was one of the candidates for the post you are now assuming. How will you defend yourself against the charge that you have undermined him?

JOŽEF ŠKOLČ: Now I should find some grandiose political words to turn this question to my advantage. But nothing grandiose comes to mind. Speaking of charges and undermining, one could say that it does not come as a surprise that I was elected, considering the fact that I have twenty-five days to the completion of my military service and that uniforms are in fashion.[8]

Comrade Sonja Lokar had a lot to do with the election of Školč as president. She took part in the election conference of the ZSMS as an executive party secretary and painted a picture for the delegates of the horrendous problems that would arise were I to be elected.

After a few farcical days of the trial (Franci Zavrl made some good notes, which I hope he'll publish some day) the sentences were meted out: four years for Ivan Borštner, a year and a half for Franci Zavrl and I, and five months for David Tasić. We were released at the same time and after two months I was a free man. And I would not trade this freedom for anything in the world.

*   *   *

In jail and also later I often wondered why, of all people, they put me behind bars. It is true that I often wrote and published things which others only whispered. For example, Jaša Zlobec persuaded me in 1986 to write for the magazine Problemi a treatise on the equality of the Slovenian language in the YNA, in which I asked for nationally homogeneous units. He very obligingly procured the required literature and very generously advised me. Only when I came under fire from various quarters and the generals called for legal action against me, did I ask myself why Jaša, whose mastery of the Slovenian language is far better than mine, had not written the article himself.

Unmistakeably and in addition to Mamula's anger levelled at me, I was chosen because of my candidacy for presidency of the ZSMS, or perhaps because of my radical manifesto, as well as my editing and publishing work on Kavčič's Diary, the publication of which meant the moral and political

---

[8] Mladina, No. 31–32, 29 July 1988. He was interviewed by Ervin Hladnik-Milharčič.

demise of Andrej Marinc, Stane Dolanc, Mitja Ribičič and indirectly also of the party reformists, because they intended to use Kavčič in another way.

They were also influenced in their choice by the misconception that with my arrest and handing over to the YNA, Slovenian politicians would score a few points in Belgrade and prove to the Army that they were also fighting the counter-revolution. Until the trial the public was not informed about the threats of arrests in Slovenia. Had there been no behind-the-scenes moves, we would have found a way to make the whole matter public. As it was they used threats and formally confiscated Mladina, which wanted to write about this. And last but not least, some hero may have emerged from among the Slovenian politicians of that time to warn me of what was in store.

From the way the trial was conducted and some of the facts which came to light during the trial and later it has become absolutely clear that the victims were basically selected in advance with the consent of the Slovenian government. The following facts support this conclusion:

1. The military prosecutor Živko Mazić in his indictment and the court senate of the military court in the wording of the sentence merely copied the indictment which was formulated or copied by state security agents Dragan Isajlović and Zvonko Hrastar in the very centre of Ljubljana in Prešernova or Beethovnova streets.

2. The so-called experts – court experts of the RSNZ – also worked out a professional opinion on the handwriting found on an issue of Narodna Armija (National Army – NA) which the state security service confiscated at the time of my arrest. On the same issue of NA someone wrote in block letters JANŠA. While we were in detention at Metelkova, the secret military police sent this issue of Narodna Armija and the piece of paper on which David Tasić was forced to write Janša several times to the Republic Secretariat of Internal Affairs and asked them for their opinion on whether the handwriting was identical. Even though the handwriting was obviously not identical – and I also know beyond a shadow of the doubt that Tasić did not write my name on Narodna Armija – so-called "impartial court experts" of the Slovenian state security lost no time in answering that the handwriting on the magazine was indeed that of Tasić.

3. These "experts" of the Slovenian Republic Secretariat of Internal Affairs had put together a comprehensive study, proving for the court that there was absolutely no doubt that the photocopy in question was underlined with the green felt pen from my desk, which is a ridiculous charge considering that there must have been thousands of green felt pens of exactly the same colour. The issue of underlining was all the more contentious because the National Assembly Commission found out that the State Security agents had performed an illegal search, that is, they broke into Mikro Ada a month prior to my arrest and prior to the officially warranted search. Considering the zeal with which they tried to argue that the passages were underlined with my felt pen, the suspicion that Miran Frumen and Dragan Isajlović had underlined the photocopy in question during the secret break-in into Mikro Ada is well--founded. This also explains why the premises were not thoroughly searched

for fingerprints. The fact is that I did not underline the passages on the photocopy and neither did Franci Zavrl, who gave it to me.[9]

4. That my handing over to the military authorities had been planned in advance is also confirmed by the fact that the appeal against police detention, which I wrote at Povšetova on the evening of 31 May, was immediately relayed to the military court, which did not reply within the legally stipulated period of time.

The Commission set up by the Assembly with a view to clarifying the background of the trial revealed some facts in its report of 8 June 1989 which were of crucial significance for the elucidation of events leading to the trial or the political grounds for the trial.

In its report, the Commission wrote on page 3 that the state security service had already performed an illegal search (break-in) in Mikro Ada on 27 April and that it had immediately notified the presidency of the Central Committee of the League of Communists of Slovenia of the results of the investigation (Kučan's tape) and the presidency of the SRS, or Marinc's Council.

The public, the Committee, and even we, the prisoners, had been convinced until the report was made by the Republic commission that the events had occurred without the knowledge of the liberal section of Slovenian political circles and even behind their backs. This was the impression – and more than just an impression – given by Milan Kučan and Janez Stanovnik in conversations recorded by Igor Bavčar. The news that the state security service, which had performed an illegal search at Mikro Ada, had also immediately came to attention of the presidency of the SRS and the presidency of the CK ZKS, and thus also Milan Kučan and Janez Stanovnik, came out of the blue. Our surprise was complete and some people could not believe that the most prominent Slovenian politicians continued to deny months after the arrests were made that this was a politically-motivated trial. They contended that it had been turned into a political issue due to the reactions it provoked.

In an interview for The New York Times (9.6.1989) given immediately after Borštner's, Tasić's and my own arrest, Jože Smole stated that "in our case this was not a political trial, but rather the theft of a military document on defence preparations against an external enemy".[10] At the session of the presidency of the RK SZDL (The Republic Committee of the Socialist Alliance of Working People), on 14 June 1988, he contended that the claim that the arrests were a political settling of accounts was pure insinuation.

Andrej Marinc assured everyone at the meeting of the Assembly of the

---

[9] The photocopy was in fact quite easily available in Ljubljana. It was in the hands of, or at least seen by many later members of the collegium of the Committee. When the arrests began, people burned such documents in panic.

[10] The portion of the military document discovered in my home and in the home of David Tasić did not, of course, discuss preparations against the threat of an outside enemy. The reader can satisfy himself of this by reading the facsimile of the document appearing in this book.

SRS on 16 June 1988 that the procedure followed by State Security during the search and the arrests was within the law.

The police did not replace Tomaž Ertl, who carried out the procedure, but Milan Domadenik, who objected to some of the methods they intended to use. In their dealings with the Committee, Milan Kučan and Janez Stanovnik protected Ertl, who, in turn, took responsibility for the events. All crucial information and some of the threads of the trial were also in the hands of the man in the background, Stane Dolanc. Through his contacts with the top echelons of power in the YNA and his adherents among Slovenian politicians he was informed of the events on an ongoing basis, and he personally intervened in some.

The public demands for clarification of the background to the trial were skilfully channelled by the authorities into the Assembly and a group of delegates was assigned to study the events leading to the arrests for over a year. Aleksander Ravnikar, the vice-president of the Assembly was appointed president of this working group, but he spent more time protecting the state security than studying the background. Assigned to the post of president of the Commission for Supervision of state security was Slavko Soršak, a party man in charge of police matters. Soršak personally (!!!) checked the archives in connection with the Mladost operation and found that the procedure followed was in order, which he duly reported to the Commission. It is obvious that the results that were achieved by the Commission were mostly the work of Matevž Krivic and Lovro Šturm, who were included in the working group thanks to public pressure.

After the elections a new commission was founded which was supposed to finish the work of the former Commission, but in fact achieved even less. Other events came to the forefront, such as independence and war. Even though dust has slowly settled on these official reports, several things still remain to be clarified. We know what the motives were, who the victims and the executioners were: those who were actively involved and those who had enough power to stop the course of events, but merely said that due legal course should be followed. Due legal course in a state where there was no rule of law, and where military courts tried civilians without legal representation or the presence of the public.

2. COMMITTEE FOR THE PROTECTION OF HUMAN RIGHTS

Immediately after my arrest my friends gathered at the premises of Mikro Ada at Cankarjeva 10 and founded the Committee for the Protection of the Rights of Janez Janša and renamed it, after the arrests of Ivan Borštner and David Tasić, the Committee for the Protection of Human Rights, or the Committee, as it was popularly referred to.[1] No one knew how things would develop, so great importance was attached to the first steps of the Committee. In addition to the courage which was required to found the Committee – since further repressive measures by the authorities could not be discounted – all its members needed a large degree of ingenuity. The Committee managed to do something which was a first in the history of Slovenia: it organised a civil society, despite the differences within it, in order to attain a common goal – the protection of human rights. This would not have been possible had the Committee not used all the avenues of non-violent action at least in the first stage of its activities. The openness of some of the media was amazing, and Mladina's open and insightful articles invited such visibility that many people who read it only at that time still consider it as the official organ of the Committee.

Even though I know a great deal about the first two months of the operation of the Committee, i.e. until my release from military prison, I was not directly involved in those events. It would be wrong to try and describe the mood of the pioneering days of the Committee or the climax of the Slovenian spring, as those summer months of 1988 were also called. People still tell me that in the summer of 1988 at Roška street they talked openly and freely for the first time in many decades, even though they did not know one another, and offered each other cigarettes and drinks; in short, they felt like members of the same community which after a long time suddenly realised it existed – a behaviour which was in complete opposition to what one would expect in this extremely tense situation. There was no fear or violence, only a sense of belonging and solidarity. Human energy was amassed, as it had been previously in Czechoslovakia and East Germany, which in a few weeks changed the political system.

---

[1] The collegium of the Committee numbered over 30 members: Igor Bavčar, Bojan Koriska, Igor Omerza, Alenka Puhar, Gregor Tomc, Spomenka Hribar, Lojze Peterle, Dušan Keber, Franc Zagožen, Ali Žardin, Slavoj Žižek, Srečo Kirn, Pavle Gantar, France Bučar, Mile Šetinc, Matevž Krivic, Anton Stres, Rastko Močnik, Dare Valič, Marko Hren, Boris Cavazza, Alojz Križman, Viktor Blažič, Rado Riha, Braco Rotar, Tomaž Mastnak, Drago Demšar, Veno Taufer, Igor Vidmar, Tone Remc, Franko Juri, Bojan Fink.

Over a hundred thousand individual members and over a thousand different organisations signed up in the Committee. The Writers Association organised unforgettable protest evenings which were a monumental reflection of the resistance of artists and intellectuals against the imminent repression. In Slovenian churches prayers were being said for us. Support came from organisations in every corner of the world, particularly from our fellow Slovenians living abroad. I leave it to those who were involved directly to provide more detailed descriptions of the emotions and impressions which they experienced during the gathering at Kongresni Trg when more or less spontaneously 50,000 people gathered in Ljubljana. I only wish I had been there as well. After this gathering, when the prison investigators inadvertently mentioned the word Committee, their voices betrayed a slight tremor. Emin Malkoć forgot himself once and began persuading everyone that "that group of losers in the Committee has no influence on the honest Slovenian nation". He soon remembered that I didn't know what he was talking about and fell silent. From similar fragments of conversation I concluded that something extraordinary was happening outside and that there existed an organisation which was the cause of great worry for the army. I noticed a great difference between the impression which these events made on the officers of KOS who lived in Slovenia and those who came from Belgrade. Even though their assessments were the same, the facial expressions and the tone of voice were quite different when they commented on the atmosphere in Slovenia during the interrogations. KOS members from Belgrade, and particularly Colonel Aleksander Vasiljević, felt that an all-out rebellion in Slovenia would not represent a problem for the YNA and Yugoslavia, since the Slovenians represented a mere tenth of the population of the country, had no arms and lacked military spirit. It was obvious that some political structures in Belgrade wished to pacify Slovenia according to the Kosovo model. The KOS members living in Slovenia, with few exceptions, were given the cold shoulder by Slovenians. They resented bitterly their neighbours who began to ignore them and were hurt by the writings in the newspapers, which even though far from providing a scathing analysis, were already too critical for their taste, accustomed as they were to praise and boot-licking.

*   *   *

After the trial and our release, Igor Bavčar briefed me in detail about everything that had taken place during my absence in several lengthy conversations. Many things became clearer after I had begun to attend the sessions of the Committee and saw with my own eyes the persons who foiled the plans of Admiral Mamula and his Slovenian lackeys. The collegium of the Committee brought together quite different people, many of whom I knew personally, and many of whom I now met for the first time. As the memory of the trial faded, their differences began to emerge. The founding of the Committee, the great membership, its informal operation, the gathering at

Kongresni Trg and the acquisition of the status of interlocutor with some levels of the Slovenian authorities altered the political scene in Slovenia. Some members of the Committee were aware of this, while others were afraid, reiterating that they had joined up only to help the Four and not to meddle in dirty politics; still others did not see beyond the surface of events. Among those who correctly assessed the changes in the political scene were France Bučar and Spomenka Hribar. Spomenka continued to include on the agenda the issue of the political engagement of the Committee. She believed that if this were not done all the fruit would be harvested by the official Slovenian political authorities even though they participated at least in part in the repression. And that is exactly what happened. Just before I was arrested for a second time and taken into custody, on 5 May 1989, Igor Bavčar, Slavoj Žižek, Marjan Hvastja (strike committee of locomotive engineers) Tone Remec and I, as a member of the Committee Delegation, were in a meeting with Milan Kučan, the then president of the CK ZKS. At the meeting Kučan calmly disregarded, without the slightest worry, the announcement of action which the Committee would take if the Four had to serve their prison terms, and uttered a sentence which completely sobered me. He said: "At the end we will balance the books and we will see who is in the black." It had become perfectly clear to me that we were going to serve at least some of the prison sentence which had been handed down by the court martial and that the official Slovenian political circles were simply looking for the most appropriate way to carry it out.

It was also clear why this was so. The Committee maintained public pressure through the long months of informal operations, which did not bring tangible results. The Assembly Commission, which was given the task of investigating the trial and was headed by Aleksander Ravnikar, did not complete its task despite the outstanding efforts of Dr Krivic and Dr Šturm. The president of the Commission and several delegates, mostly from the ranks of the monopolistic ZKS, frustrated, to the point of intolerableness, the efforts by other members which led to the disclosure of the involvement in the arrests of the local authorities and particularly of prominent func-tionaries. This was a time when the philosophy of class struggle was still alive in Slovenia. Mitja Ribičič, one of the most prominent party functionaries in Slovenia, warned against elitism and clericalism as late as October 1989:

"I have already alluded to clericalism; however, I believe that an even greater danger comes from something Kidrič called elitism. In this approach the intellectuals are considered to be a kind of salt of the Slovenian nation, and would govern in the name of the Slovenian nation and the working class. It fails to observe that the working class is in fact the elite of the Slovenian nation."[2]

We must admit that the Slovenian party authorities, which certainly had at their disposal all the required instruments, acted with great astuteness. They kept postponing the imposition of the sentence and thus weakened the

[2] Mitja Ribičič, Danas Magazine, 3 October 1989

political momentum of the Committee. At the same time members of the Slovenian secret police were busy spreading rumours and lies about certain members of the collegium and about the Four and in this way tried to diminish their prestige in the public eye. And this was also done by party politicians. Lev Kreft even went so far as to explain, during his trips through Yugoslavia, that the Four had discredited themselves. Some overzealous party commentators also went too far. In the TV News of 21 April 1989 Nina Komparič directly accused the Committee of following in the footsteps of Šolević, and also insinuated that the Committee favoured Milošević-style politics. The presidency of the RK SZDL and ZKS and their prominent functionaries promised, while the trial was still going on, that they would not interfere. However, they would initiate a thorough analysis once the verdict was final. The verdict had been final for quite some time when, instead of a thorough analysis, the same functionaries demanded that the verdict be respected since ours was a state governed by the rule of law.

After first making the mistake of treating the Committee too lightly, the authorities adopted a much harsher attitude and regarded it as opposition. They consulted the Committee, made promises, and exploited it to their advantage wherever possible. The Committee, however, had not yet decided on its identity: whether it was the opposition or not. Many were delighted simply because the authorities showed a willingness to talk.

In autumn 1988 the then president of the presidency of the SRS, Janez Stanovnik, professed that the Committee was the only body to have salvaged the liberalisation in Slovenia. Things changed, however, when Milan Kučan retorted that this was a struggle for power. The campaign continued as my prison term drew close. Before I was arrested for a second time, the Committee was accused by party politicians and the regime's media of provoking a state of emergency in Slovenia. The party authorities were even more worried when a second gathering of the Committee took place on 21 November 1988 and was attended, despite the very bad weather (the snow rendered the event even more memorable), by more than 10,000 people. I also spoke at this meeting, and said:

"The slogan of today's meeting embraces all the current topical political issues. Only a nation which is on the one hand sovereign and on the other hand allows a diversity of opinion on all the fundamental social issues can play a positive historical role in assuring living conditions fitting for a human being. But this must be determined by man himself.

Competition of ideas and goods is the basic condition for development. There is no development without one or the other, and economic reform without political change is doomed to failure. To claim that the present constitutional changes should be adopted because of progressive economic solutions is to use political ammunition without the backing of history and science. If some believe that we should accept them because of the balance of power in Yugoslavia, they should be free to say so. I am certain that their sincerity will warrant greater understanding than the pronouncements of those who pad out the truth with words which they themselves do not believe.

One should not barter with sovereignty. Sovereignty represents control of one's own territory and the rule of one's own people. That authority whose single competence is to imprison its citizens who have been tried and judged by others, in a foreign language, is not sovereign. We can speak of a partial or restricted sovereignty, but not of sovereignty as such.

National and other political passions in Yugoslavia are about to reach boiling point. People gather at protest marches in support of a variety of ideas. This is their incontestable right for as long as meetings are held in the national territory. We may polemicise with the content and the slogans displayed at the gatherings, but one cannot accede to the thesis that the political gatherings in Serbia champion Yugoslavia, while the meetings of Albanians in Priština are irredentist, and those in Ljubljana counter- -revolutionary. The slogan "Powerful Serbia – Powerful Yugoslavia" is just as backward as the slogan "Weak Serbia – Strong Yugoslavia". Yugoslavia will be strong when all her nations are strong, when each nation is free to live as it wishes and, last but not least, as it is able to live. Yugoslavia will be strong when it is able to live and develop without loans and when each of its republics is able to assure a decent lifestyle for its citizens.

If our views of some basic issues in Yugoslavia differ, we must admit the differences. Unification at any cost creates only apparent unity, under whose mantle conflicts fester. The solution is simple. Each nation should decide for itself how to implement its sovereignty and statehood. This decision may not be taken once and for all, on behalf of future generations. Who can appropriate this right? Nobody can sell it in advance. This is the essence of each and every national issue and every instance of re-inventing the wheel only prolongs the agony."

By including the above portion of my speech I wanted to emphasise its political content, and the quite open advocacy of the right to self-determination of a nation. Some members of the collegium of the Committee did not like my speech, because it was too politically charged. But the speeches by some other speakers, such as Rudi Šeliga, Ivan Oman, and Igor Bavčar were also political. The meeting itself was political and it is too bad that the Committee was not able to turn this to its advantage.

The Committee in principle insisted on the basic points. It tackled politics – even though it could have capitalised on such and similar events politically – only when it concerned its primary aim – the protection of human rights. This in politics always has fateful consequences. If one has political ambitions but does not fully exploit the space thus created, all the effort is futile.

A final test of strength occurred at the time of my second arrest, on 5 May 1989. Despite a repeat gathering at the square of Kongresni Trg three days later, which was formally under the auspices of the ZSMS, and despite public protest, we were stuck in prison. What we were concerned with was only a more comfortable serving of the sentence and a reduced sentence which the authorities were kind enough to grant us.

The political scene in Slovenia would have been unmistakeably different in the first elections had the Committee formally and factually become the opposition and had it formed a democratic forum or any other similar organisation. The collegium of the Committee, which represented a remarkable intellectual and operative political power, divided into three parties, but the Roška events did not quite lose their impact. The more or less covert expectations which had been born there were divided prior to the election, between Demos and the ZSMS. At many pre-election gatherings, in discussions and interviews, whether in Ljubljana, Zasavje, Štajerska, or the Coast, I had a distinct feeling that the people were aware that Roška was not only a symbol of freedom for four individuals, but that it also represented the democratic change which we had so intensely desired.

Slovenia would have marched more decisively into the parliamentary system had the debate in the Committee on the relationship between the civil society and state and on the differences in this relationship in a single-and multi-party system been brought to its conclusion. Perhaps this would have meant fewer parties today, which would certainly be beneficial for Slovenia.

3. FROM THE ALTERNATIVE TO THE OPPOSITION AND THEN TO ELECTION

In January 1989, when the Slovenian Democratic Alliance (SDZ) was being founded, it was already clear that the Committee for the Protection of Human Rights was not going to transform into a political organisation in the form of a democratic or national forum. There were no signs coming from the Socialist Youth League of Slovenia (ZSMS) that it was going to change from a professional interest group into a political party. The ZSMS did not know what it was going to do with itself at that time. Even in November 1989, at the congress it held in Portorož, everything seemed to end as a compromise, after which any normal person, even at his best, could still not perceive whether the ZSMS was from now on to be a political party or a socio-political organisation. It was neither one nor the other, and both at the same time. The ZSMS crossed the Rubicon only after it had ceased to exist.

I had direct encounters with the ZSMS. I worked in this organisation for a number of years and even ran for leading posts twice. Both times I was removed from the candidacy by exterior forces, in the autumn of 1984 because of the intervention of the communist party, and in the spring of 1988 by simply being arrested. After both these interventions the ZSMS became even more radical in its demands, but at the head of this radicalism were those who stayed in this organisation, or rather those who were not removed. The ZSMS, in contrast with socio-political organisations, supported the operation of the Committee for the Protection of Human Rights. It passed on the demands of this Committee to the Assembly. With the prohibition of the rally on 8 May 1989 it made a good move and called for a public meeting. Without doubt we can state quite clearly that it contributed strongly to the diversification of the political scene in Slovenia. And then it suddenly stopped. It could have proclaimed itself a party before the autumn of 1989. If it had done so, it would have gathered a mass of intellectual potential and a membership which moved to other parties. The external situation at that time already permitted transformation into parties, while the internal did not.

The ZSMS carried all that old baggage within itself that was so typical of marginal socio-political organisations during socialist self-management; an ineffective organisation, a poor apparatus, and a dependence on Big Brother. All this was nicely expressed by France Popit, who, in a lecture in 1984, stated: "The Party founded the ZSMS and can also abolish it if it deems it necessary." Developments then turned in another direction, the Party did not abolish the ZSMS but it abolished Popit and, in so doing, lost control of the ZSMS to a great measure.

It became something in-between. If the Communist Party and Socialist League still constituted the regime before the acceptance of the electoral legislation in December 1989, and Demos was the extra-parliamentary opposition, then the ZSMS was a kind of parliamentary opposition in a single-party system, for, according to the old legislation, it still had some delegate seats reserved for it in the Republic Assembly and its delegates in the last years before the elections indeed promoted, at least in the Republic Assembly, the views of the opposition. But the ZSMS held the privileged position of an old socio-political organisation, with about 160 employees, financed from the budget, good salaries, money for promotion, formal and informal connections with the government, delegates in the Assembly, in the Committees for the Slovenian People's Defence (SLO) and in the DS (Labour Council), as well as in social councils. The majority of the leading ZSMS officials, with their president Školč in the forefront, were also members of the League of Communists of Slovenia (ZKS) almost up to the elections. None of the existing team of the ZSMS at that time felt any real repercussions of the breakthroughs which this organisation actually made from 1982 to 1990. None of them lost their jobs, none of them were politically or legally persecuted or removed from the media. Those that did feel this were removed from organisation. They worked politically elsewhere, among the Greens, the Social Democrats, in the SDZ and then later in the Independent List.

The fate of the long-term official organ of the ZSMS, "Mladina", was also connected with these consequences, creeping out of anonymity during the period of liberal breakthroughs and above all during the trial against the Four. The success of Mladina conceals tough political as well as other battles, confiscations, periods of unemployment, court proceedings, threats, difficulties at work and more, behind the scenes.

*   *   *

During the period when the Committee had a big influence on the public, the government attempted to reduce the political significance of this independent organisation in a number of ways. The SZDL (Socialist Association of Working People) founded a Council for the Protection of Human Rights which, besides its beneficial work, attempted above all to convince ordinary humans of something incomprehensible, that official politics was also concerned with human rights. The president of the SZDL, Jože Smole, after having talks with the political leadership, began to summon all kinds of round tables with alternative groups and organisations, and every society which so desired could come to these meetings. They were to give an impression that the regime was holding discussions with the opposition. But the sole true joint appearance of the regime and the alternatives was a congress in Cankarjev Dom during the miners' strike. Smole's coordination, as this waste of time was called by some, seriously broke down when it attempted to formulate a joint statement regarding key points of the national programme. The official policies composed the Basic Bill,[1] which still visualised Slovenia within the framework of Yugoslavia, while the most aware sections of the alternative movements[2] were given the May Declaration[3] to sign. This Declaration envisaged the future in the formation of an independent Slovenian state. Here the basic difference between the regime and the emerging opposition was clearly shown. The Central Committee of the ZKS, under Kučan's leadership, stood decisively against the May Declaration. Viktor Žakelj, a politician in the expiring SZDL, continued to publicly defend the "legitimacy of non-party pluralism".

Meetings held at the SZDL were practically brought to an end by Jože Pučnik, who, unburdened with sentimentality, discovered that all this made no sense, for the regime would hold talks indefinitely, but would not come to terms with or relent in anything. Possibly everything could have lasted somewhat longer if Jože Smole had not been so infinitely clumsy in conducting these meetings, such that sometimes we were quite amused when he gauchely attempted to steer discussions to his own advantage.

In the autumn of 1989 the organisations and groups that were becoming the opposition to the ruling regime signed, after a difficult coordination process, a demand for free elections. This demand was called What Kind of Elections Do We Want? Relatively diffuse, frequently because of banal differences in mutual disputes, the so-called alternative crossed the threshold into true politics and delivered its key demand, which was that free elections be held as soon as possible. Many claimed that they were already satisfied with the Polish system, according to which the Communist Party would hold on to its majority in the new Assembly, but the awareness predominated that everything had to be demanded and that as much as possible had to be gained. The regime was prepared for the demand for elections and relented relatively quickly.

The demand for free elections was the last joint document which was signed by nearly all the "alternatives". After this, the existing monopoly regime succeeded, by leaning on the aparatchiks[4] in the then existing ZSMS, to deepen the rift in the alternative and thus created an opposition which, after the elections, despite the great efforts of the majority of parties in Demos, could not compose a joint government from representatives of the new political forces.

---

[1] The Basic Bill was first signed by some parties which later appeared within Demos.

[2] The May Declaration was created within a circle which even then most clearly expressed the desire for an independent Slovenian state (Nova Revija, Društvo Pisateljev, Slovenska Demokratična Zveza).

[3] The May Declaration was publicly read at a protest meeting at Kongresni Trg square after my second arrest on 8 May 1989.

[4] At that time the ZSMS was already in the hands of young professionals, mostly without having a full secondary school education and without any work or life experiences outside of the apparatus. Only this can explain their clinging to budget financing and to some incomprehensible compromises made to the detriment of their own political profile.

The Assembly of the SRS passed at the end of 1989 the Law on Political Association and the Law on Elections. Parties could register legally. In addition to Nova Revija, which theoretically initiated the demand for democracy and Slovenian statehood, and the Committee, which expanded the arena of political activities, those organisations which had already before the acceptance of the law announced themselves as parties, and acted as the opposition, in practice changed the most. The law in essence only legalised the existing legitimate state. Great credit goes to those who like – France Tomšič – at a time when this was still a counter-revolution, dared to publicly state: "We shall found a party which will not be in the SZDL."

Preparations for elections began after the acceptance of the law, where it was clear that although the regime had agreed to them, the election campaign would be far from being held on an equal footing for all. Not only because of access to the mass media, which is most important at elections and which the ZKS, save for some important exceptions, controlled, but also because it controlled other key mechanisms for influencing public opinion and the position of the voters.

*   *   *

Demos was created as a consequence of an awareness that arose from a common interest which was foremost for all the newly formed parties. This common interest was a parliamentary political system in which parties could compete equally amongst themselves for voters. The second equally important reason for founding Demos was the subordinated position of the new parties in the coming election campaign. They had no money or influence on the main media and they did not have enough political experience. The Communist Party, after it had already been forced into elections, got straight to work on this. On the one hand it wanted to take advantage of the organisational lead it held over the opposition, as it had organisations everywhere, even in companies and, on the other hand, it wanted to cash in as much as possible on the capital it had acquired with its departure from the Yugoslav party organisations and some other moves it had made in Belgrade, which the Slovenian public accepted very positively.

The leaders of the opposition parties felt that they were linked more strongly. Many Slovenians who did not want to be affiliated to any party found in Demos an alternative to the existing regime. They also supported it because their desires for change and the rejection of everything that was negative and they had lived through in the past decades were personified in it.

The Demos programme was clear and understandable. At the meeting held on 17 January 1990, a year after the establishment of the Slovenian Democratic Alliance, it became obvious even from the outside that Demos was the political force which would seriously compete for power at the elections to be held in a few months.

The question of who was to preside over the coalition could even at the very beginning have become a stumbling block between the party members and their leaders. Luckily Jože Pučnik was here, with his undisputed dissident past and long enough absence, so that he could not give offence to the over-sensitive new politicians, a person who, without great debate, took over the wheel and imprinted his own mark on Demos. This was one of the rare unanimous decisions made during the whole period of Demos which no one disputed, at least not publicly.

In the spring of 1990 a discussion flared up again – when individual young soldiers were dying in the YNA – about the justification of sending soldiers to do their military service outside Slovenia. These debates were joined by some of the parties that were included in Demos, who had from the very beginning also demanded sovereignty in the military field. As the then existing regime responded to the demands of the opposition by above all underestimating the defence capabilities of the Slovenians and by attacking it, saying that it was asking for a military putsch, I proposed to the Demos presidency that it should not only make a stand regarding recruits from Slovenia but also a stand regarding the army issue as a whole. I prepared a proposal of views[5] to which the Demos presidency at the beginning of March 1990 gave total support. Doubts were only held by a representative of the Social Democratic Party, Andrej Magajna, who stated that he respected the army.

Jože Pučnik signed this document anyway, as well as all the other coalition parties. When we were departing from the cellar premises of Demos or, should we say, the Social Democratic Party, on Strnenova street, I asked Jože Pučnik if he was aware of what we had signed. He replied that he was aware that we had stuck our heads into the lion's mouth, but that no other option existed anyway. It was then that I had warned him of some problematic activists in his main headquarters, but he did not take this warning too seriously. Only after the poor results of the first round of the presidency elections did he see his mistake and change the team.

With such views and demands Demos went in 1990 far beyond the calls of the then ruling parties, and the ZSMS as well, who through their representatives appealed to recruits to ignore their draft cards and, at the same time, assured them of "moral" aid if they were to be persecuted by the military police. We presented a concrete manifesto, politically and professionally founded in all essential points and, today, we can say that this was one of the rare "regional" programmes of Demos which was carried out very well in practice.

At the beginning of April 1990 we called a convention of the SDZ, which was also attended by party candidates for the elections and where Dimitrij Rupel, based on the example of my proposal for the Demos military programme, presented a programme to the SDZ for the area of foreign affairs. Since there had been a great response in the public to the latest publication of the Demos military programme, where the key point – the demand for our

---

[5] The basis for this was my article in the state-forming, 95th issue of Nova Revija.

own army – was not only attacked by party politicians, but also by a columnist for Delo, Boris Jež, I additionally defended the need for our own defence forces at this party convention.

"Sovereignty will not be handed to us on a plate"

"In recent months it has been trendy to speak of sovereignty and independence.

Neither one nor the other will be handed over to us on a silver plate. We will have to provide them ourselves. Those who do not make decisions about where their hard currency goes or what kind of uniform they are to wear, those are indeed not sovereign. Perhaps we would all like this not to be so. But, unfortunately, it is, and those who state an "a" must also state a "b" and a "c". It is senseless and irresponsible if, because of the elections, we pretend that some problems do not exist or that they are topsy-turvy. A treaty of confederation can, for example, be made only between sovereign states. This means that you have to be completely independent for at least one second, so that at least a part of this independence can be transferred by treaty to a confederation. This has not been clearly stated by the opposition either.

Regarding the military issue, we sharpened our views not long ago and stated what the demands for doing military service in Slovenia meant and how Slovenia could be gradually demilitarised. We stated what could possibly, in our opinion, be done today and what tomorrow."

In the Saturday supplement to Delo, 10 March 1990, Boris Jež wrote, among other things, in a leader under the heading SLOVENIAN HERBS IN THE ARMY STEW, that: "Demos, of course, has the right to have its own views on the military issue, but Janez Janša and co-authors of the above--mentioned initiative should be warned that everything has to follow a certain sequence." Then he added that Demos had a confederation in its programme and thus did not see the need for founding a Slovenian army.

As an answer to the leader I wrote that "I completely agree with the desires of Boris Jež. It would be very nice if the Slovenians could first establish economic sovereignty and then political and then, gradually, military. Or that it demilitarise completely, which would be the most ideal. This would mean that we were going in a certain sequence." But wishes are one thing, and a realistic appraisal of the possibilities something else. Military issues have throughout history very rarely been solved last, but rather, unfortunately, solved first too many times.

Our key stance in resolving the military question was as follows: we must do all we can to be able to decide in full sovereignty about the army in Slovenia. Then we ourselves will make an agreement if and what kind of army we need. In our opinion, we need it above all for the critical transition period, when sovereignty and independence will have to be finally affirmed and protected. We shall soon be placed in a position, even beyond our conscious will, when we will have to accept a crucial decision.

Accusations flew in, saying that we were not in favour of demilitarisation and even those who one year ago were openly attacking the YNA, were today standing (on paper) for the complete abolition of the army. This was not only a utopia, for they themselves knew that this could not be done under the existing conditions and in this Yugoslavia, but also throwing dust into the eyes of the voters. We could announce demilitarisation, but we could not implement it. Any thought of reducing costs or even complete demilitarisation was a total illusion, while in practice Belgrade decided on this. A few months before, the Slovenian regime agreed to a relatively large increase in the army budget for 1990 and also for the supersonic airplane project, and then, because of elections, it was demanding complete demilitarisation through its parties of the SZ and the ZKS. For as long as Slovenia was not independent or at least for as long as it was in such a Yugoslavia as it was then, we could on the one hand call for the most radical demands, while on the other hand, the processes in practice would go in the extreme opposite direction.

A nice example of this was the border zone, which in the future was to be controlled by the YNA to a depth of one kilometre. The reasons for such a proposal were not military but political. They wanted to prove who was the true master of Yugoslavia. Even if such a decision was voted for or accepted in the Federal Assembly, and the Slovenian Assembly announced (as demanded by the SZDL) that this law was not valid for us, this would not have any great practical influence on the implementation of the law. The army would simply act according to federal law. The fact was, we held no instruments by which such a decision made by the Slovenian Assembly could be affirmed or protected.

If, or should we say, when this occurred, our demand for an independent resolution of the military question in Slovenia would be even more clear.

One year later, as the greatest efforts for protecting the measures for independence with real force were reverberating, Boris Jež, with some other journalists on Delo, supported our efforts in many articles. And Delo, in the last months before 26 June and especially during the escalations of tension in March and May, played a more important and positive role than any other medium in Slovenia. Its slogan An Independent Newspaper for an Independent Slovenia was in the forefront of editorial policies at a time when this was most needed. The role of this medium in the concluding phases of the creation of the Slovenian state is comparable with the public success of Mladina magazine in 1988. We can only hope that Delo will not follow the example of Mladina and become a party-oriented newspaper.

*　*　*

Even before the results of the elections were known, a discussion was begun in Demos on forming a government. Many did not believe that Demos would actually gain a majority, but all agreed that it was better to be prepared for such an event. At a meeting of the Executive Committee of the SDZ I proposed that the SDZ form, for the meeting of the presidency of Demos, a proposal of fundamental decisions with regard to the prime minister, who selects the government, and the other principles according to which the government would be formed. Just before the second round of elections an agreement was made by which the parties in Demos would have as many seats in the government as the percentage of delegates it was to have in the socio-political chamber. The prime minister was to be proposed by the Demos party that received the greatest number of delegates in the socio--political chamber. These were not ideal principles by which we would get the strongest government, of course, but the realistic alternatives were even worse. It would be impossible to agree upon measures of capabilities and expertise as the overruling principle, and it would be even more difficult for the parties in Demos to select a prime minister from amongst their midst without prior agreement. Among the individual party champions, intolerance and disdain of others began to appear. Many were strongly disappointed with the results of the elections for the Presidency of the Republic and also with the percentage of votes which their party received in the first round of elections, then others did not know how they could get a suitable number of ministers, which by agreement their party had to ensure. So as not to risk the disintegration of Demos or at least stop internal conflicts which could be a burden on the new government at the very outset, we had to make an agreement on the questions of principle before the final election results were known.

The president of the Christian Democrats, Lojze Peterle, after consulting with the leadership of his party, which received the highest number of delegates in the socio-political chamber, first offered the post of prime minister to Jože Pučnik. He was unsure for a while, but because of his defeat in the presidential elections, he was not very enthusiastic about this proposal. Spomenka and Tine Hribar, his friends, were also very strongly against this proposal, for the two were of the opinion that Pučnik, because of his poor health, could not risk taking on such a demanding duty. Finally the offer was rejected and Lojze Peterle became prime minister, in accordance with the agreement. Long meetings and negotiations between parties began on taking over government and Assembly functions.

All parties in Demos agreed with the proposal by which the Liberal Democratic Party (LDS) would be drawn into the coalition. A few meetings then followed, during the May Day holidays, where we tried to reach an accord. Demos offered the LDS up to six seats in the government, including a post of deputy prime minister. The representatives of the Liberal Democratic Party persevered in the first negotiations on constitutive agreements on the government programme and consistently brought discussions back to the starting point. The next time they showed their true colours and for the first time demanded the office of prime minister and then the post of president of the Assembly. Because of formal (previous agreements made within Demos) and actual reasons (no one in Demos could imagine the constantly offended Jože Školč as prime minister and even less as president of the parliament) the negotiations did not come through, although many prominent members of the LDS were of the opinion that the offer by Demos was completely acceptable. Without doubt the political arena in Slovenia

39

would have been shaped quite differently if Demos and the LDS had reached an agreement. On the one hand, the LDS would have become, with six members, the strongest party in the government, and on the other hand, the government would certainly have gained several able ministers. The biggest gain for all would have been the experience which, with the take-over of specific responsibilities, the LDS would have acquired and on the basis of which its delegates would most surely not have opposed even the most rational proposals in parliament, including some key ones for Slovenian emancipation. After barely two years we could already state that the mistaken decision of the leadership of this party was most dearly paid for by the LDS itself. With a continuation of its policies of destructive opposition, it acquired the reputation of a grumbler, which is not a good electoral companion for any party in democracy. Here too is the source of the constant efforts by this party to come, in one way or another, into the government even before the elections and thus correct the poor impression it had made.

At the same time discussions on forming Assembly bodies and the presidencies of the Assembly began between leaders of the delegate clubs. As the president of the Demos delegate club, I stood for a balanced stance and for forming Assembly bodies on the basis of electoral results. In the majority of cases such a stance was considered and we organised working bodies without any great discord. Even then the representatives of parties defeated in the elections demanded the professionalisation of the great majority of delegate posts, for they saw the possibility of acquiring a relatively comfortable job. The majority of them also succeeded in this. Today I can calmly state that the urge for employment was the key reason for this perseverance and that the professionalisation of the great majority of delegates did not essentially contribute towards the more effective work of the Assembly and its working bodies, the number of which, in relation to the previous mandate, also increased to enormous dimensions. The parties did not succeed in balancing proposals for the leadership of the parliament and, in secret ballots, the candidates for the opposition, Jožef Školč (LDS) for president and Miran Potrč (SDP) for vice-president, lost very convincingly. The majority of votes, which was considerably higher than the number of Demos delegates in the Assembly, was received by Dr France Bučar, as newly elected president of the Assembly, and Vitograd Pukl and Vane Gošnik as vice-presidents.

In the procedure of forming a new government, the president of the new Presidency of the Republic of Slovenia, Milan Kučan, received representatives of the parliamentary parties for talks and conferred with them about the prime minister, who had to be formally proposed by the Presidency of the Republic, in accordance with the provisions of the valid Constitution. At this stage almost the entire government of Demos was already known, including Lojze Peterle as prime minister. This related simply to a formal procedure. The opposition did not strongly oppose the prime minister, but the candidacy of Igor Bavčar for the office of Minister of Internal Affairs and my candidacy for the office of Minister of Defence were opposed. President Kučan also warned at the discussion held with a delegation of the SDZ composed of Dimitrij Rupel, Hubert Požarnik, Igor Bavčar and myself, that the Presidency wanted to have an influence on those ministries which were constitutionally linked to his role and responsibilities. He did not express any implicit dissatisfaction. But the Party of Democratic Reform, especially Lev Kreft and Sonja Lokar, explicitly objected to Bavčar's and my candidacy at a session of the parliament, at which the new government was being elected. Their reason was so obvious that, due to their opposition, we probably got more votes, if anything. The government was elected with almost a two-thirds majority and on that day I saw many of my colleagues for the first time. Only the SDZ did not have any serious difficulties with the proposals for members of the Executive Council (IS) and easily proposed a suitable number of candidates, while all the others got their final names at the last minute. The results of such a staffing policy was a relatively unhomogeneous group which did not succeed as a united team, despite some intermediate improvements, another reason for this being the unsuitable organisation, inherited from the times when Slovenia was still a province of Yugoslavia.

All the candidates for members of the government had to prepare their own programme. The concrete activities in them could only be based on the then valid legal foundations. For me, this meant that I could not plan anything specially concrete. I prepared the following proposal of a programme of the government for the area of (what was then still people's) defence to the prime minister, Lojze Peterle:

PEOPLE'S DEFENCE (LO)

MORE THAN ANYWHERE ELSE, CHANGES IN THE MILITARY-DEFENCE FIELD ARE LINKED TO CHANGES IN THE CONSTITUTION AND SYSTEMIC LAWS.

The first task of the new Executive Council of the Assembly of the Republic of Slovenia or its ministerial body for LO will thus (in cooperation with suitable ministerial bodies) be the preparation of analytical studies and drafts of legal acts, on the basis of which a reform of the military-defence field may be carried out. The speed of the reform will depend on the speed in the change of the situation of Slovenia in Yugoslavia or on the relations of political forces.

With regard to the present competences, key decision-making (e.g. on demilitarisation) in this field will be made in the Assembly of the Republic of Slovenia or even by referendum.

Proceeding from the objectively existing situation, the work of the IS and the Republic Secretariat for People's Defence (Rep. Sekretariat za Ljudsko Obrambo – RSLO) will thus be divided into two parts:

1. Implementation of constitutional and legally defined tasks (Article 301 of the Constitution of the Republic of Slovenia, Law on SLO and DS and the federal laws on LO and military duties, etc.).

2. Preparation of legal and material foundations for a reform of the defence system.

The Republic Secretariat for LO is by its present organisation only an administrative body which does not hold any decisive links with the Republic Headquarters (RHQ) of the Territorial Defence, which is, viewed formally and legally, more subordinated to the Presidency of the SFRY, as the sole commander of the armed forces (The commander of the RHQ for Territorial Defence is, for example, appointed by the Presidency of the SFRY on the proposal of the Presidency of the RS) than to the republican bodies. Nevertheless, some jurisdiction in association with the Territorial Defence (Teritorialna Obramba – TO) was, in spite of everything, at least partly in the hands of the Republic. While the Republic Secretariat for People's Defence was above all an administrative body linked to the Executive Council and the Assembly, the Republic Headquarters of the TO, in association with Republic authority for the TO, was subordinated more to the Presidency of the RS than to the Assembly. The legislation will also have to resolve the problem of mutual relations between the RSLO and the RHQ TO.

The budget of the RS for 1990 proposed about 26 million dinars for the RSLO while the RHQ TO had about 40 million dinars. Following an agreement, up to 0.5% within the framework of the Republic of Slovenia is proposed for the needs of the SLO and DS each year, but this percentage, at least in respect of the accessible official data, was never reached. In the future budget some expenses for defence will have to be distributed differently, while some would have to be reduced and thus diminish the contributions to the SLO and DS as a whole. Precise estimates will be able to be given after a detailed survey of the balance sheet and existing plans has been made.

I propose that the Republic Secretariat for People's Defence, with an amendment to the Law on State Administration, be renamed the Republic Secretariat for Defence.

On the already existing legal foundations we shall:

1. Modernise the peace-time information system of the administrative bodies for LO in Slovenia,

2. Ensure suitable conditions for the work of employees in the administrative bodies for LO,

3. Improve the educational or staff structure of the employees in the UO LO,

4. Modernise communication means,

5. Modernise programmes for training civilians,

6. Give more attention and resources to the work of the civil defence,

7. Found a Centre for Strategic Studies and Analysis,

8. Found an institute for studying problems of war and peace.

II. In the preparation of the legal and material foundations of changes in the military-defence field in Slovenia we shall proceed from goals which are defined in the unanimously accepted and published manifesto of Demos for settling the military question in Slovenia.

III. After a detailed analysis of the situation (accessible data) we could prepare a detailed schedule, financial and staff plan for the envisaged reforms. Here I must stress again that the key decisions relating to the military question will not be accepted in the ministerial body for LO or in the Executive Council but in the constitutional committee, the Assembly of the Republic of Slovenia or by referendum.

I based the programme in the second item, which I shall not repeat here, on the previously presented Demos programme regarding the military question. When I came to my new job on my first day, where everything had to start at the very beginning or even lower, and, in addition to this, they were already confiscating the weapons of the territorial defence, I wished at least twice an hour that I had stayed in computer science or journalism. But as I was very decently accepted at the Secretariat, despite the great excitement and fear, and as my secretary, Lili, assisted me with a lot of helpful advice even in my very first hours, I set to work anyway.

The first few days after the elections, the former president of the Executive Council, Dušan Šinigoj, had to officially hand over the government business. In a discussion with Lojze Peterle, before the planned meeting of the old and new government, Šinigoj demanded that neither I nor Bavčar be allowed to attend the joint meeting. Peterle took his demand into account and during the official handing over of key government business only the prime minister and certain – according to Šinigoj – "uncontroversial" members of the government were present.

4. DISARMAMENT OF THE SLOVENIAN TERRITORIAL DEFENCE AND THE OPERATION FOR THE MANOEUVRING STRUCTURE OF THE NATIONAL DEFENCE

During the meeting of the Assembly on 17 May 1990, where we elected the new government, I received a telephone call from some municipality mayors, who reported to me that the army was driving the weapons of the TO away from the municipal storehouses to unknown locations. Similar reports were also arriving from some other sources. Immediately after the meeting ended we held a short conference in the office of the president of the Assembly, France Bučar, with President Milan Kučan, who held even more such information, but all this information was unofficial. The existing commander of the Republic Headquarters of the TO, General Ivan Hočevar, who was also subordinated to the Presidency of the Republic, according to the federal legislation regarding the commanding of the TO, had not reported to the Presidency that weapons were being confiscated from the TO, stated Kučan. Steps had to be taken immediately. I telephoned the Republic Secretariat for People's Defence, where I had taken over not one hour before, and got through to the former secretary, Janko Kušar. We made an agreement for my immediate take-over of official duties and on the same evening he passed the keys to the safe and the most important documents to me. At the same time he could not in any way clarify the confiscation of weapons from the TO, for he had no official information, he explained.

We tried in various ways to get more detailed information overnight; information which could explain the steps taken by the YNA and its branches in the TO, but without success. It was clear to me what these measures were aimed at, but I was not at all clear about the role of local factors. Next day I entered my Secretariat offices and met with a friendly reception there, which reminded me of times ten years ago, when I worked as a trainee there, after having finished my studies. The remaining part of the apparatus was visibly scared and was waiting to see what was to happen. In the middle of the morning a telegram arrived in which Miran Bogataj reported from the field that the army was also confiscating the weapons of the administrative bodies of the people's defence, although this was exclusively in the hands of our department. We composed a telegram in a few minutes, which stated that I prohibited the handing over of weapons and sent the telegram off to the municipal bodies. These steps were made in good time, for the YNA was collecting weapons from the administrative bodies only in five municipalities, and even these we got back through the decisive measures we took.

Calls from the municipal headquarters of the TO, and from the representatives of those municipalities into which new bodies were already elected, began to fly in. Numerous municipalities did not yet have the new authorities constituted when the weapons began to be confiscated. Almost all of them demanded that we halt this theft and that we give the headquarters of the TO clear instructions on how to act, for the officers in them were under great personal pressure. On the one hand, they had orders coming from a higher command post, that is Hočevar's headquarters, that they were to immediately surrender their weapons, while on the other, they knew that such behavior was counter to the interests of Slovenia, which they were bound to defend to the best of their ability.

The Presidency of the Republic, as the highest body in command of the TO, had formal and practical possibilities for actually stopping this activity. First, President Kučan demanded an official explanation from General Hočevar. At the meeting of the Presidency, Ivan Hočevar clumsily made excuses in his pidgin Slovenian, that this was simply a safety measure, that the weapons would continue to be the property of the TO and that in the barracks of the permanent guard of the YNA they would be safer from theft, of which there was supposedly a great deal in Yugoslavia. After proving that this was not so in Slovenia, and after painful arguments, he finally blurted out that he was a general appointed by the Presidency of the SFRY, and that he had received an order and that he would obey that order. Milan Kučan tried to contact the President of the Presidency of the SFRY, Boris Jović, who first feigned ignorance, and then later defended the order from the GHQ as being a technical measure of protection, as the theft of weapons was supposedly occurring.

Pressure from the municipalities continued, as the YNA trucks were meanwhile relentlessly carrying away weapons to military storehouses or to temporary premises in army barracks. In the public, rumours spread that Slovenian politicians had capitulated. Under such conditions, the Presidency of the Republic of Slovenia sent on 19 May 1990, the next day, a confidential telegram to the municipalities with which it halted the surrendering of weapons. We retained the majority of weapons in 12 municipal headquarters of the TO and part of the weapons and ammunition of the 30th development group of the TO or the defence brigade. More than 70 per cent of the formational and additional arms and equipment of the Slovenian territorial defence remained inaccessible to us in army barracks or other premises (part of the storage houses of the TO were already previously behind the fences of army barracks, and in the same way, nearly all ammunition for heavy weapons and mines were stored in special storage sites) and under the control of the YNA.

Laborious meetings and letter-sending began with General Hočevar, the GHQ and the Federal Presidency, which did not bear fruit. Each stood their ground. The generals were more or less satisfied with their action, as it had mainly been a success, and besides this, they had also simultaneously disarmed the TO of Croatia (there they had confiscated more than 200,000 pieces of weaponry) and the majority of the TO in Bosnia and Herzegovina (BH), although some municipalities in Herzegovina, which were mainly settled by Croatians, did not want to give up their weapons.

The action of collecting up the arms of the territorial defence forces was first carried out by the YNA in Kosovo at the beginning of the eighties. A similar plan had also been prepared for Slovenia, Croatia and BH.

At the end of April 1990 there was a session of the War Council in Belgrade, where they adopted the basis for disarming the TO and where they explained to all senior officers the counter-revolutionary and anti-Yugoslav character of the political changes in Slovenia and in Croatia. General Hočevar, commander of the Republic Headquarters of the TO, who participated in the session of this War Council, following receipt of a written order at the beginning of May from Belgrade, determined General Drago Ožbolt as the supervisor of the Republic Headquarters of the TO to be the coordinator of this action in Slovenia. This was a person who had had the necessary experience in Kosovo. It was he who had signed in the name of General Hočevar order no. SZ 6251-90 and distributed it to the commanders of the 13 regional headquarters of the TO in Slovenia. They had to conduct and assure the surrender of weapons by no later than 19 May 1990, at 19.00 hours.

At this same time there were approximately 40 active officers of the YNA employed in the TO of Slovenia, most of them in command posts and other more important headquarters posts. The refined staffing policies of the GHQ had been noticeable to us for quite a few years already. With its staffing policies, the GHQ tried, in any manner it could, to replace all those officers in the Slovenian TO who, in the assessment of the military intelligence service, would give Slovenia precedence over Yugoslavia under specific circumstances. It was clear during the confiscation of weapons how far Belgrade had gone with this. Only the active officers supported this, and not even all of these, and some half-heartedly, and some other reserve officers, who took a position of a more political tune. Thus the commander of the municipal headquarters of the TO in Kočevje defended his shameless behaviour, after the last truck had driven off from his storage site to the Ribnica barracks, with the words: "Better this than letting the weapons fall into the hands of Janša!"

Without doubt, the generals of the YNA, with the help of collaborators, had selected a very lucky moment for their action. Namely, they began on the day when we were constituting the new Executive Council and at a time when many municipalities had not yet elected their new leaderships. Of all the bodies, only the new Presidency of the Republic had been operating at that time. If the action had been taken a few days later, the generals would have confiscated a lot less weapons from the storage sites of the TO, which we then had to smuggle past guards with great difficulty in the coming months. The secret police or national security service passed its exam in loyalty – or rather disloyalty – on this occasion. There was no warning from it, although the almost one thousand-strong apparatus, with its connections

46

and sources within the YNA most surely knew of at least the last stage of the plan for disarming the Slovenian TO. Instead of taking care for the defence of the sovereign rights of its own people, they put their heads together and discussed the organisation of a strike on the arrival of the new Republic Secretary for Internal Affairs. Luckily, at least the uniformed branch of the Slovenian police was already then on a high professional level.

The confiscation of weapons had many bad sides but also a good side. This action showed the "weight" of individual personnel in the TO. People with prominent titles and high ranks failed the exam, and those who replaced the lack of weapons with knowledge and personal bravery surfaced. These later passed many more serious exams, and dealt decisive blows to the aggression of the YNA attackers.

The spontaneous revolt against the illegal confiscation of TO weapons, which was then "dealt with" by the Presidency of the Republic of Slovenia through a decree which affirmed it as the commander of the Slovenian armed forces, grew to become one of the best organised and best conspiratorial operations which had ever been carried out in the territory of Slovenia in the new era. The result of these operations was a 20,000-strong armed formation which was capable less than three months after the disarmament of the TO – and by relying strongly on the special and emergency units of the Slovenian police – of protecting Slovenia against any kind of armed surprise. This was the operation "Manoeuvring Structure of the National Defence" (*Manevrska Struktura Narodne Zaščite* – MSND).

It would be difficult for me to pick out which act I could denote as being the opening shot in this game. Without doubt the then secretary for Territorial Defence of the Kočevje municipality was of decisive importance, today the already legendary Tone Krkovič, who visited my office moments after I had taken over my official post. Kočevje was one of those municipalities which, together with the TO also had the weapons of the administrative bodies for people's defence confiscated. Tone Krkovič came to complain and asked with serious concern whether we were just to stand peacefully by and watch them "stripping us". He told me that as a former active officer in the defence brigade, together with the principal of the police school in Jasnica, Vinko Beznik, he had prevented the surrender of part of the weapons of the defence brigade from the storage site in Kočevska Reka. His appearance and decisiveness was a complete counter to General Hočevar, and even at the first meeting with him I knew that I could depend on him. Tone Krkovič also expressed a sharp condemnation of all the actors in this theft of weapons and demanded those responsible, from the municipal to the republic level, to answer for it, on Slovenian radio on 23 May 1990. He immediately connected himself to Rado Klisarič, who was the security agent in the regional headquarters of the TO for Dolenjska at that time. Then, through him, we regularly followed all the actions of Hočevar's headquarters and knew of all the most important measures being taken against Slovenian sovereignty ahead of time.

The Slovenian political and civil public responded loudly to the theft of the weapons of the territorial defence. In the newspaper polls more than 90% of respondents condemned Hočevar's behaviour. Municipal assemblies, societies and individuals were sending protests to Republic authorities. At a conference of representatives of regional and municipal committees of the Slovenian Christian Democrats, held on 20 May, they strongly condemned the acts of the YNA and Hočevar and discovered that it was connected to the appearance of Boris Jović as head of the Federal Presidency. They were then followed by other parties. The Union of Army Veterans, who at their assembly on 22 May 1990 changed into a non-party organisation, took a firm stance against interventions by the YNA. They said that the Slovenians had been disarmed by Yugoslavia for the third time.

At that time Igor Bavčar was taking over the Ministry of Internal Affairs. He had affirmed my conclusions that we could rely on most of the uniformed branch of the police, for it would be loyal to the rule of law. This was extremely important, for in those days the police was the only armed formation which, in the event of any kind of escalation of hostility with the army, could give us at least a little support. But neither Igor nor I knew who worked for KOS in our ministries, and great care had to be taken in those first days.

The government appointed a committee to study the problematic closed region of Kočevska Reka at one of its first sessions. As a member of this committee I then visited the headquarters of the 30th Development Group of the TO in Promiži near Kočevska Reka and with the leading staff discussed their refusal to hand over their weapons to the YNA. All were faintly worried since, until now – something which was also admitted to me by one of them – the "big boys" stuck together in the end, and those who were going too fast were then slapped on their wrists. Their distrust evaporated only at the end, when I cheered the Slovenian army and when I openly stated how we would do everything we could to get back the weapons of the TO and that I was convinced that Slovenian policies were united with regard to this question. With a survey of the facilities in the closed region of Kočevska Reka and twice of the closed region in Gotenica, the government expert committee, led by Tone Krkovič, also collected and safeguarded the weapons of the supply detachment, a unit which supplied the Republic leadership and the Central Committee of the Slovenian League of Communists, which had until the elections been under the aegis of the Ministry of Internal Affairs, and which included more than 1,000 reservists.

In the following weeks, with all the piles of other work, we also held discussions with the staff of the TO who had not laid down their weapons, and made an approximate count of the weapons and military equipment which was in our hands.[1] Tone Krkovič, who from the times of his service in the TO knew most of the leading personnel in the regional and municipal

---

[1] Weapons were retained by the following municipalities: Brežice, Jesenice, Kranj (partly), Krško, Litija, Mozirje, Murska Sobota, Radlje ob Dravi, Radovljica, Slovenske Konjice, Šmarje pri Jelšah, Škofja Loka, Trbovlje, Tržič, Velenje, Žalec.

headquarters, checked out the mood in the permanent compositions and his estimates pointed out that the majority of people would not stand around twiddling their thumbs. In some places they had already organised themselves. There, where the officers had lost even their own personal weapons, they were buying pistols and revolvers in sports and hunting shops, and many pieces of weaponry probably travelled across the border to us through private organisations. But this was nowhere near enough. We had to have an organisation which would give the entire movement effectiveness and, at the same time, prevent possible maverick actions that could do more harm than good. Although there was an item in the programme of the government for the field of defence which foresaw the integration of the RHQ TO into the composition of the Secretariat for People's Defence, I was still aware that it was a long way from a constitutional law and constitutional amendment which could offer a foundation for such a step. In addition to this, not everyone in the Republic's leading circles was so convinced that the army had to be "baited" with the organisation of our own defence forces. Thus it was necessary to find a formula for the interim period, which was extremely important and, simultaneously, extremely dangerous. According to the valid law on the SLO and DS we, in Slovenia, already had a national defence for a number of years, which was defined as a form of organisation for armed battle without rigid rules and formations. The army had been quietly sneering at this Slovenian peculiarity all the time, as those that they saw with this insignia truly did not arouse any respect with their ancient weapons and the elderly structure of the recruits. But the legal foundation was such that in case of necessity anybody could be called to perform tasks for national defence, regardless of their military status, and it is in these provisions that we found, after precise scrutiny, the legal foundation for organising the Manoeuvring Structure of the National Defence, which we called this truncated formation, mainly adopted from the TO. Looking at it from the viewpoint of a ministry, its jurisdiction was, in respect of national defence, divided between the defence and interior ministries, but some key functions were linked more to the police, as it had always been under the jurisdiction of the Republic.

On the level of the Republic, the whole operation was being coordinated by Igor Bavčar, Tone Krkovič, Vinko Beznik and myself. On the level of the then existing 13 regions, the chiefs of the national defence were appointed, who closely cooperated with the special police forces at the internal affairs offices. The chiefs of national defence in the regions appointed the municipal chiefs for each municipality. In a few weeks all of Slovenia had been covered. Contacts with the regional chiefs was maintained by Tone Krkovič, who drove thousands of miles for this. He established the contacts and tested the people. Some were rejected, while the majority accepted the task, which seemed urgent to them at that time, with great enthusiasm.

We introduced strict security measures. All documents and messages were carried personally or directly passed on by word of mouth. The archive on the Republic level mainly existed on protected computers. The documents were made by ourselves. Apart from those mentioned previously, only Milan Kučan, Lojze Peterle and France Bučar knew of the whole operation. I do not know whether they had informed any of their more confidential colleagues of this. Even my deputy, Jelko Kacin, who joined me at the Secretariat at the beginning of the summer, was only gradually acquainted with the operation and only in its final stage. The conspiracy was complete. The Republic coordination knew of the people only up to the regional level. The regional chiefs mainly knew only of the municipal chiefs, and thereafter the selection was left to themselves. The municipal chiefs entrusted the general purpose of the operation, in accordance with the law, only to the presidents of the councils for people's defence, who were still posted at municipalities at that time and their function covered the function of president of the municipality. The majority of key duties was accepted by officers of the permanent composition of the TO, who had refused to surrender their weapons, and in some places to secretaries and other employees of administrative bodies for people's defence. There were cases where the whole municipal or regional headquarters of the TO were included, except for the commander, who was an active officer of the YNA and who suspected nothing.

The basic purpose for forming the manoeuvring structure of the national defence was the protection of measures being taken by the emerging Slovenian state, which was most threatened by the YNA at that stage and at all later stages. At the same time, the Manoeuvring Structure of National Defence was also a means whereby the Republic bodies and the Presidency of the Republic actually led and commanded the Territorial Defence of Slovenia. General Hočevar could not even mobilise, against our will, one percent of the formation of the number of servicemen which he formally had at his disposal.

In July Tone Krkovič had separate meetings with Miloš Zabukovec, the former commander of the defence brigade of the TO and with General Svarun. Both strongly condemned Hočevar's behaviour. Svarun frankly told Krkovič that in his opinion a disarmed nation in the present circumstances could never become sovereign. We also received some important information through Miha Butar, the head of the regional headquarters of the TO for Ljubljana and simultaneously, for this same region, the head of the City Secretariat for Internal Affairs, and with his father, who held contacts with individual retired and active YNA generals.

On 23 August 1990 we met at the premises of the municipal services company in Kočevje, where the director of this company and the then president of the Executive Council of Kočevje, Vladislav Lenassi, assured Krkovič of a secret place for making plans and for conferring. At this meeting Tone Krkovič presented the complete organisation scheme of the MSND to the level of the municipalities, including all names and units which could still be activated. Igor Bavčar and myself approved the project and in the ensuing days the necessary provisions were issued.

In the afternoon of this same day there was a meeting in Podstene in Kočevski Rog with the defence and interior ministers of Croatia, Martin Špegel and Jožo Boljkovec, respectively, where we made an agreement on the mutual exchange of information and experience. Croatia was in a more difficult situation, for they could not rely on the majority of their personnel in the TO, while they did not have their national defence legally defined. They were left with the option of strengthening their police ranks, which later proved to have a number of weaknesses.

At the end of August and the beginning of September I made the following document, which was then used as a guideline for the preparation of the basic army plan of the MSND:

POSSIBLE SITUATIONS, where partial or complete use of the manoeuvring units of the National Defence in the Republic of Slovenia could be considered

1. Introduction

Forming the Manoeuvring Structure of the ND represents a transitional solution for the period until the staffing and organisational affairs in the TO of Slovenia are settled, above all in the Rep. Headquarters of the TO, or, until amendments 96 and 97 to the Constitution of the RS, the constitutional law for their implementation, as well as the new law on defence and protection are passed.

The existing solutions in the Republic law on SLO and DS (Articles 173 to 186) allow that for the performance of tasks of the ND, authorised bodies may also recruit servicemen of the TO, YNA and Civil Defence, for the period until they are recruited to the aforementioned structures. Such a definition of the ND allows the establishment of the Manoeuvring Structure of the ND, which would have a Republic-wide importance.

The Manoeuvring Structure of the ND is organised according to the existing regions and municipalities, and led by ND chiefs, their delegates and assistants. The organisation is more or less adapted to the organisation of the TO (regional and municipal headquarters, the existing units of the TO). In the individual regions, as many units and headquarters of the manoeuvring structure of the TO are organised as can be suitably equipped and armed. A special command assures that the arms and equipment, as well as all other means accessible to the TO, are at the disposal of the manoeuvring structure of the TO.

In the first stage those units and headquarters of the Manoeuvring Structure of the ND are founded as were determined for this in the first stage of consultations made in the regions. The further supplementation of units and headquarters of the ND is proposed by the heads of the Republic, regions and municipalities. The procedure for forming the ND is coordinated with the presidents of the councils for the LO in municipalities.

The entire organisation of the Manoeuvring Structure of the ND is coordinated with the organisation of the special and military units of the police. Joint coordination bodies are founded on the level of the Republic and regions.

The operation will be carried out in such a way that the experience acquired in it would also be applicable in the imminent reorganisation of the TO in Slovenia.

2. Possible situations where demonstrative, partial or complete use of the Manoeuvring Structure of the ND could come into consideration.

2.1. A state of emergency in the entire territory of the SFRY

In the case where a state of emergency is proclaimed in the entire region of the SFRY, such a state in the region of the Republic of Slovenia would be illegal until (in compliance with the latest amendments to the Constitution of the RS) the Assembly of the RS affirmed this. In the legal sense this means that all measures of the state of emergency, which the federal bodies, including the YNA, might carry out without the approval of the RS, must be accepted as an act of aggression on the RS. In respect of assessments available to us, no realistic possibilities exist for a proclamation of a state of emergency arising today in the entire region of the SFRY or only in the RS.

2.2. A state of emergency in Kosovo because of the national resistance of the Albanians

In this case the situation in Slovenia could sharpen if the Presidency of the SFRY decreed that units of the YNA should be deployed in Kosovo and if recruits from Slovenia were called to Kosovo. Slovenia would most surely reject such a decree, for which reason various interventions by the federal bodies (attempts at direct recruitment, collection of volunteers from among members of other nationalities in the RS, threats) could occur, which would then demand the demonstrative use of PEM (special police units) and the Manoeuvring Structure of the ND, which would give the necessary authority to the bodies of the RS. In this example the extension of the state of emergency to Slovenia is not to be expected, for there would exist no formal reasons or actual possibilities, as all the peace time and partly military potential of the YNA would be engaged in Kosovo.

2.3. A state of emergency in Croatia because of interventions by the National Defence of the Rep. of Croatia in Knin Krajina.

Despite guarantees given by the federation and also by the YNA to the leadership of Croatia, that they would not interfere with the establishment of order in its territory, wildcat intervention by parts of the YNA in the Knin Krajina could come about under pressure from the pro-Serb factions of the YNA, especially if a more serious resistance by paramilitary forces caused the intervention of the Croatian police. The organisation of volunteers in Serbia and Montenegro would follow, along with their surging into Croatia and Bosnia, and most probably into Macedonia, too. In this case not only would ethnic conflicts arise among civilians and/or between civilians and the ONZ but probably also conflicts within the YNA itself, which would then spread to Bosnia and Kosovo and would bring Yugoslavia into the worst possible situation, which could in time be solved only by the intervention of UN peace-keeping forces.

In this case the use of all forces of the Manoeuvring Structure of the ND would be urgent, for the aim of protecting the borders of the RS and to prevent the conflicts from also enveloping the territory of Slovenia and, at the same time, to protect the borders with Italy, Austria and Hungary, for the YNA would most surely no longer be carrying out this function.

2.4. A state of emergency in Croatia because of ethnic conflicts of broad dimensions, instigated by the "all-Serb congress in Jasenovac", where 2 million Serbs were supposed to have gathered.

The consequences and counter-measures would be similar to those described in item 2.2., only that with the effective action of the Croatian bodies with at least the partial help of the federation, and with a blockade of the Croatian-Bosnian border, this rally could be prevented and the situation brought under control before it came to an all-out civil war. A similar meeting could be possible in Slovenia, organised to support the all-Serb rally, which we should not allow under any circumstances.

2.5. A state of emergency in BH because of enforced ethnic conflicts

The November elections in BH would probably greatly reduce the possibility of Serb desires for the annexation of part of the territory of BH to the Republic of Serbia being realised. The strategic goal of Serb policies is thus the prevention of these elections, by applying various methods and means for this purpose. With the constant poisoning of ethnic relations, spurred on by the Belgrade media, ethnic conflicts could rapidly spread from one region (e.g. from Foča) to all regions where Serbs live, especially to the Bosanska Krajina. In this case BH would itself request the aid of federal bodies, and a state of emergency in this Republic would be announced. The further outcome of events would above all depend on whether the Republic of Croatia could succeed in preserving or at least localising ethnic conflicts in Knin Krajina, which would without doubt follow the escalations in Bosnia.

In this case the partial or entire Manoeuvring Structure of the ND could be engaged so that the RS remains out of reach of armed conflict.

2.6. The evacuation of army technology and heavy artillery from the territory of the RS

On 6 June 1990 the commander of the YNA GHQ ordered the YNA units in Slovenia to prepare a plan for the evacuation of military technology and heavy artillery from the territory of Slovenia in the event of its secession from Yugoslavia. If an attempt was made to realise this plan, which is possible long before the above-mentioned reasons and could be done gradually, an escalation of the situation would most surely arise, for any division of the property of the YNA would only be possible through a prior political agreement on a confederation or a separation of the existing federal formation. With regard to this, an attempt at evacuation would be totally illegal, and we would of course attempt to prevent this, if it could be done without greater risk.

Here, a partial or complete deployment of the units of the Manoeuvring Structure of the ND for the blockading of roads, railways and other forms of communication could come about.

2.7. Attempts at direct implementation of federal laws and regulations

The situation could also escalate through possible attempts at directly implementing federal laws, above all in the case where the federal bodies might want to prevent the implementation of amendments which specify that the Presidency of the RS appoints the commander of the RHQ TO and if the army authorities wanted to acquire a list of recruits which is safeguarded in the municipal administrative bodies for LO.

In the second example the use of part of the units of the Manoeuvring Structure of the ND for protecting the premises which contain these records and for preventing possible aggressive recruitment of individual recruits, which is less probable, would mostly come into consideration. It is not probable that in these examples a state of emergency would be proclaimed in Slovenia, while affairs proceeded through legal paths, even though this would mean giving priority to Slovenian regulations.

3. The upgrading of the possible operation and organisation of forces of the Manoeuvring Structure of the ND in regions and municipalities.

3.1. The headquarters of the ND by regions and in cooperation with the commands of the special and military units of the police, formulate a detailed assessment and plan of measures for the deployment of the Manoeuvring Structure of the ND in situations stated in item 2. If necessary, they also order the formulation of assessments and plans of measures from the headquarters of Manoeuvring Structures of the ND in municipalities.

3.2. With the formulation of assessments and plans of measures, all the headquarters of the ND must consider that this relates to a solution which would come into consideration only in a relatively short preliminary period, until the RS ensures the constitutional and legal foundations for the transfer of the TO to Republic jurisdiction, but which should be constitutively applicable while the potential sources of threats stated in item 2 existed.

4. Schedules

The schedule for formulating measures from item 2.3. is immediate.
The upgrading of measures under item 2.7. by 15 September 1990.
The upgrading of measures under items 2.2, 2.4 and 2.5 by 18 September 1990.
The upgrading of measures under item 2.1. and 2.6. by 24 September 1990.

We greatly accelerated activities after the onset of the Knin crisis in August, 1990. We were regularly informed of events associated with this by Martin špegel and Jožo Boljkovec. Despite the lack of time and although burdened with the mass of other daily jobs, I went off with Igor Bavčar, Tone Krkovič (head of the ND), Jože Kolenc (PEM) and Vinko Beznik (SEM) to Pristava nad Stično for one day at the beginning of September 1990. Tone Krkovič prepared a proposal of the war plan of the MSND, the final organisation schemes of the MSND and other measures made on the basis of the aforementioned documents. We analysed the situation and the measures that had been made by then at this meeting and also agreed upon a universal plan for the operation of the National Defence, in which the Slovenian police was included as an indivisible part. Along with some assistants, Tone Krkovič produced the necessary documentary and work charts after this meeting.

The basic war plan of the National Defence was simple and logical. In the case of armed intervention by the YNA the National Defence was to defend key structures and, at the same time, with rapid attacks on ammunition dumps and military equipment, ensure the possibility of calling up the entire formation of the Territorial Defence. Detailed plans for individual ammunition and weapons dumps, as well as for other facilities, were made. Our basic ideas for these plans were affirmed in practice during the aggression of the YNA in 1991.

The shock troops and assault troops were composed in regions and municipalities. The formation of units was adapted to the weapons and equipment which was at our disposal. The highly confidential mobilisation documents were adapted to call up new formations. The key units could be mobilised according to the self-call up principle without any additional despatch service. Coded messages were made. In the long nights, trucks, with the accompaniment of members of the National Defence and special police units, drove weapons and ammunition from Kočevska Reka and from the Gorenjska region to the municipalities which did not hold the necessary equipment. Countless secret weapons and military equipment storage sites were created. No one asked for pay or daily allowances, no one asked why. The work had a deep significance for all those cooperating. Many National Defence chiefs had great personal or family problems, for they were out all night, away from home, and their wives suspected that they had lovers. Since they were not permitted to state the true reasons for their absence, they thought up all manner of excuses, but they were mostly hard to believe. When we brought up old memories of these moments, after the successful operation, we had to laugh, but many still asked themselves how things would have ended if they could never have explained their absence publicly.

On the Republic level, the Presidency, the government and the Assembly knew of the operation in greater detail. It was supported by all three, but Dr France Bučar was by far the most fervent, frequently stressing during meetings with heads of the regions and with the commanders of regional special police units (PEM), that "the fate, safety and future of Slovenia was in their hands." Dr Bučar was one of us, who had seen what the actual proportion of forces during the critical moments was, and because of this was not giving himself any illusions.

The chiefs of the Manoeuvring Structure in regions and municipalities would have operated with difficulty without the support and cooperation of key people in the local governments. So the most responsible people in the municipalities were included in the work, these being usually municipal presidents, who, according to the law at the time were also presidents of the councils for SLO and DS. Many of them cooperated with all their soul and heart, and in the municipalities where connections were best, all necessary plans were prepared in record time. For the better notification of municipal presidents, we called a conference on 14 September 1990 at the Centre for Defence Training in Poljče, where I described the existing conditions, as an additional argument for organising the MSND.

■ "Global security depends above all on events in the Soviet Union"

The Warsaw Pact, in its true sense, no longer exists. That is, it was founded on the subordination of the weaker to the stronger and on the ideology of Marxism. When this ideology fell and when the central forces themselves began to be rent apart by opposites, the pact remained only a paper agreement, which could not work in the real world. After decades of futile options, changes became relatively rapid. So rapid, that the changes took the opposing side by surprise and NATO found itself in a paradoxical situation all of a sudden, when in the short-term it even had to deter the excessively radical desires of the Eastern European nations, which were in

55

the main prepared to immediately exchange the sanctuary of one master for the sanctuary of another, given of course that they counted on receiving certain benefits for this.

The key security problem from the NATO point of view today is the preservation of Gorbachev for as long as possible. The situation is actually dangerous. If a successful army/party putsch came about in the USSR, then the putsch regime would immediately have to find an external enemy to preserve its own position. The answer was at hand. First the question of uniting Germany would undoubtedly arise. This is why Germany is so hastily uniting and doing everything it can to help perestroika.

The question of the withdrawal of Soviet troops from the territory of Eastern European states would also arise. The USSR could make economic demands as payment for security. In a few months the situation could so sharpen that we would be on the edge of a global conflict.

Thus the key lies in the Kremlin, which is why Gorbachev has an open door and direct telephone lines to all governments and state presidents. In a certain way, the USSR has more supporters abroad than at home, where they are squeezed into a narrow space between the radical demands of the national and democratic movements and the threats of the Stalinist dogmatists in the army and state/party apparatus. In the autumn of 1989 the opinion prevailed in the world that he could hang on from two to six months. The West was getting relatively desperate. But he succeeded, even without any military intervention in Lithuania, which he could not allow (the West would have tolerated this) because of the domestic situation, for the processes would backlash in the opposite direction.

One of the reasons that the dogmatists in the Red Army did not intervene with extreme means lies in the very poor conditions existing in the army itself. The poor living conditions of the soldiers and officers, the awareness that they had lost the battle for technological prestige, the consequences of their intervention in Afghanistan and the poor living conditions of the inhabitants in general, did not give sufficient promise for a successful intervention of the army in politics. This also related to the multi-ethnical composition of the army, the influence of democratic movements and the move of Boris Yeltsin, who most seriously opened up the issue of dividing the Russian empire into a number of states. There was simply no single strict centre of rule which the army could take over and thus control the situation overnight. It had to control too many points, which, as it was, it could not do. While time was working on the side of the reforms and with the aid of the West, the impoverished Russian economy could come out well.

On the other hand, NATO was still firm, for it was based on consensus. Despite the fact that the USA has the final say, it does not impose its decisions by force. A political victory is being promised to them. And an economic one as well. This process involves new markets. For the Western economies this is much more important than the outmoded tendencies for physical subordination of a territory or a nation.

For all these reasons, NATO has even changed its position regarding the use of nuclear weapons. Now it would use them only in extreme need and not immediately after an attack by an opposing side occurred.

Due to the fact that all the eyes of politicians are fixed on events in the USSR, Yugoslavia is a disturbing element at this moment on the political scene, an unnecessary worry, a state which does not know how to look after itself, unlike the Hungarians, Czechs or Poles.

Diplomats are also afraid of conflicts between Serbia and Albania, if Serbia were left on its own. They fear the five borders between Italy and Greece. But they would accept an executed state and recognise new facts if changes came about in a peaceful manner. The USA is changing its views, and some Austrian and Italian political circles are greatly in favour of Slovenian efforts. Hungary is no problem either.

1. The term security received a new meaning with the elections. To this term we have also officially added our recognition of a second pole, the internal, Yugoslav viewpoint. The government in a democratic state must consider the disposition of the voters. The coordination between speaking and doing will have to be necessarily greater than before.

2. Slovenia must consider both aspects of security, the internal (Yugoslav) and the external. For Europe, as well as for Slovenia, the main problem from the aspect of security is Yugoslavia, except that unlike Europe, we are inside this problem. Contrary to what we have been taught until now by political army doctrine in Yugoslavia, which stated that in both political and military conflicts it was a question of material interests, history proves that this is not so. The cause of conflicts can also be entirely or mainly immaterial interests or differences, for example religious or national. Iraq and Iran are a good example. Yugoslavia is also proof of this. But economic reform alone cannot save it. An example of which is former Yugoslavia..

Democracy, economy and the national questions are strongly linked and create the main foundations for any assessment of national security.

3. Two concepts for a possible solution to the crisis predominate in Yugoslavia. These two were formed within the federation. And then there is also a third, a solution defended by Slovenia and Croatia – the confederate model.

No one with any sense thinks in terms of the current categories when speaking of the coming Yugoslavia. The latest surprises are Boris Jović and the Serbs. Marković was misled by the partial success of his economic reform, which is why Jović overtook him on the left and stole the initiative away from him.

This is important. When this concerns bankruptcy and possible reorganisation, it is very important who the receiver is. Here a strong conflict exists between the government and the Presidency of the SFRY. Jović became aware of this problem sooner than Marković, who had still not relinquished his illusion of a unified country.

For us, it is important to be aware of the fact that first we need independence, and only then can we negotiate. It is very important here

which arguments are held in whose hands. And the arguments which hold any sway under such conditions, are as follows:
- national unity, control of the political arena, at least relative social peace,
- money or currency,
- armed forces, army, weapons,
- other property,
- international support, aid, recognition.

The situation in which arms could play a key role is not excluded, although Slovenia, because of some advantages in this sense, is in a privileged position relative to Croatia, not to mention others. The advantages Slovenia holds are:
- national homogeneity of the inhabitants,
- mainly a non-conflict border with other republics (Croatia),
- relative economic development,
- strong ties with influential political circles in neighbouring countries,
- a lead in democratic processes,
- relative unity of parties with regard to strategic national goals,
- in its organisation, the MSND is a satisfactory basic defence resource for the majority of crisis situations where the use of force could arise.

We are also faced with deficiencies, the chief ones being that we have not been preparing seriously enough for a possible conflict, although we hold every possibility for the eventuality that if it does arise in Yugoslavia, we could be ready, and we could keep Slovenia out of the crisis points. In this case it is our strategic goal.

Situation in Croatia:
- Serb minority, Knin, Jasenovac, Bosnia and Herzegovina,
- mainly disarmed, key staff of TO is pro-Yugoslav,
- playing for time and the elections in Bosnia, which Milošević will try in all ways to foil.

Slovenia has good relations with Croatia because of the common interests of dissociation and since it will remain our southern neighbour, and wise politicians maintain good relations with their neighbours. But it must certainly proceed from a clean slate.

Serbia and Montenegro:
Direct contacts with the Serbs will also have to come about. In those rare contacts we have had, they expressed direct interest in assisting our dissociation and even offered a guarantee that they would oppose any military intervention, which now does not have any realistic possibility of success anyway. But they do demand that they are left with Kosovo, and the right to new borderlines. They have no claims on Slovenia, but it is my conviction that in these offers their tactics of divide and rule still exist. Similar things have been promised by them to others at the expense of Slovenia.

The Serbs would like to replace Zeynulahuya in Kosovo. The outcome of the elections is unsure because of Bogić Bogičević. Janez Drnovšek and Stipe Mesić could in this case resign and, with this, the last stage of the collapse of the federation would begin. If all the rest is solved, Kosovo still remains the problem, which is why a confederation with the whole of Yugoslavia is not realistic. Sooner or later we would be subject to international isolation because of our violation of human rights in Kosovo.

Bosnia and Herzegovina:
By national and religious structure – a powder keg. The economic problems are becoming greater and greater every day, because of its crisis in basic industries. The elections in Bosnia and Herzegovina (BH) could eliminate the Serbian appetite for Bosnia. The Serbs control the SDV (National Security Service) of BH. If the situation contains itself until 17 November this year, then we shall be able to sleep much more calmly, although nothing final will have been solved. But the possibility for a peaceful solution of relations would be so much the greater.

Macedonia:
Threatened nationally (from four sides), religiously and economically. At this moment, they are in a hopeless situation, in the long term more than Kosovo.

They will probably have to search for compromises with the Serbs, and all variants for an outcome are open.

4. Slovenia has produced its own proposal for an offer of a confederacy, which was discussed yesterday at the Republic Assembly. You know the skeleton of it, although the newspapers did not publish the latest version. The army issue will be especially sensitive during a solution.

Situation in the YNA
– two currents, pro-Serb and pro-Yugoslav
– Marković raises the salaries of officers
– anxiety predominates
– motivation is declining (deaths of soldiers)
– depoliticising, recommend SPS (Socialist Party of Serbia), prohibit Demos and the HDZ (Croatian Democratic Union) from active officer corps
– mixed ethnic structure – such an army cannot effectively mediate in internal conflicts,
– resignations from the Yugoslav League of Communists and active military service,
– danger for institutions if they continue to link themselves to the old system (Yugoslavia, socialism and brotherhood and unity), for this no longer exists and could disintegrate chaotically.

Slovenia has a grave task before it. It must protect its international borders as well as those facing the core of the crisis, as well as guarantee safety in the entire territory of the Republic. We are now settling conditions in the TO. If conflict erupts before this is done, the legal possibility of organising resistance through the MSND still exists. The mobilisation of army conscripts would proceed through a modified structure of existing units. In the case that such a necessity should arise, I am already requesting your full cooperation today, for the municipalities have important functions which, in this example, would come into consideration. The police are prepared for such a situation, its motivation and qualifications are beyond question. The problem is heavy weapons, although these in no variant play a decisive role. There are relatively sufficient light weapons for the first stage, as well as ammunition, but this is not equally distributed. In the second stage we should supply ourselves from the the YNA stocks at all costs.

Of course also the possibility that the Assembly accepts the constitutional amendment overnight or even a special law by which we can found a Slovenian army exists. There are a number of formal variants, but it is important that we are practically prepared.

The formation of the Manoeuvring Structure of the ND represents a temporary solution for the period until personnel and organisational issues are brought together in the TO of Slovenia, above all in the GHQ of the TO or until amendments 96 and 97 to the Constitution of the RS, the constitutional law for their implementation, as well as the new law on defence and protection, are passed.

The whole operation is being conducted in such a way that the experience acquired in it will also be applicable for the imminent reorganisation of the Territorial Defence of Slovenia.■[2]

Further on I presented to the municipal presidents the concept of the document on the basis of which the basic war plan of the MSND was composed. The municipal presidents were also greeted by France Bučar, who very frankly told them that they would have to rely above all on themselves in the coming months. A similar meeting was also prepared a week later for the presidents of executive councils of the municipality assemblies. They were acquainted with the safety situation and tasks of the MSND in the same great detail.

There were 20,000 men in the formations of the MSND in September 1990. All necessary plans were made, and the organisation functioned. When we proposed the key changes in the Constitution to the parliament, through which the TO was later transferred to the hands of the Republic, this measure was guaranteed by all rules. If the YNA intervened then, it would have got an enormous surprise, for it knew nothing in detail about the national defence operation.

In contrast to the intelligence held by the YNA about our activities, in a

---

[2] Introductory words of the Republic Secretary of LO at a conference of municipality assembly presidents of the RS on 14 September 1990 in RCOU Poljče (Rep. Centre for Defence Training) in the Gorenjska region.

four-way coordination (Krkovič, Beznik, Bavčar, Janša), we had regular intelligence reports on the activities at Hočevar's headquarters; this was reported to us by Rado Klisarič and was invaluable in helping us to act correctly.

We did not underestimate our potential opponent, the YNA, just because we had precise information. All our preparations proceeded in secret, so that Belgrade could never exploit the operation itself as an excuse for provocation or armed intervention. This was an exclusive self-defence organisation of Slovenia at a time when there were 32,000 YNA troops, with all their heavy technology and with the assured support of the entire Yugoslav air force based in our territory or just next to it. There were more than 4,000 officers and professional soldiers of the YNA at that time in Slovenia. Thus ten times more than there were members of the TO. The proportion between infantry weapons was many times to the advantage of our opponent, we had no heavy weapons, except for some mortars and recoilless guns. Here we should add the very diligent but luckily very inept military intelligence service with its network of collaborators, who were the most dangerous of all. We knew that KOS had collaborators in some Republic bodies, the SDV, companies and even some editorial offices. Through this network it succeeded in finding out that something was going on, but luckily we planted a counter-agent on time, and the game rolled on. We planted information that special units of the TO were collecting in Kočevska Reka with new weapons. The trucks did not pass unnoticed on the road anyway, but the YNA did not know whether they were empty or full driving to Kočevska Reka. They did not dare to check, for the transporters were heavily guarded. In Belgrade the chief of KOS in the 14th Corps, Emin Malkoć, was sending reports on military preparations around Kočevje and on the concentration of weapons. Some Serb and foreign reporters who were in close contact with the above-mentioned circle of people were adapting their stories for months later. But no one logically asked themselves what this concentration of weapons and soldiers could serve. They all fell for it, for the security reports and especially the news coverage was even more bombastic if the secret region of Kočevska Reka, foreign military instructors, contraband weapons smuggled in with the help of Slovenians abroad and so on, appeared in them. Things easy to exaggerate but not very useful.

Our advantage was that we were at home, on our own land, and thus present everywhere. That we were prepared for action solely as a response to the direct threat of the YNA and that the MSND was mainly composed of people who did not need any special reason to understand why we were doing it all. Many of them, previously as politicians or journalists, who were in the centre of events each day, finally became aware with the confiscation of weapons that moments of major decisions were on the horizon, and that with the first steps in forming the MSND a merciless race for time had begun, which ended one year later, when on 26 October 1991 the last soldier of the YNA left Slovenia.

The key reason for the fact that the formations of the National Defence did not include greater numbers was the lack of weapons. Except in the Gorenjska region, where the then chief of the regional headquarters of the TO, Major Janez Slapar, retained most of his weapons and could thus preserve the majority of the TO formation as units of the MSND, we had to compose detachments and platoons relative to the means at our disposal. To tell the truth, the quantity of weapons grew each day, for in the first months, when TO was still permitted entry into some storage sites in the army complexes, the TO drove away automatic rifles, hand-held mortars, pistols, ammunition and, in some cases, even rocket launchers, every day, under various guises. The rifles were wrapped in sleeping bags, guards were bribed, they used old friends in the barracks. This related not only to weapons, but also to the honour stolen from the Slovenian TO by General Hočevar, and those who fell for him, at least partly in innocence, who wanted to correct their slip. Frequently dangerous episodes occurred, especially when weapons left the barracks over fences at night. The commanders of the army ammunition stores usually hushed up the loss of weapons to their superiors, if they noticed it, thereby attempting to avoid responsibility. In this way we succeeded in returning to the TO a good 5,000 pieces of various infantry weapons in one year, which, for our state, was a very nice number.

Among the many events linked to the operation for national defence, the meeting of the regional chiefs and commanders of the special units of the police at a conference of the Executive Council of the Republic of Slovenia deserves special attention. This was the first meeting after the chiefs were appointed and was still held under rather dubious circumstances, for the only guarantee which the summoned people had was the word of Tone Krkovič, who held talks with each of them separately. But when Igor and I explained the whole campaign and when those present were also greeted by Milan Kučan and Lojze Peterle, all doubts faded and work began unbelievably fast. Not once did any political problem occur, no one even enquired after party affiliation. The dividing line ran only between Ljubljana and Belgrade and possibly also through the question of personal bravery. These were months where the unification of the Slovenian armed forces and its key personnel was being minted. These came to complete expression during the June–July war one year later. However I look at things, this unification appears as one of the primary reasons aiding our success in the decisive conflict for an independent Slovenian state.

5. THE RETURN OF SLOVENIAN SOLDIERS

On taking over the mandate in 1990, Slovenia was very closely wound up with Yugoslavia. Ties in the military field were especially strong. The Socialist Assembly of Slovenia decided in March 1990, just before the elections, that at the very least it would not send recruits to Kosovo, but then it even sent reserves there (a battalion of the 1st Tank Brigade from Vrhnika). Immediately after the elections, that section of the press which had attacked the demand to do military service in Slovenia the most, saying that this was adventurism and a baiting of Belgrade, launched a big campaign and began asking the new government questions about why it was sending Slovenian boys to the army hundreds of kilometres away.

The government and especially the defence department had no legal foundation, neither republican and even less federal, which could allow them to fulfil one of the pre-election demands of Demos and the old desire of the Slovenians in general, which was serving in the army in their own territory. We first began with negotiations, but the generals, Veljko Kadijević and Ljubomir Domazetović, who commanded the competent administrations at the GHQ, did not respond to letters or calls. We proposed to Belgrade a relatively acceptable variant of a gradual increase in the percentage of recruits who would remain in the army in Slovenia, so that within one year they could all be at home. Technically, the variant was, except in a few cases, implementable, but the YNA did not want to discuss this for political reasons.

Since the generals did not want to negotiate, at one session of the Slovenian Assembly held in July 1990 I proposed that we accept the stance which would allow a one-sided affirmation of the Slovenian proposal. The delegates accepted this stance with loud protests from Colonel Milan Aksentijević. Then it began to boil. That is, Belgrade became aware that we were actually serious. First, attacks came from the YNA and Serbian press. When the third administration of the GHQ did not receive a particular complete contingent, the ZSLO alerted the Executive Council and its prime minister, Ante Marković. Marković finally succumbed to negotiations and a number of meetings began, alternately in Belgrade and Ljubljana, but in which Veljko Kadijević did not want to cooperate, sending instead his deputy, Stane Brovet. At the first meeting Ante Marković agreed that up to 15 per cent of the recruits could remain in Slovenia, which was much larger than in previous practice, but still a lot less than we demanded. The meeting proceeded in

Marković's office in Belgrade and Prime Minister Lojze Peterle and I had a lot of trouble convincing the smiling and self-confident Marković that we were serious. The fact is, he was convinced that the recruits were only a bluff and that Slovenia, by exacerbating this issue, would try to bargain for a concession in the economic field. Only after some time did he become aware that the view of an assembly in parliamentary democracy was not simply spice in the Balkan melting pot, and that this time he was faced with policies of principle. We went our ways without reaching a consensus, and the following summer, too, meetings with him and Stane Brovet did not bear any fruit. The September batch of recruits went incomplete to the army and, in accordance with the position of the Assembly of Slovenia, most of them went to the 5th Army District. There was no military putsch, of which we were given frequent warning.

Negotiations continued at the end of August and September because of the departure of the October batch. The army did not relent much. The percentage of those recruited to their home republic did rise to 20 per cent, but they were in no way prepared to talk of a long-term solution and a transitory regime in 1991. Stane Brovet kept on coming to the meeting without the necessary authority to negotiate, Ante Marković kept on indirectly criticising Veljko Kadijević and threatened that recruitment and allocation of soldiers from Slovenia would be taken over by the federal bodies, as was done in Kosovo some years ago. The resolution on this was supposed to have already been passed, but Marković did not want to sign it and the document remained in his desk.

There was particularly high tension at the September meeting, again in Belgrade. A few days before this meeting the Slovenian Assembly discussed the drafts of the constitutional acts which envisaged an increase in Republic jurisdiction over the TO and military affairs. Highly confidential material was prepared as a foundation for the delegates, in which they could read that Slovenia would not be barehanded in the case of an army putsch. This material was authentic. Some members of the Liberal Democratic Party laughed, which was completely in line with their practice which, with the exception of the meeting of the Assembly during the war, they have retained to this very day, but the material did achieve its goal. Some numbers were slightly increased by us, for we expected that Milan Aksentijević would, despite the high confidentiality of this information, take it to the barracks while the ink was still drying. But he had to rely on his memory, since after the delegates had read the material we collected and destroyed it.

The meeting in Belgrade was opened by Ante Marković, with a secret smile on his face, and the eyes of Admiral Stane Brovet were very shiny despite his constant pallor. After a few introductory words Marković began making accusations, stating that the Slovenian Assembly had discussed a document in which the measures and procedures for an attack on the bar--racks and other military facilities of the YNA in Slovenia were discussed. Lojze Peterle and I easily rejected this accusation and asked where they had obtained such information. Marković and Brovet looked at each other and

Brovet replied that it was supplied to them by those who had seen these documents with their own eyes. He pulled out some kind of writing from his satchel and began to leaf through it. He did not have the original Assembly assessments in his hands but the report of the KOS command of the 14th Corps with the signature of Emin Malkoć on it. I instantly took out the original assessments which were distributed to the delegates and which had so obviously upset Aksentijević when he had seen things in it which did not exist (and probably KOS added its own also), from my folder and pushed it towards the federal premier, stating that he should rather see things in the original instead of relying on reports of hot-headed colonels. A very interesting situation then arose. Marković and Brovet thumbed though their papers and the first sent the second some rather unpleasant glances. In the assessments which I gave Marković there was a chapter missing, true, which described in numbers the actual power of our defence to the delegates, but all the rest of the assessments were in it and it was clearly visible that Slovenia was not preparing for any kind of attack on the YNA, but that it would defend itself if the YNA attacked it or attempted to prevent the carrying out of legitimate decisions of the Slovenian parliament.

The self-confident president of the Federal Executive Council needed a few minutes to compose himself, for the position which was to have brought him an advantage had turned against him. He pushed the assessments towards Brovet and muttered that they should check the information before it was supplied to the prime minister.

The continuation of the negotiations did not bring any visible results. Stane Brovet made excuses, saying he did not hold the necessary authorisations, Ante Marković called twice in between to Veljko Kadijević and Veljko finally agreed to a minimum increase in conscripts who could serve in Slovenia. Despite the poor results, after this opening lesson the talks were much more balanced and we were not underestimated anymore in the coming negotiations.

We then learned from our intelligence sources of the first information which warned that the YNA was preparing plans by which it would forcibly appropriate the records of recruits and begin dispatching draft cards itself. We upgraded our security measures in the administrative bodies for people's defence, and later moved most of the records to police stations and to some other, safer areas. At the next draft call we respected the position of the Slovenian Assembly to the letter, despite ever tougher threats coming from Belgrade and despite the obvious aggravation of some of our softer politicians at home.

After the announcement of the results of the plebiscite on 26 December 1990 it became clear to me that negotiations on the location of doing military service were practically at an end. The fact is, it would have been absurd to continue sending soldiers to serve in the army in a formally foreign country.

In the autumn of 1990 the YNA had already formed the so-called military-territorial bodies in Slovenia, which were to take the fulfilment of conscription duties into their own hands. The decree on this was passed by the Federal Executive Council in the summer, but Ante Marković had retained it in his desk and only after strong pressure from Kadijević did he sign it, with a delay of several months. The YNA constantly put off the take-over of conscription duties, for they did not know how to do it. The records of our recruits were carefully safeguarded, for the safety of tens of thousands of our boys depended on this. Relations once again sharpened in February 1991, for we had to send a portion of the March contingent to Belgrade, despite the plebiscite. The army threatened both in highly confidential letters as well as in public. Ante Marković flew to Ljubljana on 19 February. He was met at a guarded airport, while doubled guards were deployed in front of the more important buildings in the capital of Slovenia. His attempt to convince us to send recruits or otherwise the army would react lasted for some hours. He said that he could not hold them back any longer. The two of us had a private talk for nearly an hour, and he wanted to scare me, saying that in the eyes of the generals it was all my fault and not of this imaginary assembly and that I should pay the highest price for this. I rejoined that he had signed an anti-constitutional document on military-territorial bodies, for there was no basis for such in any of the federal laws. This made him especially angry. He stated that he had foundations in the Constitution, while the laws would soon be changed by the Federal Assembly. He rebuked us, saying that Slovenians were ungrateful, for he was supposedly the last barrier still holding back the generals from intervening by force. He had not signed the formally favoured vote for the decree on military-territorial bodies (VTO) for a few months and so prevented its publication in the Official Gazette, and in this way, despite Kadijević's threats, he had also postponed its implementation. "Your Drnovšek," he stated "as the president, signed the decree of the Presidency of the SFRY on introducing a state of emergency in Kosovo the moment it was brought to his desk and, through this, permitted the immediate implementation of measures there!" I reminded him that through "his brav-ery" he was also saving his position, for in the case of army intervention he would most surely not be needed any more. I proved to him that we were tied to the decision made at the plebiscite and that we would behave in the way the parliament decided. And if the army intervened with force, then we would respond accordingly. As he was leaving, Igor Bavčar showed him the guards in front of the premises and said, just let them come, if they think that they can gain anything in that way. We received an informal report from Belgrade the next day stating that the army was going to wait until the formal decision of the Slovenian parliament was made.

The public and, of course, the potential recruits and their parents explained to themselves the decision made at the plebiscite in one soul. No one wanted to do military service outside Slovenia. The biggest doubts remained in political circles and the parliament, but the latter, at the last moment, when the March 1991 contingent virtually had their draft cards in their hands, accepted the change to the constitutional law with which the obligation to serve in the YNA ceased.

Meanwhile the pressure from Belgrade continued. Among Slovenia's political elite worry prevailed, for we were all aware that there was no ideal solution to this problem, except if the army was prepared to make a deal. We also constantly wanted to hold talks with Veljko Kadijević, but he kept avoiding us. In April the situation also became intolerable for him, since he had not received even one soldier from Slovenia in March through regular paths.[1] So he agreed to direct talks, but he placed the condition that the Slovenian delegation must not include either Milan Kučan or myself. We decided that Lojze Peterle and Janez Drnovšek, who was almost convinced that it would be possible to come to a compromise with the army, should go to Belgrade. On 4 April, when the meeting was finally held, there was great disappointment. Veljko Kadijević and Stane Brovet were not prepared to discuss anything but the "method by which Slovenia would finally begin implementing the federal laws for the field of military duties and defence."

Veljko Kadijević presented the following alternatives:

1. Fulfilment of federal army duties according to the regulations of the SFRY.

2. Fulfilment by force if Slovenia does not agree to the first variant.

He agreed only that he would not intervene with force before 15 May, but that Slovenia should send half of its March generation to the YNA in May and the other half in June, and even that only if the Federal Assembly acceded to the decision of the Slovenian plebiscite.

Veljko Kadijević also offered his own proposals for settling relations between the YNA and the Slovenian TO, which were:

1. The commander of the Republic Headquarters of the Territorial Defence (RHQ TO) was to be general Marjan Vidmar, as an active officer, subordinated to the GHQ, while Janez Slapar could remain the second in command; in this case the Presidency of the SFRY would rescind its announced measures against the TO.

2. The weapons of the TO were to remain in the storage sites of the YNA, but would be temporarily available for military exercises.

3. All active officers of the YNA whom we had removed from the TO were to be reinstated.

Veljko Kadijević and Stane Brovet also demanded at this meeting that Slovenia unconditionally and immediately pay its debts to the army from 1990 (withheld funds on account of the recruits who had not been sent to the YNA), and the financial obligations according to federal regulations for 1991 in accordance with the resolutions of the Federal Executive Council.

Nothing was left of the great expectations of a "historical compromise". Both of the "acceptable" negotiators were sent back to Ljubljana empty--handed. The generals were prepared for serious talks only a few months

---

[1] The law allowed that only those who wanted did their military service in the YNA. Of the three thousand, only a few volunteers from Slovenia opted for this, going to barracks near their own homes. The YNA expected at least a few hundred volunteers.

later, when they had been taught a good lesson in defensive warfare and when they were simply left with no other rational alternative but to withdraw ·from Slovenia. Despite this, the meeting of 4 April was very helpful to us, for the last illusions on the hope that we could have civilised talks with the YNA faded away. In Slovenia even some Doubting Thomases – who had constant anxiety, asking whether we were not escalating things too much with regard to the recruits (sometimes even prominent mouths uttered statements such as what was the fate of a few hundred soldiers in comparison to the peaceful life of a nation) – finally recognised that it was the other side that was against dialogue and not us.

Many of the recruits are in the Crisis points in Croatia, though with the acceptance of the moratorium on sending Slovenian soldiers to the YNA, the second stage of the battle for recruits had practically begun. The parents founded a committee for their return, which did a good job. In various ways, negotiations, agreements and with pressure on individual officers in the YNA who could help, we succeeded in getting 75 per cent of the Slovenian soldiers back to Slovenia before the start of aggression on Slovenia. More than a thousand escaped at the beginning of the aggression and during it. Some escapes were quite spectacular and only the good organisation and the resourcefulness of individuals and their parents, as well as luck, can be thanked for everything ending well. After the Brioni Declaration a little less than 15 per cent of the normal annual contingent of Slovenian soldiers remained in the YNA, mainly in garrisons in Serbia, from where they could not escape without very great risk. These were finally saved by the resolution of the Presidency of the SFRY on the withdrawal of the YNA from Slovenia which also guaranteed the safe return of our boys. Only after the war was it possible to speak with the generals on equal terms and this task was done well by Janez Drnovšek. Even before this, Serbia had to grant its consent for such a decision of the army and the Presidency of the SFRY. With this, one of the most dramatic as well as most sensitive chapters in Slovenia's emancipation ended, a story intertwined with thousands of individual stories, hardships and joy, but with a favourable outcome. Our soldiers in the YNA were on the one hand constantly a factor for extortion by Belgrade and, on the other, a great moral obligation to the new Slovenian politicians. The safe return of practically all our soldiers is counted as one of the biggest individual successes during the process in which the creation of a free Slovenian state was proceeding. It had achieved its goal almost without any victims among those which it had, at the beginning of this process, still to send to a foreign army.

6. TERRITORIAL DEFENCE GROWS INTO A REAL ARMED FORCE OF THE SLOVENIAN PEOPLE

On 28 September 1990 the Slovenian Assembly accepted and announced amendments 96 and 97 to the Constitution of the Republic of Slovenia. With this act, authorisations in case of a state of emergency were transferred to the Republic Presidency, while in the case of an attack from outside, Slovenia still respected the unity of the joint armed forces of the SFRY. Despite this compromise, Belgrade reacted very sharply to our decision. The next day the Federal Secretary for People's Defence issued a threatening public announcement in which it accused Slovenia of violating federal regulations and destroying the unity of the armed forces. It was a Saturday and my deputy, Jelko Kacin, and I were visiting the specialised units of the civil defence of Kranj, which were training in Fažana. The news of the new threat from the GHQ caught me in the car, and when I came home the phones were already incessantly ringing. After the questions posed to me by journalists, I felt that the threat had this time caused greater consternation. And in truth, the acceptance of the amendments to the Constitution regarding the TO was, in the legal sense, a big step ahead in our acquiring sovereignty in the field of defence. Many were of the opinion that this time we would not come out of it without being punished and that we had challenged Belgrade too much. The public, for understandable reasons, was not aware of our preparations for the defence of Slovenia, which we had carried out under cover of the MSND, and many thought that we had no real force behind us. This is why I accepted the invitation to appear on television and to answer questions about the ultimatum placed by the ZSLO with the following statements:

■ Yesterday's declaration of the amendments and the constitutional law for the implementation of these amendments in the field of defence actually impedes the united line of command in one of the components of the Yugoslav armed forces, the territorial defence. I shall not repeat the reasons which forced us into the unanimous acceptance of these amendments, for you already know them. As of yesterday the supreme commander of the Territorial Defence of Slovenia is the Presidency of the Republic of Slovenia, but only in time of peace and a state of emergency, that is in the case of internal conflicts in Yugoslavia. In the case of an attack from outside, then the Presidency of the SFRY has for now still unchanged authority over the Territorial Defence of Slovenia.

Thus the fear of the army commander of the disunity of the armed forces is totally unfounded, unless, of course, it is planning to use the armed forces against Slovenia. Only in such a case could our amendments be an impediment.

Also the solutions which we accepted in association with military duty or military service envisage that we shall, under our own administration, be training only those recruits for whom the YNA does not provide their service in the YNA in Slovenia, which is technically and professionally feasible to establish. It depends on them how big this contingent will be or if it will even be necessary.

The Federal Secretariat warns that the amendments and the constitutional law are illegal and that the federal government and the Presidency of the SFRY will propose measures for their implementation to be prohibited. Let me state that the valid legal order in Yugoslavia does not allow the Federal Constitutional Court to invalidate the Republic Constitution or constitutional law. In the same way, the federal bodies cannot legally declare a state of emergency in Slovenia, for the Republic Assembly must give its consent to this.

All measures which would be in opposition to the legal decisions of the Republic Assembly, the Republic bodies will of course overrule in the defence of Slovenia. They have been prepared for some time for such extreme intervention, although it is realistically impossible, for the actual conflict zones are elsewhere in Yugoslavia.

In today's message from the Federal Secretariat for People's Defence (ZSLO) not one word mentions yesterday's acceptance of the Serbian Constitution, according to which the President of Serbia is the supreme commander of all the armed forces in the Serbian state, not only of the Territorial Defence, and not only in peace, but also in war. This solution in the Serbian Constitution is much more radical than the Slovenian amendments and Serbia can implement this in practice at any time. At this moment all the consequences which could result in this case cannot be assessed.

The ZSLO is not worried about the armed resistance of the Serbs in Croatia either, it is only disturbed by the non-mob-rule and legal solving of problems in the Slovenian TO, for which the greatest fault lies precisely in the acts of the Serbian generals and in Serbian policies in the Presidency of Yugoslavia.

All this only confirms our views of how correct the behavior of the Slovenian Assembly has been in actually accepting by consensus the constitutional amendments at the last moment, and I am convinced that we shall not resign from them under any pressure.

We in Slovenia are not prepared to pay the accounts of others with our blood. ■

The response or commentary fell on favourable ears in the public. That same night Milan Kučan called me and said that he agreed with my answer. There were very few doubts in parliament and there were no serious moves to withdraw from our accepted amendments. In Belgrade at first they did not

70

quite know what to do. Then the decision came. A plan was to be prepared for the renewed subordination of the Slovenian TO to Belgrade. Here, they counted above all on the loyal formal commander of the Republic Headquarters of the TO of Slovenia, air force General Ivan Hočevar and on all the active officers in the ranks of the TO.

Of course we expected a response from Belgrade, and we were also all interested in how General Hočevar and the other high officers in the Republic Headquarters of the TO would decide, and who would finally have to make a decision. We were ready and waiting for receipt of the amendments to the Constitution. A few hours after our Declaration of the law the Presidency of the Republic had already named its key people for the new command of the Territorial Defence, and the Manoeuvring Structure of the National Defence, which immediately after the acceptance of the law came under the composition of the TO, was battle-ready. After the threat which the ZSLO addressed to the Slovenian bodies in government and the public, we expected that the YNA would carry out a "show of force", which would be the deployment of some armoured units and sorties by the air force, and then issue Slovenia with an ultimatum. Such plans really did exist, but they became tangled up in the opening act, that is in the seizure of the building of the Republic Headquarters of the TO at Prežihova 4 in Ljubljana.

On Thursday, 4 October 1990, I sent General Hočevar a letter in which I commanded him to hand over his duties to the new acting chief of the Republic Headquarters of the TO, Janez Slapar, at 10.00 hours the next day. That same evening Hočevar went to Zagreb, to the command of the 5th Army Sector, to see General Konrad Kolšek. Since he had returned soon after 22.00 he obviously went there only to receive orders for action. We observed battle stations being implemented the whole of Thursday in some army units in Slovenia, so we too activated a part of the TO and police in the afternoon. In the evening, even before Hočevar's return, the chief of the Ljubljana Corps, Maj-General Marjan Vidmar called the duty officer of the old RHQ TO, Colonel Mežnar, and reported to him that the military police was going to seize or "additionally protect" the building on Prežihova 4. At 10.30 a detachment of soldiers from a military police battalion, specially trained, armed and equipped and composed primarily from Serb nationals, left the Šentvid barracks and seized the RHQ TO building in Prežihova street. The duty officer at the Headquarters, Colonel Mežnar, cooperated actively in this, otherwise the building was mainly empty. The units of the military police were monitored from their barracks by members of a special unit of the Slovenian police, but they did not have any orders or possibility for stopping the column without initiating a conflict. In the same way, we could not seize the building in Prežihova street without violence, for the security guards and the duty officer of the old RHQ TO, who were loyal to the army, were inside. Furthermore, the written deadline for Hočevar to hand over duties was for tomorrow. We notified Ljubljana TV, which filmed the seizure of the headquarters, and the news spread very rapidly around.

Igor Bavčar, Janez Slapar, Jelko Kacin, Tone Krkovič and a few other colleagues and I were sitting in my office at Zupančičeva 3, a few dozen metres away from the "occupied" building of the RHQ TO. All necessary orders and instructions had been issued. They were already cutting off the power and phones of the occupied block. Members of the MSND were in position or on the way, the special police units also. A high level of battle preparedness had prevailed for a few days now. All the more important buildings in Slovenia were guarded. Our intelligence men in the commands of the 14th and 31st Corps, in the headquarters of the 5th Army District and in Belgrade were attentive to any lead which could point to possible action by the YNA of a greater extent. But there was no information which suggested any greater intrigues. It was becoming clear that the YNA assessed the position only as being superficial and was of the opinion that to master the TO of Slovenia it was enough to maintain a puppet republic headquarters and General Hočevar, and intimidate people with tanks, and so the command of the 5th Army District, which led the operation, was not planning other action.

The support section for the RHQ TO was positioned in a special house in Prule, Ljubljana. There was also a garage there with a number of field and other vehicles. We sent a scout group to see what the position was like there and learned that there were no signs of life in the building, that the doors were closed, and that the keys were supposedly in the hands of one of Hočevar's men, by the name of Milošević. We had two possibilities, either break down the door and risk a skirmish, if special units of the military police were concealed in the building, or try to get the key and possibly more information on the situation in the building. Matters were taken into the hands of Jelko Kacin who, together with Janez Slapar, drove off to persuade Milošević to unlock the building of the support section in Prule. When they arrived at his flat, the man showed (feigned) panic. When he was looking for the key he cut his hand and instead of taking him to Prule they took him to a doctor. They returned to the Secretariat without having achieved anything. Meanwhile Milošević phoned the barracks and when one of our men was screening the house in Prule he was awaited with an automatic weapon trained on him. The sound of the doors being locked and a juicy eff off greeting convinced him, and, so we bade farewell to that house for some time, too.

During the night we had already notified all three presidents of the three supreme bodies of the occupation of the building in Prežihova street. In the morning Slovenian radio was already reporting the military police operation in Prežihova in its first news broadcasts and the excitement was mounting from minute to minute. I wrote a draft of an official report, but in the morning the prime minister and some colleague ministers wanted to be first acquainted with the situation, then a session of the Presidency was called. We were working over my statement and at the end it was compressed into a few sentences, which did not say much. The Presidency was afraid that I would say something which could anger the army even more. But when the report finally did reach the public in the middle of the morning, it was much too late. During this time demonstrations began on Prežihova and the people were demanding that the military police leave the building. The lieutenant who led the operation asked for support and the tanks in Vrhnika were reving up their engines. The situation was becoming serious. Igor and I, swearing at the indecisive and slow politicians, each went our own way. Igor to Prežihova to calm the people down, for unnecessary bloodshed could easily occur, and I to the TV station, where I finally explained the background of the situation in a live broadcast. At the same time we were rushing to prepare trucks and buses for barricades, if the tanks did set off towards Ljubljana to scatter the demonstrators.

Bavčar's and my appearance only partly calmed spirits down. The rage of the demonstrators was justified and the sign of the RHQ TO, which Jure Šter and his friends had ripped off the building and brought to us at the Secretariat is still hanging in our conference room. But the consequences could have been much worse, and we were not suitably prepared for them, for we were right in the middle of handing over the MSND to the Territorial Defence and this could have caused some difficulties, if we had to take more decisive measures, which was already clear from our uncertainty at the building in Prule.

People were especially offended by the visit of General Konrad Kolšek and Ivo Tominc to the headquarters. They were afraid to leave the building because of the demonstrators and only the intervention of the police allowed them to leave. Before this I had quite a "dynamic" talk over the phone with Kolšek. His voice in this conversation betrayed the first signs of fear as well as an enormous lack of understanding. Later, the army claimed in its reports that we were calling army recruits to demonstrate, and that the women were on the streets to chase their husbands home.

In the evening the situation calmed down and next day I had a platoon of YNA soldiers with weapons, ready to shoot, thirty metres away from my office which stayed there for weeks and months. But I was convinced that they were much more afraid than we were and that they were greatly relieved when they were replaced.

*   *   *

The occupied buildings in Prežihova and Prule were slowly becoming a large and unpleasant problem for the YNA. Both of the buildings were without electricity and the sections of the army which guarded them were scared all the time. The generator they had dragged over to Prežihova upset the people and many were rudely shouted at when they entered the occupied building. The officers of the old RHQ TO, who had remained loyal to Ivan Hočevar and Belgrade were coming to the building for a while in civilian clothes, and finally they all nervously moved to the barracks at Metelkova. At every contact with the YNA or the federal authorities, we reproached them for occupying Prežihova and stealing the inventory, so that they were becoming very tired of "the successful operation". After six months of perseverance they sneakily left the block. Before this, they had robbed it completely. They had even taken out the electric switches from the walls and in some places even the electric wires.

In the Autumn of 1990 we continued with our reorganisation of the TO. After posting new commanders of the TO to seven regions and the chief of the Republic Headquarters, as well as transferring jurisdiction of the units of the MSND of the TO to the new Republic Headquarters, the race with time had begun. From all views we were at the starting point, but in terms of the service of the National Protection operation, we were a few steps further. In Slovenia the Yugoslav army was organisationally, politically, militarily and, to a great measure, morally, untouched. They were still the complete master of their domain. The YNA also had some direct support from some of the media as well as in the political and regime organisations and bodies, either through sympathisers or through direct collaborators with KOS. This allowed it to play various games, which in the atmosphere of unsettled doubts existing in Yugoslavia and the future of Slovenia sometimes caused great damage among the Slovenian parties. In Yugoslavia in general the position of the army was even stronger, and the overall atmosphere was strongly disinclined even to the idea of a confederation. The rest of the world viewed our desire for independence and our attempts to form our own defence forces with disfavour.

We needed a new legislation, but things first got bogged down in the parliament, with the law on defence and protection, and then with the law on military service. The main opponent to forming our own defence were the liberal democrats and the reformers, except that the latter were allowing the naive demoliberals to get ahead. Many things were concealed in the background, from naive to utopian party programmes, to conscious and hard--headed opposition, to those concrete moves which would truly allow us to step out of Yugoslavia. Many concealed Yugoslaves knew that in the decisive moment the actual ratio of forces would decide and not one or another constitutional law, thus, under the mask of standing for non-violence and demilitarisation, they were trying to prevent Slovenian independence.

The key problem was still the poorly equipped Territorial Defence in terms of arms, military and other equipment. In September 1990 Slovenia did not send its full contingent of recruits to the YNA and, on our proposal, the Assembly passed a resolution that those who we had not sent to army training were not paid for either. Despite the decision of the Assembly, I still had great difficulties in convincing, with the help of some of my colleagues in the government, the Minister of Finance, then still a great defender of the Marković programme, that he must retain some of the sales tax and instead of sending it to the YNA propose it for the equipping of the TO. Thus we retained approximately 300 million then dinars and part of this money was proposed for the purchase of urgent ammunition, infantry and personal anti-tank weapons.

For every batch of weapons we succeeded in getting across the border there was a broad plan and carefully prepared operation behind it, and not

74

once did it occur that any operation was threatened. After we had shown the new weapons, for a deterrent effect, to the public, the KOS attempted to discredit us through the mass media – Delo Plus was in the forefront – with fabricated stories. As they did not have any real data, they made up systems and stories which they thought to be most probable. In this way they did a lot of damage to some companies, above all to organisations belonging to our fellow countrymen abroad, who were being accused of exporting weapons to Slovenia. In truth, Slovenia did not import then or later one piece of weaponry, ammunition or explosives from any of our neighbouring states, nor did any Slovenian organisation in the world cooperate in this (in contrast for example to the export of weapons to Israel during the creation of the Jewish state).

Our modest purchases abroad did not essentially improve the preparedness of the units of the TO. We organised a few smaller operations in which members of special units, mainly officers of the permanent composition of the TO, removed some of the weapons from army barracks. But, because the risk was too great, bigger operations were never taken on. So we had to adapt the formations of units to the weapons and equipment we had at our disposal, and at the same time, prepare plans for more difficult variants.

I ordered the Republic Headquarters to make an operational plan for seizing weapons and ammunition dumps in case of aggression by the YNA and for the eventuality that the Presidency of the Republic of Slovenia declared a general mobilisation. When making these plans the following tasks had to be considered:

1. Select dumps which were not so well defended and which were closer to larger settlements.

2. Include the people who knew the buildings and the location well in the preparation of the action.

3. The time for seizing the dumps had to be coordinated with the mobilisation of units which were not armed.

4. Formulate the operational plans in the regions in cooperation with the Territorial Defence.

5. Specially trained units which were to be mobilised first had to be selected. These were to be subordinated directly to the RHQ TO.

Some of the units remained in the same composition as they were during the National Defence operation, while in the municipal headquarters many new, smaller units, were composed. Mostly companies and platoons. The response time could be improved only by distributing weapons to members of the special units "into their hands", i.e. at home, while we also allocated people into units by the principle of vicinity, which meant that, for example, individual important buildings were protected by detachments whose members were living in the direct vicinity of the said building and had a phone at home. All special units could call themselves up, thus the members notified each other. Because of financial difficulties we did not have many bleepers. Only a few commanders received them.

With these methods we reduced the time of mobilisation of some of the units to as little as 30 minutes, which is good even for units which are stationed in barracks.

After the successful National Protection operation its main actor, Tone Krkovič, took command over the special units of the TO, which at that time was performing the task of a guard brigade of the supreme command. With his energetic methods he completely reorganised the brigade, he included numerous experts in its work, various types of sportsmen and had, by the beginning of the war, trained a powerful special purpose unit. At the same time a teaching centre for training special units was being founded in the hidden forests of Kočevje. Each week new, additionally trained platoons of specially picked soldiers left from there either for the composition of detachments of the special brigade or for the composition of the units of the municipal headquarters. A few similar centres were created under the organisation of the RHQ TO and in one year several thousand members of the Territorial Defence had been trained.

Tensions followed one after another during the whole autumn, winter and spring and some units of the TO had to be mobilised three times a month. The response of the conscripts was higher than all our expectations, despite the abnormal stress. The Republic Headquarters of the TO carried out the KOBRA exercise, in which the TO played out the possibility that the aggressor was the YNA for the first time seriously. The exercise was held under complete secrecy. We did the PREMIK exercise for the public, where we transferred a battalion of the TO from the north of Primorska to the southern border and tried them out in between with various variants of battle usage. The experience of both exercises proved to be very beneficial during the actual battle deployment of units during the war for Slovenia. This was a good school and the TO rapidly grew into a specific although not exactly classic army but, despite this, an effective real force for an emerging country.

* * *

At the beginning of 1991 the political administration of the Federal Secretariat for People's Defence composed a highly confidential report on the current situation in the world and in the country and the direct tasks of the YNA. The report contained great hope that the reform of the Soviet Union would collapse and that a united, socialist Soviet Union would survive. Regarding Yugoslavia, the authors of the report also wrote that "socialism here is not completed yet and the country has resisted the first blow and wave of anti-communist hysteria." This assessment was, together with the optimistic expectations that there "exist realistic possibilities for the preservation of Yugoslavia as a federal and socialist community", was the consequence above all of two facts. On the one hand it was the result of the untouched structure and functional composition of the YNA, and on the other, the eruption of optimism after the elections in Serbia, where the communists, with Slobodan Milošević at the head, won convincingly in an otherwise dubious democratic environment. On 22 January, information was sent to commanders of the most important units of the YNA in Yugoslavia.

On the evening of the following day Andrej Lovšin called me and anxiously told me that our source who was installed in an important institution of the YNA had received some very signifiant information. In half an hour I had already read it, and, although I was convinced that this related to an original document, I ordered Lovšin to check its authenticity once again, before we let this information out to the public. Later I found out that our collaborator had once again risked his head, for as evidence of authenticity he also sent a copy of the accompanying letter with all the stamps and dates.

This information was of the utmost importance for us above all because its public announcement would reveal the still present block scheme in the strategic thinking of the YNA, according to which the Western imperialists had succeeded in destroying the socialist system in some countries of Eastern Europe, but that this did not and would not succeed in countries in which authentic socialist revolution had been victorious. Authentic meant the USSR and Yugoslavia. The authors of the information accused Hungary of being the main conductor of anti-Yugoslav activities, which were directed by Western imperialists. Slovenia was threatened with the direct implementation of federal laws, and the political future was linked to the League of Communists – Movement for Yugoslavia. The end of the report stated that the "communist party had won the war from 1941 to 1945 on the idea of Yugoslavia, national equality, brotherhood and unity, freedom and social righteousness" and that "the League of Communists – Movement for Yugoslavia, will be victorious in 1991 with this same idea."

The publication of this information was a great shock to those foreign statesmen who had, until 1991, seen the YNA above all as a non-political force which could assure the integrity of Yugoslavia and prevent the creation of new states on its territory. The Yugoslav generals were exposed. The domestic and foreign mass media wrote a lot about this North Korean type of communist army in Europe at the end of the 20th century. Belgrade also received a few sharp protests from states who were directly or indirectly implicated as "imperialists".

Panic gripped the political and above all security administration of the Yugoslav GHQ. Since we had an authentic document in our hands, they could not deny the information, and apart from this, it had already been read to all the professional officers in the barracks and commands. They were more worried about the path by which the document came into the hands of our intelligence service than about the response of the world public. On the modest number of copies which had been sent to the commands and institutions of the YNA throughout Yugoslavia, it had been explicitly written that the information may be read only to active officers and then immediately burned. The chief of the KOS at the GHQ fumed over the subordinated officers in the 5th Army District. In Zagreb they promised sanctions against the leading KOS operatives in the Ljubljana and Maribor Corps, Colonel Emil Malkoć and Lieutenant Colonel Ratko Katalina.

It was then that some in the YNA first became aware that they were not dealing with "joke amateurs" in Slovenia but with a successful intelligence service, which had succeeded in getting one of the most important or most sensitive political documents which the YNA had formulated in the last two years, even sooner than it had been read to all the officers in all the barracks. And they really were in an impossible situation, for the young officers in some of the barracks were openly making fun of their superiors, when they were read the highly confidential information that had been reported by all the more important mass media.

The members of KOS in Slovenia and the 5th Army District received the task of uncovering the channel through which the information got into the hands of the intelligence service of the Slovenian defence minister, and to make the work of our intelligence impossible in one way or another.

At that time a real intelligence service at the Secretariat for People's Defence did not exist. We only had a department with four people, led by and including Andrej Lovšin, a graduate of the military academy, who soon stopped serving in the YNA and got a job with the police. But he was not well thought of there either, for during the candidacy of Igor Bavčar for membership of the Presidency of Slovenia in 1988, he voted for him despite the general distaste of his superiors. In 1990 he resisted the pressure of his bosses, who were collecting votes for the Party of Reform in the police before the elections.

When I took over the defence ministry I first met with a very unpleasant reality in the form of four officers and NCOs of KOS, who were formal military personnel and, with regard to the line of command, subordinated to Belgrade, and who were stationed at my Secretariat. First I replaced the chief without much ado, despite sharp protests from Belgrade (the ZSLO even intervened through prime minister Marković), and gave the department to Andrej Lovšin, who offered the other three either loyalty to Slovenia and its laws or the barracks of the YNA. All three opted for the barracks and not for Slovenia and thus we thanked them for their cooperation on the next day. The chief of the Ljubljana Corps of KOS tried to make a scandal of this through his connections in the mass media, saying that Janša had illegally fired honest employees, but only the editor of the Neodvisni Dnevnik, Milan Medved, was prepared to publish the article which had been written in the head office of KOS at the 14th Corps, which was not enough to make a scandal.

I immediately called Ivan Borštner to work at the security department, who, through his links in the command of the Ljubljana Corps and elsewhere in the YNA, succeeded in receiving some key information on the plans and measures of the army against Slovenia. Later, the department was joined by Franci Žnidaršič, who took over the counter-intelligence work, and then by Franci Pulko, when the experimental army training began who, took a new

job at the 710th Training Centre in Pekre. Only four posts were systemati-
cised in the department just before the war, plus one for each region. Thus a
handful of people in the defence structure resisted the entire intelligence
service of the YNA, which had over 130 officers and NCOs professionally
engaged in Slovenia. During more important operations they also received
quite large reinforcements from Belgrade and Zagreb.

Despite the inexperience, weak personnel capacities and the constant
threats of KOS (Lovšin and Borštner were told many times that they were to
be liquidated at the first opportunity that arose) the security department,
with the aid of nationally conscious Slovenian officers in the ranks of the
YNA, who, despite the risk, cooperated with us, the counter-intelligence
service successfully protected the plans for protecting the independence of
Slovenia and, at the same time, gained most of the important information on
the plans of the YNA, either against Slovenia or against Slovenia and Croatia
together. Colonel Vladimir Vauhnik at the GHQ, the most successful intelligence man of Slovenian birth, military envoy of the Yugoslav government in
Berlin, who in April 1941 reported the schedule of the German attack on
Yugoslavia to Belgrade in time had received a worthy successor. Although
the department had a staff one hundredth the size of the state security or the
security intelligence service (VIS) and although it did not have any technology, in contrast to KOS and VIS, they were far ahead in receiving key
information, because they were unburdened with old links which had
weakened the foundations of work of the security intelligence services.

The reorganisation of the national security in the security-intelligence
service (VIS) was a demanding task and up to May 1991 this service did not
operate against the YNA. We were receiving VIS reports on the operation of
foreign services but there were hardly any reports on those who were truly
threatening Slovenia, the KOS. There was a lot of bad moods and bad blood
among our intelligence agents, who saw how the higher employees of VIS
were meeting with the members of KOS which we had chased out of our
Secretariat.

Only more decisive replacements and a few retirements and the energetic moves of Miha Brejc slowly prepared this service to deal with KOS as a
possible opponent. Their first major success was reached during the events in
Pekre, when they acquired some information on 23 May on the planned
kidnapping of the commander of the regional headquarters of the TO,
Vladimir Milošević, and their work was greatly strengthened during the
conflict itself and just before it, as they assisted a great deal, with the
cooperation of the TO and other parts of the police, in almost completely
destroying or at least incapacitating most of the KOS network.

KOS, despite its great efforts did not succeed in establishing such a
dense network in Slovenia as it had succeeded in doing in Croatia. They had
a relatively large number of their own, but only a few were important. They
were receiving the most important data from two sources. One of them was
the parliament delegate, Milan Aksentijević, who succeeded in finding out
various details from behind the scenes of Slovenian politics, from his contacts

with some more "trustworthy" delegates. He was especially interested in information regarding the ratio of forces in the government, the Presidency, the relation of individual ministers and members of the Presidency with Marković, etc. Sometimes some delegates fed him "rumours" on purpose, and Emin Malkoć had some difficulty trying to explain why things which Aksentijević had stated to be one hundred per cent foolproof information did not happen.

The second important source of information for KOS was, according to some of the data collected to date, a certain retired officer of the YNA living in Ljubljana, a Serb by birth, from Lika, and a friend of Sime Dubajić. This retired officer was to have received his information from his son, employed in a high state body and an extreme pro-Yugoslav. Through Dubajić the information travelled still warm to the KOS administration in Belgrade, and some also directly to one of the Slovenian dailies, where they were used in editorials against Slovenian independence.

KOS had a few points in the Slovenian mass media, and at the same time, a number of correspondents for Serbian newspapers who were reporting from Slovenia also worked for the intelligence service. During the war, some of them reported their observations at press conferences first to the KOS and only after this to their editorial offices. Emin Malkoć had two collaborators at Ljubljana TV, one, with the code name Emona, at a more important post, and the second who was in the technical personnel, where he was pushed in a little before the war. The radio also regularly sent information to the intelligence centre of the Ljubljana Corps until the war, then this source closed down. KOS collected intelligence data and also spread disinformation through retired officers or family members of those employed in the YNA, but with very limited success.

The police and the counter-intelligence service of the TO and VIS broke down and compromised a large part of the KOS network in operations during the first days of the war. This was greatly assisted by the publication of data on key KOS members in Delo one month before. One of the key blows to the activities of KOS was at the end of June, 1991, when a unit of the TO, together with our counter-intelligence men, took over their phone tapping centre in the middle of Ljubljana and confiscated material evidence on their illegal operations against Slovenia.

7. THE PLEBISCITE

In the autumn of 1990 two other aggressive concepts, which it was attempted to realise through two federal bodies, existed, in addition to the proposals of Slovenia and Croatia on the new order of Yugoslavia as a confederate state.

Borisav Jović, who took up the initiative of Slobodan Milošević, tried, with the assistance of most of the Federal Presidency, to force upon Yugoslavia a nicely packaged Serbian model for solving the crisis. This was a proposal by which individual parts of Yugoslavia were, through a referendum, to decide on life in a united country or on secession. The proposal of the legal solution according to this model was written in such a way that decisions were made possible in individual municipalities. Behind this formulation was concealed the Serbian appetite for parts of Bosnia and Croatia, that is why these two republics did not accept such a concept.

As Ante Marković did not agree with this model, the federal government did not want to write the draft of this law, so that, in contrast to regular practice, it was prepared by the professional service of the Presidency of the SFRY.

Ante Marković, who closely linked his future and his personal ambitions to the future order of Yugoslavia, was searching for a solution in a modern centralised federation, with a modern market system and a Yugoslav (probably liberally oriented) party. He relied on the important results achieved in the reform of the economy and on greater international support than Jović, but he did not have a real political base at home. He tried to create this by calling for the foundation of his own party at the same time, and in three steps abnormally increased (by 130%) the wages of the army and federal administration. This was a cunning move by which he wanted to entice the army and all the federal administration into his party. He provided the money by increasing the federal budget.

Because he did not want to risk a final conflict, Marković allowed the obviously anti-constitutional disbanding of the Kosovo Assembly and left the Albanians at the mercy of the Serbs. With this he lost an important argument in his political contentions, for he could no longer claim seriously that he was defending the constitutional path for change to Yugoslavia. This move by the Serbs surely blocked all possibilities of legally changing the Federal Constitution for ever, since with the disbanding of the Kosovo Assembly, it could not

81

be changed. As it was difficult to expect the Serbians to change their decision, it was a waste of time discussing amendments to the federal law.

Viewed in the long term, both were in a dead end – Borisav Jović and Ante Marković. And they both caused additional chaos in the command of the YNA, which split up even more into pro-Serb and pro-Yugoslav sections.

Slowly, all eyes began to turn towards Bosnia even at that time. In November they held elections and the national parties won the majority of votes. Power was divided up between them.

In Croatia, the Serbs announced a referendum. Its short-term purpose was to brew up a dispute and create a tense situation. Then under the threat of civil war, they would force through their formula as a solution, with the intervention of the most powerful player, the YNA. But the Serb Krajina even at that time sometimes evaded the fetters of Slobodan Milošević. Thus Borisav Jović, Slobodan Milošević and Petar Gračanin had to personally calm down the volunteers who wanted to go to Knin and help their brothers at any cost.

Simultaneously with the events in Knin, the support forces of the anti-bureaucratic revolution throughout Yugoslavia were also very lively. The Party for the Equal Rights of Citizens announced itself in Slovenia, too.

Internal political life in Slovenia proceeded under constant glances towards the south for almost half a year after the elections. The collecting of volunteers, and the punitive expeditions which we could follow on our TVs, proved time and again to be a catastrophic experience for those who did not take such threats seriously. For this reason Igor and I warned many times that we should not delude ourselves that we were far from the problems of Yugoslavia and that we must do everything we could so that others might not settle their accounts with our blood.

The main political moves in Slovenia occurred after the elections in parliament. The ratio of power in the new Slovenian Assembly was an ideal relation for a stable parliamentary system with a long-term tradition. Namely, this was a relation which would not allow rapid changes to the system. This would assure a high degree of stability and anticipation in a state which would have a firm and tested democratic system. In a parliamentary life barely a few months old, without a tradition and pluralistic experience, such a ratio of power had not only the above-mentioned positive characteristics but also negative ones. These appeared in the slow systematic changes even in those affairs where there were no great political differences, and above all in the infinite possibilities of paralysing legislative initiatives. The latter was possible because of the tricameral composition of the Assembly and the lack of political experience of the delegates and above all the members of the new political parties. Despite procedural communications, the old standing orders (one of the biggest deficiencies of the new Assembly was precisely that it had not adopted new standing orders) and the overburdened delegates with their many "ballast points", without any true content, the parliamentary life of the new Assembly of the Republic of Slovenia operated similarly to the majority of other pluralistic parliaments in all its essential items. All of us who had been elected to the government from the ranks of delegates probably looked at the work of the new Assembly quite specifically. I personally was most disturbed by the overall and sometimes even strongly demagogic comments on the proposals of the government, which also came from among our colleague delegates in the ruling coalition, but by general conviction, the delegates from the ranks of the Liberal Democratic Party were far ahead in this. It was shown many times that individual delegates had not even read the proposed material properly, as a rule they did not know of positive legislation, that is of the laws which were valid at that time, so that they could not compare the new, proposed laws with the old and thus long and tedious discussions and mutual clarifications followed, from ideologically coloured criticism to actual insults.

Great difficulties in the work of the new Assembly were also caused by the huge number of commissions and boards. They wanted to guarantee the more effective work of the chamber with such commissions and boards, at the same time it was also an opportunity to employ delegates. Nearly every-one who wanted to could become a professional. The effectiveness of the work of the chambers did not improve with the increase in the number of working bodies, for the delegates at the sessions of the chamber usually repeated the arguments which they had already stated at a commission or board. Thus the daily agenda dragged on for ever, and every limitation of discussions to a normal period was immediately branded as being undemoc-ratic.

For the most part the people did not change with the replacement of the political system. In democracy anybody can, if they so desire, concern themselves with politics, and this is good, for it eliminates extremism and slowly a solution that is suitable for the majority of people begins to prevail, while at the same time, the minority can also be successfully protected. We had reached this level before the plebiscite, and the effectiveness of the system was at a critical point.

Apart from dissatisfaction with the poor operation of the government and parliament, as well as the fear of the outcome of crises elsewhere in Yugoslavia, a feeling of a lack of our own clear vision of the future predomi-nated in Slovenia during October and November. Officially we stood for a confederacy, which was becoming more and more ridiculous, since certain others, chiefly Serbia, did not want it, and it seemed as though we Slovenians were trying to force the Serbs to share a common life with us. In truth Serbia had a clearer official scheme, that was either a federation or secession, but not only were such variants unacceptable for Slovenia and also partly for Croatia, but Serbia was also actually implementing in practice the policies of a centralised Yugoslavia at any cost.

On 9 November 1990 the delegate club of Demos met in Poljče. Before the session began, Tine Hribar, Peter Jambrek and Jože Pučnik wanted to talk to me privately. We sat in the conference room and Hribar asked me directly if I would support the idea of a plebiscite for an independent

Slovenia. I was in favour, but I warned them that we were not prepared enough for the practical implementation of a decision made at such a plebiscite if it turned out to be positive. But this did not worry any of them, they probably did not have a view of the actual operative capabilities of the government – while I saw all the possible things which we would have to do before we took on any serious implementation of such a crucial move. But during this conversation I became aware that the plebiscite and actual independence did not have to be linked by time at all cost, and this made the idea feasible. These three people also had a similar discussion with the president of the Assembly, France Bučar.

The delegate club supported this idea and that same day it reached the public in a rather unsuitable manner. The proposal of the delegate club of Demos hit upon a negative response among the opposition. When the idea became a legal draft and when party conferences and coordinating began, all the parties supported the proposal in principle. Views differed above all with regard to the content of the question of the plebiscite, the time of its being held and the necessary majority for a successful result.

Immediately after the meeting of the delegate club I analysed the reasons in favour and the reasons against the plebiscite, for my own use, and came to the following conclusions:

■ **1. The collapse of the legal system of the SFRY was obvious.**
The unconstitutional decision of the Serbian Assembly to dissolve the Kosovo Assembly, the rampaging of armed roadside robbers in the Knin Krajina, the strangling of human rights in Kosovo and the issuing of money outside federal monetary establishments (Kosbanka) are only a few of the most obvious examples of the complete collapse of the legal order in the Yugoslav federation. Here we must also add the Slovenian legal path to independence and the acceptance of the new Serbian Constitution, above all the measures of the Serbian executive government which followed this.

2. The fall of the federal government and, with this, the collapse of economic reform is only a matter of time.
This, on the one hand, is a consequence of the contradictory measures taken by Marković, and on the other, the measures of the republic, including Slovenian, governments, where the obvious Serbian destruction of the federal government should be especially stressed. The federal government does not give a care for the necessity of at least a minimum operation of the federation until the outcome of the Yugoslav question.

3. The crucial nature of the outcome of the elections in Serbia for conditions in Yugoslavia and Slovenia.
With regard to the situation in Serbia, three possible variants exist for the development of the situation.

In the first, elections are not held or a boycott of the opposition is achieved. In this scenario the present regime remains in power, and at the same time relies even more directly on the YNA. Such a situation would not last long, since, due to the polarisation of the Serbian political scene, either new elections would be held or a war would break out.

84

The second possibility is an electoral victory by the Socialist Party of Serbia and the defeat of the opposition. In this case the outcome of the Yugoslav crisis could drag on greatly, and the possibility of an official coalition between the SSS (Serbian socialists) and the ZK–GZJ (League of Communists/Yugoslavia Movement) increases as well as possible intervention by the YNA outside of Serbia.

The third possibility is an electoral victory by the opposition. This brings the danger of classical military intervention in Serbia, for such an outcome would directly threaten the existence of the military command, and, taken as a whole, this variant is most favourable, for it offers the greatest possibility and space for an undisturbed exit from Yugoslavia and for a relatively peaceful separation.

4. Involvement of the YNA, either directly or through a new party of communists, in the political scene, with open threats of coercion. A political organisation and not just a military one is urgently needed for the achievement of political goals for such a hierarchical organisation as the army.[1] Irrespective of the fact that an army party in Slovenia would hardly have any support at all, its foundation would at least temporarily fulfil one of the important conditions needed for a military putsch, which is the existence of a political force to which the army after its putsch hands over power. With regard to ideological orientations similar to those in the Socialist Party of Serbia, there also exists the danger that the YNA might intervene in the preor post-electoral events in Serbia, if the socialist oriented forces do not win in the elections there.

From the aspect of national security of Slovenia it is thus better for the plebiscite to be held as soon as possible, if the Assembly of the Republic of Slovenia opts for it, and most certainly before the political image of the elections in the other republics is so clear that anyone could get the urge to make forcible adjustments in a socialist direction.

A decision made at the plebiscite for an independent Slovenian state would universally strengthen the security situation in Slovenia, for any military intervention against Slovenia after such a legitimately accepted decision would mean, from the standpoint of international law, true aggression on a sovereign and independent state (which, among other things, could request international help), while the same measures taken before such a decision was made could much more easily be explained as the settling of the internal affairs of a state. Despite this, long-term negotiations on the withdrawal of the federal army from the territory of Slovenia and for the division of the common federal property, which is in the form of military equipment and arms in our territory, would await us after the plebiscite.

5. Coordination with Croatia

At the latest meeting with the political leadership of Croatia it was stressed that both republics were aspiring to the same goals (establishment of standard foundations for the solution of relations with Yugoslavia) but in different ways. At the same time agreement was also reached about the fact that both steps (plebiscite implementation, acceptance of the Constitution) would have to be at the same time, and after this, both republics would, according to their abilities, still assure the minimum operation of the federation until the final outcome of the crisis (minimum financing of federation through quotas, non-election of new, but cooperation of the present representatives of both republics in federal bodies), for thus chaos would be prevented, more

---

[1] The YNA received this on 19 November 1990, and also with the new League of Communists – The Movement for Yugoslavia, which was founded or transformed from the Yugoslav League of Communists in the YNA, which also financed the work of the initiative committee and the founding meeting.

time for organising the secession from Belgrade would be gained, and it would also increase the possibilities for a peaceful solution to the crisis.

6. The reasons stated in the above five items could prevent Slovenian integration with Europe, which for our country signifies a conditio sine qua non not only for the suitable promotion of our economic, cultural and political life but also for the actual survival of the Slovenian nation. Thus the plebiscite opens doors to Europe.

In respect of the above-mentioned reasons which speak in favour of the plebiscite, it is obvious that political and other discords in Yugoslavia would in any delay of the plebiscite not only prevent the free expression of the will of the people on the future status of the Slovenian state but also historically threaten the already acquired independence and sovereignty of this state.■

I then used this analytical scheme either for convincing sceptics of the need for a plebiscite or for warning those who were too heated up of everything that still had to be done before the actual declaration of independence.

After forming a draft of the law on the plebiscite, inter-party negotiations began. In the end, the only disputed point was the necessary majority for a successful plebiscite result. We used up hours and hours before we came to a compromise. The negotiations showed the destitution of Slovenian politics, which was almost prepared to waste a historical opportunity over a trifle. The representatives of the then SDZ consumed an enormous amount of energy in somehow bringing a kind of consensus to the most conflicting opinions.

In the third phase of negotiations, which proceeded in the government hall on Gregorčičeva street, it was approaching midnight, and the chairman of the meeting, Milan Kučan, declared a half-hour adjournment so that the representatives could once again consult their parties. Igor and I, both very sleepy and tired as hell, dragged ourselves to the neighbouring office and sat quietly for a while. All of it was quite hopeless. I no longer remember who was the first to speak, but we both came out of the office firmly convinced to fight to the end and that the parties must be prepared at all costs to accept a reasonable compromise or agreement. We both analysed the situation and discovered that with no plebiscite – after it had been well advertised – the cart would go rapidly downhill and that all efforts which had been invested by our two departments in independence would have been in vain. Igor then went through every representative of the opposition individually, while I myself was trying to convince Malenšek and Podobnik, as well as Pučnik, to agree to the majority, as was demanded by the opposition. That is, I was firmly convinced that the plebiscite would be more than 80 per cent successful. In the late hours we finally came close to a consensus and the delegates, despite the reservations of some, almost unanimously voted in favour of the plebiscite on 6 December 1990.

All the rest was merely a technicality. The majority of Slovenians had decided long ago. They had simply never had the opportunity to express their will directly before. This time they had it and this was decisive. If, during the war, I had not had the plebiscite to back me up, but only the resolution of the Assembly, we would have been less firm. And the question is whether unacceptable compromises would not have arisen before this. The plebiscite is most surely a watershed in our history.

8. INDEPENDENCE DILEMMAS

The race for time was becoming more and more dramatic the closer we came to the end of the six-month preparatory term for the proclamation of independence and the take-over of effective power. The great majority of the public as well as politicians were not completely aware of what 26 June 1991 could bring with it.

According to a poll conducted by Variant in January 1991 only 7.2 per cent of the respondents were of the opinion that the danger of intervention by the YNA was serious. The opposition, especially from the ranks of the Liberal Democratic Party, heaped criticism on the government and the defence ministry, for supposedly putting fear into people of a danger which did not exist, and stated at every sign of a strengthening of the Slovenian defence capability that we were militarising Slovenian society, especially during the proposal of new defence laws.

The Law on Defence and Protection was submitted to the parliament in the autumn of 1990, but the Chamber of Associated Labour first did not want to discuss it in a shortened procedure. But for the operation of the defence system it was urgent, for the constitutional amendments and the constitutional law of 1990 ordered the transfer of some authorisations from the federal to republic bodies only in principle. The discussions were not only painful at times but some delegates opposed any kind of formation of our own defence forces. Thus the LDS delegate, Roman Jakič, stated that in his opinion Slovenia did not need an army, while his party colleague, Jaša Zlobec, joined in the onslaught which the GHQ of the YNA had been staging with their hunt for "illegally armed forces", and renamed the national defence a "paramilitary formation". Given such discussions Colonel Milan Aksentijević could do nothing but comment quite literally:

"I am no member of the Liberal Democratic Party, but I share the same feelings and conclusions..."[1]

After a certain sharpening of relations with Belgrade, I finally succeeded in convincing the President of the Chamber of Associated Labour, Jože Zupančič, to submit the draft for renewed voting. This time it was accepted and the government in the shortest time possible submitted a proposal which the parliament, after more heated debate, finally passed on 29 March 1991.

---

[1] Discussion in the continuation of the 18th session of the ZZD on 29 March 1991.

The Law on Military Service was experiencing a similar fate to the Law on Defence and Protection. Apart from military service it also covered civilian service. Although it was legalising the shortest military term in Europe and by far the shortest civilian service in the world, with a very liberal process for establishing the right to conscientious objection contained within it, the government was once again accused of militarism.

Peter Bekeš, a delegate of the SDP, voted against the Law on Military Service and explained his decision in the following way: "I shall vote against. There are a few states in Europe which do not even have any army conscription. The concept of defence remains a prisoner of the classical paradigm – understanding defence only as a military function... Here the danger also remains that the army will serve as an instrument for disciplining insubordinate citizens. This is a risk which I myself cannot consciously adopt."[2]

There were many such and similar opinions, the majority of them among representatives of those parties which, at that time when the army was, in a single-party system, truly an instrument of the politics of that one party, had been pressing for the greatest militarisation of Slovenia for a number of decades. The law was also opposed by the Liberal Democratic Party, especially by Jože Školč, Metka Mencin and Franco Juri, who explained their vote against before the ballot was held.

In the discussions on this law in all three chambers of the Assembly, we, the representatives of the government or the defence ministry, Jelko Kacin, Miran Bogataj and myself, cooperated one hundred and forty times, either through answers or replies to some absurd accusations. In these discussions the public became aware for the first time of the public speaking abilities of Jelko Kacin, which came to full expression at the press conferences held three months later.

On 8 March 1991 nearly three thousand Slovenian mothers received a special gift from the Slovenian parliament. Namely, on that day we passed a constitutional act by which the sending of Slovenian boys to the Yugoslav army was stopped. The draft cards which the conscripts had already received were collected on the basis of this decision only moments before their arrival at the conscription centre, to the great joy of all. Military service in the YNA after this date was no longer mandatory for Slovenian citizens. The YNA expected a large number of volunteers. Only one came.

The budget of the Republic of Slovenia for 1991 was being created in a very complex environment. Despite the plebiscite decision, the Secretariat of Finance prepared the first draft in which not all assets, which according to the old legislation, represented the so-called original income of the federation, were included. Marko Kranjc, the then Republic Secretary of Finance, was not very enthusiastic about the financial emancipation of Slovenia. Only after very sharp exchanges at a session of the Executive Council did he relent and his services finally prepared the first real budget of Slovenia, which also

---

[2] Discussion on the draft of the law in the Socio-political Chamber (DPZ) on 18 April 1991.

considered customs duties and all sales taxes among its incomes. The federation was to pay individual services indirectly though our budget, as much as would be decided by our parliament. The proposed quota for the federal budget was essentially smaller than the amount which was demanded by the Federal Prime Minister, Ante Marković. On 19 February 1991 Marković flew to Ljubljana and demanded his share. We did not relent, despite the threats.

The budget discussion in the Assembly was a reflection of the first such opportunity offered to the delegates. Almost everyone in the formulation of Assembly topics found some partial interest which he/she was of the opinion had been neglected. They would all propose the majority of assets for science, school and medical care, this or that cultural building, this or that road, etc. Only a few remembered that they were deciding on the budget for the year in which an independent Slovenian state was to be created and that if the Slovenians were left without one, the Belgrade Assembly would still, and even more so, decide on the results of our work in the next year. The opposition paid special attention to the defence part of the budget, which still envisaged a partial co-financing of the YNA (costs of soldiers who were doing military service and part of the army pensions) and at the same time also reflected the needs of our own defence. There was not much talk of the funds earmarked for the YNA, although it was nearly as much as the share proposed for our own defence and protection system, but they proposed many more comments and corrections to the share proposed for the Territorial Defence.

Lev Kreft, a delegate of the SDP stated that believing an army would bring independence and sovereignty was like being blinded by utopia.[3] Sonja Lokar, who shared similar thoughts, asked "what the price of one bow was in comparison with the price of one apparatus which could save the life of one prematurely born baby."[4]

The delegate club of the reformers and liberal democrats, as well as the socialists, proposed a great reduction in or even a total cancelling of all funds for our own defence. The items of the YNA did not disturb them so much. A delegate of the socialists, Jože Smole, stated that the first priority must be a reduction of money for defence, Jožef Školč stated that mere threats that someone was attacking us could not force anybody to accept such or another constitutional solution.[5]

The opposition delegates, all of them, accused the government, and explicitly my department, of scaring them with a danger which did not exist. So Peter Glavič, a delegate of the LDS stated that "the events in the Gulf showed that the occupation of Slovenia is not a realistic option. It is not possible to join Europe through weapons and the police but through reason and knowledge."[6] Milan Aksentijević was very active in the discussion. He agreed with the proposal of the LDS delegate, Roman Jakič, which was that

[3] 13th session of the DPZ, 5 March 1991
[4] 16th session of the DPZ, 27 March 1991
[5] Same session, see[4].
[6] Session of the Chamber of Communities, 5 March 1991.

the money should not go towards the military training of our Slovenian boys but towards the development of roads, railways and so forth, and our common borders should be safeguarded by the YNA.

Only after serious discussions which I had with the prime minister, so that he too decisively supported the defence part of the budget and after gaining nearly unanimous support from the Demos delegate club, to which I once again explained the consequences of undefended emancipation, did the parliament accept the budget together with the defence item, which was reduced to just over a third of the 1990 level, at a joint session of all chambers on 30 March in a simple majority vote.[7]

Exactly two months and 26 days remained to the day of the fateful decision. Time densified into an intertwined mass of all kinds of activities. My department finally received the green light for preparing trial army training and the urgently needed funds. It was clear that there was not enough time to call up a greater number of conscripts and that also those who we could call up would not be adequately trained by 26 June. We searched feverishly for paths and methods for the importing of the necessary anti-tank weapons, and there was a great lack of all other weapons and ammunition.

Anyone who has ever concerned themselves with military affairs probably knows that in barely three months it would be almost impossible – with the strict control of the borders by the federal authorities and especially KOS, as well as the international embargo – to find, order and safely bring to Slovenia a quantity of weapons and military equipment worth mentioning, and then to correctly distribute it to units and, at the same time, train the soldiers in the proper use of the new hardware. Nor did we own the necessary communication equipment. We tried everything possible and we can thank our lucky stars that the most urgent equipment finally arrived at the last minute, which I shall describe in the following chapters.

Apart from the obvious delays in the acceptance of the defence legislation and budget, the project for emancipation was also threatened by a number of other things. It is above all worth mentioning the disinclination of the more important countries and international organisations to our independence, the unpreparedness of the majority of other government departments for the actual take-over or transfer of power from the federation to the Republic and the great resistance against the construction of a defence system, which was illustrated in the signing of the so-called "declaration of peace".

After the plebiscite vote in favour of an independent Slovenia, serious warnings began to arrive from abroad, saying that we were not to rush in our withdrawal from Yugoslavia, for in the case that the YNA responded nobody would offer us protection. Even the German parliament in its debate in February 1991 did not support our dissociation from Yugoslavia, and harsh words on the subject of certain selfish national interests of some republics in

---

[7] In 1990 Slovenia contributed 857 million US dollars to the federal budget for the needs of the YNA. The budget in 1991 proposed less than 340 million US dollars for the YNA and the TO together.

Yugoslavia were heard. A similar stance was adopted by representatives of the European Community in February and by the president of the EC Commission for the Mediterranean, Abel Matutes, in discussions with Lojze Peterle.

On 14 February I travelled secretly to Brussels. Along with Dimitrij Rupel, who had gone there a few days earlier, for he was cooperating in visits to government delegates in the Benelux countries, I met in the evening with John Kriendler, the assistant to the secretary-general of NATO for political affairs, and his consultant for Eastern Europe and the Balkans also cooperated.

The greatest emphasis in the discussions was placed on the following:

1. NATO views the Balkans and Yugoslavia as an especially unstable region. Yugoslavia and the conditions in it are more and more frequently on the daily agenda of the political committee of NATO, presided over by Kriendler.

2. The political position of NATO regarding Yugoslavia and Slovenia does not differ from that of the Twelve or the West in general. They were also repeated in their known form at this discussion, although Kriendler specially stressed that he spoke as a representative of NATO, which does not represent the interests of the US or any other country, but only the joint interests of its members.

3. NATO was satisfied with the outcome of events in the world lately, for they had reached great successes "without them having to do anything at all". We assess the present situation in the USSR as serious, but from the discussion one could not get the impression that they were overly worried. At this moment they were not thinking of bringing new members into the organisation, for it was "unnecessary". Their strategic interest was to press the borders of the West as far East as possible, to the end if possible. Time was not the most important factor here.

4. He was especially interested in what the relations were between Slovenia and Croatia and, in association with this, the joint statement signed in Otočec a few days earlier.

5. Kriendler was advised especially that conditions in the USSR (near the Baltic) could have a decisive influence on the possible intervention of the army in Yugoslavia, especially if the conflicts in the Gulf dragged on and the major military potential of the West was engaged there. He was also advised of the actual differences (economic, historical, religious etc..) between the individual parts of Yugoslavia as well as of the seriousness of the process of Slovenian emancipation.

6. Kriendler also promised that the contents of the discussion would be stated in detail both to Secretary-General Manfred Woerner and the entire political committee of NATO, over which he presided.

7. In our mutual interest the discussion proceeded informally.

Both Rupel and I assessed that NATO was well aware of the conditions in Yugoslavia and that it was very probable that they had formulated detailed political and other measures in the case that conflicts arose in Yugoslavia or even if civil war broke out, and that their first goal then would be to limit the conflict to Yugoslavia. Most certainly NATO, at least in the first stage, would not intervene militarily, but their indirect cooperation would be under the auspices of the UN, if the intervention of the UN Security Council came about.

No great enthusiasm could be read for the independence of Slovenia from this discussion, despite the friendliness and the even sympathetic stance of Kriendler to the democratic changes in Slovenia. My impression was – and this later proved to be true – that NATO would adhere totally to the American policies for Yugoslavia and that its stand would be more firm than that of Europe.

The USA unrelentingly supported a united Yugoslavia in the spring, and the International Monetary Fund resolutely supported Marković's economic policies. On 31 May two representatives of the Twelve flew to Belgrade and in a discussion with the leaders of individual republic and federal bodies succeeded in reaching a consensus with regard to a united Yugoslav market, monetary and foreign policies as well as defence. Milan Kučan and Lojze Peterle separately visited Italian Prime Minister Andreotti at the beginning of June, who warned of the need for an agreement within Yugoslavia. Foreign Minister De Michelis was even more unequivocal, and he always put his opposite number, Dimitrij Rupel, in a bad mood every time they met with his constant repetition that it meant a lot to the Twelve that Yugoslavia was preserved.

The closer the allotted day came, the greater was the pressure from abroad. On 21 June 1991 US Secretary of State James Baker came to Belgrade. A day later he met with President Kučan, who arrived from Belgrade very agitated and upset. Baker told him frankly that neither the USA nor any other country would recognise the international subjectivity of Slovenia. When Igor Bavčar and I passed on this information to members of the coordination group, I read from most of their faces that they were aware that the devil had had the last laugh and that a blood bath was to ensue, in which we would be able to depend only on our determination, wits and bravery. This feeling was affirmed even more by Baker's public statement on television, which he gave during a talk with Federal Prime Minister Marković. Marković acquainted Baker with the resolution of the federal government to directly implement the federal laws on the crossing of the state border, which the Federal Executive Council passed on 20 June. In other words Marković at that time predicted a limited military intervention in Slovenia in the case of actual emancipation, and the American Secretary of State publicly supported this measure after the meeting was over. Two days later we received a report from the intelligence department, according to which Baker, after being presented with the ratio of forces between the defence capabilities of Slovenia and the units of the YNA, which was preparing itself for intervention, convinced himself of the possibility that the federal bodies could put Slovenia in order in a little over two hours. One of the generals supposedly even stated to him that this would be a Desert Storm operation in small and that after two days no one would think of secession from Yugoslavia as being a realistic option. Thus, the strongest superpower in the world, with such an emphasised democratic and freedom-loving tradition, gave the green light for the last communist army in Europe to bring a nation to its knees, a nation which wanted nothing else than by peaceful means to fulfil the principles of the American Declaration of Independence. Instead of aid or at least warning, the American government sent a military envoy to Ljubljana a few days before the aggression to observe the Yugoslav version of Desert Storm at close range.

One moment earlier the European Community also said its final and enphatic "NO". On the 25 June the Twelve decided they would not recognise the declarations of independence of the republics of Slovenia and Croatia, and to strengthen this resolution they approved a loan of 807 million ecus of aid for the infrastructure of the SFRY.

The Liberal Democratic Party and the Party of Reform, in cooperation with some once independent civil social groups, presented to the public on 6 February 1991 the so-called "Declaration for Peace". Apart from the many generally acceptable and undisputed civilisational views which the text contained, there were also some crass simplifications and demands which my then deputy, Jelko Kacin, in the journal *Obramba,* absolutely correctly marked as a "demand for a rapid unilateral disarmament". The Declaration, which the two parties offered for signing as a petition, also contained the sentence that "any armed conflict in the territory of Slovenia would be a national catastrophe." The Declaration was timed to coincide with the heated parliamentary debate on both defence laws and on the budget. It was signed by numerous party leaders and civil workers, including Janez Drnovšek, Ciril Ribičič, Jože Mencinger, Jožef Školč and four members of the high command or, should we say, the Presidency of Slovenia – Milan Kučan, Dušan Plut, Ciril Zlobec and Matjaž Kmecl. Of course many of them signed the petition after only a cursory reading, for the zealous activists, including some members of the Presidency, carried it around through the government offices. Jože Mencinger admitted to me that he did not even read it.

The impact and influence on the public was not so superficial. A few months before the fateful day of the decision, the actual capability of emancipation was very unsure and I was becoming seriously worried. Luckily at least the socialists did not opt to hinder the practical preparations for independence, which is why a small Assembly majority was still assured. Despite everything, many things hung on a thread for a few days. I sent the following letter to the members of the Presidency who had signed the petition:

To the members of the Presidency of the Republic of Slovenia and members of the Executive Council of the Republic of Slovenia who have signed the so-called "Declaration for Peace"

Dear Sirs,
Allow me to take up some of your precious time and completely informally

notify you of some thoughts and questions which occurred to me while reading the aforementioned Declaration.

A peace initiative is necessary, even if it is not realistic in a given time. On the one hand, this is a vision of the future, which is, as much as such is possible, to be without violence, and on the other, a challenge to the desires for force as the dominant instrument for solving conflicts as well as control over state institutions of repression. For society as a whole, it is always good if strong peace movements exist in it and if these peace initiatives have support.

But it is one matter if signatures are collected in a civil initiative and another if this is a powerful political campaign by different parties or if this is done by members of a body which is the supreme commander of the armed forces in the Republic and who, according to the existing Constitution, not only has the right but also the duty to conduct and organise defence perhaps even including armed conflict. Even if we ourselves think that it is practically possible to differentiate, for example, between Mr Milan Kučan the citizen and Milan Kučan the President of the Presidency of the Republic of Slovenia, the people, of course, will not differentiate. This is a fact, like it or not, and the consequences of such acts, even where a politician has done these acts completely privately, are political.

The Declaration among other things also contains a political falsehood (in Saturday's Delo supplement, in the article by Janez Švajncer, so I shall not dwell on it here) and at the same time at least one formulation is stated which misleads the public and from the professional aspect does not hold water. I am thinking here of the sentence which states that in the coming period we shall ensure safety with the "police and TO in its present dimensions."

The TO has no soldiers in its composition now. The TO is composed of reserve army formations, from mainly older generation conscripts. If we do not provide for the military training of younger generations, the structure of the reserves will become old without any suitable replacements. Even if somebody does think that the "period of insecurity" will last for only two years, such an aging would represent a serious problem. The moment we stop sending conscripts to the YNA, without suitable replacements in our own army training system, the input of young conscripts with fresh knowledge would stop for the TO.

Apart from this, who, during this period, will explain to people that some (older!) generations are conscripts and others (younger) are not? That is, in all countries defence is mainly founded on generations between the ages of twenty and thirty, while in Slovenia there would be those who are forty years old. And with what rights would some be conscripts and others not? Where is there equality before the law? No, this affair is not as simple as it seems at first sight. The national security project must be taken seriously. This question has a fatal significance for Slovenian emancipation and for safeguarding Slovenian independence, when it is reached and recognised. If anybody can decide that we disarm or that we ensure our own safety without an army, then these can only be Slovenians and citizens of the future sovereign state themselves. The solution which we could achieve in such a manner must be clean. It is impossible to play our cards somewhere in between, as is being attempted by this Declaration with its formulation on "the police and the TO in its present dimensions." Either the transformation of the present defence structure of Slovenia and partly the YNA into a normal, parliament-controlled and economically powerful society-adapted structure or the complete abolishment of all armed formations (with the exception of peace-time police). The composition of the armed forces must, namely, by quality and quantity, be such that it is satisfactory or, should I say, that it corresponds to the goal. According to the relatively balanced opinions of the professionals, Slovenia is capable of providing a relatively well armed defence in terms of quantity and quality without placing too great a burden on society. If this is not satisfactory, then it is truly better that we do not play around, for in this case we will only irresponsibly expose to sacrifice that handful who would, in the opinion of the composers of the Declaration, defend us. In this case I of course also propose that the emancipation project is hung on a peg and that we do not play with the destiny of a nation, for we would be behaving like someone stepping out into the cold, and taking off his jacket instead of putting on a coat.

We are living in very sensitive times. We have no guarantee that this sensitivity will not transform into armed conflict or even civil war. In this case, you can be one hundred per cent sure that the people will demand security. Unfortunately, this cannot always be assured simply through declarations. No one who has been legitimately elected for any responsible post in any branch of government in Slovenia has any right to ignore reality and say that the world with all its conflicts and weapons is a utopia. Just the opposite. Unfortunately such a world is a very brutal reality and it will be no less brutal if we do not see this or if we pretended that nobody could do anything to us. Feigning ignorance can only increase the danger and, at the same time, also threaten the processes of realistic demilitarisation which, in at least some parts of the developed world, are actually underway. But with the fact that there it is based on the transformation of the consciousness of the people and not on the physical throwing away of weapons. The basic problem of violence lies in the person and not in the economy or in weapons. If no one is forced or even prepared to use weapons, they are relatively harmless anyway. Demilitarisation represents a process which cannot be absolutely limited to one state or nation or municipality. Moreover, a completely disarmed state surrounded by neighbours who are strongly armed, is in practice a negative factor for stability in a region or continent. Ask foreign diplomats what they think of this. It is true that globally more weapons mean more danger, but the even greater danger for peace is represented by a sudden upset in the balance of a region, which could end in armed conflict even if it then has less weapons.

In Slovenia the YNA contains a greater number of Slovenian and non-Slovenian officers who are at the beginning or in the middle of their commissions, and to whom we have assured, in one way or another, that in the case of the independence of Slovenia they will not become unemployed. A guarantee of a similar nature also has another, political significance, besides a personal one. If we say: "We shall retain the TO in its present dimensions," then nobody will see any special possibility of pursuing their professional career e.g. in the TO, and they will cling more firmly to the job they have now.

American senator Denis De Concini stated the following thought at the end of January of this year in the American senate, which, with all we know together but which is not publicly known, can be offered as an additional matter for thought and concern. That is, he stated that the situation here is such that it is entirely possible that the 20th century will end as it began: with war in the Balkans.

The sensitivity of the national issue demands, from all who are in one way or another professionally involved in it (and members of the parliament and government most surely and without exception fall into this category), professional behaviour, which does not allow for the constant cheap collection of political points. I myself am convinced that for the vast majority of the signatories of the Declaration for Peace this is not a case of political game-playing, nor is it an opposition to Slovenian independence, rather it is an honest stand for that which the document offers in its title, that is a stand for peace. The problem lies in the fact in its details the Declaration (which the majority have not read in detail) does not offer only a stand for peace but that in its content it "demands a rapid unilateral disarmament", which will bring us neither peace nor independence. Since there are strong political parties among the signatories, the statements in the Declaration are automatically points of a political programme and not only a civil initiative.

Let me finally remind you also of the results of the Slovenian opinion poll of 1990, which in December last year revealed that only 15% of the inhabitants of Slovenia favoured a rapid unilateral disarmament, and all the rest favoured our own army, at least during the transitional period.

And possibly as the stimulus for a small thought, the following quotation:
Winston S. Churchill, Second World War, Chapter 1: Path to Catastrophe:
"As one of those who have lived and worked in those times, I would like to explain how we could have prevented the tragedy of the Second World War and how the evil of villains accelerated the weaknesses of respectable people... We shall see how advice on precaution and moderation can become the main reason for fatal danger, how mediocre paths, selected in the desire for safety and a peaceful life can bring us directly to the greatest evil."

I would ask that this letter remains of an internal nature,
with best wishes, and no offence intended,
Janez Janša
Ljubljana 25 February 1990

Circulated to:
President of the Assembly of the RS
President of the Executive Council of the RS

The letter remained a secret to the public, but it did achieve a certain change. Some read again the text which they had signed, and in the last two months before the Declaration of Independence, the Republic Presidency, after detailed study of its own defence capabilities and the assessment of the imminent danger very soberly and responsibly carried out its share of responsibilities.

While the demagogic discussions were in full swing in parliament and certain idiotic newspaper articles, which warned against some kind of militarisation, were circulating in public, I began to ask myself how we would see the decisions made today with the benefit of hindsight six months later. And what would we have experienced in between? Would not those who were speaking grand words today repeat their behaviour? Except that then they would be talking of the victims who could have been fewer if we had been better prepared, and they will ask themselves, without even a hint of guilt, who was responsible for this. What had the competent bodies who were paid for this been doing? Why didn't we have enough weapons?

We tried to explain to some delegates in vain that a state which is not capable of ensuring its own safety is not a factor of stability and peace but, in surroundings when the appetite of one or the other neighbour has been whetted, is a source of instability and potential conflict and such neighbours are not desired by the well intentioned.

We explained also that it was high time for us to start thinking soberly, and that we rid ourselves of the illusion about how all major problems could be dealt with overnight and that it was enough if we seized one grand idea of salvation; that we had had enough bad experiences with salvation projects which wanted to fundamentally change the world and mankind, and are today collapsing in absurdity; that mankind would not be saved by big ideas, from electricity to demilitarisation; that we should not repeat the mistakes of those who wanted to take a short cut into the future. We had been listening for many many years now about how Slovenia was the most developed republic in Yugoslavia and that thus it would be the first to develop authentic socialist self-management. The result had been standing before us for some time.

This time we heard that we could demilitarise immediately and show the whole world the right path. As though everybody was waiting for our salvational move and as though anybody would be asking us for advice. We heard that Slovenia did not need defence forces as one of its guarantees for independence and sovereignty, and at the same time we were witness to new escalations and threats each month which were trying to block and prevent our path to independence.

The polemics which we had in the spring of 1991 in public and in parliament during the aggressive initiatives for demilitarisation or a rapid unilateral disarmament reminded one in many ways of the years before the Second World War in Britain and France. When I was reading Churchill's memoirs, I found numerous descriptions which after an analysis of the atmosphere, are beautifully apt for the months before our Declaration of Independence.

At 15.30 on Sunday, 28 April, there was a meeting of the party presidents of Demos and some members of the government at Brdo pri Kranju. The meeting came about after the discussions Igor Bavčar and I had first with Dr Jože Pučnik, and then with Dr France Bučar; at this meeting we presented them with the delay that the government was falling into with its preparations for independence, and which was seriously threatening the implementation of the project.

Dr Jože Pučnik, Dr France Bučar, Lojze Peterle, Ivan Oman, Franc Golja, Dimitrij Rupel, Igor Bavčar, Dušan Plut, myself and two or three more vice-presidents of the parties in Demos were present at the meeting.

The meeting was begun by Dr Jože Pučnik with an assessment of the political situation. He stated that gossip was circulating in the public about the unsettled relations in the government and that these problems were so much the more obvious the closer we came to 25 June. In his opinion, the latest public appearances of some ministers, above all Mencinger and Kranjc, were such that they provoked serious doubts about whether we were capable of implementing independence. The government had no clear economic or social policies, some establishments did not feel this crisis at all, but it was being felt in the economy. The people had to be told the truth, and not blinded to the true situation, on the one hand, and on the other, scared by doubts about our capabilities. The independence project must leave no room for party interests and this week we must discuss all open issues. At the end of his introduction, Jože Pučnik proposed that every party clarify without any doubt whether 26 June was still the date for the transfer or take-over of actual government and independence.

Dr France Bučar spoke after Pučnik, saying that uncertainty was prevailing, for we had nothing in our hands. Many were of the opinion that independence would not be able to be implemented. Communications between the government and the Assembly, between the parliamentary parties and between the parties of Demos were not proceeding as they should, given the gravity of the situation. The basic legislation, which should be accepted by 26 June still did not even exist. The delay was catastrophic. In the end, Bučar was firmly in favour of the take-over of actual power on 26 June and stressed that if this did not happen, the "South" would deal with us summarily.

France Bučar was also supported by Ivan Oman. He stated that we had no image of our economy and above all no answer to the question of what costs there would be in one or the other case, so that we might be better prepared for our fateful step. In his opinion there was no dilemma; 26 June must be the date of the take-over of effective power.

The president of the Liberal Party, Franc Golja, stated that doubts were becoming more and more serious in the "field" and that they did not know what kind of legal order would be valid after 26 June, for we were in horrific delay in the passing of our own legislation. In his opinion the government was composed hastily, but it should hold until independence and, until that time, he was of the opinion that no replacements should be made. In his opinion the plebiscite left no doubts. The date of 26 June must be the date for the actual take-over of effective power.

Prime Minister Lojze Peterle tried to avoid the basic question in his address – which Jože Pučnik set as the starting point for the meeting – and restricted himself to the field of the economy. According to him the basic problem was how to take things on. Mencinger had all the jurisdiction, but defended a slow, inoffensive path. Regarding privatisation, three parties were against Mencinger's law and thus it came about that Sachs was invited in. Mencinger wrote to Sachs, and in the letter and invitation even wrote that there were no differences between them. Later, it became clear that there were differences, although Mencinger also agreed to Sachs' thesis that a parallel currency was senseless. Boris Pleskovič, Ivan Bernik and Marko Kremžar were not in favour of a step-by-step method but of Sachs' method of eliminating the crisis in one go. When Sachs explained his concept, all parties accepted it, except the SDZ. In the elimination of the economic difficulties, only shock treatment could achieve success, was the conviction of experienced experts. In his opinion the difficulties and differences were more of a verbal nature and among the public, rather than real. Finance Minister Marko Kranjc did not believe in the possibility of the project succeeding, but despite everything he was prepared, under certain conditions, to accept the post of deputy prime minister and replace Mencinger. Peterle stated finally that he understood that some people had lost faith in the project, but that in his opinion nothing was lost yet, and 26 June could remain the deadline in the sense of passing the law (meaning the Constitutional Law – author's note).

Dimitrij Rupel warned of the unfavourable attitude of the world to our plebiscite and stressed that the SDZ, in spite of this, stood firmly by 26 June as being the actual day of independence. He was also interested in by whom and when was the decision confirmed that shock treatment was generally accepted for salvaging the economy.

Dušan Plut agreed with the assessments of France Bučar and Joče Pučnik. The conditions in the government were having a negative influence on the disposition of the public. The delay in the preparation of the basic independence legislation was obvious and the response that nothing was lost yet was not convincing. The decision made at the plebiscite was clear and his party understood 26 June as the date for actual independence.

Igor Bavčar warned that Lojze Peterle was throwing the problem of privatisation and the question of actual independence into the same basket too much. The privatisation law could, although there really should be more haste, be passed after 26 June, when we were no longer burdened with more decisive steps. The deadline of 26 June was a question of survival and this date could not be done away with by saying that it was understood as the deadline for accepting the law. Already the adoption of the 1991 budget had shown that some things were not clear. Despite the very good results of the plebiscite and the law on the plebiscite, the first drafts of the budget, the coordination of which was in the hands of Lojze Peterle, still envisaged the payment of customs and sales tax to Belgrade for the whole year. As Bavčar said, only after Janša's perseverance and then the clear stance of the SDZ, to the loud muttering of Mencinger and Kranjc, was the draft, corrected. Igor Bavčar found in the end that it was becoming more and more clear that our acts, if it came to it, would be more or less one-sided, that there was no clear script for such a scenario or any true coordination.

I myself also warned of the unacceptability of the avoided answers, for this concerned totally clear alternatives. Either Slovenia truly becomes independent on 26 June or we adopt another declaration or law which would have no realistic effect on our situation. Next week we would have to clearly decide and pass resolutions on customs, the ultimatums issued by the YNA, the question of borders, citizenship, and this is why we needed a clear line in principle. In brief, I also described the situation in Yugoslavia, the situation in the YNA and our assessment of the measures which were expected to be taken by Marković.

The meeting once again proved that priorities were not in the least bit clear to the prime minister. His evasive answer that "26 June can remain the deadline in the sense of the law", aroused displeasure in the majority of those present. For this reason Jože Pučnik proposed at the end that we were once again to make a definition of 26 June. This time Peterle was clear. He stated that he agreed with the standpoint of the others, for Slovenia to take over effective power in its territory on 26 June.

After this meeting, work began to proceed in the government in the tempo it should have started on 27 December 1990. The prime minister cancelled some already announced visits abroad, and the project councils[8] for the individual fields which were of key importance for independence and the independent operation of the Slovenian state stepped up their activities. Work was coordinated by a small group led by Lojze Peterle, and in his absence he was replaced by Igor Bavčar. First we made an inventory. In a small log cabin in Brdo meetings followed one after another with representatives of bigger companies and infrastructural organisations on whom we played out possible events after independence, counted our stocks, composed lists of problems, that is, we investigated whether the individual vitally important parts of the economy and public infrastructure were capable of operating after emancipation even in the case of embargoes from Belgrade and the indisposition of neighbouring states. The meetings were mainly led by Igor Bavčar. The result of the inventory was better than I had expected. Slovenia had enough stocks – some had already been supplemented by the government – to allow a relatively normal survival even during any month-long embargo. The directors of more important companies were prepared to take risks and many claimed that if we had survived for 70 years in Yugoslavia we would also survive our farewell from it. In the case of an embargo, Slovenia would also hold a counter-weapon, for many communications, from PTT lines to the road and railways, linking the rest of Yugoslavia with Western Europe passed over our territory. Finally we also got a useful list of pressing problems.

The government departments who until now had been operating under their old rhythm began zealously to prepare themselves for independence legislation in the fields of monetary policies, citizenship, crossing of national borders, passports etc. It was shown that Slovenia had no hard currency reserves. The new finance minister, Dušan Šešok, received a very poor dowry from his predecessor, who was so mourned by the opposition. But the regular work in the economic part of preparations for independence, with the arrival of him and Ocvirk, were relatively eased, for in contrast to Mencinger and Kranjc, they did not doubt the success of the entire project, and furthermore, they were used to working more than eight hours a day and they had suitable experience from operational work.

On my proposal the Presidency of the Republic of Slovenia had already, on 18 March 1991, founded the OPERATIONAL COORDINATION

---

[8] Project councils were founded for the following fields: The economic system (Ocvirk), foreign economic relations (Ravbar), foreign financial contacts (Šešok), foreign affairs (Rupel), cooperation with some republics of Yugoslavia, supplies (Bastl), infrastructure (Kranjc), borders (Bavčar), defence and security (Janša), legislation (Janko), the media (Kacin).

BODY IN THE EVENT OF A STATE OF EMERGENCY.[9] This is how we named the operations group for the sake of legal diction, which did not allow any doubts, while in practice this concerned a body which coordinated all defence and security preparations and during war performed the task of being the headquarters of the commander-in-chief. The role of the commander-in-chief was, according to the Constitution, performed by the Presidency of the Republic, expanded by the prime minister and the Assembly. In practice the ministers of defence, internal, and foreign affairs, information as well as the commanders or chiefs of republic headquarters for territorial defence and civil defence cooperated in the work of the Presidency.

The foundation of the coordination group was one of the most important operational decisions for the defence and protection with real force of measures of emancipation. If all activities were not coordinated to the best possible level, our advantages could not be exploited and the enemy, because of its superior numbers and technology, would sooner or later achieve better results, thus any war would claim incomparably more victims.

*　*　*

On 29 April, the day when the Assembly of the Republic of Slovenia finally passed the law on military service, the last urgent systemic act for independence in the defence field, my hopes for the success of the enterprise once again grew. At the same time I was aware that an impossibly short time remained until the crucial day. We had lost at least two months because of the complications in passing laws and the budget as well as the barren polemics on demilitarisation. The work of the project groups of the government had hardly begun. In my car on the way home from the parliament I was thinking intensively about how to gain back the lost time. It was becoming clear to me that it would be impossible to wait for the other departments and then, after the formulation of their measures, make plans for their protection. It was necessary to imagine the situation on the day of declaration, we must foresee the response of Belgrade and above all the armed forces and, on the basis of this projection, make plans for measures, both to protect individual procedures of emancipation and plans for defence in case of armed intervention by the YNA.

I went from my car directly to my computer and, on the next day at three in the morning, it printed out the draft of a document under the working title of:

---

[9] The coordination group was composed of: Igor Bavčar, Janez Janša, Jelko Kacin, Miran Bogataj, Janez Slapar, Tone Krkovič, Vinko Beznik, Miloš Bregar, Miha Brejc, Pavle Čelik, Milan Domadenik, Marjan Fekonja, Franc Kokoravec, Jože Kolenc, Bogdan Koprivnikar, Lojze Kuralt, Danijel Kuzma, Andrej Lovšin, Rudi Merljak, Stane Praprotnik, Janko Stušek, Bojan Ušeničnik, Anton Vereš, Ludvik Zvonar, Franci Žnidaršič. The law defined that such work was headed by the principal of the Republic authority for internal affairs. In the operational part of the group individual duties were also performed by: Lojze Bogataj, Janez Švajncer, Zoran Klemenčič, Miha Butora, Dominik Grmek, Bogdan Avbar et al.

POSSIBLE VARIANTS OF DISSOCIATION
FROM THE DEFENCE ASPECT

Legend:
D = day of declaration of independence and take-over of the greater part of
effective power (borders, customs, monetary system, foreign affairs)

From the defence aspect there exist six possible variants of emancipation, which
are divided into three different systems:

I. system – agreed dissociation

II. system – attempt to prevent dissociation by force
variant II1 (simple variant)
variant II2 (rough variant)

III. system – chiefly unilateral dissociation
variant III1 – operative preparedness
variant III2 – partial mobilisation and passive assistance
variant III3 – complete mobilisation and active assistance
variant III4 – combined variant
after the implementation of variants III1, III2 or III3 the Federation responds
with force

REFINEMENT OF SYSTEMS AND VARIANTS

I. SYSTEM – AGREED DISSOCIATION
Presupposition
Dissociation develops gradually and has been agreed upon, all republics accept
the proposal of Slovenia for dissociation, the Federal Assembly accepts an act on the
technical implementation and distribution of inheritance, a withdrawal or reformation
of the YNA units in Slovenia is made.
Slovenia offers or demands the following conditions:
- gradual withdrawal of the YNA from the territory of the RS within a period
  of three years
- evacuation of 1/3 of the military buildings in the hands of the YNA by 1
  August 1991
- financing of social care functions of the YNA until final withdrawal
- take-over of social and status obligations for military personnel and service
  pensioners living in the RS
- non-intervention of the YNA in the political solution of the crisis

---

II. SYSTEM – ATTEMPT TO PREVENT DISSOCIATION BY FORCE
Presupposition:
In the period before the planned the day, a military intervention occurs with the
goal of preventing the dissociation of Slovenia.

VARIANT II1 (SIMPLE VARIANT)
Show of force and closure of national borders, attempt by the YNA to take over
police jurisdiction for the purpose of causing economic crisis and chaos, as well as to
convince the inhabitants of the mistake of attempting dissociation.

COUNTER-MEASURES
- partial mobilisation (PEM, special units of the TO)
- strengthened protection of facilities and personnel according to plan
- mass media counter-propaganda
- international activities through all channels
- coordination with allies in Yugoslavia
- introduction of rationing
- in the example of the acceptance of a prepared constitutional law some measures from variant II/2 follow

VARIANT II/2 (ROUGH VARIANT)
- show of force and closure of national borders, attempts to take over police jurisdiction by the YNA and
- liquidation and/or interning of members of the Presidency, the Executive Council, the Assembly and representatives of the local government, according to prepared plans (actually exist)
- occupation of seats and offices of Republic and some local government bodies, the radio and television, infrastructure centres (PTT, electricity network, railways, airports), facilities of the ONZ and headquarters of the TO
- blockade of all communications
- bombing and rocketing of mobilisation centres of the TO and VEM (para-military police) from the air and sea (plan being prepared by a special group of the GHQ of the YNA)
- attempts to establish military-civil rule with the aid of members of the ZK–GZJ and part of the personnel and collaborators of the state and military security services – DV and VVS – (plan being prepared by a special group at the GHQ of the YNA)

COUNTER-MEASURES
- total mobilisation of all structures of the ONZ, TO and ND, implementation of measures for preparedness
- evacuation to safer locations according to plans
  resistance at all levels and with all disposable means
- passing of necessary legal acts (Assembly or Pres. of the RS)
- recall of all citizens of the RS from federal institutions
- renaming units of the YNA into units of the TO, disbanding and partial take-over of these units
- occupation of federal property, recruitment of new TO units
- introduction of rationing
- strengthened protection of facilities and personnel according to plans
- mass media counter-propaganda
- international activities through all channels
- coordination with allies in Yugoslavia
- opening of some border crossings, establishment of direct international communications
- organisation of international aid
- take-over of control of national border
- protection of border with the Rep. Croatia, take-over of complete control over the territory of the RS
- beginning of negotiations on the exchange of military personnel who are

citizens of other republics in Yugoslavia with citizens who in the time of conflict were in units of the YNA outside of the RS

III. SYSTEM – MAINLY UNILATERAL DISSOCIATION

Presupposition:

Slovenia defines the day, irrespective of the standpoints of the other republics and federal bodies or only in partial compliance with some republics and with unclear agreements with individual federal bodies.

VARIANT III1 – OPERATIVE PREPAREDNESS

D–3
- Introduction of duty shifts in the ONZ, UOLO (local defence), TO headquarters and centres
- testing of preparations for the take-over of border crossings, customs posts and branch offices
- testing of preparations for partial and complete mobilisation

D–2
- testing of preparations for partial and complete mobilisation
- concealed strengthening of the protection of facilities and buildings

D–1
- testing of preparations for partial and complete mobilisation
- testing of preparations for the take-over of border crossings, customs posts and branch offices
- strengthened duty shifts in the ONZ, UOLO, TO headquarters and centres
- partial call up of police reservists and additional establishment of new customs posts

D0
- start of border crossings, customs posts and branch offices take-over as well as strengthened protection of occupied border crossings and facilities by the police

D0+0.30
- announcement of decree over radio and television
  – content of constitutional law or some other act
  – recall of citizens of the RS from units of the YNA, if they so wish and if they do not expose themselves to risk in doing so
  – guarantee for recognising the social and status rights of military personnel and service pensioners, guarantee of personal safety to all military personnel and their families
  – renaming of reserve units of the YNA into units of the TO (decree of the Presidency of the RS)
  – announcement regarding take-over of borders and the regime at border crossings

D0+2
- final take-over of border crossings, customs stations and branch offices as well as operation according to new regime

D+1
- beginning of talks with individual units and headquarters of the YNA on

solving problems during the transition period, the operation of the infrastructure as well as the gradual disbanding of individual units, take-over of facilities and military hardware etc.

VARIANT III2 – PARTIAL MOBILISATION
AND PASSIVE ASSISTANCE

D–7
- acquaintance with plans for the narrower composition of TO and ONZ headquarters

D–5
- acquaintance with plans for commanders of special units by segments

D–4
- view of locations, tour of commands
- start of permanent operation of the Republic operations headquarters

D–3
- introduction of duty shifts in the ONZ, UOLO, TO headquarters and centres
- testing of preparations for the take-over of crossings, customs posts and branch offices
- testing of preparations for partial and complete mobilisation
- testing of plans for preventing the withdrawal of the military hardware from the territory of Slovenia

D–2
- testing of preparations for partial and complete mobilisation
- strengthening of the protection of important buildings and facilities
- mobilisation of the reserve composition of the police, recruitment of the PEM
- partial mobilisation of TO (headquarters and special units)

D–1
- testing of preparations for partial and complete mobilisation
- preparation and additional equipping of the mobilised compositions of TO and PEM
- testing of preparations for the take-over of crossings, customs posts and branch offices
- strengthened preparedness in the ONZ, UOLO, TO headquarters and centres
- protection of infrastructural centres and exchanges, activating parts of the ND
- preparation to block communications for preventing the manoeuvres of special units of the YNA

D0
- start of border crossing, customs post and branch office take-over as well as strengthened protection of occupied border crossings and facilities with the police
- protection of some selected border crossings with PZO (anti-aircraft) and POO (anti-tank) units
- protection of borders with the Rep. of Croatia, establishment of border crossings

- take-over of airspace control
- partial blockade of individual units of the YNA in their barracks – in communications

D0+0.30
- announcement of decree over radio and television
  - content of constitutional law or some other act
  - recall of citizens of the RS from units of the YNA, if they so wish and if they do not expose themselves to risk in doing so
  - guarantee for recognising the social and status rights of military personnel and service pensioners, guarantee of personal safety to all military personnel and their families
  - renaming of reserve units of the YNA into units of the TO (decree of the Presidency of the RS)
  - announcement on take-over of borders and the regime at border crossings

D0+2
- final take-over of border crossings, customs posts and branch offices, as well as operation under new regime
- operation of air space control according to new regime

D+1
- beginning of talks with individual units and headquarters of the YNA on solving problems during the transition period, the operation of the infrastructure as well as the gradual disbanding of individual units, take-over of facilities and military hardware etc.
- demobilisation of some special units

VARIANT III3 – COMPLETE MOBILISATION
AND ACTIVE ASSISTANCE

D–10
- beginning of constant functioning of operations headquarters
- acquaintance with plans for the narrower composition of TO and ONZ headquarters

D–7
- acquaintance with plans for commanders of special units according to segments

D–5
- notification of plans to the commanders of all units of the rank of commander of battalion and colonels of units with special tasks
- view of locations, tour of commands introduction of duty shifts in the ONZ, UOLO, TO headquarters and centres
- testing of preparations for the take-over of border crossings, customs posts and branch offices
- testing of preparations for complete mobilisation of TO
- recruitment of PEM
- testing of plans for preventing the withdrawal of the military hardware from the territory of Slovenia

D–2
- testing of preparations for complete mobilisation

- strengthening of the protection of important buildings and facilities
- mobilisation of the police reserve, recruitment of VEM
- mobilisation of TO

D–1
- preparation and additional equipping of the mobilised formations of TO and PEM
- testing of preparations for the take-over of crossings, customs posts and branch offices
- strengthened preparedness in the ONZ, UOLO, TO headquarters and centres
- protection of infrastructure centres and exchanges, activating parts of the ND
- blockade of communications for preventing the manoeuvres of special units of the YNA
- preparedness for carrying out all types of battle deployments

D0–2
- deployment to starting positions for PEM and special units of TO
- notification of Rep. of Croatia of the start of operations

D0
- temporary cut-off of civil communication infrastructures of all federal bodies in the RS
- blockade of internal YNA communications
- beginning of border crossing, customs post and branch offices take-over as well as strengthened protection of occupied border crossings and facilities by the police
- protection of some selected border crossings with units for PZO and POO
- protection of borders with the Rep. of Croatia, establishment of border crossings
- take-over of airspace control

D0+0.30
- announcement of decree over radio and television
  – content of constitutional law or some other act
  – recall of citizens of the RS from units of the YNA, if they so wish and if they do not expose themselves to risk in doing so
  – guarantee for recognising the social and status rights of military personnel and service pensioners, guarantee of personal safety to all military personnel and their families
  – renaming of reserve units of the YNA into units of the TO (decree of the Presidency of the RS)
  – renaming of peace-time units of the YNA into units of the TO and announcement of the order for their subordination to authorised military-territorial TO commanders
  – announcement of take-over of borders and the regime at border crossings

D0+2
- final take-over of border crossings, customs posts and branch offices as well as operation under new regime
- operation of airspace control according to new regime
- take-over of individual YNA facilities and units

D+1
- take-over of individual YNA facilities and units

D+2
- take-over of individual YNA facilities and units

D+3 to D+7
- demobilisation of individual peace-time units of the YNA
- organisation of transport for members of demobilised units of the YNA to the border of the Rep. of Croatia and their hand-over to border authorities of the Rep. of Croatia.

D+7
- demobilisation of some larger TO units
- demobilisation of part of VEM

D+10
- total take-over of control of national border

Variant III4
AFTER THE IMPLEMENTATION OF VARIANT III1–III3
THE FEDERATION RESPONDS WITH FORCE
If violent intervention occurs in the period before D0, then the RS implements measures envisaged in system II, variant II1 or II2 in combination with the measures envisaged in system III, variant III3.

If violent intervention occurs after the start of implementing measures on day D0, the RS first acceleratedly implements measures of variant III3 (if this was not the basic variant) in combination with variant II2.

SOME CONCLUSIONS

1. In the example when we can justifiably expect a violent attempt to prevent Slovenian independence just before day D0 or immediately after, then variant III3 must be selected at the very beginning, for the end consequences will be smaller.

2. If variant III2 or II3 is selected, then the time for the session of the Assembly must be selected accordingly, the decision must be passed at around 21.00 hours, 5 to 7 days before the logical expectation (and semi-officially envisaged) date.

3. The procedures must be coordinated with the groups for supplies, borders, foreign policies and the media.

4. At least the technical procedure regarding the border must be coordinated with the Rep. of Croatia.

5. In the example of the selection of any variant from system III, a part of the means proposed for the training of soldiers must, without delay, with the beginning of autumn 91, be redirected into accelerated equipping and training of existing and the formation of new TO structures.

6. The critical time is D0 to D + 2 (D+10) and the time D+60 and on, if the other republics (Serbia and Montenegro) organise their own armies and
- greater disputes in questions of secession were to arise
- a civil war between Serbia and the Rep. of Croatia were to arise

---

NECESSARY GENERAL (STRATEGIC) DECISIONS

1. SELECT SYSTEM
(not to decide, means to wait for I or II)

2. DEFINE D DAY
(could be temporary only as a framework, plus/minus 15 days, precisely to D-30)
3. SELECT VARIANT
(no later than by D-45)

WHO TAKES DECISIONS:

---

1. General decisions (selection of system) is (has been?) taken by the Assembly of the RS
2. Detailed decisions:
   a. defining D Day
   b. scheduled operational plans are passed by the Executive Council of the RS and partly by the Presidency of the RS
3. Decision on deploying TO is taken by the Presidency of the RS

All the necessary normative foundations (constitutional law, laws and non-statutory acts) have already been passed or partly passed and frozen.

Measures stated in individual variants are refined or are detailed within the framework of the following documents:
1. defence plan of the RS
2. security plan of the RS
3. Plan of ŠČIT (SHIELD)
4. Atlas plan
5. Purchase plan
6. Preliminary plan for preventing the withdrawal of the military hardware from the territory of the RS
7. Preliminary plan for counter-measures in the case of a show of force
8. Operational plans for the operation of the mass media under a state of emergency
9. Preliminary plan for operating of police at the border in a state of emergency

Maps:
- map of the RS including border crossings, commanders of border sections and sentry posts
- map of Yugoslavia including YNA strategic facilities
- map of western part of Yugoslavia with the precise positions of individual YNA units drawn in
- map of the RS showing weapons, ammunition, MES (mines) and other military hardware storage sites under the control of the YNA

* * *

The document incorporated all possible circumstances for the last stage of emancipation. The key factor for the preparation of any measure was the clear projection of the possible outcome. On the general or strategic level, the basic question was whether reason would triumph in Belgrade and emancipation would be mainly a process of making agreements or whether

110

they would attempt to prevent by force the plebiscite decisions of Slovenia from being carried out. The question of the timing of possible armed intervention was also of crucial importance. The fact is, it was not obvious that it would come about immediately after the declaration of independence. It is true that in the majority of perspectives this was an unsuitable time, but they could do so, in agreement with some powerful foreign countries which did not support our independence. Ante Marković and the YNA could wait for ten days and then, when it became clear to the people in Slovenia that the world was not going to recognise Slovenia, carry out armed intervention under conditions when the Slovenians might possibly be less motivated for defence.

The draft of the document which I finally completed on 19 April was a good basis for the clarification of numerous dilemmas in the "non-defence" fields. First I coordinated with Igor Bavčar some main issues linked to the cooperation of the police and the question of the borders. Then a discussion followed at the staff meeting of the RSLO, and I presented the plan to the entire coordination group which was set up by the Presidency of the Republic.

The first serious discussion followed in Villa Podrožnik after a few days, when we submitted the plan for a thorough going-over at a working meeting, where Milan Kučan, Lojze Peterle, France Bučar, Igor Bavčar and myself cooperated. I remember very well that there were no superfluous words spoken and that all of them had very serious faces. I think that after this meeting there was no one at the top of Slovenian politics who was unaware of the great risk of this enterprise. Since the meeting was informal, we did not adopt any conclusions, but we all agreed that during the time which was left to us, we were to invest the greatest efforts in those points which could possibly assure us the greatest degree of consensus from the remaining Yugoslav republics and international public for our step. Indeed from the document it was possible to read very vividly the link between the degree of agreement for dissociation and the degree of risk.

At the same time we all knew that the possibilities for dissociation by complete agreement were virtually nil and that we also had to prepare for the worst variants. We had the data and plans of the YNA and its counter-intelligence service (KOS) in our hands for the rapid disarmament of the Slovenian TO and police as well as the "neutralisation" of part of the Republic leadership and the leaderships of some municipalities including the delegates of the Republic parliament and presidents of some parties. A delegate of the Chamber of Associated Labour, Milan Aksentijević, gave the KOS the addresses of the delegates in the Republic Assembly. Their arrest was built into the plans of the special units of the YNA military police.

At the beginning of May there was a meeting in Poljče of members of the expanded Presidency of the Republic, part of the staff committee of the secretariats for defence and for internal affairs, commanders of the regional headquarters and special brigade of the TO and the chiefs of police units in

Poljče. The members of the expanded Presidency of the Republic were first acquainted with the document Possible Variants of Dissociation from the Aspect of Defence, then we very precisely explained to them what the capabilities of the potential enemy were and what the actual might of our defence forces. In reports and talks at this meeting, which was extremely important for the later outcome of events, the key views on the question of defence in the case of the aggression by the YNA were formed.

After this meeting, Miran Bogataj, my deputy, on the basis of the document Possible Variants of Dissociation from the Aspect of Defence, prepared a formal draft of guidelines on measures for preparedness, in which the procedures and tasks of individual bodies were precisely detailed. Special attention in these guidelines was devoted to the measures for civil defence, for we had to replace the lack of weapons and military equipment with various improvisations, which it was låter shown were extremely effective. The Presidency of the Republic accepted these *Smernice* (Guidelines)[10] in their final form on 15 May 1991, or five minutes before the clock struck midnight. Only a week later the YNA provoked an incident in Pekre and some measures from the Guidelines, which we refined on the municipal level on 22 May, were applied before the ink on the stamp had dried.

Very strict security measures were constantly in force for handling documents with important contents. These were observed everywhere almost without exception, both in the Republic bodies as well as in companies and municipalities. Here it is interesting that the general plans or documents under the title of Possible Variants of Dissociation from the Defence Aspect did not even exist on paper. It was made on a computer and stored on a protected diskette, which I always carried with me. At sessions and work meetings, the text of the plan with individual additional explanations were displayed on canvas with a data show projector.

All plans for the deployment of the TO were supplemented on the basis of the Guidelines of the Presidency. The Republic Headquarters formulated a very detailed procedure for the units of the TO in the event that the YNA tried to completely block the border, and coordinated it with the police. The plan was called Kamen (Stone) and had four stages.

I also studied some foreign historical examples of successful resistance against a stronger opponent. From the organisational aspect, the Finnish experiences during the aggression of the USSR on 30 November 1939 were especially interesting. At that time, the technically and numerically vastly stronger Russian divisions were deployed in Finland as though they were going for a stroll. The Finnish army, which numbered only some 200,000 soldiers resisted very competently. The columns of tanks were left in the interior, then they blocked them and destroyed them, and, in winter conditions, took advantage of their territory. The Soviet Union had to admit

---

[10] The Guidelines ordered the immediate uninterrupted operation of intelligence centres, the strengthened protection of the more important defence facilities and introduced constant duty shifts in the coordination groups. At the same time it assigned the implementation of those measures which were already envisaged in the basic plan to individual implementors.

defeat during the first attack, and in the second offensive they had to put together much stronger forces. Despite this Finland was never defeated. On 29 March 1940 it had to sign a very unfavourable truce, but this was far from unconditional surrender.

Later events showed that the majority of tasks were planned very realistically, for the plan was applied in nearly all of its variants, of course, in different intensities in different regions. The acting out by the headquarters of events if the units of the YNA really broke through to the border crossings and surrounded members of the border police proved to be particularly welcome. In this example previously determined units of the TO would shut off the path of the attackers from behind, cut off their supplies, prevent the arrival of reinforcements and surround it. They would find themselves in a vice between crossfire and the situation in the battlefield would change immediately. In many cases during the war precisely such a situation appeared and a number of detachments of the YNA surrendered after being surrounded.

9. PRESSURE MOUNTS

The YNA had in practice initiated its preparations for war at the beginning of May 1991, when it tried with all the means at its disposal to raise the battle preparedness of its units in Slovenia and the 5th Military District, and week in week out it was reinforcing in particular its border, armoured and special operations units. During this period they were intensively transporting reserve infantry weapons from Slovenia to Serbia and Knin Krajina, for they no longer envisaged the recruitment of our reserves. They wanted to replace them with dependable units mainly composed of Serbs and Montenegrins. The YNA used the GHQ military exercise "OKOP" as a mask to disguise their preparations for war, which truly did envisage the use of the YNA against a so-called external enemy, but these were also to include anti-socialist and anti-Yugoslav oriented Slovenian and Croatian parties.

These preparations coincided with the convulsive attempts by Serbia to ensure the passing of a resolution on the basis of which the YNA could, relatively autonomously, but with the legitimacy of the supreme command, apply extreme measures before Stipe Mesić replaced Boris Jović in the Presidency of the SFRY. When these attempts failed or only partly succeeded, the battle began for preserving relative dominance in the SFRY and the later blockade of this body by opposing the election of Mesić.

On 7 May 1991 the session of the Federal Presidency began in Belgrade. The presidents of the republics and Ante Marković participated in them. After the fatal incident during the demonstrations in Split on 5 May, the YNA implemented a partial mobilization of some units, above all in Serbia, and demanded from their commander-in-chief authorizations for taking measures. But at the session they did not even achieve a consensus on the text which was to be the foundation for discussions. For this reason Boris Jović stopped the session. It continued in the late afternoon next day. The demands of the generals and the "spirit of the suspended session" caused considerable turmoil in Slovenia (and even more in Croatia), where the parliament met behind closed doors. With the mandatory "vexation" of the demo–liberals, we passed a constitutional law which remained "frozen" until its need arose. It allowed us the use of all disposable military capabilities for the defence of Slovenia. I also acquainted the deputies with the latest intelligence information on the plans of the army commands.

Around noon the Presidency of the Republic of Slovenia met in its expanded composition and discussed measures with which Slovenia would

114

protect itself if the YNA received extraordinary authorizations that evening at the Federal Presidency. All that we had at our disposal was prepared, but we were desperately lacking even the most simple infantry weapons and ammunition, not to mention anti-aircraft and anti-tank weapons. We did not carry out any larger mobilization. The units for which we had weapons were able to assemble in a relatively short time. The deployment of larger units for a longer time would mean a big expenditure. I strongly hoped that the YNA would not decide to intervene, since we needed at least another month for preparations. We were still only negotiating for the main delivery of equipment. The budget was accepted at the end of March and the money had come too late. The law on military duty was also accepted with great delay. We would not have one trained regular soldier in the most crucial days. The bridging variants were in the process of realization, but all depended on whether the weapons would arrive on time. The deputies of the Slovenian parliament were walking past the president's conference room, where the meeting was going on. No one was aware of how fatal the delays were that we had made these last months.

Some members of the Presidency of the Republic of Slovenia were opposed to Milan Kučan cooperating in the continuation of the session of the Federal Presidency. Dušan Plut was convinced that he would not be seen again if he departed that day for Belgrade. Kučan decided for himself, and after the passing of resolutions, flew to the session. After painful discussions, a compromise was accepted in Belgrade which gave the YNA only limited authorizations in Croatia, but their public accepted this as being too soft and some even understood it as capitulation. The resolutions actually did ensure the YNA undisturbed performance of its function according to federal law. All decisions of the Assembly of the Republic of Slovenia regarding defence were placed under question. Boris Jović unwittingly confirmed in a dialogue with Milan Kučan our suspicions that the army was preparing to intervene in Slovenia in case of its independence. This session did not reflect any goodwill from Serbia either, which some politicians in Slovenia had constantly emphasised, either through mistakenly falling for the "Balkan" way of conducting of politics or simply from the exaggerated desire for a "solution from above". I myself accepted the compromise of the session as a tactical step backwards, which we needed, for we were not sufficiently prepared. The consequences for Croatia were worse. I knew also that the YNA was not capable of taking on any bigger operation without an extensive mobilization of its reserves in Serbia and that this was more a psychological pressure on people, who slowly fell for it. In those days the amount of doubt among the leading politicians in Slovenia once again reached a critical level.

On 15 May 1991 Stipe Mesić should have become the president of the YNA high command. But it only remained as a sincere desire on his part and that of the Croatian president, Franjo Tudjman. On the basis of the "resolution on compromise" of the Presidency, the YNA was preparing to transfer the centre of its pressure from Croatia to Slovenia. It selected two of our teaching centres for military training as their goal.

* * *

On 17 May 1991 the commander of the Fifth Military District, General Konrad Kolšek demanded from the Slovenian government that it immediately discontinue activities at both training centres of the TO, which a few days ago began to operate in Pekre and Ig. We immediately called in two anti-commando companies to protect both training centres.

In the afternoon the chief of the GHQ of the YNA, General Blagoje Ađić, personally telephoned Zagreb, Ljubljana and Maribor and issued the basic instructions to the commander of the Fifth Military District and to both corps of the YNA in Slovenia for the operation with which they would force Slovenia to close both training centres. The basic idea was that the YNA should trigger a tense situation, then demand negotiations and bargain for concessions from the Slovenian leadership.

They assessed that the 710th training centre in Pekre near Maribor was the more favourable to surround. The coordination of this operation was taken over by the KOS chief in the 31st Corps, Lt-Colonel Ratko Katalina. For this purpose a number of special sections of the YNA from Varaždin and Zagreb arrived at the Maribor barracks with armoured vehicles. For a few days they were sending reinforced patrols of scouts to the vicinity of the 710th training centre and trying to spark an incident.

On 20 May 1991 I held a press conference at the press centre in Cankarjev Dom where I presented to domestic and foreign reporters the "defence and safety" project which I headed under the aegis of the project council. Basic stress was given to the following:

■ "We are making efforts for dissociation to proceed in agreement and without conflicts.

In the proposals sent to the Federal Executive Council we offered the following:

a) the general approach for solving the military question is gradualism,

b) the final deadline for settling all questions was 31 December 1993,

c) by this deadline the YNA, if it reached an agreement, would still perform some functions for the needs of the RS, which the RS would also finance,

d) the RS is prepared and will take over the provision of social and status rights of:

– citizens of the RS who are serving in the YNA and for whom the Executive Council has demanded that they be discharged by 10 June 1991

– citizens of the RS who are currently in military schools and academies,

– citizens of the RS who are doing active military service in the YNA,

– all those active military and civilian personnel employed in the YNA who have permanent residence in Slovenia and would like to stay here on contract or in the TO of Slovenia, which will gradually take over some functions which the YNA now performs in Slovenia,

– all military pensioners who have permanent residence in the RS and wish to remain here.

116

"All these rights will be ensured in compliance with Republic regulations and with the dynamics which will depend on the take over of competences in other fields.

"From the above it follows that Slovenia does not desire to realise its decision made at the plebiscite through conflict, for the proposed measures and principles of gradualism and the principle of ensuring social and status rights to the affected would allow, with at least a minimal preparedness of some federal institutions to negotiate, a perfectly proper solution.

"The deepening of the Yugoslav crisis, the collapse of federal bodies, the confiscation of some of the jurisdiction of civil institutions by the military commands of course also dictates to us the preparation of measures by which the RS shall protect its steps with real might.

"In the last year the Slovenian parliament has passed:
– constitutional amendments for the field of defence,
– three constitutional laws from the field of defence with a two-thirds majority,
– the law on defence and protection,
– the law on military duty,
– a number of resolutions and adopted positions primarily in association with military service and the situation of Slovenian soldiers in the YNA.

"The Presidency of the RS adopted corresponding guidelines for the preparation of some measures, and the Executive Council, the Secretariat of Defence and the RHQ TO have issued the majority of sub-laws.

"Attempts at training army conscripts are proceeding in two training centres as well as conscription activities in all municipalities for the generation of 1973. The reorganization of the TO and the RSLO is in the final stages. We have carried out a few smaller military test exercises.

"All the adopted regulations allow the RS to provide suitable protection of its steps to independence and to realise its plebiscite decision.

"Some steps have also been coordinated with Croatia; these relate primarily to the question of protecting our south-eastern border, which measures over 600 kilometres, and to the question of certain measures if anybody tried to prevent our independence through force.

"Viewed subjectively, and considering the situation at home, in Yugoslavia and the world, it would be virtually impossible to do more. In the material sense we were of course dependent on the means provided in the budget and on the time available for preparations. There has not been a lot of either.

"Despite the relaxation of the situation in Croatia and irrespective of the completely peaceful situation in Slovenia, the state of battle preparedness continues, for apprehension is being generated by the increased battle preparedness of the YNA, and it seems increasingly so that this is connected to the Serbian intervention in the Presidency of the SFRY. Other more logical conclusions do not exist as yet.

"We will prepare everything necessary for the protection of the take-

-over of effective power in Slovenia by 26 June 1991. If we are politically unified in this step, this is the all-important factor now, and no-one can prevent us." ∎

On 21 May the commander of the Fifth Military District, General Konrad Kolšek, came to Ljubljana for negotiations. Lojze Peterle and Dušan Plut also cooperated in these talks, which were very polite. Kolšek constantly repeated that they would not interfere in politics, but that they would uphold federal laws, which was the demand of the Presidency of the SFRY, to which Janez Drnovšek and Milan Kučan had also conceded. They demanded the conscription records and the closure of both training centres. We proposed negotiations on a higher level and a moratorium on any kind of army intervention until 26 June. There would be no sense in escalation when the situation was only partly evolved, if Slovenia would definitely be declaring independence in a little over a month.

In the afternoon Lojze Peterle called the chief of the GHQ of the YNA, Blagoje Adić, in Belgrade. Surprisingly, the chief of "one of the strongest armies in Europe" was on hand. Even before Lojze could fully explain what he wanted to negotiate about, Adić very crisply clarified his position, saying "we can only talk about how you are going to carry out federal laws!" Thus no progress from the visit by Drnovšek and Peterle to Veljko Kadijević on 4 April.

On 23 May 1991 the activities of the YNA units greatly increased in Slovenia. In some barracks they were intensifying battle preparedness, and the roads were full of trucks from the early morning hours, transporting additional battle kits of ammunition from the storage sites to the armoured sections. From 7.30 a.m. unknown uniformed people armed with automatic weapons were spotted in the direct vicinity of the 710th training centre. The detachment of the TO protecting the centre carried out a rapid operation in compliance with battle rules and caught two of them. After interrogation they turned out to be an officer and soldier from a unit of the 31st Corps. At 8.15 a.m., after signing statements, both were released and returned to their barracks.

At 12.30 a special unit of the YNA hurtled to the 710th teaching centre with six armoured personnel carriers (APCs) and loaded weapons and demanded the handing over of the recruits. A little later seven T-55 tanks placed themselves in battle formation at the nearby firing range which faced the training centre, while additional reinforcements arrived in four APCs and a detachment of infantry. The head of the centre, TO Major Andrej Kocbek refused the demand for the recruits and began to negotiate with the leaders of the operation, Lt-Colonels Ratko Katalina and Stevilović. Meanwhile the centre was preparing for defence. The instructors placed themselves at key positions, and displayed one or two hand-held anti-tank rocket launchers of the Armbrust type to the cocky YNA soldiers in the transporters. They only had one or two, in fact, but this balanced the situation a little and Katalina slowly toned down his demands. Finally he wanted only those who had

118

arrested their scouts in the morning. Meanwhile the public found out about the YNA ultimatum and a number of people and journalists gathered in Pekre. Representatives of the Maribor municipality also arrived. Time passed. General Mićo Delić, commander of the 31st Corps sent additional infantry reinforcements to Ratko Katalina, but the people of Maribor blocked their route a little after 4.00 p.m. and forced them to retreat back to their barracks. Meanwhile the majority of exits from the Maribor barracks had been blocked.

That Thursday morning we were working over the preparations for independence in the government conference room in Gregorčičeva street. The session had hardly started when I was called to the phone. The duty officer in the operations group reported that the unit of the TO which was protecting the 710th teaching centre in Pekre had caught two armed and uniformed persons without identification markings in its direct vicinity. Then telephone calls followed every few minutes. I notified the Prime Minister and the Presidency of this event. At about 11 a.m. I left the meeting of the project council and went across the road to the operations hall, which was improvised on the fourth floor of the building opposite the government secretariat in the conference room of the then Secretariat of Planning. Reports were coming in from everywhere on the movement of smaller military units. Military traffic between Varaždin and Maribor and Zagreb and Maribor was especially lively. They were calling the regional headquarters of the TO in Maribor and the training centre from the command of the 31st Corps and demanded the release of their soldiers (they had been released ages ago) and the handing over of all those who had cooperated in their capture. We established a direct telephone inductor connection between the operations hall and the centre in Pekre. Then I spoke with Lt-Colonel Vladimir Milošević and the commander of the regional headquarters of the TO issued appropriate orders, moving some units of the TO which were in training in other municipalities, closer to Maribor. A few minutes after 12.30 a report came in that the military police had surrounded Pekre with six APCs. I spoke to the commander, Major Kocbek, who passed on the army's demands to me. His voice was a little shaky but otherwise he was determined. He muttered only about the inadequate quantities of Armbrusts, for he did not even have one for each armoured vehicle. I ordered that the defence should be organised with the instructors and the units which had been protecting the centre, while the soldiers who had been in Pekre for only a week were to retreat to shelters. We would summon reinforcements and try to push through Belgrade and the Fifth Military District for the YNA to withdraw. We left the telephone lines open and the person on duty in the centre in Pekre gave us a running commentary on events via this.

I tried to ring up General Kolšek in Zagreb, but I could not get in touch with him or his deputy, Andrija Rašeta. It was becoming more and more obvious that this was a prepared game. Meanwhile the situation in Pekre was at boiling point. Mićo Delić was moving in reinforcements. The Maribor mayoress, Magda Tovornik, telephoned Milan Kučan and demanded instructions. I called my assistant, Marjan Fekonja, and sent him to Maribor as a laison officer. The journalists who broke through to Pekre began to raise the temperature in the public with their dramatic reports, while I attempted to calm matters down, for I was almost certain that the YNA would not go all the way and attack the centre. Above all it was important that we hold out under the psychological pressure, which was gigantic. The loaded weapons in the armoured vehicles were trained at close range directly at the unfortified facilities of the 710th teaching centre. The defenders did not even have flak jackets. We called a few more of the most responsible members of the coordination group to the operations hall. Igor Bavčar came directly from his hospital bed – he had caught mucus angina a few days ago because of the constant work in the preparation of the project for independence. When he joined us he had lost his voice. In a few hours, when the tension had increased, the angina rapidly left him and he got back his voice. The commander-in-chief of the TO, Janez Slapar, had activated the narrower section of the headquarters. The afternoon passed with talks with the centre, the issuing of instructions to the headquarters of the TO and the bodies for internal affairs, as well as attempts to reach an interlocutor in the YNA who could do anything at all.

The YNA had selected a good tactic for putting pressure on us. It was directed towards local authorities, to the leadership of the Maribor municipality. In this way they wanted to create a rift between them and Ljubljana, so that Maribor would finally demand that we close the training centre, which was only bringing problems to this otherwise peaceful town. The leadership of this Styrian city was quite scared of the possible consequences of conflict, but the mayoress also showed a lot of determination and dexterity in warding off the constantly new demands and proposals of the YNA. Meanwhile Marjan Fekonja arrived in Maribor, so that we were informed about all events at first hand. After a number attempts at negotiations in the centre and in front of it, they finally agreed to negotiate in the building of the municipal assembly. At 18.30 Ratko Katalina withdrew his armoured vehicles from the centre, two hours before he had received additional reinforcements, which had avoided the blockades and arrived in the vicinity of Pekre through side streets. Some units of the YNA arrived in Pekre fully armed in cars with the Red Cross insignia on them.

When it became clear that negotiations would be serious, we also sent my assistant Miran Bogataj, who was well versed in negotiating – it was he, after the war in Slovenia, who wore out General Rašeta so much during the negotiations with the YNA, that the general, otherwise a non-smoker, began smoking – to Maribor, after having conferred with Igor Bavčar and Milan Kučan.

In the late afternoon we held a special session in the operations hall. Reports were coming in regularly. Our sources in the units of the YNA reported increased excitement but, except for some special units, there was no alarm anywhere. The police were monitoring every slightest movement of military vehicles. We activated a special brigade of the TO, and a special unit

120

of the police was prepared. Within the limits of the means we had at our disposal, we were in complete control of the situation. It was critical only in Pekre and Maribor, where the people were gathering on the streets, and the YNA was revving the engines of its tanks in the barracks, digging foxholes and sending groups of KOS armed to the teeth in civilian cars onto the streets of Maribor.

At 1.15 the following day (24 May) negotiations began with the delegation of the YNA in the building of the Maribor assembly house. The YNA delegation was made up of the commander of the 31st Corps, Mićo Delić, his assistant, Colonel Alojz Lipnik and the chief of the Corps KOS, Lt-Colonel Ratko Katalina. In addition to Miran Bogataj, who had meanwhile arrived in Maribor, our group of negotiators was made up of the president of the Executive Council of the Assembly of the Municipality of Maribor, Anton Rous, deputy of the Republic Assembly, Janez Gajšek, and commander of the regional headquarters, Vladimir Milošević. Miran Bogataj had precise instructions according to which he was allowed to agree only to say that we ourselves would investigate the seizure of both soldiers and report our findings to the 31st Corps. But as was quickly evident, Mićo Delić did not come to negotiate, and the meeting was simply a camouflage to capture Vladimir Milošević.

At 23.35 hours our source near the headquarters of the 31st Corps reported through VIS that the YNA were preparing to kidnap Vladimir Milošević, and Franci Pulk, who had captured both scouts that morning. We immediately passed this news to the regional headquarters of the TO and the authorities of the internal affairs in Maribor, but they did not take this news seriously. They even withdrew the special units of the police from in front of the municipal assembly building just before the negotiations, and the commander of the regional headquarters came without suitable protection. A detachment of YNA commandos from No. 5 Commando, under the command of Lt-Colonel Milan Šuput, had already been circling through the streets of Maribor in six field vehicles since 23.40. This information (six vehicles full of armed soldiers) was passed on to the competent bodies in Maribor in good time.

Soon after the start of negotiations, General Mićo Delić asked for a glass of water, so Lt-Colonel Ratko Katalina stepped into the corridor and gave a signal to one of Delić's armed guards, who were thoughtlessly allowed into the assembly building. He radioed the leader of the units in the field vehicles which were traversing the city. They turned towards the assembly building and, in a lightning operation secured the exit, "covered" the street and a section of them stormed into the building. At the same time Delić's guards, armed to the teeth, disarmed Miran Bogataj's escorts and the members of the TO who were standing in front of the conference hall in which they were negotiating. Lt-Colonel Milan Šuput, who led this operation, then broke into the conference room with two aides, he "leaned" the negotiators up against the wall, whereupon his assistants handcuffed Vladimir Milošević and, taking the two members of the special police units who were guarding Bogataj and the Captain of the TO, Milko Ozmec, shoved them all into the cars waiting in front of the municipal assembly building. Immediately after this, Delić, Lipnik and Katalina also left the building. As a farewell, during their withdrawal Colonel Lipnik threatened deputy Gajšek with a military court. The column of military vehicles with the kidnapped officers and the conniving negotiators drove off at full speed to the Vojvoda Mišić barracks. The whole operation lasted only a few minutes, and it succeeded because of the colossal negligence of safety measures made by both the Maribor TO and the police. The basic mistake was that the road in front of the assembly was not blocked and that the entrances were not guarded. If they had taken care to do this, the break-in of such a small unit would have been impossible. When the members of the YNA were already in the building, the behavior of the guards in the building was correct, for any kind of resistance would have caused unnecessary sacrifice.

When Miran Bogataj called from Maribor after this event and told me what had happened, at first I could not believe my ears. Despite all the warnings they had received, on time, they had even reduced the safety measures instead of increasing them. Luckily, they reported from the 710th training centre nearly at the same time that the army was withdrawing from its positions. And indeed, the sections of the YNA which had surrounded Pekre had returned to their barracks by 5.00 in the morning. We notified the Prime Minister and the Presidency of this kidnapping. All of us in the operations group were mad enough. First because of the despicable behavior of the YNA, which had violated basic civil norms of behavior and international conventions on negotiations and then also because of the unbelievable naivety of our negotiators. Various proposals were centred around possible retaliations, but I proposed sober thinking. I looked at the guidelines which the Presidency had accepted on our proposal on 15 May and, on their basis and after a short conference, we decided on a limited blockade of the infrastructure of military facilities, with the exception of the military medical establishments. We woke up the duty people in the electricity administration and the PTT companies. The couriers took out orders and instructions and at 5.25 the barracks in Ljubljana were without telephone lines. At six the same fate befell the Maribor barracks, and an hour later the majority of the other barracks. We cut off their electricity supplies at the same time.

Meanwhile Igor Bavčar succeeded in calling the commander of the 31st Corps, General Mićo Delić, before the telephones were cut off. The "brave" negotiator was very arrogant and extremely proud of his successful operation in grabbing Milošević. Igor firmly demanded that they immediately release both illegally captured members of the police and the TO. The lads in the special unit to which both the kidnapped policemen belonged were very tense. But Delić only laughed at his proposal: Bavčar, who got his voice back completely, responded to this by raising his voice to the same high tone of pressure in his conversation with Delić, and stated that they were in Slovenia, that they were paid by us, that they were eating our food and that for the coming days they could prepare their tinned rations and dry food, for they would soon be without electricity, refrigerators and the other benefits of civilization. Delić, who was not expecting such a reply, slammed down his phone, and both members of the police were soon released after this. They even had their weapons returned.

After cutting off their electricity and telephones, chaos ensued in the barracks. The commanders were completely lost. The water pumps were not working, water was slowly dripping out of the refrigerators, the electric cookers were totally useless, the soldiers were unshaven, the officers were irritated and surprised. Most of the generators in the barracks were broken down. Some commanders began to issue ultimatums to municipal chiefs, others called through their radio links to the headquarters of the 5th Military District in Zagreb and demanded that they should stop having to take the rap for the politicians' talk.

At six in the morning a session of the Presidency of the Republic was called in its expanded composition. After my report on the counter measures (blockade of the infrastructural services) a question arose as to whether this was not unnecessary harassment, and some of the members of the Presidency had to be reminded of the content of their own resolutions passed at previous sessions. Milan Kučan proposed a talk with the presidents of the parliamentary parties and met with them after the session of the Presidency. It was even worse there. Jože Pučnik very strongly criticised the tepidness of our counter measures and our negligence in the safety precautions taken in Maribor, owing to which Milošević was able to be kidnapped. The representatives of the demo-liberals attacked us from another flank, saying that by opening the training centres we ourselves had baited the otherwise peaceful YNA and that with the blockade of the infrastructure we were escalating this. Igor Bavčar and I remained pretty isolated in this session, and without doubt, they would have pointed to us as the chief culprits if things turned out badly in whichever direction.

Tension mounted. While the party leaders tried to weigh up their political manifestos, their consciences, personal calculations, the results of the plebiscite and the true situation among themselves – in which they did not succeed very well – more and more planes and helicopters of the Yugoslav Air Force (YVL) were flying over Slovenia, and the second battalion of the armoured brigade was preparing to move to the Ljubljana barracks in Polje, which they had officially announced. Here they would, of course, have to drive through Ljubljana. We prepared everything necessary for the blockade of the most dangerous barracks. In Maribor people began to gather in front the Corps command and protested against the kidnapping.

In the operations group we followed the escalation of internal pressure in the barracks. The command of the 5th Military District was in a difficult position. It did not have enough units for a serious intervention, and so it was looking for a way out through compromise. The conscripts and the training centres had been forgotten. We were demanding Milošević and Ozmec, they electricity and telephones. We were prepared to turn on the power and phones immediately after the YNA released both kidnapped officers. All of a sudden we were able to get in touch with any general. We spoke with Konrad Kolšek, Andrija Rašeta, Praščević and again with Mićo Delić, who was a lot less arrogant than before.

Meanwhile, a new incident occurred in Ptuj. A soldier, Jasim Moharini from Belgrade, shot at an unarmed employee of the electricity company and wounded him in the leg. Later he received 22 days' leave for this "exploit".

At 16.35 hours the army finally relented. They released Vladimir Milošević and Milko Ozmec. This was the end of Ađić's plan by which they would demand the closure of the training centre and the renewed sending of recruits to the YNA in exchange for Milošević. The judge of the military court, Ferlinc, contributed to this outcome also. He was a Slovenian who was to conduct the criminal proceedings against Vladimir Milošević, but despite pressure, he discovered that Milošević was not the one responsible for the act for which he was being charged by the KOS. Jelko Kacin flew to Maribor and organised a press conference after Milošević's release. At 17.00 hours we revoked the measures of the services blockade around the barracks. The Maribor Assembly met and demanded an apology from the YNA for the break-in into their building and for violating negotiation principles.

Afterwards, when the situation was calming down, the YNA brought upon themselves another provocation, this time with more serious consequences. At 19.00 hours an APC made in the TAM Maribor factory and under the command of Vojislav Šišljak, callously ran over and killed Josef Šimčik, from Maribor, in front of the barracks. New demonstrations followed in Maribor. At 23.00 hours there were nearly a thousand people in front of the Corps command. As all other indications showed that the situation was temporarily calming down, we also tried to calm down the situation in Maribor.

Janez Drnovšek appeared on TV in the evening. Half of the coordination group was collected in the operations hall, the other half was resting. Those who were there were staring at the TV screen in surprise after Drnovšek explained that he had spoken to Veljko Kadijević and at the same time felt that Slovenia had increased tension too much when it cut off the services to the army barracks. In the end, his appearance on TV sounded like a condemnation of some of our measures, as though they had only worsened his negotiating position, when he and Kadijević had already made some nice agreements. According to the information we had, Veljko Kadijević did not promise anything to Janez Drnovšek, not to mention that it was not he who had bargained for and obtained the release of Milošević. Kadijević's stance during those days was very firm, for the YNA was already very seriously preparing itself for intervention on 26 June. I called Drnovšek by phone after this. We had a long and unpleasant talk after which both of us stuck to our positions. But I had to admit that Drnovšek was a master in political appearances and that he knew how to take advantage of his position for his own promotion excellently. His short discussion with Kadijević and his half--hour appearance on TV was enough to convince a large part of the public that it was he who had saved the situation and achieved the release of

Milošević. Only a few noticed the constant and uninterrupted work of the coordination group and the Presidency in its expanded composition, or the 710th training centre, where a group of instructors with a few Armbrusts maintained a balance of power for a few hours with armoured cars a dozen metres away and with the most modern equipment; last but not least, the contribution of the citizens of Maribor, who repulsed some army columns destined for Pekre with their bare hands, when they blocked the exits of several Maribor barracks.

Next day I went to Maribor. I visited the "scene of the crime", the municipal assembly which was this time guarded like Fort Knox and where, during my discussions with the leadership of the Assembly and Executive Council, I became aware of what a good lesson this last event in Maribor had been. I knew that the likes of General Delić would not be able to draw them onto thin ice again. Then we joined the commemoration in the town hall in Miklavž for the deceased Josef Šimčik. When I spoke to a packed hall I noticed tears in the eyes of those present as well as determination, which filled me with new hope. We were saying our farewells to the first victims of the conflict with the YNA. But there in that hall in Miklavž there was much more bravery than, for instance, at the meeting with representatives of the parliamentary parties and presidencies the day before. After the commemoration I met with the former presidential candidate, Ivan Kramberger, who had said many unpleasant things at my expense in the preceding months. This day he was very serious. When we shook hands, I said "So this time you're with us!" He gave me an affirmative and during the war, a good month away now, he proved that despite his eccentric appearance, he could be of true Slovenian backbone when necessary.

After the commemoration we also visited the 710th training centre in Pekre, which, during this time, had changed into a regular little fortress. New lines were imprinted on the faces of our officers, from which I could read, as though from the rings on trees, the events of the last days and especially the critical hours of that Thursday afternoon, 23 May 1991. Despite the traumas of the past days, work continued normally and the instructors were already preparing their groups for the swearing-in ceremony.

In the night of 26 to 27 May 1991 we took off with four complete APCs from the TAM factory in agreement with its management. Everything had to be carried out in complete secrecy. Ludvik Zvonar, who led this operation, developed a few grey hairs that night. The first thing that happened was that the elevator with which they were loading the armoured vehicles onto trucks broke down. Then the members of the police who were protecting the operation noticed a column of military police nearby. But everything turned out fine and in a few hours the vehicles were safe. We wanted to get a new trump card with this operation and to turn attention and pressure away from the conscripts, for we wanted to have peace at least during the swearing-in. At the same time,

125

we all had bad consciences because of these vehicles, for the YNA had used vehicles made in our factories against the civilians of Maribor. In association with this event, the coordination group issued the following message to the public:

REPUBLIC OF SLOVENIA
Coordination group of the Republic authorities

Date: 28 May 1991
No.: 358

To the mass media
Notification of measures carried out

On 26 and 27 May, 1991, the Republic authorities received a number of indignant calls and messages from the citizens of Maribor and the employees of TAM in association with the ruthless behavior of the armoured car team which killed civilian J. Simčik in front of the army barracks in Maribor. The protest mainly referred to the fact that the producers of armoured cars are chiefly companies from Maribor. This is what the employees of TAM reported to the Republic bodies, that there were a large number of armoured cars in production and they are demanding that they should not be supplied to those who are terrorising the citizens of Maribor. Some messages also contained threats in the sense of sabotaging the production lines for armoured cars.

In order to avoid possible complications and incidents and considering the fact that the arms and military equipment manufactured by Slovenian companies should not be used for the most brutal interventions by units of the YNA against civilians, the coordination group has carried out some preventive measures through the competent bodies, including the prohibition of active military persons entering the official premises of some authorities and those of companies manufacturing specific products. In the same way, the competent authorities have ordered companies with specific products to temporarily halt any delivery of arms and military equipment to units of the YNA. Some arms have been taken out of production and have been suitably safeguarded. This measure will remain in effect until the authorities of Slovenia receive firm assurance that the YNA will not again use such equipment against the citizens of Slovenia.

The Federal Secretariat for People's Defence has also been notified of this.

On Sunday, 26 May 1991, the Republic coordination group met at 12.30. We analysed the events during the Pekre incident and issued a message to the public in which we explained the background to these events. On Saturday we received more precise intelligence from Belgrade, with which Adić's role in the events was explained, as well as Kadijević's stances, which he had defended in his discussion with Janez Drnovšek or his views on the Slovenian project for independence in general. On the basis of these analyses, the competent bodies eliminated a number of deficiencies in their work. That day information came in about the prohibition of watching TV in barracks, which we took as a bad omen.

On Monday a military exercise by the Yugoslav Air Force began, which also involved Slovenian airspace. Since for that day we had also announced a drill against hail, the airplanes flew quite high up. We restricted the use of petrol derivatives for the needs of the YNA and thus it had to eat into its stocks. The next day, the Air Force exercise continued, despite our protests. Andrija Rašeta visited the 31st Corps and discussed the blocking of our borders with the commanders of the border units. Some officers of the YNA had doubts about the success of such a foray.

Ambush at Karteljevo

Tonči Vrdoljak, a film director and, directly following the elections, a member of the Presidency of the Republic of Croatia and director of TV Croatia, called me on Sunday. He invited myself and Igor Bavčar to Zagreb for a special live broadcast which was to be transmitted on Tuesday 28 May at eight in the evening. For this day Croatia was preparing in great secrecy the swearing-in of its national guard assembly, and the evening was to be enlivened with the TV show, on which not only ourselves but also the Croatian Defence and Internal Ministers Martin Špegelj and Joža Boljkovac, respectively, were to appear. The topic of the show was to be the current military and political situation. As at that time cooperation between Slovenia and Croatia was very good in the defence and police fields, Igor Bavčar and I confirmed our cooperation.

The next day HTV was already advertising the names of the guests for its programme.

The commander of the battalion of the military police in the Šentvid municipality in Ljubljana was called on Monday to the headquarters of the Ljubljana Corps, to the KOS Corps chief, Colonel Emin Malkoć. They told him that Igor Bavčar and Janez Janša were travelling next day to Zagreb. He received orders to prepare a special strike unit of military police and at the slope by Karteljevo before the town of Novo Mesto set an ambush.

They put together a unit equipped with a number of light armoured and field vehicles and additional arms with chemical agents for a temporary "knock out". The ambush plan was:

When the car with the ministers or cars and accompanying vehicles reached the incline and slowed down, several armoured cars were to block the road in front, and a part of the unit were to block the rear, under the incline. If the escorts resisted they were to be disabled through an ambush or liquidated by snipers or by the nearby crews of the armoured cars. Both ministers had to be caught alive – if necessary, use chemical agents – then bundled into the armoured cars, an army column was then to be formed and driven to the barracks in Novo Mesto at full speed. From there the prisoners were to be taken by Air Force helicopter to the military prison in Zagreb, and, if necessary, on to Belgrade. The entire operation, from attack to the handing over to the military law authorities, must not last longer than 60 minutes.

The military prosecutor in the 5th Army District already had his charges prepared. Both would be charged with violating federal laws, and I would also be accused of setting up illegal armed formations (here they were thinking of the trial army training centres).

On Tuesday morning it was very tense, and the outcome of the situation was very unsure. I proposed to Igor Bavčar that we should not go to Zagreb in the evening, for anything could happen at home in the meantime, and apart from that, a meeting of the Presidency was called in the afternoon. He agreed and we called Anton Vrdoljak at HTV. He was very disappointed, but understood our situation. He congratulated us on our brave stance and said that the Croatian public was following our counter-measures during Milošević's kidnapping with open enthusiasm. Soon after this we received a warning from our source at the Šentvid barracks about the ambush. We were not completely convinced, but after the war we received absolutely reliable data on the plans for this ambush as well as a description of the preparations.

During our operational work we watched the swearing-in ceremony of the units of the national guard in Zagreb on TV. We knew that with the presentation of their units and arms they were throwing a little sand in our eyes, but the swearing-in made a strong impression, at least on TV, although the ceremony was a little pompous. The GHQ without doubt also had some deep thoughts about this event, since this presented to them the same challenge as our first 300 trial generation of soldiers. Most surely this exhibition of Croatian military power had an influence on the yielding of the YNA after our counter-measures, for a new factor had suddenly appeared in their calculations.

The show on Croatian TV (HTV) passed without us and thus without the ambush either. We asked ourselves a number of times what would truly have happened at the hill by Karteljevo if Igor and I had actually driven off to Zagreb. As the situation was tense, we would most surely have had a reliable escort with us, and both of us had travelled with an automatic on our knees many times. I relied completely on our guards, the lads of our special police unit, and the department of the YNA military police, despite their armoured cars and possible surprise, would not have had an easy job, especially since we had our man in their midst.

On Tuesday, 28 May, the Presidency of the Republic of Slovenia met in its expanded composition. The daily agenda was full once again of moaning about our counter-measures, which had supposedly aggravated the YNA. Ciril Zlobec and Dušan Plut were especially determined in their criticism, albeit without any foundation. The meeting at the Presidency was once again followed by a meeting of the parliamentary parties. The talks were dominated by the proposal that Ljubljana organise a congress in which we would express our solidarity with the bravery of the people of Maribor and, through this, show the determination of Slovenian policies against the ever worsening threats from Belgrade. This proposal was immediately attacked by the demo-liberals of Školč, who appeared quite extreme at this meeting. They named Igor Bavčar and myself as the main perpetrators of this escalation. No one wanted to listen to my explanation that the reason for the escalation

The Arrest (photo: Tone Stojko)

Document from file No. 81452 (photo: Tone Stojko)

J A N Š A Ivan
(priimek in ime)

Formula

| 0 | 1 | U | i | o | o | i | 0 | g |
| 0 | 1 | U | ṅ | o | o | o |

Rojen	17. 9. 1958		(dekliško ime)	
v	Ljubljana	Ime	očeta Janez	Posebna znamenja
SO	Ljubljana		matere Frančiška	
SR	Slovenija		Dekliški priimek Erjavec	

Narodnost Slovenec   Državljanstvo SFRJ

Šolska izobrazba visoka   Poklic dipl. obramboslovec

Kraj bivanja stalno: Plešivica 1a, Grosuplje
začasno: Gornji trg 44, Ljubljana

Stan samski   ime moža (žene)

Bivališče zakonca   število otrok 2

Identiteto potrdil

Lažna imena

št. os. iz. 14486
Lj. center

Desni kazalec

na podlagi fotog. št.

Št. spisa

Vzdevek Janez   Opomba:

Govori jezike angleško

Podpis opisane osebe:

KT 9   jm 7544-86

Priimek   J A N Š A   Formula | O 1 | | U | i | σ | σ | i | 0 | g |

Ime   Ivan | O 1 | | U | i | σ | σ | σ | | |

Letnica rojstva
1958

KT 10

	palec	kazalec	sredinec	prstanec	mezinec
		Ui	σ	σ	σ
Desna roka		16		8	
	16		8		4
		Ui	σ	σ	σ
Leva roka	4		2		1
			2		1

Documents from file No. 81452 (photo: Tone Stojko)

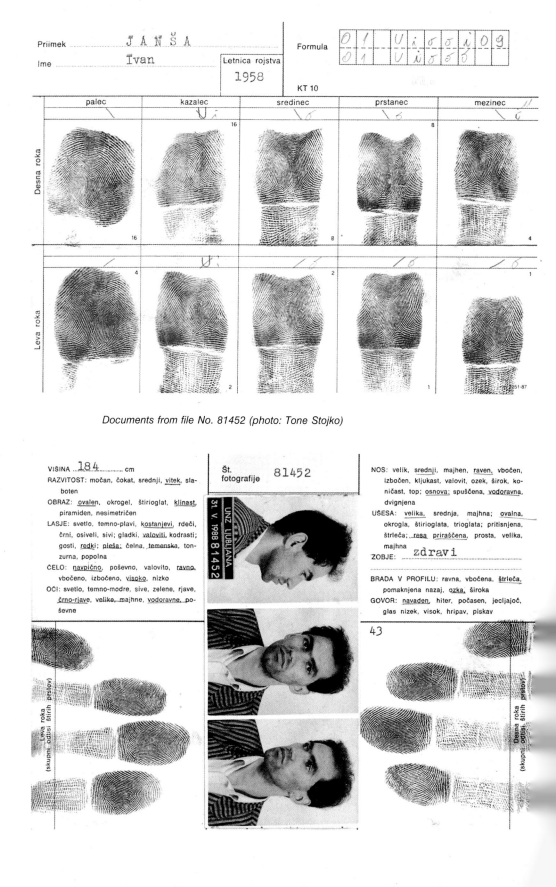

VIŠINA 184 cm
RAZVITOST: močan, čokat, srednji, vitek, slaboten
OBRAZ: ovalen, okrogel, štirioglat, klinast, piramiden, nesimetričen
LASJE: svetlo, temno-plavi, kostanjevi, rdeči, črni, osiveli, sivi; gladki, valoviti, kodrasti; gosti, redki; pleša: čelna, temenska, tonzurna, popolna
ČELO: navpično, poševno, valovito, ravno, vbočeno, izbočeno, visoko, nizko
OČI: svetlo, temno-modre, sive, zelene, rjave, črno-rjave, velike, majhne, vodoravne, poševne

Št.
fotografije   81452

UNZ LJUBLJANA
31. V. 1988   81452

43

NOS: velik, srednji, majhen, raven, vbočen, izbočen, kljukast, valovit, ozek, širok, koničast, top; osnova: spuščena, vodoravna, dvignjena
UŠESA: velika, srednja, majhna; ovalna, okrogla, štirioglata, trioglata; pritisnjena, štrleča; resa priraščena, prosta, velika, majhna
ZOBJE: zdravi

BRADA V PROFILU: ravna, vbočena, štrleča, pomaknjena nazaj, ozka, široka
GOVOR: navaden, hiter, počasen, jecljajoč, glas nizek, visok, hripav, piskav

Leva roka (skupni odtisi štirih prstov)

Desna roka (skupni odtisi štirih prstov)

Poster calling for a gathering in support of the detainees (photo: Tone Stojko)

Founding of the Committee for Protection of Human Rights, 3 June 1988 (photo: Tone Stojko)

Gathering in Congress Square, 21 June 1988 (photo: Borut Kranjc)

Roška Street during the trial (photo: Tone Stojko)

The Four at liberty (photo: Tone Stojko)

Consultation following the latest ultimatum from Belgrade (photo: Borut Kranjc)

First government of Slovenia elected in a democratic parliament (photo: Borut Kranjc)

Vitodrag Pukl, Franc Bučar and Vane Gošnik on the proclamation of the Declaration of Independence (photo: Borut Kranjc)

Dr Franc Bučar, president of the Assembly of the Republic of Slovenia, proclaims on 25 June 1991 the Constitutional Charter for the Independence of Slovenia (photo: Borut Kranjc)

Guard of honour of the Territorial Defence of Slovenia during the raising of the new Slovenian flag, 26 June 1991 (photo: Borut Kranjc)

On 23 May 1991 the YNA in armoured units surrounded the 710th training centre at Pekre near Maribor, demanding surrender (photo: Majda Struc)

Consequences of air raid at Medvedjek (photo: S. Živulović)

Gornja Radgona, 28 June 1991 (photo: J. Pojbič)

Ljubljana railway station during air raid warning, 3 July 1991 (photo: Joco Žnidaršič)

Consequences of tank fire near Ormož (photo: Zoran Klemenčič)

Rocket attack on a bridge over the Sava (photo: Ernest Sečen)

T-84 tank, the pride of the YNA, in flames (photo: Borut Kranjc)

Remains of a tank after the clash near Prilip (photo: Borut Kranjc)

They came in tanks, but went home in coffins. The consequences of Marković's incomprehensible decision (photo: Borut Kranjc)

Ruins (photo: Borut Kranjc)

Continuing attack by members of the TO and police on YNA units which had occupied the international border crossing at Rožna Dolina (photo: Marjan Pavzin)

Slovenian delegation at the Brioni talks (photo: Joco Žnidaršič)

The YNA finally left Slovenia on 26 October. A special ceremony was held to mark this occasion (photo: »Obramba«)

Igor Bavčar

Vinko Beznik

Miran Bogataj

Tine Brajnik

Miha Brejc

Miloš Bregar

Pavle Čelik

Milan Domadenik

Marjan Fekonja

Janez Janša

Jelko Kacin

Franc Kokoravec

Jože Kolenc

Bogdan Koprivnikar

Anton Krkovič

Alojz Kuralt

Danijel Kuzma

Andrej Lovšin

Rudi Merljak

Stane Praprotnik

Janez Slapar

Janko Stušek

Bojan Ušeničnik

Anton Vereš

Ludvik Zvonar

Franci Žnidaršič

9th ARMY COMMAND   MILITARY SECRET
Str. class.no. 5044-3   Strictly classified
08. 01. 1988

OONP Chief

On the basis of the order of the SSNO GHQ str.class.no. 80-24 of 21 Dec. 1987 and on the order of the Command of the 9th Army, class. no. 2256-1 of 3 July 1987, and due to the visible need and for the better organisation of the BOiV units of "A" and "B" categories, and their training for strengthening units under permanent and increased state of battle preparedness,

I ORDER:

1. – All units of "A" and "B" categories, of the level of battalion/division are to be expertly militarily and ideologically trained through drills and education to reinforce "battle strength" and train them in defined directions.

Through a test of "battle strength" (and in a specially defined time), plan and implement a test of the battle preparedness of the units of "A" and "B" categories and train them in strengthening "battle strength" and for action.

Plan and implement a complex test of the battle preparedness of units "A" and "B" categories once a year on the level of brigade and regiment.

Permanent task

2. – The commands of garrison 44, Kozina, garrison 64, Sežana and garrison 65, Murska Sobota, are to plan and implement a complex check of battle prepared-ness of their border anti-tank detachments once a year. In planning and implementing these tests, verify the practical work and training from red alerts of units, sending of draft cards and implementing mobilisation, to allocation to anti-tank regions (positions) and organisation of a firing and coordination system.

Permanent task

3. – In the garrisons of Ljubljana, Postojna and Maribor, select units and train them militarily and professionally, through drills, for taking over and implement-ing tasks of units of the military police with permanent tasks at garrisons, as follows:

– in the Ljubljana garrison, designate one mechanised company (mtč) from the 14 ppp. 14 pmtd

– in the Postojna garrison, designate one rifle unit from 228 motorised brigade (mtbr) and,

– in the Maribor garrison, designate one rifle unit from 195 mtbr, 31 pd.

Incorporate these systems into the mobilisation and other plans.

The deadline is 1 February 1988.

4. – In every first subordinated command and in the ONO of the 9th Army Command carry out a modernisation of the security guard by introducing new technology and carbine belts. After receipt of standardised technology, carry out the necessary training of the guards with officers versed in using this technology, and then incorporate them according to priorities and, in this manner, reduce the number of soldiers on guard.

The 9th Army ONO Command will, in cooperation with the commands of the border detachments, withdraw the technology from those sectors of the state border where they cannot be used technically or tactically and allocate them to units according to priority.

The units for intervention in facilities are to be trained for carrying out their planned tasks and tested regularly.

Permanent task. (also after new technology arrives).

5. – in all the first subordinated units/divisions, independent brigades/regiments and in the Operations Centre of the Command maintain a daily SITUATIONS DOSSIER and, at the end of the month, summarise the data. Then write a political security report for their zone of responsibility in which flashpoints and the appearance of unfriendly activities, destructive and peaceful demonstrations have to be specially registered and analysed so that the units are not surprised in terms of security or threatened in terms of combat.

To implement this, organise action with the bodies of security and self-defence as well as with other structures in the zone of responsibility.

Task leaders: Security bodies of divisions, independent brigades/regiments.

Deadline: 1 February 1988, and on, as a constant task.

6. – The personnel on duty at the Operations Centre of the 9th Army Command and the duty personnel of the leading teams will, on the basis of reports from RSUP and RCO reports and the exchange of intelligence and information, enter data relevant for the assessment of the political security situation with regard to the situation in the units and in the territory, on the announcement of larger strikes, gatherings near military facilities, as well as all other possible activities which could threaten the security of the units and military facilities.

Permanent task.

7. – Carry out MANDATORY FIRST LESSONS every working Saturday in the month within the complex of general military training for informing officers of professional army, ideological and political, security, and other issues. Urgent information is to be passed on immediately through necessary lessons. Inform the army composition regularly and to the necessary dimensions. The PKPR and PP, with the security chief of the 9th Army Command is to forward short and concise political security assessments of the situation every three months to subordinated commands.

Permanent task.

8. Acquaint all officers and commands with this order to the necessary extent. Reports in association with this order are to be submitted according to the schedules of implementation.

MT/JP

COMMANDING OFFICER
Lt-Colonel-General
Svetozar Višnjić

Circulated to:
– original to the ONO 9.A,
– all first subordinated commands and units,
– all assistant commanders and chiefs of detachments and sectors.

Order of the 9 Army Commander, Gen. Svetozar Višnjić. no. 5044-3. The photocopy which was circulating in Ljubljana contained only item 3 of the first page and the entire second page. The beginning and end of the document containing the official marks and top secret stamp were removed by Ivan Borštner

Chairman

I did not understand. Are you in favour of us opening up the standpoints at all or the reworked ones? I feel that we have to make ourselves clear here.

Štefan Korošec:

I am not in favour of such a concept of standpoints. I must state this. Now it is a question of whether we go for another approach, and I have already stated what I think this approach is.

Chairman:

Okay.
Comrade Kučan has the floor.

Milan Kučan:

I am naturally speaking of the problem of the SLO, the way we see this problem. I shall start from the weight of the problem and from the standpoints and the conclusions of our last meeting, that the ideological political activity in the whole of the League of Communists of Yugoslavia (SKJ) has to be strengthened, but above all in those places where these phenomena are in their greatest stride. For the leaderships in these centres are the most called and most responsible for the principled solving of the problem, which is the practice of the SKJ anyway, its principle of work, and it is good that it is so.

We had, because of the Plan of Standpoints, a meeting of the Presidency yesterday. We could not have it sooner, unfortunately, for I had only received the papers on Friday, we copied them, the meeting was expanded. Except for two, all members of the Central Committee of the SKJ from Slovenia were present, the leaders of Slovenia, except for the president of the Trade Union, who was in Belgrade, and members of the Presidency of the Republic of Slovenia. This is what was agreed here, if I remember correctly, that I did not come with only my standpoints, but with the standpoints of all.

We studied the document very carefully, no one defended the situation, no one claimed that the situation was good. Just the opposite. All the colleagues, except for two, had a word. it was our unanimous opinion that the document points out many relevant questions, warns of the mistakes of the political work in general, that the ideological political action of the League of Communists is directed towards beneficial activities, but that it contains things that, in our estimation, cannot be agreed upon, most surely because the problem is moved to Slovenia.

Page from a recording of a session of the CK ZKJ 29 March 1988.

DECLARATION OF PEACE

Arming oneself does not bring security. The latest events in the world and in Yugoslavia only confirm this. Investment in military facilities is a blind alley, which reduces the possibility of politically non-violent solving of political disputes, while within individual countries, it means a constant threat to democratic order. Arming oneself is a bottomless abyss, which, especially in less developed countries or countries in a development crisis, means an unbearable burden on the economy.

We are convinced that the state can only assure security to its inhabitants and all its neighbors with a security policy which is founded on human rights, political freedoms and social and ecological safety, in relation to neighbouring countries and people, if it integrates intensive social and diplomatic measures for a non-violent solution of disputes and the pacification of those with whom a dispute or tension exists.

The Republic of Slovenia has an especially good opportunity to opt for such a concept.

As a country which is still only being created, it must define anew its system and policies, and the issue of the army here is one of the basic developmental questions.

Even if the Republic of Slovenia sets up the strongest possible army, it cannot compare itself with its neighboring states. Besides this, a military conflict in Slovenian territory would mean a catastrophe for the Republic.

The founding of our own army would dramatically threaten the already very modest accumulation of the Slovenian economy and its inhabitants, while the relaxation of those assets which have, until now, been proposed for the military machinery, would mean an exceptional development incentive at the most critical moment of the restructuring of the economy. The Republic of Slovenia provides more for its army than it does for education and more than it does for medical care, and ten times more than it allocates to culture, social security or employment.

Slovenia is situated in a relatively conflict-burdened region, or at least on its edge, which is why the abolishment of the army, with the development of institutions for the non-violent solution of disputes and with a pacifist policy, we could make an important contribution to a peaceful outcome of relations in Yugoslavia and further afield, and Slovenia would present itself to the world within the framework of its efforts for international recognition, as a state of good-will, which nurtures a comprehensive understanding of world peace, a peace which cannot be achieved by closing into national military-defence concepts.

The Republic of Slovenia has a professional, civilised and democratically controlled police and professional and well organised units of civil defence.

Last but not least, Slovenia has a positive historical experience in non-violent efforts for political democratisation and state independence.

DECLARATION OF PEACE

We stand for:

Slovenia as a sovereign, peace-loving state which actively contributes to world peace, for a Slovenia without an army or arms industry.

– An Article on peace in the new Slovenian Constitution, which should read: "The Republic of Slovenia is a demilitarised state. The transition period which is necessary for demilitarisation is determined by a constitutional law."

– A transition period until complete demilitarisation, during which the police units and the existing units of the territorial defence will take care of the safety of the borders of the Republic of Slovenia.

– Freeing of all contingents of Slovenian recruits from service in the YNA as a constituent part of carrying out the decision made at the plebiscite.

– Cessation of further arming in Slovenia and Yugoslavia.

– Beginning of negotiations with the federation on the withdrawal of YNA units from Slovenia

– Compiling a peace option for solving the Yugoslav crisis.

– Introduction of the values of culture and non-violence into the system of upbringing and education, and the establishment of peace institutions which will study and create new security systems on the foundations of social, ecological, economic and spiritual freedoms and safety and on good international relations.

In Slovenia, emancipation, demilitarisation and peace security policies are to be three parallel processes.

Name and Surname   Address   Signature

P.S.
The Declaration was composed by: Primož Bulc (SKD/youth), Marko Hren (NDG list), Lev Kreft (SDP), Rastko Močnik (SDUS), Dušan Plut (ZS), Mateja Poljanšek (ZS), Vika Potočnik (LDS), Janez Sodržnik (LDS), Mile Šetinc (LDS), Jožef Školč (LDS) and Jaša Zlobec (LDS)

On Thursday, 7 February, there will be a public presentation of the Declaration and the first signatories at a press conference which will be conducted by Vika Potočnik, Dušan Plut, Jožef Školč and Marko Hren.

Send your signatures to the Centre for the Culture of Peace and Non-Violence, Mestni Trg 13, 61000 Ljubljana, no later than by the evening of Tuesday, 6 February

"Declaration of Peace"

COMMAND MILITARY SECRET
5 CORPS RV and PVO STRICTLY CLASSIFIED

Information submitted to THE COMMANDER OF THE 350 vp PVO
(91.b.VOJIN)

In the supplement to this act we enclose the "Information on the current situation in the world and country and the direct tasks of the YNA".

The commanders of units are obligated to acquaint all active military personnel with the contents of this Information. In a corresponding manner (executively) use it to inform soldiers and civilians employed by the YNA.

On the basis of the standpoints expressed in the Information at a collegium of the command, view the situation in your own units and, in association with this, also the direct tasks for units, with special emphasis on command officers and key bodies in the command units.

The commanders of units will, by their own example and authority, aid the President of the Committee of the League of Communists and Secretaries of the basic organisation of the League of Communists in their own units in activities on recruiting members for the League of Communists – Movement for Yugoslavia (SK-PJ). Defend and patiently explain the sense and character of the existence of the SK-PJ through direct political work and discussions with officers and civilians employed in the YNA. Here it is important to apply all positive experience from the work and operation of the KPJ-SKJ, and especially of the experience of the work and operation of SK organisations in the YNA. Here we have to begin from the standpoints of the Federal Secretary, that in solving the situation in our country the army cannot solve anything by force and is thus appealing to the officers to join the SK-PJ and, through political battle and action, contribute to the SK-PJ in its battle for Yugoslavia. Joining the SK-PJ is the personal stance of every individual, and when explaining the significance of joining this organisation, no-one is to be forced to become a member. Through direct political campaign, this should be a confirmation and definition of the majority of the active army personnel and civilians employed in the YNA.

AFTER READING   COMMANDING
DESTROY BY BURNING   Major-General
OFFICER   Marijan Rožič

INFORMATION
on the current situation in the world and our country as well as the
direct tasks of the YNA

In this notice we point out the more important characteristics of the most recent events in the world and our country and of the main tasks of the YNA in 1991, especially those which stand directly before us.

I

The basic conclusion drawn from the present situation is that one stage of development has been concluded – of Yugoslav society and relations in the international community. The end of the 90's marks the beginning of a new stage, which will be essentially different from the previous one. Naturally, we are not thinking here of brutal division, but of the essential quality and constituents of what has happened, what is current and what is on our doorstep. There is no doubt that the international scene is characterised by many processes and phenomena, of which some will most surely have a significant and important influence on the events in our country.

Since future developments in the USSR cannot be predicted, we can say at this moment that the process of disintegration of this huge country has been slowed down. The Soviets have begun to assess themselves and see that the path they have taken does not lead to the success of reform, but to destruction. The forces which favour the preserving of a united state and its institutions are reaffirming and increasing themselves. These days they are adopting more decisive measures for stopping the separatistic tendencies of individual parts of the country. In some regions they are effecting this in a manner which is very problematic, with great resistance in the country itself and pressure from abroad. The Soviet army is also actively involved. Such a development in the situation of the USSR, irrespective of its outcome, restricts the free action of the West and the extent of its influence on world events.

Information on the current situation..., which revealed the ideas of the YNA and presented it to the world as a communist army of a North Korean type.

PROJECTED ACTION
OPERATIONAL TIME: D-10 AT 07.30 A.M.

Map 1:500,000 Munich, Prague, Vienna,
Milan, Zagreb, Sarajevo

1: MILITARY/POLITICAL SITUATION

1. The military and political situation in the world is increasingly unstable. With the dismantling of the Warsaw Pact the focus of tension in Europe has shifted from Central Europe to the Balkan peninsula and the USSR, to both its European and Asian parts.

Explicit aspirations towards secession from the USSR on the part of the Baltic republics, Moldavia, western Ukraine and some of the Soviet Asian republics, and the creation of parallel national military formations in these republics, have led to armed clashes between these formations and the Red Army as well as the police force, threatening to escalate into a civil war with unpredictable consequences.

Pressed by numerous economic and political problems after internal changes, and intent on realizing claims on Yugoslavia, former Warsaw pact members – Hungary and Bulgaria – and Albania are increasingly leaning towards the U.S. and NATO, with Hungary and Albania wholly espousing the policies of NATO.

2. The economic and political situation in Yugoslavia is characterised by extremely tense inter-republican and inter-ethnic relations and overt separatist tendencies on the part of certain republics and their governments. The socioeconomic situation is very difficult. Efforts at reaching an inter-republican agreement on redesigning relations in Yugoslavia and the future of the country have been deadlocked owing to the intransigent and mutually opposing views of republican governments.

OKOP plan

PRESIDENCY OF THE SFRY   STRICTLY CLASSIFIED
No. 244/3-4-1170
BELGRADE, 27.09.1990

TO THE PRESIDENCY OF THE REPUBLIC OF SLOVENIA

LJUBLJANA

WE HEREBY NOTIFY YOU THAT THE PRESIDENCY OF THE SFRY HAS STUDIED YOUR LETTER OF 30 AUGUST 1990, IN CONNECTION WITH THE TEMPORARY APPLICATION OF THE "DOCTRINE OF TERRITORIAL DEFENCE OF THE ARMED FORCES OF THE SFRY" AT ITS SESSION HELD ON 25 SEPTEMBER 1990. HERE THE SFRY ALSO CONSIDERED THE INFORMATION OF THE FEDERAL SECRETARIAT FOR NATIONAL DEFENCE ON THE SUPPLEMENTING OF THE TERRITORIAL DEFENCE DOCTRINE.

THE PRESIDENCY OF THE SFRY HAS ESTABLISHED THAT THE DOCTRINE OF THE MILITARY DOCUMENT IS BASED ON THE CONCEPT OF GENERAL NATIONAL DEFENCE AND CIVIL DEFENCE, WHICH HAS BEEN PREPARED ON THE BASIS OF THE CONSTITUTION OF THE SFRY AND THE LAW ON NATIONAL DEFENCE IN COOPERATION WITH THE AUTHORISED BODIES IN THE REPUBLICS AND AUTONOMOUS PROVINCES AND INITIATED ON TEMPORARY, TEST USE, TO HEADQUARTERS AND UNITS OF THE TERRITORIAL DEFENCE UNTIL THE END OF 1991. THE GOAL OF THIS TEST USE OF THE DOCTRINE IS THAT THROUGH A TEST IN PRACTICE AN OPTIMAL SOLUTION FROM THE ASPECT OF THE USE OF THE TERRITORIAL DEFENCE MIGHT BE FOUND, AND FOR THIS REASON IT IS DESIRED THAT ALL THE REPUBLICS AND AUTONOMOUS PROVINCES, THROUGH APPLYING THE SOLUTION ENVISAGED IN THIS DOCUMENT, INSPECT THEIR FOUNDATIONS IN THEIR SPECIFIC CONDITIONS, AFTER WHICH THEY MIGHT SUBMIT COMMENTS AND IDEAS ON THE BASIS OF WHICH A FINAL TEXT OF THIS DOCUMENT WOULD BE MADE. THERE IS NO DOUBT THAT HERE OBSERVATIONS OF SUCH A CHARACTER AS YOU HAVE IN YOUR LETTER CAN ALSO BE SUBMITTED.

HAVING ALL THIS IN VIEW, THE PRESIDENCY OF THE SFRY HAS ASSESSED THAT THE REASONS UPON WHICH THE REPUBLIC OF SLOVENIA HAS GIVEN ITS JUSTIFICATION FOR THE DOCTRINE NOT BEING APPLIED IN THE TERRITORIAL DEFENCE OF THIS REPUBLIC AND WHICH HAS BEEN STATED IN THE LETTER, IS UNACCEPTABLE, THE MORE SO, FOR IT IS NOT AUTHORISED BY THE CONSTITUTION OR LEGAL JURISDICTION TO MAKE SUCH DECISIONS.

INSOFAR AS THE PRESIDENCY OF THE REPUBLIC OF SLOVENIA IS OF THE OPINION THAT THIS DOCUMENT IS NOT IN COMPLIANCE WITH THE CONSTITUTION OF THE SFRY OR THE LAW ON NATIONAL DEFENCE IT WOULD BE A MATTER OF COURSE THAT SUCH COMMENTS ARE STATED AND EXPLAINED AND SUBMITTED TO THE PRESIDENCY OF THE SFRY FOR DISCUSSION.

SECRETARY-GENERAL
ANTON STARI

Notification from the Secretary-General of the SFRY

REPUBLIC HEADQUARTERS   PEOPLE'S DEFENCE
FOR NATIONAL DEFENCE   STATE SECRET
THE REPUBLIC OF SLOVENIA

DIRECTIVE

OF THE CHIEF OF THE NATIONAL DEFENCE OF THE REPUBLIC OF SLOVENIA FOR A DEMONSTRATIVE, PARTIAL OR COMPLETE APPLICATION OF THE MANOEUVRING STRUCTURE OF THE NATIONAL DEFENCE

Topographical map: 1:200,000 Klagenfurt, Graz, Maribor, Trieste, Ljubljana, Zagreb, Rijeka, Gospič, Bihać

The directive has been made on the basis of an integral assessment of the possible consequences of the acceptance of the constitutional law, on the basis of which the RS would itself order a part of military duties, and the assessment of possible situations in which partial or complete use of the manoeuvring units of the National Defence in the Republic of Slovenia could come into consideration.

I.

REASONS AND POSSIBLE OPERATION OF FORCES FOR MEDIATING IN THE REGION OF THE REPUBLIC OF SLOVENIA

1. Due to the complicated internal political conditions within the SFRY and the escalation of conflicts, both between republics and between the Federal bodies and individual republics, the YNA is appearing as the only "healthy" force and cohesive strength, with all its competences as well as with its "arbitrary" or ultimative demands. The foreseen changes of amendments to the Constitution of the RS and above all the law on SLO and DS, as well as other laws which affirm the subversiveness of the RS, are the cause of the extremely escalated situation in Slovenia. The most responsible individual YNA representatives and Federal bodies are making statements concening the illegitimacy of the elections and the operation of the Assembly and bodies of the RS, as well as threatening to introduce a state of emergency.

a) The reasons for intervening in the area of the RS could be as follows:
– State of emergency in the entire territory of the SFRY
– State of emergency in Kosovo because of national revolt of the Albanians
– State of emergency in Croatia because of the intervention of the Administration of Internal Affairs of the Rep. of Croatia in Knin Krajina
– State of emergency in Croatia because of inter-ethnic conflicts of wide dimensions due to the "all-Serb assembly in Jasenovac"
– State of emergency in Bosnia-Herzegovina because of forced inter-ethnic conflicts
– Evacuation of military technology and heavy artillery from the territory of the RS
– Attempts at direct imposition of Federal laws and regulations.

b) The Federal bodies, in the possibility of an operation of forces for intervening in the region of the RS in each of the above possible variants, with the introduction of an emergency state in the RS, would above all deploy units of the YNA.

2. The YNA is composed of peace and war-time compositions. The war units of the YNA are mostly nationally homogeneous, while the peace-time forces are ethnically mixed because of the ex-territorial manner of fulfilling its ranks with recruits.

Directive of the chief of the Manoeuvring Structure of the National Defence of Slovenia

REPUBLIC OF SLOVENIA
REGIONAL HEADQUARTERS OF
TERRITORIAL DEFENCE
WEST ŠTAJERSKA

MILITARY SECRET
STRICTLY CONFIDENTIAL

NO. SZ
CELJE 15.05.1990

ON THE BASIS OF THE ORDER OF THE COMMANDER OF THE TO, REPUBLIC OF SLOVENIA, NO. SZ 625/1-90 FROM 15.5.1990

I ORDER

ALL WEAPONS AND AMMUNITION OF THE TO MES, WHICH ARE OUTSIDE OF YNA FACILITIES MUST BE SURRENDERED FOR SAFEKEEPING IN YNA FACILITIES AT THE DEPOT AT BUKOVZLAK BY 19 MAY 1990, 23.00 HOURS. ALSO GIVE UP ALL WEAPONS AND AMMUNITION OF OTHER BODIES (SECRETARIAT FOR PEOPLE'S DEFENCE, UNITS OF COMMUNICATION CENTERS, AMMUNITION FOR TRAINING, ETC.) WHICH ARE STORED IN DEPOTS OF THE BUKOVZLAK DEPOT. IN FACILITIES OUTSIDE OF YNA COMPLEXES, ONLY ANTI AIRCRAFT GUNS ARE ALLOWED TO REMAIN.

THE RELEASE OF WEAPONS AND AMMUNITION FOR TRAINING IS CARRIED OUT ACCORDING TO THE INSTRUCTIONS AND APPROVAL OF THE RŠTO ON THE DEMAND OF THE HEADQUARTERS FOR TO THROUGH THE PŠTO AT LEAST FIFTEEN DAYS BEFORE TRAINING COMMENCES.

TRANSPORT AND WORKFORCE WILL BE PROVIDED BY THE PŠTO, IN ACCORDANCE WITH THE PLAN OF HAND-OVER.

THE SMALL ARMS DISTRIBUTED TO OFFICERS IN THE PERMANENT COMPOSITION ARE TO BE APPROPRIATED AND HANDED IN WITH THE OTHER ARMS AND AMMUNITION.

PREPARE RESERVES FOR ALL WEAPONS AND AMMUNITION

IN THE CARRYING OUT OF THIS ASSIGNMENT CONSIDER AND BEHAVE ACCORDING TO THE ORDERED MEASURES FOR THE DEGREE OF SECRECY APPROPRIATE TO THE SERIOUSNESS OF THE ASSIGNMENT.

OŠTO CELJE IS PREPARING STORAGE PLACES FOR THE TAKE OVER OF THE WEAPONS AND AMMUNITION FROM OŠTO ŠENTJUR TO ITS STORAGE SITE IN BUKOVZLAK

AFTER THE IMPLEMENTATION OF THE ORDERED TASKS NO AMMUNITION OR WEAPONS MUST STAY OUTSIDE THE FACILITIES OF THE YNA.

GS/RS
COLONEL
IVAN GORENJAK

COMMANDER OF THE TO ZSP

Order for disarming the TO in the west Štajerska region

COMMAND OF THE 1ST armoured brigade   MILITARY SECRET
13.03.1991   STRICTLY CLASSIFIED
Horjul
D-7 16.00 hours

Deliver personally to Commander _____

PREPARATORY ARRANGEMENTS

1. – Due to the deterioration of inter-state relations with NATO members, the armed forces of the NATO Alliance are at battle readiness. Movements towards our borders have been observed, and an act of aggression against our country is expected to come within 6 or 7 days.

On the commencement of aggression it is expected that the "P" will initiate the deployment of stronger VD (fire power) in the regions of Vrhnika, Kamnik and Brezovica.

Before aggression begins there will be accelerated DTG and deployment of special commando forces in the regions of Menišija, Krim and the west part of Ljubljansko Barje.

2. – Our battalions have to carry out PDB (anti-commando operations) in the regions of Vrhnika, Kamnik, Brezovica and active military action in the line of Vrhnika, Postojna, Razdrto and (Postojna Pivka).

3. – For this purpose I order! Carry out mobilisation of troops and allocation to OR. Supply units with ammunition, fuel and other means. Execute necessary control of arms and equipment. Carry out morale preparations and rest your people.

4. – 1/mč I allocate for battle against DTG and IDG and other special forces of "P" (the enemy)

5. – The majority of the anti-aircraft battalions are to monitor air space and measures of the PVZ.

6. – Units should be prepared for PDB in their regions.

7. – Nuclear Chemical and Biological agents should be prepared for use.

COMMANDING OFFICER
Major
Danilo Radovanović

Execution document of the command-headquarter exercise OKOP

SOCIALIST REPUBLIC OF SLOVENIA
REPUBLIC HEADQUARTERS
OF TERRITORIAL DEFENCE

No. SZ 16/4-90

Ljubljana, 24.01.1990

Inspection of storage facilities
and OVO (municipal defence) equipment
stored outside of YNA facilities

To provide necessary data for planning the development of the TO in the coming period and for the construction of facilities for storing OVO material of the TO SR Slovenia, on the basis of the Order of the GHQ OS SFRY, SZ831-5 from 05.01.1990 and in accordance with item 35 of Instructions for a Register of Weaponry and Military Equipment of the Territorial Defence (UPPRFF-13) conduct:

An inspection of storage facilities and stored material of the OVO which are located outside of YNA facilities.

Carry out the required survey in accordance with the enclosed forms which we are supplying to you as supplements no. 1, 2 and 3, as follows:

1. – The survey according to suppl.1 must be made for all storage facilities which fall under the OOŠTO, MŠTO, PŠTO or 30. RSk and are not situated within a protected military complex of the YNA (barracks, storage site, border guard posts), with a precise statement on who owns the structure and the quantity by types of basic army equipment which are found in it and, under item 7, the manner of safekeeping, and in item 8, the general conditions of storage (space, moisture, access and so on).

2. – Surveys according to suppl. 2 and 3 are to be made on the basis of surveys in suppl. 1 for OŠTO, PŠTO, MŠTO, 30 RSk and for regional TOs as a whole.

The actual state of the weapons, ammunition and MES recorded in suppl. 1 and 2 must be in accord with the actual state and quantities in the structures.

3. – The storage structures in which the technical material means are stored for training and drilling are to be shown equally, and then write in the comment: means for training with total weight in kilos (tons).

4. – The necessary number of forms no. 1, 2 and 3 have to be copied for making the required surveys in the OŠTO, MŠTO, PŠTO for submitting to RŠTO and for regularly updating created changes.

The required data has a great significance for the further development of the TO, which is why the ordered task must be carried out responsibly and well, and the required surveys are to be submitted to the RŠTO of the SR of Slovenia no later than by 20 February 1990.

Demand other possible clarifications for making the required surveys from Lt-Colonel Ivan Kapitler of the interior sector of the MŠTO.

PF-FN

C O M M A N D E R
TERRITORIAL DEFENCE OF THE SR SLOVENIA
Lt-Colonel-General
Ivan HOČEVAR

Order by General Ivan Hočevar, who was creating the conditions for disarming the TO

CONSTITUTIONAL LAW FOR IMPLEMENTING THE CONSTITUTIONAL ACT ON THE INDEPENDENCE AND SOVEREIGNTY OF THE REPUBLIC OF SLOVENIA

Article 1

In accordance with this law, the authorities of the Republic of Slovenia take over the implementation of rights and duties which were, according to the Constitution of the Republic of Slovenia and the Constitution of the SFRY, transferred to the authorities of the SFRY.

Article 2

The delegates from Slovenia cease their mandates in the Federal Chamber of the Assembly of the SFRY.

The delegates of the Assembly of the Republic of Slovenia in the Chamber of Republics and Provinces of the Assembly of the SFRY, who performed this function until the affirmation of this law, and the delegates of the Assembly of the Republic of Slovenia for the Chamber of Republics and Provinces of the Assembly of the ON6 SFRY who were elected at a joint session of all chambers of the Assembly of the Republic of Slovenia on 30 June 1990, cease their mandates.

The Assembly of the Republic of Slovenia elects a twelve-member delegation which, on the basis of its authorisations, cooperates in the Assembly of the SFRY, in the negotiations for carrying out the process of dissociation from the present SFRY, in negotiations for resolving regular issues and in agreements on the possible formation of a community of sovereign states in the territory of the present SFRY.

The draft of the Constitutional Law for Implementing the Constitutional Act on Independence and Sovereignty of the Republic of Slovenia was until the session of parliament marked as a document of the highest level of confidentiality.

On the basis of the 37th Amendment, item 3, sentence 3, of the Constitution of the Socialist Federal Republic of Yugoslavia, the Executive Council announces a

RESOLUTION

ON THE DIRECT IMPLEMENTATION OF FEDERAL REGULATIONS CONCERNING BORDER CROSSING POINTS IN THE TERRITORY OF THE REPUBLIC OF SLOVENIA

1. In order to assure the fulfilment of Federal regulations at state borders and ensure movement in the border zone in the territory of the Republic of Slovenia, as well as to assure the fulfilment of international obligations of the SFRY, the undisturbed flow of international traffic and the free movement of people over the state border, the Federal Secretariat of Internal Affairs (hereinafter, Federal Secretariat) approves or assures the implementation of control of border crossings.

2. In the direct assurance of implementing the Federal regulations regarding border crossings, the Federal Secretariat will directly cooperate with the Federal Secretariat of National Defence, so that the border guard posts of the YNA will also be directly engaged in the protection of the state border, both at border crossings, as well as the regions in the border zone.
   The manner of implementing decisions of the first paragraph of this item will be mutually agreed upon by the Federal Secretariat of Internal Affairs and the Federal Secretariat of National Defence.

3. If the Federal Administrative Authority or Federal Organisation meet with physical or other resistance, or if such resistance can be expected in the performance of its control of the traffic of goods and passengers in its jurisdiction at the border crossings, the employees of the Federal Secretariat are obligated to give their assistance to these Federal Authorities or Federal Organisations.

4. Detailed conditions and manner of implementation of this decision will be defined by the Federal Secretariat of Internal Affairs.

5. The Federal Secretariat of Foreign Affairs will notify the authorised bodies of the neighboring states of the temporary measures applying to the state borders in the territory of the Republic of Slovenia, in compliance with this resolution.

6. The resolution comes into force on the day of its publication in the Official Gazette of the SFRY".

FEDERAL EXECUTIVE COUNCIL

E.p.no._____
25 June 1991   PRESIDENT
Belgrade   Ante Marković

Resolution on the direct protection of the implementing of Federal regulations on the crossing of the state border in the territory of the Republic of Slovenia

On the basis of Article 347, Item 5 of the Constitution of the Socialist Federal Republic of Yugoslavia, the Federal Executive Council passes a

DECREE

on the prohibition of establishing so-called border crossings within the territory of the SFRY

1. Prohibits the establishment of so-called border crossings within the territory of the SFRY.

The day this Decree comes into force, the so-called crossings which have been established must be removed.

2. The Federal Secretariat of Internal Affairs and the Federal Secretariat of Defence will implement this Decree.

3. This Decree comes into force on the day of its publication in the "Official Gazette of the SFRY".

THE FEDERAL EXECUTIVE COUNCIL

E.p.No.   PRESIDENT
25.6.1991   Ante Marković
Belgrade

Order on the prohibition of establishing border crossings within the territory of the SFRY

COMMAND OF THE
195th MOTORISED BRIGADE
Conf. no. 330–91
26.06.1991

Report on the state of morale,
    submitted by –   TO THE COMMAND OF THE 31st CORPUS /OMV/

1. The latest events in Slovenia and Croatia have aroused great interest in the entire composition, above all from the aspect of "what and how to continue and where is the place of the YNA here?" The units have just completed a round of discussions with soldiers and officers, as well as civilians, with specific lessons and messages on how to behave in various situations, with various confrontations and provocations, and even possible calls for desertion. The opinion prevails that DEMOS and the HDZ must "go all the way", for too much money has been spent on arms and other things, symbols etc, so that probably a lot of money has been received from abroad, and this will not be allowed to stop half way. This is why they do not regard even the more energetic messages from the entire world. The people have been brought to social poverty and this "must be justified in any way possible". There also exists a specific opinion, which is not without foundation, whereby the biggest problem is the illegal arming to date, for which about 8 billion dollars has been given and there exists a potential danger that, in the goal of proving the right to arming, an armed conflict could be instigated. This could be done by any mercenary group from abroad, but not by the members of the TO, police or civilians.

– We are receiving information from civilians on a general mobilisation, which is also written on the draft cards, the great absence of reserves, or, their great unresponsiveness, even up to 50%, and the state of morale of the TO is also very low.

The greatest concentration of the reserve composition of the TO is on and around Jerenina and Polički Vrh, while in Smolnik it appears that there has been fighting between them.

2. The soldiers are now most concerned about the possibility of leave to take entrance examinations, due to which they could lose a whole year, as well as trips to the city in civilian clothes. We assess that this state should be corrected, although it is stable, for from 20 to 30% of the problems would be immediately solved with the issue of civilian clothes, if only we had them in store. Precisely because of this, the officers of the units state that we do not have to wait for the centralised arrangement of the wardrobe and that until this equipment arrives, every unit can find a solution for itself, especially when light clothing for the summer is in question.

3. The officers and the civilians employed by the army are very concerned about the possibility of GO, and the civilians have their work made very difficult; eg. the work team neither has a wardrobe or a bathroom, they do not even have tools, so they are using their own, they do not even have a means of transport, and thus frequently use their own vehicles to get to the borders, or even all the small

vehicles of the duty bodies, whereby they themselves are then left without a vehicle, so it is essential that we resolve the question of transport for them.

– The active military personnel and civilians are burdened with tax questions, as well as with purchasing places to live.

– For the adapting of one wardrobe and bathroom we must be approved about 20,000.00 dinars, for the RE already has the necessary material.

– The adapting of plumbing systems has been promised and work has already begun on this, and we are of the opinion that this could also have a significant positive influence on the state of morale.

– It is demanded that the accommodation of those who have left the YNA and have not acquired housing rights have their accommodation taken away from them.

– Some officers are burdened with their social problems, for their wives are unemployed, and the kindergartens charge most to active army employees, because their entire incomes are calculated as the basis, which does not happen in companies, so we have situations where a NCO pays more than a director.

4. We have not noticed any organised hostile acts, but we noticed that on 26 June a group of Slovenian soldiers in one unit went to inspection without their stars on their caps. This case is under investigation and we shall inform you whether they took them off on purpose or whether they did not have them. In any case they now have their stars.

– There are also circulating specific jokes, kidding among soldiers, or, should we say "paying back debts" to those who are predicting that they will be going home on the 26 June, and now the others are taunting them with "no going home, no private country of yours either". We reacted immediately, at a meeting of the units it was stated that under the present conditions all such jokes must be terminated, and this question will be pointed out before the whole barracks also.

– We are continuing to record and show "Yutel" on TV at 19.30.

5. All other tasks and obligations are regularly carried out, the units are prepared for all tasks, and we estimate that morale after the latest events is stable, or should we say, that possible "recalls" from the YNA will relate only to individuals; above all to those who are already on leave and whom Janša has summoned over the TV to enroll at the secretariat, and that they will be registered as though they have served their military term in the YNA or, that those that have not been in the army for 7 months will be sent to collection centers and finish their military service to the full seven months.

AM/AM

Assistant to Command of MV
Lt-Colonel
V. Aleksandar Mihailović

– Please solve the question of the VK chief as soon as possible, for the same owes enormous material assets which are now left to the soldiers.

Report on the morale of the 195th Motorised Brigade of the Maribor Corps of the YNA

PROCEDURE FOR TAKEOVER AND SECURING OF BORDERS WITH ITALY, AUSTRIA AND PART OF HUNGARY, AND FOR DISMANTLING THE ESTABLISHED BORDER CROSSINGS WITH CROATIA

1.

Proceeding from the decision of the Federal Executive Council, the YNA and the Federal Police (SSUP) take over the complete section of the state border in the Republic of Slovenia and dismantle border crossings established by the Rep. of Slovenia between Slovenia and the Rep. of Croatia.

Only the most important road and railway border crossings will be left open, and all airports except Brnik will be closed. The port of Koper will be left open.

At all crossings, airports and ports which remain open, border services will be performed by Federal agents (SSUP and Customs).

The most important light-traffic border crossings (those used by people employed in neighboring countries, in particular) will not be closed. Police duties at these crossings will be performed by the Slovenian police (if they agree) under the control of military officers. In the event that they refuse, a solution will be sought in assigning new police officers (retired, if they accept) or in entrusting these duties to the army (soldiers must be trained for this).

The SSUP forces should be transported by military aircraft to Cerklje airport and from there by helicopter to the border crossings.

II: Method and procedure of taking over crossing

1. Take the forces earmarked for individual border crossings to the corresponding regions, give them specific tasks and deploy them for the execution of the tasks.

2. In principle, the combat order should be as follows:

a) Border-guard post at the border crossing with direct reinforcement.

b) Forces for circular blockade of the facility earmarked for intimidation and pressure and, at the worst, for battle and seizure of the border crossing. These forces are deployed in a semi-circle 100–400 meters from the border. They must include armoured combat vehicles at all major crossings, or direct support armament (recoilless rifles, bazookas etc.) at less important crossings.

c) Groups which operate the crossings are composed of SSUP members at all the crossings which remain open, and of army members at the crossings which are closed and will be directly controlled by the army.

d) Patroling unit occupies the corresponding area and prepares it for defence.

e) The combat order may include other elements, if necessary.

3. After the tasks have been assigned, the units completed and the positions taken, the officer of the group selected for operation of the crossing (a SSUP or YNA officer) goes with his escort to the police commander at the crossing and tells him that under the decision of the Federal Executive Council the SSUP and YNA are taking over the border crossing and its operation. He asks him to take his men, leave the office building and withdraw to the police station until further notice, peacefully and without resistance.

If the commander agrees to hand the crossing over, the SSUP group for the operation of the crossing occupies the office and continues work. The customs officers follow suit. The work of these officers is detailed separately.

4. If the border crossing officers of the Ministry of the Interior of the Rep. of Slovenia refuse to do as requested, the SSUP officer returns to the initial position and the YNA officer categorically demands for the police commander to promptly do as requested and leave the premises at the crossing in 15 minutes.

If the request is refused again, the officer shall undertake combat action as follows:

– Fire a warning round from a combat vehicle (BsT or RB) at a place near the building but at a safe distance from the impact of the shell. Shortly thereafter demand that the militiamen go out and lay down their arms. If the demand is met, put the disarmed militiamen under guard in the station and later hand them over to SSUP agents.

– If the request is denied, fire another warning shot at the building but choose a place where there will be no casualties (roof, cellar, corner of the building etc.). Repeat the request.

After that, fire new repeated rounds at the building, taking care that there are no casualties.

This gradual pace is applied only if the other side has not opened fire. If fire has been opened at the YNA units, combat rules are applied fully.

The same procedure is applied to units of the territorial defence, except that in this case the officer first warns the territorial defence operative that he is a member of the armed forces of the SFRY and, as such, is answerable for his acts under military regulations and laws.

After the seizure of the border crossing, the SSUP group for operation of the crossing starts work, and the YNA units guard the crossings which have been closed.

5. Sea ports are taken over in the same way as road crossings. However, the specific features of these facilities are taken into consideration.

6. After the takeover, the YNA units retain the same combat order as in point 2. From among the group securing the takeover, a manoeuvre group is formed to secure the frontier.

7. All elements of the combat order, the facilities at the crossings and military facilities must be protected against any subsequent attacks; in other words, their combat protection must be ensured.

8. YNA units which protect the border perform their duties according to the rules of the border service, cooperate with SSUP agents and with the population.

In the event of attack, they act in accordance with combat rules.

III. Dismantling of border crossing points with the R. of Croatia

– SSUP agents (groups assigned to the task) come and order that the crossing be cleared, the barriers dismantled and that the entire staff withdraw.

If the request is denied, an armoured mechanised unit of the size of a platoon arrives and, together with the SSUP, pulls the border crossing station down.

IV. Special attention must be paid to securing safe movement of units towards the border – rule number one is that the unit must arrive at its destination.

Order on seizing border crossings

TO THE EXECUTIVE COUNCIL OF THE REPUBLIC OF SLOVENIA
TO THE PRESIDENT OF THE EXECUTIVE COUNCIL
Mr Lojze Peterle

Dear Prime Minister,

We hereby notify you that the 5th Military Sector has been ordered to take over all border crossings and defend the state border of the Socialist Federal Republic of Yugoslavia.

We count on the cooperation of all authorities and citizens of the Republic of Slovenia.

This command will be fulfilled unconditionally, which means we shall act according to the rules of military combat.

All resistance will be crushed, and the consequence will be borne by those who issued commands and executed them

COMMANDING OFFICER
Lt-General
Konrad Kolšek

REPUBL.   INTELL.   CENTER
No.telegram 10705 . . . .
Accepted: . . . .
day: 27 JUN 1991   hour 07.20
Released:
day . . . .
Signature . . . .

Ultimatum given by the 5th Army District a few hours after the start of aggression

Order for the procedure and
action on the night of 29/30.06.1991

FOR THE COMMAND OF
_____

We have received the following telegram from our superior command:

At your present positions, structures, border posts and barracks and commands prepare for the decisive defence of all structures.

During the night be totally alert and prepared for the defence of the region in which you are situated.

If the enemy attacks exact from him the highest losses.

Any person who wishes to escape, surrender or shows hesitation must be detained.

The defence of Yugoslavia and the latest movements for its integrity and unity are under question.

The high command shall this night send an ultimatum to the Republic of Slovenia, and if Slovenia does not respect this, we will deal with Slovenia most energetically in the course of tomorrow.

The end result will be positive for Yugoslavia.

I demand from all my officers and every individual and soldier extreme sacrifices, decisiveness, bravery and endurance, irrespective of the conditions in which you find yourselves. Have complete faith in your Supreme Command.

You must endure through the coming days to the end.

Convey this to the every single soldier of the unit.

COMMANDER
Maj-General
Mićo Delić

The accuracy of this telegram has been checked by:

COMMANDER
Lieutenant-Colonel
Slobodan Tripković

Battle orders of General Delić, commander of the Maribor Corps of the YNA

Citizens of Slovenia

By the decision of the Federal Executive Council and in accordance with constitutional authorisations, the Federal Ministry of Internal Affairs and units of the Yugoslav People's Army are taking control of the state borders.

This step has been forced upon us. The territorial integrity of Yugoslavia, the peace and safety of its inhabitants, and implementation of international obligations of the Socialist Federal Republic of Yugoslavia have been threatened.

Citizens of Slovenia

Stay at home and at your workposts. Do not let anyone damage your essential interests.

We invite you to peace and cooperation!

Units of the Ministry of Internal Affairs and the Yugoslav People's Army will perform their task consistently and vigorously.

All resistance will be crushed.

Copy of a leaflet scattered by the Yugoslav Air Force over Slovenia.

PRESIDENCY OF
THE REPUBLIC OF SLOVENIA
Ljubljana, 9 July 1991

    The Presidency of the Republic of Slovenia has in its session of 9 July 1991 affirmed the decision which the members of the Presidency accepted by telephone at the corresponding session held on 7 July 1991, during discussions held on the island of Brioni, which is that the prisoners of war who have fallen into captivity during military operations in Slovenia after the date of 26 June 1991 are to be released. It has also affirmed the decision that the 88 officers of the YNA who have been interned in the prison of Dob are to be released and handed over to the YNA.

    The Red Cross of Slovenia, the Red Cross of Yugoslavia and the International Red Cross will cooperate in the carrying out of these decisions.

PRESIDENT
Milan Kučan

Copies to:
- Matija Malešič, vice-president of the Executive Council of the Assembly of the RS
- Janez Janša, Minister of Defence
- Dimitrij Rupel, Minister of Foreign Affairs
- Rajko Pirnat, Minister of Justice and Administration
- Igor Bavčar, Minister of Internal Affairs
- Janez Slapar, acting chief of RŠTO Headquarters

Resolution of the Presidency of the RS on the release of prisoners of war

AGREEMENT,

made on 18 October 1991 between the delegation of the Republic of Slovenia and the delegation of the Federal Secretariat of People's Defence on completing the withdrawal of the Yugoslaw Army from the Republic of Slovenia

1.

With this agreement the signatories set down the manner of completing the withdrawal of the Yugoslav Army from the Republic of Slovenia, on the basis of talks held on 12 and 15 October 1991 and the exchange of written standpoints received on 16 and 17 October.

2.

The members of the Yugoslav Army withdraw from the Republic of Slovenia through the port of Koper, with their personal arms and personal equipment, but the first part of the withdrawal includes at least 50% (1,200) of the members of the Yugoslav Army who are still in the Republic of Slovenia, no later than two days after the signing of this Agreement or by 21 October 1991 at 07.00 hours. The remaining parts of the units are to withdraw in no more than two groups and no later than 25 October 1991.

In the organisation and implementation of the withdrawal, the Republic of Slovenia guarantees safe passage to the members of the Yugoslav Army to the borders of the territorial waters of the Republic of Slovenia and offers its aid in organizing and preparing transport. Transportation to the port of Koper is carried out by the Yugoslav Army with its own vehicles and via the rail network.

Each transport towards the port of Koper must be announced in advance and a permit is to be issued for this no later than 6 hours before departure at the Republic Intelligence Center, tel.: 061/131-323. The vessels with which the withdrawal from the port of Koper is effected must be reported to the harbour master at least 6 hours before entering the territorial waters of the Republic of Slovenia.

3.

For effecting the transport of the units from item 2, up to 200 motorised non–combat vehicles for the transport of the units can be used, according to the selection of the Corps commission.

4.

Immediately after signing this Agreement the units of the Yugoslav Army shall carry out the dismantling of mines in structures and transporters and surrender the transporters to the TO within a period of 24 hours. Here the Republic of Slovenia guarantees the safety of all members of the Yugoslav Army and the material technical means on these transports and in structures against physical attack until the period for withdrawal has expired.

. . . .

The Republic of Slovenia regulates the manner of implementing and payment of the health care of insured army personnel as well as the payment of pensions to retired military personnel in the Republic of Slovenia in the transition period. During this time the Republic of Slovenia will also be given the entire documentation on service pensioners in the Republic of Slovenia.

13.

The costs of the withdrawal, the concentration of the material technical means and the maintenance of the material and technical means which will remain in Vrhnika, Cerklje and Mačkovci as well as part of the Corps commission shall be borne by the Yugoslav Army. The Republic of Slovenia will cover costs in association with the withdrawal of only those services which have been especially agreed upon.

Both signatories will, in accordance with the agreement of 12 October 1991, ensure the immediate settlement of outstanding obligations to enterprises and other organisations and vice-versa in the territory of the Republic of Slovenia.

14.

The Republic of Slovenia obligates itself to allow the export of complete training packages from the Bregana Technical Refurbishing Institute in Bregansko Selo for outside purchasers through the port of Koper, in accordance with the current agreements.

15.

This Agreement represents the mandatory instructions for the work of all commissions which will be implementing the initial hand– over of property or other work in association with the withdrawal and can be supplemented or changed only with the consensus of both signatories. The delegation of the Federal Secretariat of People's Defence has been notified that from 24.00 hours on 18 October 1991, members of the Yugoslav Army in the territory of the Republic of Slovenia will be treated in accordance with the law and this Agreement. The delegation of the Federal Secretariat obligates itself to draw the attention of all members of the YNA in the territory of the Republic of Slovenia to the consistent observance of the laws of the Republic of Slovenia and the Provisions of this Agreement.

16.

The delegations agree that on 24 October 1991 they assess the realisation of this Agreement and solve possible contentious issues at a meeting in Belgrade.

Delegation of the Federal Secretariat of People's Defence	Delegation of the Republic of Slovenia
CHIEF Ljubivoje Jokić, Admiral	CHIEF Miran Bogataj

The first and last page of the Agreement ... on the withdrawal of the YNA from Slovenia.

SLOVENIAN BATTLEGROUND 2 JUNE 1991 at 15.00 hours

KEY:
>clashes and incidents
>air strikes
>deployment of YNA armored units
>units of the Slovenian TO
>Krško Nuclear Power Station
>Destroyed transmitters of RTV Slovenia

BATTLE IN KRAKOVO FOREST

could only be the decision made at the plebiscite which (at least so they claimed) the demo-liberals also supported. Once again we listened to lectures about how we could not resist the army and that the solution lay in negotiations. As though we had never wanted to negotiate more fervently!

I had a talk with Jože Pučnik and Milan Kučan before our meeting and both supported the idea of a congress. Kučan also accepted my argument that it was better to organise some meetings and express our unity in that way rather than, when it was too late, express it with weapons. In this sense Kučan also had sharp exchanges with Jože Školč, but it was like bashing your head against a brick wall.

Before the rally, Bavčar and I had a talk on the balcony in front of the operations hall. Both of us were worried about the attitude of many politicians, which was far from the decisiveness needed at that time. We ruminated about individuals and agreed that in the end it would be all our own fault if anything went wrong. It was then that I also told Igor a story about the character of the Slovenians, which I had read in a biography on Henrik Tuma. This is what Tuma narrated:

The teacher I liked most at grammar school was a tough German fanatic called Anton Heinrich. He hated the French and Slavs, and considered the Germans to be a chosen race. But he lectured very nicely and as a free thinker of a pure mould he developed in fact the liberal revolutionary notion. He spoke to me from his soul. The thing I liked most about him was that he liked to see that a pupil held his own opinion. Since during assessments I spoke my thoughts, he felt the revolutionary blood in my veins. He frequently praised me, especially because I wrote my home and school work in quite a joking way. The Slovenian pupils in general hated him very much, as he had no time for farmer's sons and favouritised the bourgeois. He always exposed a certain Zelnik to ridicule – a tough Kranj farmer's boy who had no talent for German. Once, after a certain incident, Heinrich depicted the Slovenians as a low and coarse people and called us "Slovenische Hunde". The desks in the back of the room muttered out our dissatisfaction and nothing else. At the end of the school term the pupils of the fifth, sixth and seventh grade planned to take revenge on Heinrich. He lived on the second floor of a house in Poljanska street which now houses the financial administration. About fifty of us collected in the "Zum Kaiser von Oesterriech" tavern for the purpose of celebrating the end of our school term by breaking Heinrich's windows. We drank and sang until midnight. When I impatiently reminded everyone of our plan, all but four chickened out. So only four of us went to work. Ljubljana was blanketed in its thick and smelly summer fog. When we got to the Franciscan Bridge, a certain Pogačnik – a Gorenjska lad and a good pupil – pulled out a six-shooter from his pocket. For me this was the height of bravery. After this we went along Špital (today Stritar) street past the Saintklavž Church. Two guards were coming towards us from the square now called Vodnikov Trg. We did not see each other in the fog but we judged by the rhythmic steps that they must be officers of the law. We were just at the edge of the church when our heroes with the revolver darted behind the houses along the embankment of the Ljubljanica river. I was left alone with rage in my soul for the lowness of the others. I calmly walked on and met with the guards approximately where Vodnik's statute now stands. They looked at me suspiciously but went past. I slowly made my way to Poljanska street, under the window of my teacher,

Heinrich. I waited until the last steps of the guards had faded away. Then I grabbed a fistful of gravel and threw it with all my strength at the darkness of the shutters, which opened up under the assault. I grabbed another fistful of stones – and the windows fell to the ground. Immediately after this a man came to the window in only his shirt. It was Professor Heinrich. I grabbed another fistful of gravel and waited. Heinrich calmly looked towards me. I let the gravel from my fist and peacefully went away. I went to the end of Poljanska street and back behind the water to Gradišče. I was spiritually depressed. I could not comprehend that fifty pupils who had given their word, left me in the lurch. All my life I held a grudge against my own nation, that the Slovenians lacked bravery and that one could not count on their word. Next morning, the last day of school, our teacher Heinrich ordered us to stand. He said that he had always been good to us: that we should not take offence if he was too strict at times: but that he did not deserve what had happened last night. Then he added: "I know very well the pupil who did this (he did not say what), and I am convinced that he made this plan with others, but that he was the only one who had the bravery to carry out the agreed plan. I shall not expose him," he concluded, "but I hope that he has learned a lesson from this." This was a cold shower for my rebellious character. I never again joined a conspiracy.[1]

Many things that the former German teacher unmasked one hundred years ago have been preserved to the present day in the character of our nation.

The rally in the central square of Kongresni Trg was held on that Friday, but it was attended only by the parties in the Demos coalition. The opposition attacked this event, and the majority of the media supported them. Relatively few people collected in the square and its impact on the public was weak. In spite of this, all the speakers at this rally, including both the Prime Minister, Lojze Peterle, as well as parliamentary president France Bučar and representatives of all the parties, promised to fulfil the obligations of the plebiscite, irrespective of any threats. In my speech I spoke above all of the new sharpening of tension with the YNA and once again offered negotiations.

The partial failure of the rally and especially its poor media impact caused immeasurable glee in the barracks. The chief of KOS of the Ljubljana Corps, Emin Malkoć, sent a message to Belgrade in which he again assessed that because of its nationalistic and anti-Yugoslav policies Demos was losing support among the people in Slovenia and that the time to make a decisive move was approaching.

The glee of Emin Malkoć and the generals would have been much greater if they had known of the hidden ally in their efforts to weaken the Slovenian defence or if they had known of the content of the letter which Jožef Školč sent, on behalf of the delegate club of the Liberal Democratic Party, to Milan Kučan on 30 May, just before the inauguaration of the first generation of Slovenian soldiers. In this letter Jože Školč proposed the immediate closure of the training centres in Pekre and Ig. He founded his proposal on the following political base: ✳

---

[1] Henrik Tuma, Iz mojega živlejenja (From My Life), Naša Založba, Ljubljana 1937.

"A poor peace is better than a good war. Actually, there is nothing worse than a good war. Once again our conviction is being affirmed that demilitarization is the only starting-point for establishing Slovenian sovereignty... The path to the independence of Slovenia has no short cuts or unilateral acts – the shortest path to sovereignty lies in long-term, at this moment, even hopeless agreement-making and negotiations."

Of course Školč was not upset by the old truth that there have to be at least two sides to negotiate and that in realpolitik one-sided yielding leads sooner to greater conflicts and, in the end, many times into a bloodbath anyway, than to any mercy being shown by the stronger. Where would Slovenia be today if we had considered their formula? *IN SLAVERY*

Such a stance in an important area of Slovenian politics did not promise anything good at a time when pressure was increasing on us.

After the rally on 31 May 1991, exactly three years after my arrest, Igor Bavčar and I met with General Andrija Rašeta and Marjan Vidmar. The meeting was held at 21.00 hours in the premises of the Republic Secretariat for Internal Affairs in Ljubljana, and the theme of the talks was the armoured cars taken from TAM. The two of us demanded a guarantee that the armoured cars, in the event that we did return them, would not be used in the territory of Slovenia. Rašeta claimed that they were destined for Montenegro. Finally he acceded that he would give a guarantee of this in writing and, in a few days, General Konrad Kolšek really did send a letter confirming that the armoured cars would not be used in Slovenia. Many did not believe that the army had truly given us written confirmation, and even later, when this letter had arrived, they still would not believe it. We returned the armoured vehicles on the border with Croatia, and they had to be removed from Slovenia at once.

On 2 June 1991 the first generation of Slovenian soldiers were sworn in at Pekre and Ig. This was a historic day, not only for the new soldiers but for all who understood this act as an omen of announced sovereignty additionally in the military field. Milan Kučan was the main spokesman playing the role of the representative of the supreme command at both the events, which were very well organised and attended. His speech was very much peace-oriented on both occasions, but he allowed for no doubts regarding the basic decision. I myself also spoke in a similar style, although we had not coordinated one word with each other, and the message of the oath was clear and very acceptable for the majority of our citizens. The parents of the new Slovenian soldiers were very pleased, for the majority of their boys had been expecting to spend twice the service time in the YNA, far from home. I wrote my speech at three in the morning and fell asleep twice in between. Possibly this might have been the reason why there were some shorter and better thoughts in it. Some, linked to both events, I state here;

■ **"Officers, non-commissioned officers and soldiers of the Territorial Defence, most respected guests!**

Young Slovene men and women have given their oaths to various causes

131

throughout history. They have already sworn an oath to their own homeland during two wars. Today you will be giving an oath to your homeland for the first time in peace. In peace so that it will not have to be done during war, for war can nearly always be prevented through sensible policies.

The Slovenian TO is a defence force. Its task is to defend freedom, independence, sovereignty and the territorial integrity of the Republic of Slovenia. Our TO is organised according to democratically enacted laws in the Slovenian parliament. Our laws also recognise conscientious objection.

You will be serving your homeland in an army with one of the shortest military service terms in Europe and the world. Internal relations within the units have been organised on modern European lines. In the future some things will be improved still further.

As an armed force of the Slovenian Republic, the TO is politically neutral. It will not interfere in political decision-making nor serve the interests of one party or one ideology. This is a guarantee that the Slovenian nation will never again in the future be affected by division, the consequence of which was internecine murders.

It is fair that here, too, we remind ourselves that our soldiers also include all those Slovenian boys and citizens of Slovenia who at this moment are still wearing the uniforms of the Yugoslav army. They are the same as you, a part of our first guard. We must not neglect their interests.

Only a few days divide us from the events which began at this location and which in the form of TV pictures and journalistic reports, will be sent throughout the world. At this location and with the support of the whole of Slovenia, you have proved that we are at home here, that Slovenia will no longer be a servant to anybody, and that a people who have made a decision cannot be suppressed.

Particularly because we do not accept a logic which violent Yugoslav policies are trying to affirm. We answer force primarily with other means. Here we are incomparably stronger. Our strength is in our will, knowledge, intellect and bravery. And in the 90 per cent result of the plebiscite, that is, in the unity of the people's will. We are not trying to assure our independence directly by military means, but through sensible and rational policies, economic development, the honouring of human rights and tolerance.

But we must be aware that our problems will not end on 26 June.

An independent Slovenia will, especially in the early period, require certain preconditions in order to survive and develop. One of these is the greatest possible stability. And this is closely linked to security, to a feeling of security and actual security. The state will need stability based on the effective operation of the parliamentary system, a firm economic policy, a firm currency, the protection of human rights, gradual integration into the currents of the European economy, culture and civilization in general. One is linked to the other.

It is impossible to have a stable economy if even the threat of an encounter or incident on the border can empty the hard currency deposits, cause panic among people or dissuade foreign capital from its purpose of

132

investing in the Slovenian economy. Unfortunately, we will be surrounded by smaller or larger conflict crisis points for quite some time to come. Dissociation from Yugoslavia will not pass in a manner whereby we will all satisfy our interests, for this is simply impossible. If it was, then there would be no conflict and we would not be saying today that Yugoslavia is on the threshold of a civil war.

Some European states will also have to recognise that Yugoslavia cannot be unified and democratic at the same time. The fact is, it has never been like this. We are too different. Some are a few decades behind with this formula. It can be unified only by force, it can be democratic only by not being united and by those nationalities which are capable of carrying this out being given the right to self-determination. The sooner this awareness predominates, the sooner the problem will be solved at the right place. Let us just look at the last few years. The world supported a united Yugoslavia, but this unfortunate creation is less unified every day and is becoming more and more riddled with inter-ethnic conflicts. Today, in its very centre it is on the verge of civil war.

Soldiers, officers and non-commissioned officers of the Slovenian Territorial Defence!

Given what we have said, take your work extremely seriously.

You are wearing the uniform and insignias of the Slovenian armed forces. The insignia of the TO is a shield in the national colors, the symbol of defence and protection. Carry this insignia with pride and dignity.

Finally, allow me to thank all those who have in one way or another contributed to the fact that the Slovenian TO has been created and remained the armed force of the Slovenian people and all those who have assisted in the preparations and implementation of this first attempt at training. This thanks also goes to you, the parents, who in these turbulent times, have entrusted your sons to the armed forces of the Slovenian state.

A special place will always be given in the history of the nation to the first generation of Slovenian soldiers who in these days of exceptional trials of will are testing not only new programmes, statutory and non-statutory solutions, but also – themselves and us.

I sincerely congratulate all those who today, a few weeks before independence, are to solemnly give their oath to our common homeland." ■

This swearing-in had a very favorable impact on the public. No pomp or exaggerated ceremonies. People involuntarily compared all this with the swearing-in of the National Guard in Zagreb a few days before. Even some foreign journalists, who, as a rule, doubted our capabilities against the YNA, if it really intervened, expressed recognition of the dignified presentation of the swearing-in. The chief merit for this goes without doubt to Janez Švajncer, a major in the TO, and the commanders of both training centres, Bojan Šuligoj and Andrej Kocbek. All three understood that we were constructing something new and the oath was so different from similar ceremonies in the YNA, that this difference was felt by even the most malevolent observers.

10. IN EXPECTATION

After the events in Pekre, after the first generation of Slovenian soldiers were sworn in and after the episode with the APCs smuggled from TAM, a short lull ensued in the military field. The GHQ of the YNA had, without doubt, assessed that the Slovenians were serious. The policies of pressure and demands for observance of federal legislation in the field of military service were continuing to come from the federal authorities, while at the same time they were polishing the battle plans for deploying units of the YNA in operations for seizing and blockading the national borders in the Republic of Slovenia and the key infrastructural facilities.

Within the framework of projects which coordinated measures of independence on the government level, the projects Meja (Border) and Obramba in Varnost (Defence and Security) were important from the aspect of taking over effective power. Since the plebiscite it had been clear to me that the national borders were that concrete point upon which national sovereignty was decided in the final sense. That is why the replacing of border signposts and flags after the declaration of independence was not only a symbolic act but a key step across the Rubicon. Thus a coordinated take-over of the customs, border and other functions which would at a specific moment become alive as functions of the independent state of Slovenia had to be organised. As in June the so-called customs war was being escalated, some key decisions were made every day, with the great help of the majority of the chiefs of the customs offices. From the aspect of the project which I was heading (Defence and Safety), the protection of the measures for independence, in its essence, was centred precisely on protecting the taken-over national borders (together with the police), air traffic control and the customs services. The main interventions by the YNA units and the federal police were also directed at these three key points and we had known for over a month before 26 June that the question of success or failure hung on this triangle.

If the Slovenian army had been stronger it would – due to the logic of affairs – have had to direct its key measures during the declaration of independence towards the foreign army which was at that time in our territory and thus nip in the bud its intervention against the civil measures of the new country on the border. With a prior solving of the military question the danger for other measures of emancipation would of course, also fall away. But for such a step as that we were in the military sense not one tenth as strong as we needed to be, and on the other hand, we would have had to be the first to apply force, which, irrespective of our justification, would have greatly reduced the moral power of our enterprise as a whole, and confirmed those claims that declared our path to independence to be an aggressive act, that is, an attempt at dissociation by force. Instead of escalations, we offered the YNA a three-year term for its final withdrawal from Slovenia and the co-financing of some of its needs during this time.

Given the material and moral reasons, we planned emancipation, and above all, the take-over of the greater part of effective power after 26 June, as a political act, during which we would not apply force. But we did not renounce the right, in the event that the other side used force, if anybody attempted to prevent the implementation of the will of the people expressed at the plebiscite with force, to defend ourselves with means appropriate to our times and environment.

In June the government project council finally determined the measures which would, in the sense of taking over effective power, be able to be implemented – the day. According to the guidelines of the Presidency and its detailed workings, which included all the more important subjects in Slovenia, the measures with which the emerging Slovenian state was preparing to protect its independence were determined. On the basis of these decisions and the accepted documents and considering the document Possible Variants of Dissociation from the Aspect of Defence, which I had composed in April and which also served as a guideline in the making of strategic decisions, I made a draft in the first half of June of the final Operational Plan of Defence and Safety Measures in which we, in the coordination group, finally coordinated the plans of the Territorial Defence, police, civil defence and civil protection: this was, at the same time, the basic document for controlling preparations which were performed every day by the operational duty coordination group.

OPERATIONAL PLAN FOR PROTECTING THE MEASURES FOR THE EMANCIPATION OF SLOVENIA

(final version)

STATE SECRET

Measures of protection:

1. Take-over of customs services and customs facilities
2. Take-over of border crossings
3. Take-over of air traffic control
4. Take-over of other federal institutions in the RS except for the YNA
5. Take-over of some DKP (diplomatic/consular offices)

Manner and methods of implementing protection:
Partial mobilization and active assistance

THOSE COOPERATING

RSLO (TO RS)
1. Headquarters of the TO RS army composition (1,200)

135

2. Units of the TO RS in protecting facilities and authorities
3. Strike detachments and TO troops trained according to OŠTO (6,000)
4. Anti-tank, anti-aircraft and other special departments of the TO for blockading units and facilities of the YNA (3,000–4,000)
5. Part of the 30th development group of the TO for special operations (200)
6. Members of the NZ for the protection of buildings and the infrastructure (600)
7. Republic detachment for communications (200)
8. Regional units for communications (210)
9. Municipal units for communications (600)
Total: 15,210

(All available anti-tank, anti-aircraft and other heavy weapons of the TO are activated, if necessary they are transferred from the PŠTO to the OŠTO – Regional to Municipal TO HQ, respectively – and in the same way, units may be transferred between the PŠTO and OŠTO, if necessary)

INTERNAL AFFAIRS AUTHORITIES (ONZ – POLICE FORCE)
1. Regular composition of the ONZ (3,200)
2. Reserve composition of the ONZ (4,000)
3. PEM (600)
4. SE 1 (120)
5. SE 2 (120)
Total: 8,040
Total activated: 23,250
Reserves:
20,000 members of the TO RS (unarmed)
2,000 members of the NZ

STARTING POINTS:
if no agreement is made the units of the YNA in the territory of the RS are forced to perform only those two functions which cannot be prevented without the use of force, these are:
1. Protection of the green belt with Austria, Italy and Hungary
2. Control of air space with units of the Air Force and PZO
The manoeuvring of the special units of the YNA and the transport of new units of the YNA to the RS must be prevented – this is the point of conflict which changes the scenario.

DYNAMICS:

D–8
• notification of plans for coordination group and sub-group leader
  implementor: project leader
• call-up of officers of newly formed TO units
  implementor: OŠTO
• checking of complete Republic defence plans
  implementor: all Republic bodies

D–7
• notification of plans for implementors on the regional level without revealing – the day
  implementor: RSNZ, RSLO (RHQ TO)

D-6

- notification of plans for implementors on the OŠTO and municipal level without revealing – the day
  implementor: Regional bodies
- call-up of newly formed units of the TO for seven-day training
  implementor: OŠTO
- preparation for establishing operational (PTT, courier and radio) communications with a coordination group from the Rep. of Croatia
  implementor: Republic coordination group, the RSNZ

D-5

- call-up of officers of other cooperating units of the TO and ONZ and preparation for the call-up of these units
  implementor: competent headquarters and bodies
- notification of unit commanders of their tasks, without revealing – the day
  implementor: competent headquarters and bodies
- checking of preparations for operation NABAVA (procurement)
  implementor: according to plans

D-4

- tour of locations, command trips
  implementor: commanders of the PŠTO, OŠTO, commanders of cooperating units
- checking of preparation for operation PLEBISCITE
  implementor: RSNZ
- checking of preparation for operation SHIELD
  implementor: according to plan
- harmonization of operational plans with coordination group of the Rep. of Croatia
  implementor: RKS

D-3

- last checking of preparations for protecting border crossings, customs posts and branches
  implementor: ONZ and headquarters of the TO according to plan
- final checking of preparations for partial and total mobilization
  implementor: UOLO, competent headquarters and bodies
- checking of plans for preventing the removal of military hardware from the territory of Slovenia
  implementor: Republic coordination group and sub-groups
- checking of plans for blocking the entire infrastructure of the units of the YNA
  implementor: Republic coordination group and sub-groups
- checking of plans for blockading manoeuvres of YNA units
  implementor: Republic coordination group and sub-groups
- establishing operational (PTT, courier and radio) communications with coordination group of the Rep. of Croatia
  implementor: Republic coordination group

D–2

- establishing operational communications between border municipalities of the Rep.of Croatia and the Rep. of Slovenia through municipal intelligence centres
  implementor: sub-groups in regions
- mobilization of the reserve composition of the police, call-up of PEM, partial mobilization of TO (headquarters of the army composition and special units, units for blockading, the PO and PZ defence)
  implementor: according to plans
- strengthening of the protection of important buildings and facilities (at night)
  implementor: according to the plans and previous decisions of the RKS
- checking of preparation for activating collection centres
  implementor: UOLO and OŠTO

D–1

- preparation and additional equipping of mobilised compositions of the TO and VEM
  implementor: according to plans
- checking of preparations for taking over border crossings, customs posts and branches
  implementor: RSNZ
- protection of infrastructure centres and networks, activation of parts of the NZ
  implementor: according to the plans and previous decisions of the RKS
- activating of operation ATLAS
  implementor: RSNZ
- establishing reserve TV and radio transmission locations
  implementor: RSI
- mobilization of Republic, regional and municipal units for communications and establishment of reserve locations for the work of the bodies of the DPS
  implementor: according to plans
- establishment of operational plans for jamming internal communications of the YNA
  implementor: according to plans

D0–7

- activating implementors for blocking the infrastructure of the YNA
  implementor: according to plans

D0–6

- concealed assuming of starting positions for the blockade of communications for preventing manoeuvres of the special units of the YNA
  implementor: according to plans

D0–6

- activating operation PLEBISCITE
  implementor: RSNZ

D0

- start of take-over of border crossings, customs facilities and strengthened protection of taken over crossings and buildings
  implementor: according to plans
- protection of borders with the Rep. of Croatia, establishing border crossings
  implementor: according to plans

138

- take-over of control of air space
  implementor: according to plans

D0+2
- final take-over of border crossings, customs posts and branches as well as their work according to the new regime
- operation of air space control according to the new regime

D+1
- call-up of recruits of units which were on the 7-day training (as needed)
  implementor: UOLO and OŠTO
- advance of units for carrying out operation NABAVA to their starting positions (as needed)
  implementor: according to plans and previous decisions of the competent bodies
- call-up of reserve TO units (as needed)
  implementor: according to plans

In June 1991, as a result of day to day analyses and our knowledge of conditions in Yugoslavia and thanks to our good intelligence data, we were almost convinced that the YNA army would not be capable of carrying out an attack deploying a great enough number of forces during the declaration of independence of Slovenia and Croatia and that it would only be intervention and pressure on some key points, which could be escalated later by introducing new units of YNA reserve forces. But despite this I had no illusions about whether we had foreseen everything and that affairs would proceed only according to our expectations. I knew and respected Moltke's thesis, according to which no operational plan can remain unchanged after meeting the main forces of the opponent, which is why we made very precise plans for protecting our moves, but for the reaction of the enemy we foresaw its general framework, and above all the coverage of the terrain with our forces and enough reserves.

The political atmosphere was radiating intrigues and doubts during the last month before independence. On 5 June the new Minister of Finance, Dušan Šešok, told parliament that he had received a poor dowry and that there would be no new Slovenian currency on 26 June. After his appearance, the impression was once again created that we were not prepared for independence and the opposition once again began to bring the decision made at the plebiscite into question. The SDZ criticised the Prime Minister for the delay in the preparation of measures in the economic field. And he in turn accused Dimitrij Rupel of "attacking him behind his back" at critical moments. It all became even more confusing when Janez Drnovšek suddenly supported the Gligorov – Izetbegović project for some kind of new Yugoslavia a few weeks before – the day and, in the opinion of many, had dangerously played a solo game in a direction which was completely opposite to the will expressed in the plebiscite. This move made by Drnovšek did not only cause bad feeling but also among some left-wing party politicians and members of the Presidency of the Republic it once again deepened doubts about the correctness of our steps. Most of the doubts were expressed by Ciril Zlobec, the Academician, with whom I had many unpleasant exchanges. He did not approve of more decisive moves, and he always had thoughts along the lines of were we not harassing too much? What would the consequences be? Why were we rushing into it? Who was going to take responsibility? What would the people say, they quickly change their minds, etc, etc. At that time we frequently asked ourselves if the military intervention succeeded, on whose side we would find Mr Zlobec and his son, Jaša, who in parliament frequently made offensive accusations to oppose the majority of steps which established the defensive capabilities of the emerging state.

Ante Marković came to Ljubljana on 12 June. As on his previous visits, he again demanded the money (from customs), and in exchange he was offering to mediate with Veljko Kadijević. To reinforce these demands, he brought along Admiral Stane Brovet with him. After Marković's appearance in the Assembly and discussions in the government, where we did not get far, for we were demanding that Marković recognise the result of the plebiscite in Slovenia as a legitimate fact, dinner followed in the Podrožnik Villa. Dinner turned into an all-night bout of persuasion and negotiation, so that Marković and Brovet flew to Belgrade in morning. Both these two guests from Belgrade were playing a weird game. Marković persisted all night of the discussion in the demand that we "obey federal laws in respect of possible different decisions of the Federal Assembly", while Brovet appeared "soft" and promised that until the independence of Slovenia was declared they would not take conscripts by force. He frequently repeated that the YNA would respect the decision of the Slovenian Assembly on 26 June, where Marković always added "if this is affirmed by the competent federal authority". We knew that the units of the YNA already had plans to close the national borders, which is why we did not trust Brovet, but his peaceful and, at moments, even relaxed appearance only placed Marković under a strange light, for he looked like an extremist compared to the military representative.

In a few days, on the basis of additional information from our source in the GHQ of the YNA, it became clear to us that the army was indeed not planning any smaller skirmishes like the one at Pekre before 26 June, but that it was planning to solve "all its problems in Slovenia in one go".

On 14 June we called a conference of members of the coordination group, with the addition of the sub-group chiefs in the regions.[1] We went through the content of the most important independence laws and up-to-date intelligence information and agreed that our main attention in the future had to be focused on conditions on the border. On this same day there was also a session of the government where we discovered, among other things, that

---

[1] Seven coordination sub-groups were founded. They coordinated the measures of the armed and civil defence, the police and intelligence activities on the level of regions. During this time they were led by: Ljubljana region: Starc, the Dolenska region: Gutman, Gorenjska: Hočevar, East Štajerska: Komar, West Štajerska: Kranjc, South Primorska: Žele, North Primorska: Vidrih.

with the take-over of the customs service according to the implemented preparations there would not be any major problems. A great service to the development of such events was made by Franc Košir, later the director of the customs administration and the then chief of the Ljubljana customs office, and Alenka Markič and Vojka Ravbar, who coordinated the jurisdiction between finances and foreign affairs in association with customs.

That day the security administration of the GHQ of the YNA issued a circular which contained data on the escalating situation, with stress on the situation in Knin Krajina. Two days later it also issued information on "attacks on the YNA and its members", with which they wanted to convince the officer corps of the YNA that Slovenia and Croatia were preparing attacks and assassinations of members of the army. By such methods, KOS wanted to arouse the animosity of the officers towards the local authorities and to prepare them for the planned intervention against Slovenia and Croatia.

On 19th June the Slovenian Assembly discussed the new Slovenian symbols. Franco Juri, who defended his membership of the Liberal Democratic Party by stating that this party was closest to anarchistic ideas (which is a very accurate finding), strongly opposed the new symbols at this session, stating that Demos was playing with the emotions of the voters in this way. All these arguments on new state symbols, mutual accusations, party calculations and the escalation of pressure from abroad against Slovenian independence had a negative influence on the members of the recruited units of the TO which we had newly formed and were training in the event of armed intervention by the YNA after 26 June. The bad atmosphere was also influenced by the fact that the five-member supreme command (the Presidency) did not deem it necessary to visit some of our units. Some were asking themselves who they were supposed to fight for. But these were problems, in comparison with the lack of arms, ammunition, communications and other military equipment, which could be solved in one way or another through the great efforts of the officers of the TO and police. Despite all our efforts, we did not have much more than 23,000 pieces of infantry, with not enough ammunition, and a little more than 1,000 pieces of various light anti-tank weapons, because of the delay in accepting the budget on 15 June 1991. Anti-aircraft weapons, except for light cannons, hardly existed.

The main delivery was only on its way. The days and nights from 10 June, when they were supposed to have arrived, dragged on like a nightmare. We expected both communications equipment (Operation KANAL) and weapons and ammunition (operation BOR). The government of one of the more distant Western countries officially approved the export of army radio communications systems with data transmission protection to Slovenia on the request of our government. When the delivery was already in the plane the ambassador of this country in Belgrade received a sharp protest from the Yugoslav government which contained a threat that the plane would be shot out of the sky. We were warned of this and thus had to bring the radio stations across in trucks, thus over a longer and more risky path. Finally, we luckily received our radio equipment on 17 June and by the beginning of the war we had organised the urgent protected communication network to the level of municipal headquarters. Unfortunately, because of our lack of money, there was not enough radio equipment for the majority of units, and this proved to be a great deficiency in our later conflicts. Luckily, the TO and police closely cooperated and thus many communication difficulties were circumvented through the technical equipment of the bodies of internal affairs.

It was obvious that due to the delayed acceptance of the law on military service and the budget it would not be possible to provide through army training at least a minimum number of regular soldiers, so we searched for a reserve variant. The administrative bodies for people's defence received instructions that the territorial defence would provide about 6,000 army reserves, who had done their military service in the last five years in special units of the YNA. From them we composed more than 30 assault detachments and platoons which, in compliance with the operational plan, were to be called in for training a week before – the day. We had no weapons or new uniforms for these units. Each day new intrigues arose. As we were working very conspiratorially it was difficult to solve problems in a rush.

From 10 June on the difficulties were so frequent that Igor and I slept in the premises of the Executive Council, next to the operations hall. I went home only once or twice a week for the needs of logistics. To defend the coming delivery, in which there were 5,000 automatic rifles and five million rounds of ammunition, more than 1,000 anti-tank weapons, including a few rocket launchers of the Fagot type for medium distances and even a few dozen Strela 2M anti-aircraft rockets, Tone Krkovič, in cooperation with the special police units and some regional headquarters of the TO, made a special plan. The path over which this vital equipment was coming was so protected that even a tank brigade could not prevent it. We had been waiting too long and we needed this equipment too badly to afford to make a mistake at the end. Despite the complicated operations which, under the surroundings of a strict embargo, lasted from April to June, not even the smallest crumb of information fell into the hands of KOS or any other foreign intelligence service.

On 21 June the delivery arrived. Operation BOR had happily ended. Almost half of the members of the coordination group who were not on duty went to Kočevski Rog in the middle of the night. We wanted to see with our own eyes if this was true and that we would finally be able to give people effective weapons. Despite being very tired, a large weight fell off my shoulders that night between the Kočevska Reka pines. I still ask myself today if the Presidency of the Republic could have proposed its decision on armed resistance with a clear conscience on 27 June, if we had not received those weapons, which increased our capabilities for anti-tank combat by more than 100 per cent.

On the next day, the headquarters of the TO divided the arms and ammunition among the units at training. The boys who were wearing old uniforms and were virtually without any weapons were already moaning strongly and there were also a couple of examples of absent with-out leave and drunkenness. But when they received these new automatic weapons, enough ammunition and even anti-tank weapons, their disposition changed in the blink of an eye. Battle morale increased and 24 hours later all reports of the unit commanders indicated an effectively more optimistic picture.

On the morning of 21 June some of the units of the YNA in Slovenia raised their battle preparedness. A day earlier the construction of improvised control points was started between the border of the republics of Slovenia and Croatia. A battalion of military police from the barracks in Šentvid reinforced the guard of the army section at Brnik airport, where there were ten old Kragulj type planes, which once composed the aircraft squadron of the TO, but General Ivan Hočevar, after his replacement by Janez Slapar left them to the YNA, and these were under constant guard at Brnik.

At 10.20 federal air traffic control closed Brnik airport, while six MI-8 helicopters flew with pilots for the Kraguljs from Cerklje airport, together with a special unit. They landed at the military part of the airport and dropped off the pilots and then took the Kraguljs to Cerklje. This operation was directly commanded by the headquarters of the 5th Air Corps, and Colonel Topolovšek, former commander of this squadron, also cooperated. The operation was constantly under the protection of several pairs of interceptor fighters.

We had heard of this operation in the morning, when the closure of the airport was being prepared, but we could not do anything without the use of force. Only the Presidency sent a protest to Belgrade, but this did not excite any one over there much. But the theft of the TO aircraft caused quite a storm in the Slovenian public. Jože Pučnik told me that we could not afford something like this a few days before independence. Even those who had accused us of being the cause of incidents in May, when we took the armoured cars from TAM, were equally sharp with the theft of the Kraguljs – this time in the opposite sense – saying that we had not dared do anything. One of the members of the operations group cynically commented during these "turns" by our leading politicians that this was no surprise for even Ivan Cankar (Slovenian writer) had discovered that the Slovenians' greatest misfortune was themselves.

That same day the Presidency of the Republic met and passed the final acts up to the stage of a draft law in case escalations occurred after 26 June. Everything was prepared and when not even a week later we had to respond to aggression, the supreme command pushed through all the necessary measures with only one decree. The session was greeted by Belgrade twice. Once with the above described theft of the squadron of airplanes of the TO, and then with a letter in which they demanded our conscripts, and that no later than by 30 June 1991.

On the evening of 23 June (Sunday) the coordination representatives of the parliamentary parties met. They were to harmonize the final wording of the independence acts, for in the coming days the decisive session of the Assembly was to be held. We acquainted the party representatives with the final preparations for taking over effective power. Consensus regarding key affairs was actually not an issue any more, except for the Liberal Democratic Party. Jožef Školč had the feeling that evening that he had to be different at any cost. He himself did not even know what he was actually against and could not explain this to us either. Because of this, even the usually calm Milan Kučan had his nerves strung. After a fruitless attempt to persuade the eternal youth someone said let him be against and we split up dissatisfied and with a bitter taste in our mouths. If anybody had taped that meeting held a few days before our crucial step and transmitted it to the public, most of our voters would most surely have fled across the border on 26 June. Some leaders of the opposition, with Jožef Školč in the forefront, had been trying to create a forked tongue position. This was a political position which in the case that independence came out well, would allow them to boast of how with their patient stance and reining in of the adventurous ambitions of Demos, they had prevented an armed conflict, but if a conflict did arise (no one among them did believe that we could successfully defend ourselves in this case) they would load all the blame on the ruling coalition, saying that they had been constantly warning of the urgency for long-term and patient negotiations. Fortunately something else happened and even Jožef Školč at the meetings of the presidents of the parliamentary parties gradually became aware that this war could also cost him his head.

The following day the constitutional commission, irrespective of the poor harmonization of the previous night, approved the key acts, and in the evening the parliament, despite everything, defined the new Slovenian coat-of-arms and flag. Miloš Bukavec, who was coordinating the preparations for the celebration on 26 June was blooming with satisfaction. The whole month before this he was angry and muttering, saying that he would not be raising the old flag on independence day, and that without flying the flag the independence celebration would be making a "pig's ear" of things.

That day our intelligence people obtained the content of the lectures of the head of chief security bodies of the 5th Air Corps of the Yugoslav Air Force, which was held on 22 June, in which the chief acquainted his subordinates with the contents of the briefing meeting held in Belgrade. The Belgrade meeting was between 15 and 20 June and the Federal Secretary for People's Defence, Veljko Kadijević spoke there. The following is a summary of his talks:

Veljko Kadijević:

Italy supports a united Yugoslavia and is trying to deter Austria and Germany from their pretensions for the north-west of Yugoslavia. In the past month Yugoslavia has received its only true support from Britain and France. The Federal Secretary of Foreign Affairs is working badly, which is why General Kadijević had to make contact personally with these countries.

The influence of Germany is becoming stronger all the time and the Fourth Reich is gradually growing. The YNA has the support of the US and the USSR.

The powerful expansion of the anti-army campaign confirms that the time for a decision is closing in. Attacks on the accommodation of active military personnel in Split and Zadar are following one after the other. In Đakovo the security agents of the YNA have found an explosive device in the building in which the files of recruits were stored. If the YNA tried to get to these lists by force it would have exploded. In BH extremists are planning attacks on barracks. And a national guard was started to be set up in BH three days ago.

Macedonia:

The Executive Council of Macedonia has lately been cooling down its relations with the YNA. Not long ago a dispute arose during the visit of the Federal Secretary to Macedonia, because of which the Federal Secretary had to leave the joint dinner prematurely. Immediately after this an order was given that the SDV of Macedonia was to cut off all contacts with bodies of KOS and the YNA. Kiro Gligorov stated that if Slovenia and Croatia seceded from Yugoslavia they too would found a national guard to protect Macedonia.

Everyone was preparing for day X in Kosovo – the day of secession. Foreign forces were monitoring the activities of the YNA. Military representatives supported the unity of Yugoslavia in the majority of cases.

Germany supports Slovenia and Croatia in their desire to secede. As it does not want to expose itself, it is verbally standing for a unified Yugoslavia, but has been putting pressure on Austria and Hungary. These three countries are prepared to recognise immediately the independence of Slovenia and Croatia after their secession.

Italy still stands for a unified Yugoslavia and assesses that foreign intervention in Yugoslavia would not be good, for this would signify a long-term war.

In Croatia concrete preparations for conflicts with the YNA are underway. Intensive courses are in progress. The Croatian units are being trained by the Livajić brothers and other known Ustashi, as well as by foreign legionaries. There exists data that Yugoslavia will be infiltrated by units composed of extremist Croatian émigrés from Germany. They will come from Stuttgart and from certain other cities in which they have been preparing for commando raids on military facilities. Given all the data the Federal Secretary demands that the security bodies of the YNA should be in complete control of the flow of information so that on the level of the Federal Secretary it can formulate decisions. The system of security in the SFRY has broken down, such that we can only depend on information received from YNA security bodies.

The YNA security bodies must fulfil the moral and constitutional obligation of defence of the state. At present the state is threatened by forces both within and outside it. In view of this the security bodies face a test of their morale and of their attitude towards their work. Every person in these bodies must recognise that their solemn obligation is not simply a formal but a moral obligation.

The policies of Slovenia are a policy of fait accompli. The attacks on the army are not because of the army itself, but in order to destroy the state. This we must and will not allow. The Federal Secretary told Kučan if the Slovenian recruits do not come to the army, others will not come either and that would mean the end of the YNA. We would have only republican armies and this would bring about war. Kučan had no reply to this and was left speechless.

It is unacceptable that Konrad Kolšek shook hands with Špegelj. For us Kolšek is not an enemy but extremely naive. At the same time they duped him and took pictures.

The military police has to train for its tasks everyday. Anyone who appears incapable of these tasks must be immediately removed from these units.

On the whole, everything will depend on the YNA. The YNA will fight for a united Yugoslavia. This it will try to do through peaceful means. If it does not succeed, the army also has other solutions. The YNA will not allow anyone to win secession through force.

The security bodies must acquire sources everywhere the YNA is being attacked. The security bodies in units must above all operate in these units, while the counter-intelligence groups will operate in the field. In their work, they must be as active as possible. They must operate without restraints, for the opposite side has also been constantly collecting intelligence on the YNA. New collaborators must be recruited and the situation in the field must be monitored attentively.

The YNA must accept as allies all who fight for Yugoslavia and among them the SPS and SDS.

The officers of the YNA are superior compared to those in the Ministry of Internal Affairs of Croatia and the officers of the TO in Slovenia. Every officer in the YNA is worth more than 10 mobilised in the TO. Slovenia has issued an order that all doctors must be at their work posts from 21 June on and no one is allowed to go on holiday.

The Federal Secretary has stressed that the positions of the ZSLO and ZIS (Federal Executive Council) are after a long time once again completely coordinated. Ante Marković has become more aggressive and has accepted the stance of the YNA, which is that political issues must be solved first and only then those of the economy.

At this moment there are three options to resolve the crisis:
1. The YNA continues its observations, as it has been doing until now.
2. The YNA takes action independently.
3. Only the ZIS goes to the republics, but very radically.

The YNA does not know which option will be used, but the army will be present in the solution in any case.

The YNA will not withdraw from Slovenia or Croatia under any circumstances. It must be energetic and take steps against any attack on any member of the YNA or a member of their family, it must also take measures if any facility is destroyed.

The recruitment system will be taken over by the YNA, even if it has to apply force. The Federal Secretary stressed that this had also been conveyed to Lojze Peterle, along with the news that, if so deemed, Peterle himself was to be arrested."

This information was extremely precious for us, especially the information that Ante Marković and Veljko Kadijević were on the same side.

From April on, when even the most responsible Slovenian politicians became aware that 26 June, the calendar day, would most surely be coming, and when serious preparations began, I was constantly warning that the formal resolutions on the declaration of independence must be passed before 26 June, in a closed session, which would then allow us to gain a lead on possible responses of the federation, especially military, and that we establish our sovereignty in the key triangle, border–customs–air traffic control. If the opponent beat us to it, then we would find ourselves in circumstances where

146

we would be forced either to use force or to relent. One can imagine what the replacement of sign-posts on the border or the seizure of the Brnik flight control tower would be like if, on 15 June, the army placed a detachment of military police or paratroopers armed to the teeth there. None of these two variants would be good, which is why we had to take over effective power in this triangle without violence, and this could only be possible if we were dexterous, quick and conspiratorial enough. I myself proposed the day to be between 15 and 20 June. Milan Kučan agreed with this, others had doubts. Because of delays in coordinating the constitutional documents on independence, the change of the national symbols and other complications, as well as delays in the BOR and KANAL operations, this variant fell into the water. In the first half of June the expanded Presidency of the Republic of Slovenia decided that the formal acceptance of the constitutional documents be proposed to parliament on 25 June, and the celebration on 26 June. Belgrade took the bait and despite just one day's difference between the announced and the actual passing of the decision for independence, it was this one day that was of key importance. For on 25 June, Immediately after the declaration of the laws, we took over the customs, border crossings and air traffic control without letting off one shot. In Belgrade they were convinced until virtually the last second that the declaration of independence would be on 26 June, and that the assumption of effective government would come on the following day. For this reason they planned the beginning of their intervention for the early hours of 27 June, for the time, they thought, when the Slovenian decision was still to have been on paper. But a surprise was in store for them, for, due to our timely measures, and despite the great advantage they had in being present in our territory, they could not implement things in such a way that in the eyes of the public we (despite their undoubted aggression) appeared the first to use force.

Although we had agreed that the date of assumption of effective government (25 June) was the greatest national secret and only a few people knew about it (the expanded Presidency, some members of the government and the key operators), not everyone held to the agreement and the law, on the basis of which even the constitutional and other acts for parliament were stamped "state secret". A "most courageous" Slovenian politician had already blabbered out the actual date of independence to a foreign diplomat on 17 or 18 June and this foreign diplomat immediately informed his government. From there, this information came officially or unofficially to Belgrade, but it was too late to change their plans. The army could not raise its units a day sooner, and in particular a special unit of the Secretariat for Internal Affairs, which was being assembled in Serbia, was late. Thus only part of the 13th Corps in the Primorska region performed a deployment before 27 June, but we could not determine if this was the consequence of an order from Belgrade, after they had found out the actual date of taking over effective power, or the self-initiative of General Marjan Čad, who was commander of the Rijeka Corps. When we received a different report a few days later in the midst of the war from our source in Belgrade, on how information (date of issue) travelled there, our blood pressure rose significantly, but we did not take the report as gospel. Unfortunately, it was later confirmed that this report was true.

On 25 June the parliament passed the Constitutional Act on the Independence and Sovereignty of the Republic of Slovenia, the Constitutional Law for its implementation and a Declaration of Independence which was coordinated between the parties. At a meeting two days before, we tried to reach an agreement that the passing of these acts would proceed with dignity, as befits such an occasion. The parties and delegate clubs were represented in the constitutional committee anyway, where there was plenty of opportunity for wild debate. But some delegates could not shed their skins. The most enthusiastic were Peter Bekeš and Jože Smole with their procedural proposals and supplements. Milan Aksentijević warned the Slovenians for the last time about what kind of adventure they were letting themselves in for. Of course, the Liberal Democrats were not behind either. When it was finally time for voting, some souls were really quite upset and the president even counted a few votes against independence. Some cat calls at the expense of the Liberal Democrat woman delegate were heard, for she had voted in accord with Milan Aksentijević.

Immediately after the passing and announcement of the Constitutional acts on independence, the carefully prepared and planned measures for taking over effective power were activated. The coordination group sent an order to all operational sub-groups and some Republic bodies and, in a few hours, the customs facilities, border crossings and air traffic control were taken over without the use of force and without stopping their operation.

11. WAR

1. Generally taken, in war it is most expedient to conquer a country; and far less so to destroy it.
2. It is better to take the enemy army captive than to destroy it.
3. To win a hundred battles is not the highest skill. The highest skill is to win without a battle.
4. To attack the enemy's strategy is therefore that which is most important in war.

Sun Tzu, The Art of War

The take-over of power in the Republic of Slovenia was in line with the parliamentary decisions adopted a few hours after the declaration of the Constitutional Act on Independence. While the delegates and other guests were jubilantly drinking champagne within the halls of parliament, the take-over was in progress. This included taking control of the customs and its facilities, air traffic control towers at our airports and the replacing of border signs and national flags at the border crossings. Along the border with Croatia eight border control posts were established. The police assumed direct supervision over them while the TO units moved in to protect vulnerable border facilities. The take-over of other sections of federal administration (inspectorates, public institutions, etc...) did not present major difficulties. In the operations centre the coordination group monitored the development of events. Everything was done in earnest without the smallest incident. The telephone conversations were kept short and in low voices, only to confirm the receipt of reports or provide additional explanation of issued orders.

The operation proceeded unobstructed despite the decisions taken on that day by the Federal Executive Council (ZIS) headed by Marković. According to this act entitled "Direct implementation of federal regulations on the crossing of state borders in the territory of the RS", the federal government ordered federal police and army units to take control of Slovenian borders, with the use of force if necessary. At this session of the ZIS a decree was also adopted forbidding the installing of border posts inside the SFRY, authorising the federal army and the police to destroy all those installations already erected. The Federal Secretary for National Defence immediately implemented the contingency plans, namely, the order on the manner of taking control and securing the borders with Italy, Austria and partly with Hungary and the removal of erected border posts with Croatia, as

149

well as the methods and procedures for closing the border crossings. The start of the operation was given the code name MEJA.

The Republic of Croatia, like Slovenia, also declared its independence on the evening of 25 June, although without actually taking control of the borders and the customs administration. On 22 June, during our meeting with the Croatian delegation at the highest level, it was already evident from the reports presented by the members of their government that Croatia was not prepared to take such measures, largely for technical reasons, since its authorities were in some areas physically unable to reach the borders (Knin Krajina). Contrary to the statements made by Gregurić and Ramljak, President Franjo Tuđman gave his assurances that on 25 or 26 June Croatia would adopt identical measures to Slovenia and take effective control over its territory. We agreed in detail on all the border posts and the border regime to be established on 25 June, between the two newly declared states. Our talks at this meeting led us to the conclusion that the Croatian project had little chance of success. After this became indisputable, Kučan said to Tuđman over the table that we should at least agree that the Croats would prevent the Army going through to Slovenia. He did not receive a definite reply.

On 26 June at 11.10 a fax sent by Jože Slokar, who was then still a member of the ZIS, arrived at our information centre addressed to Milan Kučan, informing us of the two decisions which were drafted by ZIS in its session which lasted until 3.30 that morning. We thus had an official declaration of war sitting on our table. At 12 noon the first session (until now the only one) of the Presidential Defence Council[1], was held with a single topic on the agenda: discussion of the national security situation in Slovenia. The official press agency Tanjug launched its propaganda assault, full of threats against Slovenia. The Federal Air Traffic Control Administration closed Slovenian air space to all civilian flights. At some of the border crossings the YNA border patrols tried to prevent the exchange of flags and border signs. We observed the increased frequency of movements by army units, especially the 13th (Rijeka) Corps. At the meeting of the Defence Council we made a final review of the prepared measures and concluded that nothing of significance had been left out. During the meeting we received countless messages in which prominent guests from abroad, who were invited to attend the ceremony marking the declaration of independence, one after the another "excused" their absence.

A horde of foreign journalists descended on Ljubljana, such as the city had never seen. Fortunately Jelko Kacin had full control over the situation. We were also receiving reports on the movements of the Italian army. A state of alert was declared for the Ariette armoured brigade in Pordenone and for Pozzuolo del Friuli in Palmanova, as well as for the mechanised brigades at Udine, Trieste and Pordenone, for the Alpine brigade at Udine and for the

---

[1] According to the Law on Defence and Security the Defence Council is an advisory body of the Presidency. It was composed of the following members: Milan Kučan (President), France Bučar, Lojze Peterle, Igor Bavčar, Dimitrij Rupel, Miran Bogataj, Janez Slapar, Janez Janša.

air force in northern Italy. A number of Italian navy assault ships arrived in Italy's northern Adriatic ports.

The Austrian army and the NATO command for southern Europe in Naples and Verona were also on alert. The American military attache in Belgrade arrived in Ljubljana "incognito" to watch the "show" at close range.

A festive atmosphere prevailed at the YNA GHQ in Belgrade. They were finally given an "official" authorisation for action signed by Ante Marković, who had greater support from abroad than at home, which could only mean that the West had given him a green light. The generals could not have wished for more favourable conditions for action. They also had a guarantee which Ante Marković obtained in Zagreb, stating that although Croatia would declare its independence it would not take effective control of its territory (borders, customs) and would remain passive during the attack on Slovenia. Looking at the battle map the operation seemed ridiculously simple, almost too easy. An attack using armoured brigades and the air force unleashed on an opponent which did not possess even a single tank or plane. The blue colours on the map (representing our TO and police forces) were almost indistinguishable. The generals made jokes about the "Slovenian Johanns who never were or will be soldiers" and made references to the Desert Storm. It was said that if Americans needed several weeks to defeat Iraq the YNA would need only a few hours to defeat Slovenia. The order that was issued ran as follows: to secure border crossings and airports by 12 noon on 27 June 1991. "The only serious threat to our armoured columns will be the congested roads filled by the mob of frightened Slovenians fleeing across the Šentilj and Ljubelj border crossings to Austria, with Kučan and Janša at the head", was the conviction of the generals and a favourite sentence that Blagoje Adić especially liked to hear.

On Wednesday 26 of June, while preparations wereunder way for the ceremonial declaration of independence, the operations headquarters was continually receiving reports confirming my apprehensions. The airspace above was hot from the exhaust fumes of Yugoslav air force planes flying over all the major cities. At the Vrhnika barracks the tanks were moved to where their crews could reach them quickly.

We expected the flights to become much more intensive over Ljubljana just before the start of the ceremony, taking place on the square in front of the Assembly building. At 19.30 hours, therefore, I called the commander of the 5th Air Corps of the Yugoslav Air Force, General Rožič. Without hesitation I told him that we would start shooting down his aircraft within the hour if the flights did not stop. With surprising calm he replied that the flight plan for the day was almost completed and that there was no cause for anxiety. We finished our conversation and I left for the Assembly building.

Until now we had been unable to determine whether this decision was taken by Rožič himself or whether the disruption of the ceremony was not their intention, which seemed highly unlikely. Perhaps the answer lies behind the replacement of Rožič, which was made a few days later. His replacement,

151

colonel Ljubomir Bajič, was much more unpleasant to deal with, although he sometimes almost managed to amuse us with his extreme verbalising.

Despite the anxiety felt by those better informed, the ceremony held for the declaration of independence was worthy of the event, and apart from a hitch when the Archbishop had to speak without a microphone, everything passed off in a celebratory atmosphere. The TO guard of honour which at the time when the scenario for the ceremony was being prepared, annoyed the demo-liberals and especially Ciril Zlobec, performed its function perfectly. Following the ceremony Igor Bavčar and I went for a short time to Cankarjev Dom where the solemn atmosphere was transforming into a jovial celebration. While I was there I received a number of urgent messages from the operations centre. I also intended to take a short walk through the capital city of an independent nation but my plans were interrupted. The reports we were receiving from the field confirmed that the decisions taken by the ZIS were being implemented. At around midnight I was recalled to the operations centre where the national coordination group was stationed. I again reviewed the most important information of the previous day.

THURSDAY, 27 JUNE

During the celebration itself we received a message form the Croatian defence headquarters (Špegelj), informing us that on 27 June 1991 a team from the Federal Secretariat of Internal Affairs would be flown from Belgrade to Slovenia with orders to take control of the border crossings. At 0.57 hours we received information from Varaždin that three detachments, stationed at the Kalniški Partizani barracks and composed of approximately 300 soldiers, would at 4 a.m. move towards Slovenia, each having at its disposal about 10 APCs. In addition an armoured brigade was also preparing for the assault. Immediately afterwards we received a call from the duty officer at the Croatian Defence Headquarters informing us that a YNA armoured unit had left Karlovac heading towards Metlika. Without delay we sent a message to the 2nd operations subgroup in Novo Mesto, although the information was too late since the motorised armoured unit (12 APCs, each carrying one 20 mm three-barrel anti – aircraft gun, 7 trucks and 4 cross-country vehicles) raced over the Republic border at 1.15 passing Metlika and heading towards Novo Mesto. The advance of the column was monitored by the police and based on the information which they provided the TO set up the first road block, but at 2.00 this managed to stop only the hindmost section. The forward section composed of six armoured vehicles and carrying the commander, Major Boško Prodanović, was by then already at the village of Mačkovec. By radio link the blocked section of the light anti-aircraft armoured battery called Major Prodanović for help, and supported by six armoured vehicles he quickly returned as far as the village of Poganovci and, stopping just short of the road block, stepped out of his vehicle and from an automatic weapon fired the first round of shots in the war for Slovenia. The time was around 4 o'clock in the morning. One of the members of the TO

152

who manned the barricade[2] returned fire. His bullets hit one of the trucks, wounding a YNA second lieutenant in the hand. Because the TO still had not received orders for attack and could only return fire, negotiations began at the barricade. The wounded second lieutenant was taken to the civilian hospital in Novo Mesto. Major Prodanović ordered the artillery guns to be pointed towards the village and threatened to start shelling the nearby buildings. Since the barricade at Poganci was set up at an inappropriate location and blocked only the last section of the advancing column, the regional TO headquarters deliberately dragged out negotiations in order to establish a stronger road block at Medvedjek. After repeated threats by Prodanović the TO removed the barricade and allowed the column to proceed along the main road towards Ljubljana. Due to the traffic slow-downs (police) and because Prodanović was not prepared to take another risk, the column advanced at a slow pace. At 4 o'clock it arrived at the Medvedjek rise where it was met by members of the 1st battalion of the 52nd TO brigade, the 174th TO anti-diversion unit, a few squads of TO special forces, as well as the TO units which first encountered the armoured column and moved from Poganci to Medvedjek.

From the moment of receiving information the operations centre monitored the movements of the armoured column from Karlovac. In the meantime we were informed that the column was heading towards Ljubljana and then on to Brnik airport. Around 2.00 in the morning, when a section of this column was stopped at Poganci and the negotiations were in progress, we made a quick review of the situation as it looked on the map. Except for the highest state of alert which existed in the key YNA units no other troop movements were detected. It was not self-explanatory why the YNA would first deploy only a few armoured vehicles which in addition were not moving in battle but rather in cruise formation. It still seemed most logical to us that the officers leading the operations to block the borders of Slovenia would be intending to reinforce the units in positions from which they would launch the assault, before operation MEJA was given the green light.

All of our sub-groups were already in place and ready for battle. We could do no more. Igor decided to take a short nap, saying that the next few days would not be conducive to satisfying such basic needs. I agreed but before I could follow suit the armoured brigade broke out of the Vrhnika barracks.

After the war a number of false conclusions were made about how it all began with the break out of the armoured brigade from the Vrhnika barracks and that the first shot was fired in Trzin. Both are false. The aggression officially began on 26 June at 3.30 when ZIS adopted a decree on the blockade of Slovenia's international borders and in reality on 27 June at 1.15 when the mechanised light anti-aircraft battery from the 306th LAP PZO YNA formation crossed the border at Metlika. Individual army units had

---

[2] The barricade was defended by the members of the anti-diversion unit from Novo Mesto and the PDD unit from Trebnje. The Fire was returned by a TO member named Robert Vidmar.

from the beginning of May started arriving at the borders, border posts and in the vicinity of border crossings.

On 27 of June 1991, precisely at 1.00, the commander of the 1st armoured brigade of the YNA, attached to the 14th Corps, Lt-Colonel Pane Matić ordered the commander of the 1st armoured battalion, Major Danilo Radanović, to advance from the army barracks and surround Brnik airport, thus securing the return of the customs administration into the hands of the federal authorities. The battalion should have divided in two and according to the previously practiced "OKOP" plan advance in the following directions: 1. Vrhnika–motorway towards Ljubljana–ring road (Maribor exit)––Trzin–Mengeš–Moste–Brnik and 2. Vrhnika–old road towards Ljubljana–Brezovica–Dobrova–Toško Čelo–Ljubljana Šentvid–Tacen–Smlednik––Trboje–Brnik. The brigade commander ordered that the assigned task be completed at all costs.

Without sounding any alarm Major Danilo Radanovič moved into action at 2.40 and partly carried out his orders. At 5.35 both advancing columns arrived just short of their objective, although at a high price and along different routes. The price was paid both by Slovenia and the YNA which along the way lost almost a third of the armoured vehicles in the columns, either due to mechanical falts or later because of action taken by the TO and the police.

Some time after 3.30 the duty officer rushed into my room located near the operations centre saying: "The tanks have left Vrhnika barracks! They are moving towards Ljubljana." I almost suffered a stroke. Not because I did not expect it but because we were certain that the regional TO command and the operational sub-group of the Ljubljana region, who from the 23rd of May were ready to set up a blockade, would succeed in blocking the advance of one of the most dangerous army units in Slovenia. Despite explicit instruction and ample stocks of explosive devices, they failed. The first barricades were set up by the police using their own vehicles. If the consequences were serious, the courts would certainly have a lot of cases to plough through. As it was, there were simply some personnel changes made[3].

I woke up Bavčar who only a short time ago had managed to fall asleep. He too could not understand how it was possible for the tanks to leave the barracks. Where were the barricades, where were our defence units?

Bavčar called Milan Kučan and the others while I telephoned the commander of the 14th (Ljubljana) Corps, General Pavlov. His assistant picked up the receiver and at first tried to persuade me that the General was still sleeping. After a few angry words on my part General Pavlov took the call. I asked him what his tanks were doing on the road. He tried to act surprised, replying: "Well, listen, the 1st armoured brigade is probably on a routine

---

[3] During a subsequent detailed investigation of the reasons why the tanks were allowed to leave the army installation, as well as the consequences of this happening, we reached a conclusion that despite different recommendations an opinion prevailed that the police should be able to block the tanks through the blocking of normal traffic. However, traffic during the early hours of 27 June 1991 was non-existent.

exercise, on the way to a firing range. I don't know any more, ask my superiors." I made a few more choice remarks and realised that there was no point in talking to him. He had arrived in Ljubljana only a few weeks ago. He did not seem to be the vehement type of an aggressor, and rumours had it that he was totally useless. Later his comrades who defected to the TO said that more than anything he was very frightened. After the YNA pulled out of Slovenia the following joke began circulating about him within the military circles:

Who is the most successful Yugoslav general?

???

General Pavlov, commander of the Ljubljana Corps!

???

He came to Ljubljana with just a briefcase, but after only one month he left with the entire army!

Meanwhile Milan Kučan first spoke without success with Ante Marković and afterwards with the deputy commander of the 5th Army District Andrija Rašeta, who said that it was not tanks but armoured vehicles on wheels, that it was not an attack and that the army was acting according to the law.

The destination of the armoured column was still uncertain. Because it broke up into several sections, each of which were heading in a different direction, it was possible that their destination was Ljubljana city centre. I doubted this but it was not entirely impossible.

I decided to try somewhere else. I called the number of the special office of the commander of the Ljubljana Army Corps, General Marjan Vidmar. Although I knew that the army did not entirely trust him and was withholding important information from him, I called nevertheless. He answered instantaneously. His voice was full of anxiety, uttering a single word: Brnik!

I said thank you, went into the operations room and issued instructions. The commander of the Gorenjska region, Peter Zupan and the commander of special police units in Gorenjska began sending reinforcements to the airport, while the armed units already on the scene mined the barricades. Despite the badly placed barricades, which were unable to block the departure of the tanks from the Vrhnika barracks on the way to Ljubljana, Brnik airport was never taken due to the prompt information that became available on their intended destination. Although a section of the tank battalion did get to the perimeter of the airport, its obstruction meant that it was no longer a key but rather a burden for the operation against Slovenia.

Meanwhile reports of a skirmish were coming in from the barricades at Poganci, saying that one of the YNA soldiers was wounded. The barricade still stood. We received the news with mixed feelings but in general the feeling was optimistic due to the fact that at least this advance had been halted.

Immediately after my conversation with Vidmar I was on the direct line to Martin Špegelj at the Croatian operations headquarters. That day we first spoke after the armoured column left Karlovac. I briefed him on the current situation in Slovenia, incidents occurring at the borders and the tank advan-

155

ces towards Brnik airport. He said he was on his way to a meeting and that we could count on their assistance. Prior to the meeting of our Presidency I gave him another call. He was still in the meeting of their National Council, but he was called out. His voice was subdued when he said that he did not understand what was happening because their authorities were not prepared to act. He did not mention names but I knew he was referring to President Tuđman. His absence during our independence celebrations the day before was a good enough reason for concern. I asked him at least to try and propose the adoption of a decision on neutrality, which would mean that they would not allow the free passage of tanks and other reinforcements which the YNA would attempt to send from or through Croatia towards Slovenia.

During the mid-morning he called back and said that they had not adopted such a decision. The argument against getting involved was based on the fact that since Croatia was already in a war with Četniks over a third of its territory it could not afford to risk a fight with the YNA. We nevertheless agreed that they would at least assist us and provide us with all relevant information. Špegelj did do all he could to provide us with detailed information on the time of take-offs of military aircraft from Croatian airports or about the movement of army units towards Slovenia. He was unhappy because he was well aware of the situation, knowing that Croatia would not be able to escape the conflict and was missing the most favourable moment for action. When subsequently it was finally forced into a war it was not any better equipped with armaments. Moreover, it no longer fought against the multinational units composed of regular YNA soldiers but faced determined Serb and Montenegrin reservists.

Shortly after four o'clock we received a report that the commander of the column advancing from Karlovac had begun firing and that our units had returned fire. The YNA suffered its first casualty.

The decision to deploy the TO units in active engagements had not yet been taken and thus our forces could use force only while defending buildings and in self-defence. It was essential that the Presidency of the Republic met as soon as possible. Before the meeting was called we sent out the following instructions to our sub-section units:

REPUBLIC OF SLOVENIA
Coordination group

No. 1097
Date: 27 June 1991

To all operations sub-sections

I. CURRENT SITUATION

1. At 2.45 a column of 40 tanks and 20 armoured vehicles left the Ivan Cankar army installation at Vrhnika and on its way towards Ljubljana broke through a number of barricades. The column is heading towards Brnik airport. The TO and ONZ units are attempting to stop it.

2. A YNA column is blocked between Metlika and Novo Mesto. Another column is also blocked between Zagreb and Novo Mesto.

3. A column of 30 armoured vehicles is on the way from Varaždin to Ormož.

4. Intense communications with various Belgrade authorities are in progress. For now there are no signs that Belgrade is ready to ease off. In our assessment the objective of these and other activities is to use radical measures for taking effective control of the following locations:

– borders
– customs
– air traffic control

and subsequently replace the legal institutions of the Republic of Slovenia.

II. IN CONSEQUENCE ADOPT AND COORDINATE THE FOLLOWING MEASURES:

1. Ensure 100% effectiveness of sub-section.

2. Tighten security at all key protected installations.

3. Barricades at key locations should be supplied with explosives. Use these with great caution.

4. Set up strong road blocks. If they are easily overrun this will have a negative effect on the battle morale of the RS defence forces.

5. In anti-tank combat use squads and individuals with appropriate training.

6. All YNA soldiers and officers who request to join the TO should be sent to the collection centres. All others who are likely to switch sides and who are not Slovenian nationals should also be held at these centres.

Head of the Coordination Group
Igor Bavčar

Shortly after six in the morning Milan Kučan succeeded in getting hold of the rest of the members of the extended Presidency. Wandering around the Presidency building was the president of the Liberal Democratic Party, Jožef Školjč who, when on returning from a night of celebrations at Podpeč, came across the destruction caused by passing tanks at Brezovica. Although clearly shaken he was still not certain whether the YNA tanks were really out on the roads or whether it was just a provocation caused by the Slovenian Ministry of Defence through which it was trying to militarise Slovenia. Similar doubts were being expressed by some of the other leading members of his party. Much has been written about the meeting at which Lojze Peterle and I were to be accused of instigating the war in Slovenia. That very morning a member of this party was in front of the Assembly building, while tanks were advancing through Slovenia, explaining to the passers-by that there was no difference between Janez Janša and Veljko Kadijević.

The session of the Presidency (which was, in addition to its regular members, attended by Bučar, Peterle, Drnovšek, Rupel, Bavčar, Kacin, Bogataj, Slapar, and myself) began with a short description of the current situation and an assessment of events presented by Igor Bavčar and myself. Prior to the session we both spoke to Milan Kučan, Lojze Peterle and France Bučar. None of them seemed to be disheartened. Although no one hid their

157

anxiety, the atmosphere was nevertheless encouraging. Some were afraid of Drnovšek's reaction, but on that day and throughout the war he bore himself surprisingly well. During the session, at 7.20, a telegram came from the commander of the 5th Army District, Konrad Kolšek, addressed to the Prime Minister Lojze Peterle. it read:

"Prime Minister,
We hereby inform you that the 5th Army District has been ordered to take control of all border crossings and secure the SFRY border.
We are relying on the cooperation of all authorities and the population of the Republic of Slovenia.
We will execute our orders unconditionally, which also means through the use of force.
Any resistance will be crushed and the consequences will be the responsibility of those who ordered resistance and those who acted on such orders."

Some of us were wondering what the order which Kolšek received from Belgrade must have been like, since his formulation was so threatening. When I proposed at the end of the session that the decisions which the Presidency discussed at its previous session be confirmed there were practically no opposing arguments. Milan Kučan summarised and added the following conclusion which officially confirmed the state a war:

1. The YNA intervention can only be taken as a direct and violent attack and an attempt at permanent occupation of Slovenia.

2. The RS is recalling all active and civilian persons from the RS who are serving in the YNA and calls on YNA officers and soldiers not to take part in the aggression on Slovenia.

3. The Presidency of the RS commands the implementation of the prepared measures for obstruction of YNA units, the blockade of infrastructural facilities and the use of TO forces in the defence of facilities and communications. The implementation is the responsibility of the Coordination groups.

4. The Prime Minister should contact Marković and demand the termination of military activities by the YNA in the RS.

5. The Presidency of the RS shall inform the presidencies of the Yugoslav republics of the current situation and demand the recall of its citizens from those YNA forces which are participating in the aggression against RS.

6. The Republic Secretariat for International Cooperation shall inform the governments of neighbouring countries and the international public of the current situation.

7. The President of the Assembly shall inform the presidents of the parliamentary parties of the current situation and the adopted proclamations.

8. The Presidency of the RS proposes the calling of a session of the Assembly.

The resolutions were adopted unanimously. Janez Slapar immediately left for the operations centre and in accordance with the measures that were prepared in advance sent out the following fax message to the sub-sections:

On the basis of the Decree of the Presidency of the Republic of Slovenia No. SZ 800-03-1891 dated 27 June 1991 concerning the orientations and measures for the state of alert

I ORDER

1. Through decisive military action, with an emphasis on engaging the armoured units and other technical systems, ensure the realisation of the planned tasks. By the use of the available military means ensure the protection of facilities, the borders and communications. Obstruct the manouvres of the YNA units.
2. Coordinate activities within the Coordination Groups.
3. Prepare the units for activating the Nabava plan.
4. These tasks should be performed immediately, and keep me informed of all measures taken and results attained!

When the session continued we decided that Milan Kučan should make a television address while Lojze Peterle, Janez Drnovšek and Dimitrij Rupel should make contact with as many members of foreign governments as possible, informing them of the current situation and requesting that pressure be applied on Belgrade to stop the military operations. During the session Rupel drafted a couple of letters for his "connections" abroad. Fortunately the telephone lines were working and after a few hours the world gained first hand information about the events in Slovenia which differed from what the Yugoslav propaganda through its consular offices and the Tanjug press agency were trying to disseminate.

Meanwhile new reports were coming in of YNA units breaking out of their installations and heading towards the borders. The 345th Mountain Brigade from Kranj began preparations for the march towards the northern border crossings; the motorised detachments at Vipava followed suit. No one tried to stop them. Those heros who very vocally and aggressively protested against the TO moving into the army installations when the YNA had already left, were nowhere to be seen.

A motorised battalion in Maribor prepared to break out of the Franc Rozman Stane barracks. At nine o'clock the tanks broke through the barricade and secured a free passage. Until they got to the next barricade.

A detail of ten tanks from Varaždin was advancing towards Lendava. A barricade was waiting for them at the bridge over the Mura river. A detachment of troops from the Tolmin barracks started towards Bovec. From Postojna two tank regiments and two motorised units moved towards Vipava.

Gradually a picture was forming of the degree of success of our defences. The defenders in Štajerska (Slovenian Styria) and Dolenjska held up well. In the Gorenjska and Ljubljana regions the defence was weaker, while in Primorska the situation was even worse. In Ljubljana defence was in the hands of the TO and police special forces from the national reserves. A few anti-tank units followed the trail blazed by the tank battalion from Vrhnika, destroying the tanks that fell behind. A member of the national Coordination

Group, Janko Stušek, left for the regional TO headquarters in Gorenjska while Ludvik Zvonar went to the Ljubljana regional headquarters. Their reports provided us with a true picture of the situation.

Kučan's TV speech was unambiguous. In clear sentences he reiterated the assessments and decisions adopted by the Presidency. It subdued the hopes of those who expected us to be defeated and disarmed, accepting "long and at times unproductive negotiations". A number of parliamentary parties soon issued their statements. They all supported the decision for a decisive but carefully weighed defensive action.

The tactics adopted by Ante Marković and the Army were obvious. In anticipation of a quick occupation of border crossings, airports and other infrastructure centres they pretended to be uninformed or were simply not responsive to the calls from Slovenia. That morning no one among them even considered negotiating with us. If all went as planned – as Admiral Brovet's report seemed to suggest, with its statement that "all the objectives have been achieved" – they would issue the first ultimatum during the early afternoon which, along with pressure from international public opinion, would then be followed by more ultimatums.

Some time after 9.00 a.m. the information centre finally established contact with General Rašeta who was evidently chosen to communicate with us. I reminded him of our conversation that took place after the seizure of four armoured vehicles from TAM when he repeatedly stated that the YNA would not resort to force. He burst into loud guffaws, and after an arrogant "How are you Mr. Minister?" said that although he really enjoyed our discussions and would like to continue them, since orders were orders they must be obeyed. There was nothing left to discuss. Perhaps later with someone else. He ended with the following words in Serbo-Croat:

"At last we are on the move. In two hours you will be finished!"

I was neither frightened nor satisfied by the conversation. It provided me with two important facts. I realised that Rašeta, who was not one of the less intelligent or more extreme Yugoslav generals, was passionately caught up in the spirit of war and certain of victory. Unintentionally he also let me know that the deadlines set for their operations were very short. This could have meant that they were not prepared for a prolonged battle. I was very sure that those two hours would seem very long to the comrade general.

At 10.45 a report came that our forces had stopped a tank column advancing from Varaždin at the bridge near Ormož. They could not break through the barricade, even after trying to destroy it using their cannons, which for the duration of the war represented a very significant practical and moral factor of support.

During the early afternoon on 27 June 1991 Tanjug released Admiral Stane Brovet's message saying that the YNA had achieved its objectives and secured the international borders of SFRY. That was the plan. The two hour deadline had passed. According to the plan, during the second phase of the operation the YNA was to transfer control of the border crossings to a special brigade of the Federal Secretariat for Internal Affairs which was flown in from Belgrade. Regardless of the fact that the first phase was not yet completed, General Blagoje Adić ordered the start of the second phase. The helicopters carrying the federal police took off for the borders. The operations headquarters attached to the 5th Army District, which was greatly put out because we had blocked many of their outfits which consequently had not yet reached their destinations, saw during the extremely premature start of the second phase a chance to load some of the helicopters with members of the special forces (gathered at Pleso, Zagreb and Cerklje airports) and to send some of them as reinforcements to the surrounded armoured columns and other units in order to attack those few border crossings which were still under our control. They hoped that they would thus be able to make up for lost time and finish the operation by the evening.

Telephones at the headquarters of our operations group were ringing constantly. Reports of helicopter fly-overs were coming in from all over, followed a little later by reports of their attacks on the border crossings, their vicinity or near the blocked armoured columns. YNA Air Force planes were also in the air providing protection for the second phase of the operation. Their flight paths and assaults were being charted continuously on maps and after only a few minutes it became clear that the second phase, which we expected to begin after the control of at least two of the larger border crossings had been secured by them, had started prematurely. A look at the second map on which the enemy's available forces and armaments were marked revealed that while having plenty of fighting men, the aggressor lacked the helicopters which could be used to fly them in. Since the distances involved were relatively short the army headquarters in Zagreb planned on three to four helicopter transports in one day. We immediately concluded that it would be necessary to shoot down as many helicopters as possible in order to last until nightfall when flying conditions would prevent further take-offs.

Although single or groups of helicopters were following prearranged flight paths, avoiding dangerous areas, we had the territory covered to such an extent that it was almost impossible to fly over Slovenia and to the borders unobserved.

We immediately issued all necessary orders but the incoming reports only spoke of more helicopters, not mentioning that any of them had been shot down. Despite clear orders we were receiving enquiries from some of the sub-sections whether the helicopters may be shot down. I was furious but Igor Bavčar and Danijel Kuzma were even more so. Danijel personally called some of the units at their battle positions and almost pleaded with them to shoot down at least one of the helicopters. Several times the sound of helicopter engines reached us at the operations room. Our anti-aircraft defence units were located on all the higher points in Ljubljana but since the helicopters were flying so low they could not shoot at them without endangering civilian targets. Bogdan Koprivnikar, a one time professional anti-aircraft gunner, rushed off with some 2M missiles towards

161

Brnik saying that he would at least get one of them. Major Janez Švajncer and Captains Jože Hrčič and Matjaž Vrhunc went off with him.

The reports on helicopter assaults flooded in for the next hour but none were as yet shot down. I knew that the reason for this was not only due to the lack of appropriate weapons – we had less than 30 2M missile launchers in the whole of Slovenia – nor to the inadequate training of our crews, given that most of the missiles were obtained only a few days ago, but was mainly due to psychological barriers. Most of the members of the Territorial Defence were only a few days ago common civilians. From the time they were drafted they had not even got used to wearing uniforms, let alone to the feeling of being in a real war situation. Many of them were also under the influence of the media, which over the past few moths had tried to suggest that Slovenia was not in any danger and that those in power were only trying to frighten the people in order to militarise the country. Besides this, everyone knew that we are short of effective anti-aircraft weapons and on seeing helicopters flying overhead remembered that Slovenia did not possess anything as a counter-balance. Consequently many of the commanders in the field were uneasy about issuing orders to fire. Under such circumstances it was even more difficult to keep one's aim on the target or to hit anything at all. Tanks, planes and helicopters – in the eyes of many TO defenders these were targets which at first seemed indestructible. A perfectly understandable reaction when you consider what the enemy has and you don't. Such reactions can usually be overcome only if the people are able to see with their own eyes (here the TV played an irreplaceable role) a burning tank or a shot down helicopter.

I called Tone Krković – apart from anti-aircraft guns located on the roof tops of Ljubljana, his unit also had a few anti-aircraft missiles – and asked him what the hell his men were doing. He promised to look into it personally.

The time was seven in the evening and the sun was still treacherously high in the sky. I wished for a heavy storm so at least it would prevent the aggressor's vertical take-offs. The time for a turnabout was running out. We had to think how to use the approaching night to regain at least some of what we had lost during the day. I was about to turn on the computer and begin drafting an order to activate that part of the operation "Kamen" which envisaged the regaining of some of the more important border crossings. Just as I held the telephone receiver waiting for Slapar to give me his opinion on the possibility of deploying a sufficient number of units to accomplish operation Kamen that same night, I heard a loud bang. The window panes rattled and both Igor and I jumped to the floor to take cover. Below in the courtyard of the Executive Council building a uniformed security officer was running wildly to and fro calling on people to take cover. Windows were opening and the members of the security brigade, who for days had patiently kept watch, now looked out in surprise. Then into our office came a pale Marjan Šiftar and somewhat calmer Milan Kučan. At first I thought that the Presidency building had been hit by a rocket launched from a plane or a helicopter. I blamed our carelessness since the operations centre was still located at a peace time location on the ground floor of the building which was totally unprotected against air attacks (the same premises now serve as a press conference room). The emergency telephone rang and the duty officer of the security forces reported that a Gazela type helicopter had been shot down near the government building. Meanwhile the commander of the security forces, Tone Krkovič, appeared in the middle of Gregorčičeva street, and through a SAR 80 megaphone issued a few decisive orders which were heard over half of Ljubljana, bringing the duty crews to order.

The news spread instantly. All of Slovenia heard it on the radio. Within the operations centre many of those present uttered a single word in unison: "At last!" All of a sudden reports on more downed helicopters began flooding in from all over, just as if someone had turned over the hour glass. Two of them were hit at Trzin, one with only an anti-tank gun. The Gorenjska subsection reported that one had been shot down and another badly damaged at the village of Suha. A report came from the Ig 510th Training Centre that a missile had been fired at a MIL 8 transport helicopter flying over the Ljubljana marshland. A few minutes later the downing was confirmed. We later learned that only two of the helicopters were totally destroyed (hit by anti-aircraft rockets), and the others that were hit by artillery fire were only badly damaged and were able to return either to the nearest airport or an army installation. Some of them never flew again while most of them were grounded for several days.

Thus the helicopter assaults of any significance ended and were not resumed until the end of the war. In only an hour's time the situation changed drastically. This was the first reversal of the war and was much more significant than it appeared at first. The psychological barrier was broken. From then on the aggressor had great trouble convincing its pilots to go on flying missions since they were afraid to fly over Slovenia even during a cease-fire. They painted their iron birds with huge red crosses, although they mostly used their aircraft for troop transports and replenishment of used stocks of ammunition of those units that were in a blockade.

The first day of the war was immeasurably long – not that we were timing it. Despite long periods without sleep no one thought about getting any rest. The armoured units and smaller companies of YNA troops from the border regions spread out through the majority of the roads leading to the border crossings. The units of the 13th, 14th, 10th, 31st and 32nd Corps advanced. They moved as though they were on a peacetime parade, although not everywhere. After encountering road blocks, the units of the Mountain Brigade from the Kranj barracks proceeded towards some of the border crossings in battle formation.

In the operations centre it was like an ants' nest. Due to lack of time, orders were issued over the phone. There was a lack of communication links between the regional headquarters and the field units. The commanders complained about the shortage of anti-armour and anti-aircraft weapons. In reply we gave them the locations of the nearest army arsenals. Janez Slapar and Danijel Kuzma began utilizing additional units. Miran Bogataj was

163

trying to improve the civil defence, especially its tactics of obstruction. We cut off the telephone links and electricity supply to the army installations. In the meantime Jelko Kacin conducted the press conferences held at Cankarjev Dom as a military instrument, turning our insufficient material assets to our advantage. The reception centres began receiving the first deserting soldiers, particularly Slovenians, Croatians and Albanians. Special centres for prisoners of war started filling up, and their numbers grew rapidly, causing logistical problems.

On the second day after its independence and the first day of war, the Slovenian leadership performed like a well-oiled machine. The Prime Minister formed a war cabinet, which was responsible in as much as was possible for general supplies and other essential public functions. In truth it must be said that during the war the most important decisions were taken by the government and the Presidency at the extended sessions of the Presidency, and that as far as the most important decisions were concerned there were no major disagreements between the most prominent politicians. The most far-reaching decision, however, was passed in low whispers in one of the corners of Milan Kučan's office by himself, Drnovšek, Bavčar and myself.

Local community authorities were for the most part well prepared for the deteriorating circumstances. Apart from some of the overwrought city mayors who wished to make peace treaties with the YNA all by themselves, no other major difficulties were encountered.

That evening, following the main news, the Prime Minister and I appeared on a joint TV programme produced by Slovenian and Croatian TV. Present in the Zagreb studio were the Croatian Prime Minister Manolić and Deputy Minister of Police DeGoricija. They were unable to give an explanation as to why Croatia remained passive even after we were attacked from their territory. In a few sentences I tried to explain to them – and in particular to the Croatian public – that Croatia was making a great mistake. If Slovenia was defeated, Croatia was next in line. Both of them got up and left the studio before the end of the programme with the excuse that they had been called to attend an urgent meeting. In a very calm manner Lojze Peterle told the audience that we were prepared to negotiate but not if that meant forfeiting the plebiscite decision. I described the current situation on the battlefield without concealing anything. At that time there were already more than one hundred dead and wounded (fortunately only lightly wounded) on both sides which some found hard to believe but which was nevertheless true. In addition a large number of helicopters and tanks were put out of action. The situation was far from rosy, however. In the afternoon we had a call from Veljko Kadijević who said that an agreement was reached with Ante Marković and that the Army would suppress any kind of secessionist aspirations. Janez Drnovšek informed France Bučar that he would no longer perform the duties of a member of the SFRY Presidency.

They had taken control of most of our border, destroyed some of the border control points with Croatia and they kept on coming. From the Lora navy base near Split a squadron of missile carriers was sailing for the northern Adriatic. The battles spread particularly in the Dolenjska, eastern Štajerska and Ljubljana regions. The helicopter assault, assisting one of the sections of the 3rd tank company of the 1st tank battalion of the 1st armoured brigade, was repulsed at Trzin. The major role here was played by a special police unit led by Vinko Beznik and Dušan Gorše, whom we sent in support after receiving disturbing reports from Trzin.

Before I left for the TV station, Igor Bavčar, Miran Bogataj, Janez Slapar and the other present members of the operations group assessed the current situation while standing in the corridor. We concluded that we were close to establishing a balance of power but still needed arms and equipment from the army arsenals in order to equip additional units. Psychologically we were prepared for a prolonged struggle.

For this reason I made certain bold statements during my TV appearance. "We will never surrender. We consider the protection of human life as the highest priority and will consequently resist only in places where we are in an advantageous position. This is our home, while the aggressor will soon realise that he is in a foreign land and that tanks and airplanes are not sufficient, since their troops must have food and water to survive – and each night there will be fewer of them."

I also displayed the documents that were captured from a tank at Toško Čelo which showed that the armoured unit from Vrhnika was acting according to the OKOP plan of operations.

During the TV programme I was called back to the operations centre. Despite the onset of night the fighting was becoming more intensive.

FRIDAY, 28TH JUNE

Night passed without any sleep. We were involved in reinforcing the barricades and drafting reserves. The newly drafted TO units were heading towards those border crossings which the aggressor had taken over the night before. The morning greeted us with the sound of aircraft engines. The aggressor was going mad. Because we had succeeded in blocking the largest section of his most powerful armoured units, he called in the air force. With missiles and bombs the YNA attacked our positions and a civilian line of trucks at Medvedjek, Brnik airport, television and radio transmitters, Šentilj and the Karawanken tunnel. A dramatic battle for the border crossing at Holmec began. The tank company attached to the 32nd Corps reached as far as Radenci.

We had to maintain a balance of pressure in every way possible. There was a threat of a drop in morale. We were without aircraft and only had a very limited supply of anti-aircraft missiles. The enemy did not care. Civilian targets were hit indiscriminately. There was only one thing left to do: attack on all points where we were superior. On the ground. At eleven o'clock I wrote a message which was immediately sent out:

165

NATIONAL COORDINATION GROUP
dated 28 June 1991

To all coordination sub-sections

Due to the insensitive bombardment of civilian targets at Brnik airport and the TO positions at Medvedjek by the air force of the occupying Yugoslav Army and the threat of the further bombardment of civilian targets

I ORDER

1. At all points where the defence forces of the Republic of Slovenia have a tactical advantage they should engage in offensive actions against the aggressor's forces and facilities. Call on the enemy to surrender immediately and attack with all available means. Apply all heavy weapons including MES.
2. During the operation undertake evacuation measures and see to the protection of the civilian population.
3. Activate plans code named "NABAVA", putting them into practice as soon as possible at an appropriate time and at your own discretion.
4. Secure captured weapons and explosives, call in reserves and place them in position.
5. In each region you must immediately carry out at least one successful attack. Concentrate on the destruction of command posts, especially those where the commanding officers are demonstrating extreme attitudes.
6. Report back on all undertaken activities.

For the Coordination Group
Janez Slapar   Janez Janša   Igor Bavčar

The TO and police units gradually established a balance of power. Following the air strike at Medvedjek the Dolenjska TO forces caused considerable damage to the armoured column, but not enough to put it out of action permanently. A special unit led by Beznik captured an elite enemy squad at Trzin. At Gornja Radgona the residents burned a few of the trucks themselves. The commanders of the regional TO forces moved their units back to their starting positions in preparation for an attack on those less heavily guarded military facilities. Sections of the TO protection brigade attacked the YNA barracks at Ribnica, and those in Koroška (Slovenian Carinthia) attacked the Bukovje barracks near Dravograd. The YNA garrison commanders were in a panic forming intervention squads, sending them to assist their blocked comrades. The majority of them were turned back as they tried to break out of the installations, while the rest were halted soon after their exit. At 11.30 after a short clash the TO forces from Maribor destroyed and captured a squad at Limbuš which was hurrying to help the crew of an armoured vehicle at Ruše. TO Captain First Class Milorad Popovič described the dramatic battle in the following report:

The war in the Republic of Slovenia broke out on Thursday 27 June 1991. At Šentilj the YNA tanks fired on road blocks and the aircraft fired rockets on the barricades and on our positions. An armoured column broke through the barricade at Ruše and continued towards Koroška. One of the self-propelled guns carrying a 90

166

mm cannon and armed was stopped at the bridge in Ruše. During the afternoon, negotiations began on the surrender of the crew along with their weapons. The YNA sent reinforcements from Franc Rozman Stane barracks to assist the beleaguered crew, including a reconnaissance unit, military police unit and two T-55 tanks.

All together there were 25 armed soldiers. On 27 June 1991 at approximately 19.00 this column was stopped at the road block at Limbuš. During the night three YNA soldiers escaped through a nearby farm house.

On 28th June at 6.30 the commanding officer of the Maribor regional TO headquarters ordered the nearest TO unit to surround the column and demand its surrender. At 9.00 the TO unit commander reported that the YNA unit refused to surrender and was threatening to open fire. We were undecided because of the possible danger of a large explosion and the unfavourable balance of power.

At 10.00 the commanding officer of the regional TO headquarters gave me a brief assignment: A PDD (anti-commando) squad from Ruše would be waiting at Limbuš. When you make contact take over command and take up battle positions; assess the situation and if possible attack and destroy both tanks.

I immediately made a plan of the assigned task; there was no time to prepare documentation. I called my father in-law who lived nearby to provide me with detailed information on the YNA positions and on what the soldiers were doing. At the same time I armed myself with a revolver, a Manlicher sniper rifle and a PRG-22 anti-tank gun. It took me twenty minutes to by-pass all the barricades and get to Limbuš. When I arrived I still could not spot the YNA unit. I sent two civilians to warn the residents and evacuate the houses in the vicinity of the enemy target. I told the people who were gathering to take cover and call ambulances because of the ensuing armed attack. In the meantime the commando squad from Ruše arrived on the scene. I was relieved because I knew most of them personally. I explained why they had been called in and that they should prepare for battle. No one had any questions. I divided the men into sections in perfect silence. The time was 10.50. I made a final check of the arrangements and could not notice anything which I might have forgotten. We were about 70 meters away from the YNA target, separated from it by fences and back yards. The first fence had to be taken down and from then on we proceeded unimpeded. Within fifteen minutes we had reached our attack positions. I sent one of the sections to the barricade. We had to prevent the enemy cutting us off from the road leading towards Ruše. The anti-tank squad consisted of two men carrying hand-held rocket launchers, two men with automatic guns and a commanding officer. I moved into position above the road. I decided to command both squads directly. I had one of the rocket launchers trained on the left of the first tank with orders to shoot at the tank's engine. The second one I positioned directly facing the second tank and ordered it to be aimed at the tank's turret. I remained approximately 70 m back from the enemy tanks. After breaking off negotiations I ordered everyone to be ready to fire. The tanks began to move, looking for a target. I immediately had to give the order to fire so as not to lose the advantage in our position. The decision was difficult. A direct hit on a tank means a detonation of 80 grenades – there would be casualties on both sides. I heard the sound of the sirens from the approaching ambulances. I looked around and saw everyone waiting for my order. I must act, this was a historical moment for Slovenia. Not to act now would be a historic error. I managed to get above the deafening rattle of the tank engines with a loud shout of "fire". Both squads immediately fired their rockets. The first tank went quiet, the crew stumbled out and ran for cover. The sound from automatic weapons dispelled the feeling of uncertainty. The battle had begun. I made my contribution using my

167

sniper gun. I aimed at the helmets lying in shelter. I was looking for the yellow insignia worn by the commanding officer. If I was to put him out of commission the battle would perhaps end sooner. I exchanged my bullet clip and looked around the battle field.

The second tank was moving closer, firing its machine gun. The nearest man with a rocket launcher was looking at it without firing. Two rockets ricocheted off the tank's turret. I had to incapacitate it before it had a chance to launch a grenade. The turret slowly turned towards me. Heat, a dry mouth, the heavy sound of gun fire...it demanded quick action. I was familiar with the weapon only theoretically. I opened up the RPG-22, armed it and raised the sight. "I must hit it. I should aim for the tank's turret, not its mid-section". I aimed just below the antenna and squeezed the trigger. The blast was deafening – I had forgotten the ear plugs. A rocket was also fired from another side. The turret was momentarily engulfed in smoke – the tank stopped moving. The firing ceased. My head hurt, I could not feel the right side of my face and was momentarily completely deaf. The dizziness passed shortly. Sweat was running down my back. I waited for the tank to explode. Nothing happened. I shouted: "Surrender, stop the engines, cease firing!" Two to three minutes passed after which a white T-shirt appeared. The battle was over. All that remained to do was to secure the area, collect the arms and assist one of the wounded. The commanding officer, Captain Blagojević, was wounded in the left arm. A soldier brought me his gun. The ambulance took him to hospital. A jubilant atmosphere ensued among the soldiers, the press and the local people; it was only disturbed by the announcement of the arriving helicopters. The time was 11.30 on 28 June 1991.

Due to the seriousness of the situation the Presidency of the Republic also met on the second day, adopting the following decisions:

PRESIDENCY OF THE REPUBLIC OF SLOVENIA
No.: 800-03-02/91
Ljubljana, 28 June 1991

CONCLUSIONS AND RESOLUTIONS OF THE 45TH SESSION
OF THE PRESIDENCY OF THE REPUBLIC OF SLOVENIA
– DATED 28 JUNE 1991

The Presidency of the Republic of Slovenia has in its 45th session, in the presence of the President of the Assembly of the Republic of Slovenia Dr France Bučar, the Prime Minister of the Republic of Slovenia Lojze Peterle, a member of the SFRY Presidency Dr Janez Drnovšek, Republic secretaries Dr Dimitrij Rupel, Igor Bavčar, Janez Janša and Jelko Kacin, acting commander of the Republic Headquarters of the Territorial Defence Janez Slapar and the commanding officer of the Civil Defence of the Republic of Slovenia Miran Bogataj, reviewed the current military situation in Slovenia, the consequences of the brutal bombardment of civilian and military targets and other consequences of the aggression of the Yugoslav Army on the Republic of Slovenia, and debated the latest international attempts to stop the aggression.

The Presidency also discussed the contents of the telex which was this morning sent to Lojze Peterle by the Commander of the 5th Army District, Colonel-General Konrad Kolšek. In it Kolšek repeated the threat that unless the TO and the police of the Republic of Slovenia immediately cease endangering the lives of Yugoslav Army soldiers, the YNA would be forced to utilise all its available fire power. He also wrote that the YNA units had not at any time used force other than in self-defence.

The Presidency of the Republic of Slovenia expressed its deep regret for all the casualties that were the consequence of the aggression by the Yugoslav Army, particularly the deaths of those YNA officers and soldiers of Slovenian nationality. In connection with the downing of the YNA helicopter, when its pilot Captain First Class Anton Merlak lost his life, the Presidency emphasised that this occurred ten hours after an official announcement by which the Presidency of the Republic of Slovenia, on the basis of article 14 of the Constitutional Act related to the Founding Charter on the Independence of the Republic of Slovenia (Official Gazette of the RS, No. 191) recalled all Slovenian officers and civilians serving in the Yugoslav armed forces.

Based on the reports provided by the Coordination Group and the evaluation of the possible turn of events, the Presidency adopted the following measures:

1. In view of the real danger from air attacks on inhabited areas and military targets it adopted measures for the protection and rescue of the population, and material and other property.

2. It authorised the Prime Minister Lojze Peterle to send a reply to the commanding officer of the 5th Army District Colonel-General Konrad Kolšek saying that it was the YNA which had begun military operations in the territory of an independent and sovereign Slovenia, that Slovenia was only acting in self defence and that all responsibility for the violence and human casualties fell on the aggressor.

3. It was decided that the Republic of Slovenia should immediately set up a commission to assess the war damage and other consequences of the aggressor's activities. The Presidency invited the assistance of Slovenian citizens, especially in the provision of relevant data.

4. The Presidency again called on all officers and enlisted soldiers serving in the YNA not to take part in the aggression against the RS and to leave their YNA units. The Presidency hoped that the officers and soldiers who were citizens of other republics, would no longer follow orders which through military force threatened the sovereignty of the Republic of Slovenia.

5. The proposal that the President of the Presidency of RS, Milan Kučan, meet with the three foreign ministers, who would that afternoon arrive in Belgrade as representatives of the European Twelve was met with approval, but due to the intensity of the fighting and air attacks the President would be unable to leave for Belgrade. In this regard the Presidency stressed that there can be no negotiations based on the assumption that it was a case of civil war and that the adopted constitutional acts regarding the sovereignty of RS be suspended.

6. The Presidency of RS on the basis of article 75 of the Law on Defence and Security (Official Gazette of RS, No. 15/91) ordered military conscription into the TO of RS to the degree necessary for the defence of the sovereignty of the RS and in this regard authorised the commanding officer of the RHQ TO to determine the types of units and the numbers of conscripts required.

7. The Presidency of the RS concluded that there was no need to declare a state of war or a state of emergency because yesterday, 27 June 1991, in the early hours the YNA began military activities on the territory of RS which represent an act of aggression of the YNA and an attempt at permanent occupation of the RS.

8. The Presidency of the RS, in accordance with the opinion expressed by the Supreme Court of the RS determined that there was no need for the setting up of TO military tribunals and that in all cases where the aggressor had, through military

169

activity committed a criminal offence, be tried by the existing regular courts of justice and public prosecutors according to standard procedures.

9. It was also agreed that the competent authorities should forthwith begin legal proceedings against officers and other YNA members suspected of committing unlawful acts, especially against those who are citizens of the RS.

10. The RS secretariat for international cooperation should inform all Slovenian representatives at the Federal Secretariat for Foreign Affairs that from this day they were serving as the representatives of Slovenia within the Yugoslav missions, except of course where they were not allowed to do so. In the latter event they should remain at their present posts and act on instructions from the RS authorities.

11. The Presidency of RS recommended that the Executive Council of the RS evaluate the economic situation and adopt urgent measures for the protection and advancement of economic activities.

12. At this meeting it was also decided that all the legal acts which were essential for defence, security and other activities should, by the next session of the Assembly which was expected to be held on Monday, 1 July 1991, be adopted by the Presidency of RS.

During the meeting of the Presidency I was called away to the emergency telephone which was in Mr Kučan's office. As I waited for the connection I noticed lying on his table a copy of an article entitled "Declaration of War!", published in the current edition of the Neodvisni Dnevnik newspaper. Certain passages were underlined and on reading them I could not believe that in the middle of a war which was forced on us anyone could write against the right to self-defence. Later I asked Kučan what was behind it but he only shrugged his shoulders in reply.

It is true that in Slovenia, apart from the existing political differences mentioned in earlier pages which were expressed in parliament against the movement for independence, there was also substantial opposition to it from the moment more decisive steps were taken towards the achievement of independence and sovereignty, not only disagreement with the method but also with its substance. Such opposition is only legitimate up to a point but not after it turns into blatant collaboration and support for those who try through force or undemocratic means to stand against the freely expressed will of the people or the electorate.

In its essence, democracy presupposes a minority opinion and when it is a question of democratic decision-making the minority opinion must represent an adequate insurance, otherwise democracy is transformed into a dictatorship. Although the decisions which were adopted through a democratic process (constitutional or legal acts) apply to everyone alike, all those who voted differently should not be persecuted in any way, even if it is a question of such a grave decision as was the Slovenian plebiscite held on 23 December 1990. In such decisive moments the minority must not be repressed when defending its opinions through the media, in parliament or through other legitimate political instruments. One crosses the Rubicon only through violent acts against legal and legitimate decisions or when engaged in terrorist activities or blatant wartime collaboration with the enemy.

During the rather sensitive and unstable period which we lived through during the past few years, especially from the plebiscite until the end of the Brioni moratorium, political freedom in Slovenia, despite the many dangers we faced, was not threatened for a single moment. Our progress towards independence and statehood must surely be unique since even in wartime not a single measure was imposed whereby the status nor the rights of an individual were infringed.

All of the European states which we took as our example, not to mention Israel, our neighbouring Croatia or any other state which was created during the latter half of this century, passed through a period when everything, including individual rights and freedoms, not to mention broader political freedom, was subordinated to a single objective – the state and human survival. Slovenia on the other hand did not adopt a single legal act which restricted human rights. In the midst of the fiercest battles a session of the National Assembly was called, even though the constitution provided the legal basis whereby the Presidency could take all the necessary decisions in its place. We did not impose censorship even after some of the news reports disclosed the dispositions of our defence forces. We did not set up military tribunals. None of the pro-Yugoslav political parties were prohibited, not even the Communist Party – The Movement for Yugoslavia which openly supported the armed aggression against Slovenia. Some will perhaps say that there was no time for this but that is not true. On the first day of the war the Presidency considered such measures but what might seem to some as illogical, on the proposal made by the Ministry of Defence and the Supreme Court, it was unanimously decided that despite the state of war no military courts would be established and no decrees adopted that would replace the existing civil laws.

It was not an easy decision since the peace-time legislation does not foresee circumstances which arise and must be dealt with every day during a war situation. Let us consider the case of the prisoners of war for example. In this regard and for some other issues we found a Solomon-like solution since we decided to rely directly on international conventions.

We survived and won the war without changing the system. After the war or the Brioni declaration the whole of Slovenian society returned to a peace-time life style without the difficulties which are usual for such a transitional period. Overnight the old issues became current, such as privatisation, denationalisation and even demilitarisation. This was possible primarily because of the short duration of the war and relatively low price which had to be paid. Another reason for this is that there was no need for authority to be transferred from a provisional government to peace-time institutions. The Republic Coordination Group which during the war held enormous power made a strict distinction between political and military decisions. Considering the strained circumstances, occasional frictions did arise but only at those times when it was not objectively possible to harmonise two points of view or when due to the intense activity there was no time to bring one or the other type of decision into line with the development of events.

Recently Slovenian journalism was confronted with two important tests. The first was during the trial of the Four in the summer of 1988, when it gained broader freedom of speech considering that it still operated within a one-party system, and the second during the 1991 June-July war, when the uncensored reporting of journalists and editors surpassed even the most effective of professional censorship. It is thus not surprising that many foreign diplomats and especially the American administration rightfully noted that during the war we had a large propaganda corps which were involved in psychological and propaganda warfare and which through the media portrayed a war that in reality was not a real war at all. Such an assessment was certainly not only due to injured pride because the events in Yugoslavia did not follow the course outlined by the great powers but was also a reflection of a conviction that through the form of a peace-time political system and particularly without media censorship it was impossible to wage a successful war (the Falklands, Desert Storm – in both cases strong censorship was imposed by both sides). In this respect our experience is certainly an interesting subject of study for the military analysts who will have to abandon some of their hitherto generally accepted convictions or at least consider them as relative.

Even under ideal conditions, however, there must be exceptions. One such conviction, which on the second day of the war many judged to have come close to national betrayal, was aroused by a circle centred around the Editor-in-Chief of the Neodvisni Dnevnik newspaper, Milan Meden. This "circle", with pro-Yugoslav orientations consisted of the members of the Communist Party of Yugoslavia – The Movement for Yugoslavia, as well as of the members of Marković's political party which in Slovenia acted under the wing of the Social Democratic Union Party. Milan Meden had for some time before maintained close ties with the army. In the days when tensions were high, he would make room for articles which were authored by KOS in the Ljubljana Army Corps and signed by Colonels Mihajlo Terzić and Jovan Miškov – without mention of their ranks, of course. In his editorials and commentaries Milan Meden challenged many operations that were implemented and which in practice proved to reinforce Slovenian independence. This is not an illegal act in a democratic country. It raised public controversy which would have ended or continued as long as circumstances did not take a turn for the worse. A Dnevnik photographer was given the task of finding and photographing a drunk TO soldier but refused to carry out the assignment. A few days prior to the declaration of independence Dnevnik published a short article that was signed under the pseudonym F.W. Dornseiff in which the author quoted Stalin: "Intelligence of small nations is the greatest misfortune of today's civilisation."

As it got closer to 26 June, the opposition from some of Dnevnik's editors, columnists and collaborators increased. In the 20 May 1991 edition of Dnevnik, Milan Meden defended Veljko Kadijević himself by writing that "in all of this no one is surprised by the restrained conduct of Veljko Kadijević, the Federal Secretary for National Defence, who is disconcerted neither by the non-existent Federal Presidency nor the Federal Government and even less by the politics of gentility that consider the armed forces to be the root of all evil."

On 24 June he sheds a tear for Yugoslavia and writes "history will certainly not be kind to those who portrayed it wearing an ugly face."

On the second day of the war, 28 June, at a time when it was a matter of life or death, Meden wrote an editorial in Dnevnik entitled "Warriors" in which he accused all those who were fighting of being against "the principle of free choice".

More forceful than Meden's editorials were the commentaries written under the pseudonym of Veno Karbone. On 24 June, two days before war broke out, the brave man hiding behind this pen name wrote that "the Territorial Defence forces are transforming into some kind of defending brotherhood, adorned with peculiar insignia, designed by Janez Švajncer and are at this moment their own worst enemy... Although this may sound paradoxical, the Yugoslav economic area will for some time to come be the most effective mitigator of Slovenian economic difficulties."

After the declaration of independence, in the 27 June edition of Dnevnik, published on the first day of the war, this same author mourned the loss of mother Yugoslavia, saying "all of us who in our hearts said our last farewells to Yugoslavia must now say good-bye to peace."

The following day and in line with the editorial by Milan Meden, Dnevnik published his column entitled "Declaration of War!", which by coincidence I happened to see on Kučan's desk, which caused bitter public reactions, as well as among the people who for two days had fought for life or death against the aggression. Veno Karbone wrote: "A different outcome was not possible, too many mistakes were made through wanton impatience. This had to happen! And we all knew it would happen!... I never imagined that our President, who through his words and actions proved that he was above party politics, a whole-hearted Slovenian and above all peace-loving, would be forced into the position of calling on the use of arms. In the same way I have not even in my dreams seen an officer of the Territorial Defence amusing the people with his sword."

It was a cause of much conjecture who was hiding behind the pseudonym of Veno Karbone, and the majority believed that it was Milan Meden in disguise, used when stating things that were even too pungent for his own taste. Some argued that it was a pseudonym for Branko Ziherl, a former member of UDBA, the old Yugoslav secret police and afterwards an editor at Dnevnik. The price for publishing "The Declaration of War!" was paid by Milan Meden who, due to pressure exerted by his own colleagues, had to resign. Most of the journalists, photographers and others employed at Dnevnik did not agree with the conduct of Meden and his supporters. Despite his resignation Meden and his circle retained a strong influence in this newspaper.

Later some people concluded that the style of the commentaries written under the pseudonym Veno Karbone, which included some dealing with economic issues, was surprisingly similar to the style used by Neven Borak, the son of the retired YNA officer and adviser to the Presidency of the Republic of Slovenia.

By 17.00 on 28 June, the time when I was leaving for the news conference, we already held seven of the border posts while the number of captured YNA soldiers had doubled. But the main operations were still to follow.

From the early morning we had been receiving reports from the Koroška region describing the battle for the border crossing at Holmec and the neighbouring border post. The commander of the first company of the 62nd TO detachment described the combat in his report:

"Our company was mobilised on the night between 24 and 25 June at Kotlje. On 25 June we moved into the Dravograd area where we secured the routes of communication. At midnight we received written orders from the regional TO headquarters and proceeded to the area of the Holmec border crossing. Our orders were to organise a circular defence and to assist the units of the border police in case they were attacked by the YNA. We arrived at Holmec on 26 June at 4.00 a.m. That day we organised a circular defence, set up patrols over a wide area, but kept out of the agreed 1000 meter belt which was at that time still under the control of the YNA border guards. We established contact with one of the border police units stationed at Holmec but nothing of significance took place on Wednesday. On Thursday afternoon around 15.30 we got information that a helicopter was heading our way but we were ordered only to observe and take cover. The helicopter landed at the border crossing and we saw two YNA officers step out. Later we found out that one of them was a lieutenant who later started the attack on the Holmec border crossing. At approximately 16.30 we received a call from our people at the border crossing informing us of an ultimatum demanding that they had to leave the area within fifteen minutes or be attacked. We immediately reacted and surrounded the area. While setting up the blockade we realised that the YNA organised the defence so that the farm house, belonging to farmer Kralj, and the road from which they probably expected to get support was behind them. Our company took positions approximately 200 m from the border crossing. At 17.00 a grenade was fired and landed close to the border crossing. This time we returned fire. The firing lasted about one hour and fifty minutes with short pauses. All this time the border crossing was open to civilian traffic. Immediately after the shooting began we noticed an Austrian helicopter circling above the Austrian side of the border. We were incapable of taking the guard post but we did force the YNA to stop firing at the border crossing itself. During the night we continued patrolling the wider area of the border crossing. In the meantime the Slovenj Gradec police station inspector Halilović arrived at the border crossing. With his assistance we found a possible way of securing or even taking control of the crossing, provided that we were supplied with additional men and weapons. In our first encounter with the YNA we did not suffer any casualties. At 21.00 Halilović arrived with a radio transmitter and another policeman. Around midnight we expected a call from our positions at Kralj's farm house where additional units were already waiting and where we were to make plans for the attack which was to commence on 28 June at 4.00 hours. After the first armed encounter we were now familiar with how the YNA units were positioned at the crossing. The bunker located to the left of the crossing, from where we were fiercely attacked on 27 June and were prevented from taking control of the area below the railway line, presented a problem. During the night between 27 and 28 June all of the commanders and members of the police met at Poljana. We agreed on a plan of action. We postponed the start of the attack until 5.00 because we were afraid to move our units since we did not know how much territory the YNA was controlling. At 4.00 we got our orders and we immediately proceeded to form mixed companies because some of the men were more familiar with the terrain than others. One section was sent towards Reht with the task of attacking the bunker from behind and securing the Reht-Holmec route in case a YNA unit patrolled this area. The Reht crossing was blocked by our mountain regiment. The second group headed in the direction of Gulak's farm house with the task of setting up a blockade and thus protecting its back in case the YNA soldiers attacked or patrolled the area from the direction of the Sonjak guard post. The main segment of our company attacked along the left and right side of the road. Those that were on the left side at the Hauser farm house joined in the attack only after we knew what had happened to the bunker in the forest. The attack began on 28 June at 5.30, immediately after the bus took workers to the valley below. At that time the first shot was fired from the guard post and the main section of our company returned fire. The battle lasted until 7.00. At 6.30 the first ambulances started to drive away the wounded YNA soldiers at which time we ordered a cease-fire. Most of the wounded and dead were suffered by the YNA in the area in front of the group of houses facing Kralj's farmhouse. A little after 7.00, farmer Vušnik came running towards us saying that on the upper positions the situation was grave and bloody and suggested we should start negotiating with the other side. I agreed and he took the short cut to the guard post (he was the closest neighbour to the guard post) and later informed us that a cease-fire should take effect at 8.00 so that the YNA could assist their wounded and establish contact with their command headquarters to arrange for the negotiations. We waited until 8.10 for their reply. In the meantime they removed all their dead and wounded from the frontal positions but they were still not prepared to negotiate.

To our surprise the ambulances first took away their wounded soldiers before they took ours even though we had called for emergency assistance before the YNA did. I heard this over the radio link with the border police. We had great difficulty in keeping in contact with our units because we lacked radio communications and could only rely on messages sent by courier which due to the impassable mountainous terrain posed the danger that we would start killing our own troops. At 10.30 the first group of YNA soldiers surrendered. As we were later told by the officer in command of the guard post, they could only do this after the lieutenant escaped. Before his escape he allegedly shot one of the soldiers in the back because he attempted to surrender. It is sad that the YNA officer tried to maintain the morale of his soldiers in this way and at the same time expected of them to defend the guard post and attack the border police units and the border crossing itself. The second large group of YNA soldiers surrendered at 13.30. They sought refuge at the farm close to the Austrian border. When we established contact with the farmer he told us that all of the soldiers were in his basement, that they had left their weapons in front of the house and that they wished to surrender. After a thorough search of the area we took all of the soldiers to Kralj's farmhouse. At 14.30 two of our commanders entered the guard post, followed by the policemen who inspected the installation. Afterwards we were criticised for leaving the captured weapons behind. Allow me to explain why we did not first collect these weapons. When the soldiers were surrendering they left their weapons at their former positions. We began collecting them after 15.00 hours because our primary duty was first to thoroughly inspect the surrounding area for any remaining soldiers that had stayed in hiding since we did not know precisely how many soldiers were in the guard post originally or how many were wounded or dead. The danger existed that some of them were still hiding and could attack us. At 19.00, after we collected all of the armaments, we raised a Slovenian flag on top of the guard post. We were proud that we had taken it over. We left one of the regiments at the Holmec guard post and additionally reinforced its protection because we feared another attack from the YNA. The second regiment led by Pogorevčnik headed for the Sonjak guard post where the YNA soldiers surrendered without a fight at 16.00. None of the YNA officers were there, as they had all fled to the Strojna guard post. On 29 June we proceeded to blockade the Strojna guard post. Lieutenant Dragan from the Holmec guard post was already here, and he prevented the soldiers from surrendering. As we later learned from a subaltern, the lieutenant arrived at Strojna very tired and hungry, saying that this post would be defended until the last drop of blood. The subaltern and soldiers wished to surrender but they were afraid of the lieutenant. The subaltern therefore recommended that Dragan go out and check whether the troops were holding up in their trenches. There he encountered our own troops and had to surrender. All of the others then surrendered without a fight. We also secured this guard post and like all the others held it until the signing of the Brioni declaration and the subsequent demobilisation.

Because this was not a standard type of attack formation, since we were all in the front lines, I cannot single out any particular soldier. We did not have any wounded or dead (one of us suffered light injuries from a fall), while the border police suffered two casualties. Although I suggested to Halilović that his unit withdraw from the border area and join our forces, he remained holding his ground. Five members of the border police were among the main section of our company – four machine guns and a marksman. I must emphasise that our conscripts exhibited a great amount of patience which was important since we had to act gradually and effectively and not quickly and emotionally. Since we had the protection of anti-aircraft guns we felt secure and were in no hurry. We could have proceeded quickly but in my opinion this would have caused many more casualties on both sides.

According to unofficial information the YNA had 13 dead and 14 wounded. All of them were young soldiers ranging from 16 to 18 years of age. Three of them were Slovenians.

At the press conference, which I wished to end as quickly as possible so I could return to the operations headquarters, but where on this and all other occasions I was prevented from so doing, I tried to explain to the press the presupposition of the battle plan "Okop". The foreign journalists in particular were noticeably surprised over the stereotypes which were still deeply rooted within the ideology of the Yugoslav army. The catchphrase "tank communism" was after this press conference used to a much greater extent when referring to the nature of the Belgrade authorities.

After I returned to the operations headquarters I learned of the two Austrians who were killed at Brnik airport. During the withdrawal of the YNA from Slovenia via Koper we seized a report made by the commander of the tank battalion Danilo Radovanović describing the event.

The NCO who was given the task of monitoring the landing strip informed Radovanović that a field vehicle was heading in their direction. According to the report it had the appearance of a military vehicle carrying rocket launchers. He gave the order to fire and second lieutenant Stanko

Ignjatović released a burst of explosive bullets from his 12.7 mm anti-aircraft gun. The vehicle caught fire instantly. Radovanović explains the fire as proof that the vehicle was carrying tanks of fuel with the intention of incinerating his troops.

The report was written by Radovanović after he got back to the Vrhnika barracks when he already knew that the vehicle was neither equipped with rocket launchers or tanks of gasoline but carried two Austrian journalists. In addition, a professional who had at his disposal all the latest optical equipment for day or night surveillance should have been able to observe that the jeep was not a military but a civilian vehicle.

In the afternoon Milan Kučan talked with Stane Brovet and the first proposal for a cease-fire which was to take effect at 21.00 was made. We were to negotiate the conditions with the 5th Army District but when I received a call from Andrija Rašeta an hour later I could tell that the YNA was not prepared for any kind of compromise and that it still counted on crushing us by force. Their readiness to negotiate was their idea intended to blind the international community, which was exerting strong pressure on Belgrade, and throw sand in our eyes. Rašeta demanded that we allow all military columns a safe passage in any direction they choose and that we immediately stop all military operations, which of course meant that we were to stop defending ourselves. Despite this we agreed on the cease-fire to take effect at 21.00 under the condition that the opposing side followed suit.

Many believed that the premature cease-fire could do us more harm than good. We had only just managed to relieve the pressure and achieve our first successes. Stopping military activities at a time when one has gained an advantage can only favour the other side. In case negotiations got under way our diplomatic arguments were still an open question, but many of us believed that these would to a large extent depend on the balance of power in the field, which later proved to be the case. We were reminded of similar cases in the history of warfare whereby when any side gave up the advantage it gained in the field, it never regained the strategic advantage again. Long after World War II it was still debated whether Hitler, by explicitly forbidding the advance of his forces across the Lens-Gravelines line during the invasion of France, unnecessarily allowed the retreat of the British forces over the Channel and thus prevented the destruction of the core of the forces which later in 1944 participated in the Normandy invasion and sealed the fate of the Third Reich.

Meanwhile the fighting continued. At 18.25 our forces attacked the Rožna Dolina border crossing at Nova Gorica and took control of it, destroying three T-55 tanks, seizing three of them and more than 20 other vehicles and taking 98 YNA soldiers prisoner. Two YNA soldiers were killed and sixteen wounded. Our side had no casualties whatsoever, although some of the civilians who were observing the fighting at close range were also wounded. This was a great victory and was received at the operations headquarters with notable satisfaction because it meant that we were taking the initiative in all regions. Almost at the same time the TO unit from the 5th

PŠTO with the assistance of our counter-intelligence took control of the YNA communications monitoring centre in Ljubljana. The mission was accomplished without casualties. A great amount of recorded tapes and technical equipment was seized which proved that since the elections the YNA had eavesdropped on state authorities.

In the evening, YNA planes bombed Kočevska Reka thinking that the military and political leadership of Slovenia was hiding there, while we still met at the regular meeting halls and did not even move our headquarters to a protected shelter. Our security brigade, which in peace-time was stationed at Kočevska Reka, had not been there for some time. The command headquarters was located beside the operational headquarters and the security forces were on various duties. On this same day the security brigade performed its most significant mission. At 15.40 it seized a large army depot at Borovnica, capturing 32 soldiers and a second lieutenant who was wounded. More significant was the wealth of seized armaments consisting of more than 100 tons of explosives, guns and ammunition, grenade launchers, vehicles and other military equipment. During the next few days we distributed the seized supplies because we feared an air attack. But our fears were apparently unjustified since the YNA learned only after the war that the Borovnica depot had fallen into our hands. Tone Krkovič brought the captured soldiers from the depot directly to the Executive Council building. When I looked them over I saw young frightened faces of mainly Serbian soldiers. I told them that for them the war had ended and that they would be taken to the reception centre where they would be under the authority of the international Red Cross until the end of the war when they would be allowed to return home. Sighs of relief could be heard, some of them even smiled or muttered words of gratitude. They returned home much sooner than any of them expected. Unfortunately many of the captured soldiers who were returned after the cease-fire were later detained by the YNA military police and returned to the front lines.

In the afternoon we got a call from Ante Marković, who in the meantime had received considerable criticism from some dozen presidents of foreign countries because of the escalation of the conflict and his promise that he would "settle the issue of Slovenian secession in a matter of hours". He urged both sides to stop the fighting immediately. He did this prior to the arrival of the three European foreign ministers (De Michelis, Poos, Van den Broek), who flew to Belgrade that evening. A meeting with Slovenian representatives was also planned. Milan Kučan and Dimitrij Rupel left for Zagreb and met the Troika late that night. Also present at this meeting were the Federal Prime Minister Ante Marković and the Croatian President Franjo Tuđman. At that time Tuđman still acted as though he was the wise man and someone who was rescuing Slovenia from a muddle. The night was peaceful, but not the cease-fire, since the YNA continued to shell our positions with heavy artillery.

12. THE SECOND OFFENSIVE

SATURDAY, 29 JUNE

On the night from Friday to Saturday we were engaged in coordinating military and other activities as well as holding telephone conversations with Zagreb where Milan Kučan and Dimitrij Rupel were participating in negotiations. We were a bit worried how they would bear up under the pressure. Despite the subsequent criticism that they forfeited the plebiscite decision, at the operations headquarters we believed that the negotiated issues (end of hostilities, undefined postponement of the implementation of the constitutional charter on independence, reinstatement of a part of the SFRY Presidency) provided enough space for manouvering since during those days the actual military conditions and the balance of power in the field were much more significant. The circumstances faced by the blocked YNA in Slovenia were becoming similar to the circumstances faced by the French army in the battle for Dien Bien Phu, where elite French forces defended fortified bunkers but were entirely prevented from engaging in ground manoeuvres.

After the Zagreb meeting the radio began carrying reports of a "moratorium on the decisions adopted on 25 June" so we immediately sent detailed instructions to all our units regarding the new circumstances following negotiations with the European Troika and about our future actions. In the instructions we gave our interpretation of the negotiated agreement to give ourselves enough room in which to manoeuvre.

REPUBLICAN COORDINATION GROUP
No: 29
date: 29 June 1991

TO ALL SUB-GROUPS

Following the Zagreb negotiations held between the representatives of Slovenia, the three European ministers and the Prime Minister of the SFRY the situation is as follows:

1. Immediate halt of aggression on the RS; the end of hostilities by the YNA must be guaranteed by Prime Minister Marković.

2. Slovenia will not give up its achieved independence and sovereignty (border, customs, air traffic control administration), while other steps will be taken gradually.

179

3. Only the approved and supervised movements of supply and other YNA vehicles will be permitted; all YNA activities in the air will be considered to be a breach of the cease-fire; the blocked YNA units may return to their barracks only without the armoured or other vehicles which they must leave behind intact.

4. In respect of the above order 1.:

a) Every breach of the cease-fire must be neutralised (capture, destruction).

b) The situation within those military installations and in the field under YNA control must be supervised at all times.

c) Battle positions on the barricaded barracks and roads must be reinforced by all available heavy artillery. From the RHQ TO request all the required quantities of ammunition. If necessary the barricades should be mined.

d) Prevent the arrival of any additional YNA units to Slovenia.

e) The police authorities should detain any military personnel – YNA members – who are present in RS territory without a permit.

f) Prisoners of war should be treated strictly according to international conventions.

g) Prisoners of war may only be exchanged for captured members of the RS defence forces or those YNA soldiers of Slovenian nationality who are still serving in the YNA under duress. Prior to any exchanges or negotiations you should contact the Republic Coordination Group.

h) All the measures regarding the blockade (disconnection of infrastructures facilities) of the military installations remain in force.

i) Repair the captured military armoured vehicles, man and move them to appropriate positions. Mark them beforehand with clear TO markings.

j) The representatives of the OŠTO and the police force must be present at the funerals of TO and police force members; ensure that the commemorations are performed according to regulations.

k) Casualty reports should be sent regularly to the Republic Operations Group.

l) Medical assistance to those YNA members who are under the blockade should be offered in accordance with humanitarian principles.

m) Document (photo, video) all breaches of the cease-fire by the YNA.

n) Repeatedly call on YNA soldiers to defect and joint the TO. Offer guarantees of social and status rights in accordance with the law.

o) Conduct activities within your units in such a way that the troops will be rested and ready for battle.

p) Do not position your units at locations where they would be open to air attacks.

5. Despite the cease-fire the status of the YNA in Slovenia is clear, it is an invading force. In this regard perform all activities which are not specifically defined in section 4. When uncertain request instructions from the Republic Operations Group.

For the Coordination Group

Janez Slapar   Janez Janša   Igor Bavčar

In the morning the Presidency met in an extended session after Kučan and Rupel returned from Zagreb. Both of the negotiators complained about Tuđman's conduct and the somewhat firm attitudes of the Europeans. We reviewed the situation. Militarily we were already over the worst shocks. There was the danger of a second wave, which however could not have been stronger, and a danger from air attacks. We were apprehensive about the constant breaches of the cease-fire. The YNA acted as though it only applied to the Slovenian defence forces. We decided that Janez Drnovšek, Dimitrij Rupel and Lojze Peterle intensify the daily contacts with the prime and foreign ministers of the European countries, as well as with their presidents.

According to the agreement reached the day before Andrija Rašeta arrived in Ljubljana to finalise the conditions for a cease-fire. He was met at the border. His large retinue was refused entry so that he was brought safely to Ljubljana with only one of his assistants. Igor Bavčar and I received Rašeta on the second floor of the Ministry of Internal Affairs. Rašeta agreed that the conversation be recorded on video tape. His assistant was disarmed and waited under supervision in the hallway. The General's facial expression showed that his "two hours" dragged out substantially. Like the two of us he, too, perhaps had not had a night's sleep since the start of the war. I could not help myself but remind him of our telephone conversation of Monday. He could not find words in reply. He gave the impression of a man who still did not fully realise what had happened to him. He spoke like an automaton with a colourless voice. He proposed 12 points which should be contained in the cease-fire agreement. One of the essential points related to the lifting of the blockades around YNA installations and columns. 'On this particular point we could not come to an agreement because he was still defending the demand that the columns be allowed to move in any chosen direction, while our offer included only retreat without the military vehicles, since anything contrary to this would have presented too much of a threat to us.

The fact that their proposal was just an intrigue became clear the same day when the YNA, despite the termination of our offensive activities did not first pull back those columns or armoured units which were not under siege. The price the YNA paid for such an approach was that more and more of their soldiers defected to our side. The prisoners were thus becoming a great burden to our authorities. In the evening the YNA unit holding the Vrtojba border crossing surrendered. Five more tanks were seized. At the fuel depot at Mokronog an NCO, Dragomir Grujević, shot and wounded his commanding officer, who wanted to surrender, and threatened to blow up the depot. A few soldiers nevertheless escaped over the fence, while Grujević – threatening an ecological disaster – for a few days presented us with a delicate problem. The special police squad sent to the scene could not resolve the problem. For his "bravery" Veljko Kadijević promoted Grujević to the rank of lieutenant.

Meanwhile in Belgrade the attempt to elect Stipe Mesić did not succeed. On Belgrade TV the commander of the YNA counter-intelligence, Marko Negovanović, issued an ultimatum which was also sent in writing to our government and the Presidency. The ultimatum signed by Veljko Kadijević in practice demanded the capitulation of Slovenia and the retraction of the adopted decisions on sovereignty by 9 a.m. the following day.

That evening the parliament met in a closed session to discuss the plan

181

code named "Plebiscite"[1]. The atmosphere was special, almost solemn. The president, France Bučar, broke the statutory rule and allowed me to speak first. I described the situation exactly as I saw it without adding or concealing anything. I said that we would be able to survive militarily if there was political unity. I also commented on the 12 points proposed by General Rašeta as the conditions for a cease-fire which were in line with the ultimatum issued by Kadijević. My suggestion that we take a firm stand against them was taken into account by the members of parliament in their subsequent deliberations. Milan Kučan gave his account of the negotiations in Zagreb. I must admit that after my speech I dozed off and did not hear the other speakers. After all the sleepless nights I sometimes dozed of for a few seconds while standing up. Fortunately I was soon called to an emergency telephone when I was informed of the state of alert imposed at military airports and the start of the air strikes against Slovenia.

SUNDAY, 30 JUNE

The parliamentary session lasted until the early morning hours. The decisions adopted were positive, exhibiting an unequivocal desire for a peaceful resolution of the crisis but not at the expense of the basic decisions already reached regarding independence. Milan Kučan and Lojze Peterle had accordingly drawn up an eight-point reply to Kadijević's ultimatum. We finalised the reply at the morning meeting of the presidency and the government's war cabinet. During the night many reports cited take-offs of military aircraft. We were aware that some of them could be false but due to the lack of technical facilities for the control of our air space we could not do otherwise but to sound air raid alarms to protect the population. The parliamentary delegates also had to seek underground shelter and were informed to do so by President Milan Kučan himself who just happened to be the one answering my call in Bučar's office and was the first to be told of the impending air attacks. Numerous flights which caused disruption were not, however, made by attacking aircraft but by transport aircraft flying in special units from Serbia as part of the second wave of attack which the YNA intended to organise. After the first setback the Belgrade generals started to act under the belief in the proposition made by young Clausewitz that "in war it is absurd to act under the principle of moderation because war is an act of extreme violence." We could only hope that they would not deploy all of the available force which would have meant that they were no longer interested in invading Slovenia but rather in retaliation, thus causing for its own sake as much destruction as possible. We were taking a great risk.

The operations group was preparing all the necessary measures for protection and rescue in case the hostilities increased. The civil defence headquarters which was functioning well throughout the war emphasised some of the already adopted measures:

---

[1] The plan foresaw the calling of a parliamentary session under the state of emergency.

182

REPUBLICAN CIVIL DEFENCE HEADQUARTERS (RCDH)
date: 30 June 1991

TO ALL REGIONAL CIVIL DEFENCE HEADQUARTERS

1. Conduct basic preparations for sheltering the population.
2. Position visual observers so that the air raid warning can be triggered on time.
3. VOP (visual observation post) members must wear civil defence uniforms.
4. Warn the population of the impending air attack and double check all reports on incoming aircraft so as to prevent cases of panic among the population.
5. Issue preventive warnings or move the civilian population away from areas of military activity.

Commander of RCDH
Miran Bogataj

We expected that in case of repeated air strikes, when our forces and the civilian population would be in underground air shelters, the possibility existed that commando squads might be parachuted in. We decided to engage the land watch element of the National Defence to keep watch.

REPUBLIC OF SLOVENIA
Republic Coordination Group
No. 1339
Date: 30 June 1991

TO ALL UOLO

1. Immediately prepare to activate the National Defence in all local communities. Draw up lists, markings, plans for the protection of all vital facilities and territory. Engage civilians owning guns (hunters and others). The National Defence shall be activated if and when it becomes necessary.
2. Enhance the preparations for protection and rescue.
3. Enhance and increase the degree of permanent functioning of administrative bodies for the task of material and medical assistance to the TO and the civilian population.

For the Coordination Group
Janez Janša

Our reply did not seem to have satisfied the army leadership, which in those days independently – without Ante Marković, who was no longer needed – took far reaching steps. In the morning the flights continued. At around 9.00 the flights intensified and the air raid warning was sounded. The Operations Group was of the opinion that the YNA would not venture a mass destruction of civilian targets, since for one thing they would imperil. their own forces that were under siege (the generals were primarily worried about their billions of dollars worth of equipment), and for another they might trigger off international reaction that could have led to military intervention. Despite such logical conclusions we were uncertain whether the Belgrade generals still had the ability to make reasonable judgments. Even

183

greater apprehension in this respect was held by certain politicians and a section of the population who were now for the first time – and under the sound of the air raid sirens – under a direct threat.

Fear...It was present everywhere and in all of us who made crucial decisions. It was intensified by defeats and relieved by victories. On the first day of the war we were receiving telegrams of support as well as those urging us not to put up resistance. They were sent by people who did not believe in success or were not prepared to pay a high price which any war demands. Some of them were sent by the parents of the soldiers serving in the aggressor's army. How terrible must their predicament have been! In the face of the possible bombardment there was an increasing level of anxiety in those whose voices had at first betrayed no tremble of fear. The ventilation ducts from the underground shelter of Cankarjev Dom, where many took refuge that day, exuded fear.

When entering the operations headquarters one could not even in the worst of times sense the smell of fear or unease. But I would tell a lie if I was to say that there was no apprehension. It existed and was of two kinds. The first in reference to the consequences of war and the second against the fear which could have taken root in some of us. The people who worked within the Coordination Group were chosen for their unalterable belief in the plebiscite decision and in ultimate victory after we were forced to defend ourselves. All of us, however, were afraid of causing too many casualties and were several times on that edge when fear almost overtakes courage. We did not fear the moral principles of the people within the operations group, who did not have the power to decide between war and peace or a cease-fire. When Igor and I entered the operations room after returning from the meetings of the Presidency we would usually be greeted by an unusual silence. No one ever asked any questions. At one time they even left the telephones ringing for a time before answering. They only stared at us questioning: "Are we still holding up?" No one had the balance of power in mind. They were all familiar with it. They were apprehensive that we ourselves would give way to fear due to moral pressures, the "well-meaning" advice and the pressure coming from those who were even before the war demanding a quick and unilateral disarmament. "The only constant in war is change" said Sun Tzu, one of the first theoreticians of war. More than for war, this definition holds true for politics and public opinion. We were much more easily able to foresee the events in the battlefield than the reactions of politicians and the public.

We never informed our colleagues of the doubts and uncertainties which due to the difficult circumstances were expressed during the sessions of the highest body of the newly emerging Slovenian state. We never brought back the feelings of fear which were at times and in a grotesque manner personified by Ciril Zlobec. Almost always the moment of silence was immediately followed by action. First the short report from the duty officer on the latest dispatches followed by the urgent measures that had to be taken. Igor then usually proceeded to take care of the urgent matters while I would dictate the instructions that would be sent to the sub-groups regarding the new circumstances and the decisions taken by the supreme command. Janez Slapar or Danijel Kuzma would draft the orders for operations. Miran Bogataj would coordinate the measures of civil defence and civil protection. Meanwhile Jelko Kacin would already be informing the public of what it needed to be told.

Only on two occasions were we not convincing enough. The first was after the cease-fire when Danijel exclaimed: "But we only needed another 12 hours", and the second after we received an order from Brioni stating that we had to release all of the captured YNA officers, when we did not understand what had really taken place on that island. But on both of these occasions there was not a single instance of doubt that anyone would take decisions into his own hands. The discipline or trust exhibited was surprising. We always found a solution.

An all-out air attack never happened but in place of it some of the ground battles again flared up. The columns under siege attempted to break through the barricades, which we did not allow. The YNA commanders sometimes acted independently, attempting to reach their destination at all costs but without much success. Hour after hour more of the YNA soldiers surrendered. We began receiving disturbing reports, however, of the new formations which were preparing to attack Slovenia, namely the 32nd (Varaždin), the 10th (Zagreb) and 13th (Rijeka) Corps.

Later in the afternoon the Federal Prime Minister Ante Marković, the under-secretary of the Federal Secretariat of National Defence General Mićo Čusić and Admiral Stane Brovet arrived in Ljubljana. We did not accept Brovet as one of the negotiators, of which we had already informed Ante Marković in advance, but he did not comply with our demand. The police had instructions to refuse entry to Brovet at the border but due to a mistake he arrived with Marković nevertheless. His efforts were in vain because we could under no circumstances accept him as a negotiator, since he was considered by our people and especially by the TO members and the police as a national traitor of the first degree.

We reached an agreement on a cease-fire but due to the differences in opinion we could not agree on the how the army would withdraw to their barracks. While Mišo Čusić proposed that his units withdraw with their heavy armour, Bavčar and I defended our position saying that the soldiers should withdraw without arms and heavy artillery because any other way would be unacceptable, not simply for security reasons but also for technical reasons, given all the barricades and obstructions. The YNA negotiator did not accept this because he was not familiar with the existing circumstances on the barricades and because he was opposed to it in principle. We finally agreed that both sides would try to resolve the situation after the establishment of the inter-state commission and with the cooperation of international observers. Until then all attempted movements should be considered as breaches of the cease-fire.

As one of the conditions for the cease-fire Igor Bavčar and I demanded that the YNA aircraft do not operate within Slovenian air space, because we were not given any guarantees that they would not be used for attacks against civilian targets. Neither the YNA negotiator nor Ante Marković had the necessary authorisation to be able to agree to this point. Ante Marković admitted that he no longer had any influence on Veljko Kadijević, which was to be expected. The army had got from Marković what it wanted, formal authorisation for military action in Slovenia, but now that he was no longer needed was now simply redundant.

In the evening Milan Kučan and Dimitrij Rupel again went to Zagreb for talks with the EC representatives. This time the EC delegation was led by the Dutch foreign minister Hans Van den Broek who then – and later – proved to be antagonistic towards Slovenia. After this round of talks the situation was unchanged but they were at least a prelude to the subsequent Brioni agreement. The status of the YNA in Slovenia, which we held in total blockade, still remained a point of dispute. We held the blocked YNA units hostage in case of any further air attacks. In any case, this kind of strategy (blockade instead of destruction), excluding the fact that time was on our side, had in the long-term almost identical results to the destruction of the enemy but with incomparably fewer casualties on both sides. If we loosened our grip we would no longer have any guarantees against the aggressor's renewed attacks which would be more effective because the aggressor would have learned from his mistakes. I still cannot believe that this simple but essential point, which even the commanders of our armed forces could understand, could not be grasped by some of our politicians who were constantly expressing doubts about whether our side was rather over-antagonistic. At the following day's session of the state presidency such views seemed to the majority quite logical, but when within 24 hours the YNA attacked again along with the air force, some more loudly, and others more quietly, began to change their opinion.

MONDAY, 1 JULY

The commanding officers of the YNA forces under siege in the barracks faced increasing difficulties from hour to hour. Almost all soldiers of Slovenian, Croatian and Albanian nationality had already defected. There was strife among the officers. Despite strict disciplinary measures and shots at the backs of the fleeing soldiers, discipline was breaking down rapidly. From the loudspeakers which our troops and information centres had placed in front of the barracks we called on the other side to hold the cease-fire and read out the constitutional guarantees of their rights, in case they decided to join the TO, as well as the proclamations of the Presidency and the Republic Secretariat of Defence.

A little after 3.30 a massive explosion destroyed the TO arms depot at Črni Vrh. Our units arrived too late. While at some locations they successfully took control of the more heavily guarded depots and other facilities by the second day of the war, in this case there was way too much hesitation and unprofessionalism.

From the early evening hours General Rašeta kept calling with a demand that we remove the road blocks and was particularly concerned about the column which had come from Karlovac and essentially began the aggression against Slovenia. Meanwhile Major Boško Prodanovič, commanding officer of the blocked LPA (light anti-aircraft) battery of armoured vehicles at Medvedjek, had succeeded under cover of darkness in digging a path from the main highway to a side road and rapidly made his way towards Cerklje. When we learned of the break out I immediately called Albin Gutman, commander of the Dolenjska regional TO headquarters. From his voice I could sense his exhaustion but he nevertheless promised that his men would stop the column at the most appropriate location. It was very important that it did not make its way to Cerklje where our units were surrounding the military airport and to Krško, where they were protecting the nuclear power station because an attack with strong fire power from behind it could have caused great chaos and many casualties.

Our forces placed barricades on side roads and diverted the column along the main road towards Krakovo Forest. Before 4.00 the column was blocked in Krakovo Forest from both sides and surrounded by the TO under the command of Captain Mitja Teropšič. The crew of the first tank surrendered immediately. Andrija Rašeta called again demanding that we let the column through the forest. It seemed unusual that they should have been concerned with just one of the columns, and it seemed clear to us that it was due to some friendship or family ties between the officers in the column and some top ranking general. I was also called by colonel Bajić from the headquarters of the 5th Airborne Corps. He tried to talk down to me as though he was in total control of the situation and demanded the disbanding of all the anti-aircraft defence units in the territory of Slovenia. When I in turn requested that air attacks and the violations of our air space should stop, he replied that Slovenia did not have its own air space and that his forces were merely defending the "free Yugoslav skies". Our conversation ended without results but during the future calls he was either calmer or frenzied but never again entered into a political discussion

The situation at border crossings of the Republic of Slovenia as of 1 July 1991 at 8.00 was as follows:

BORDER CROSSING	OPEN	CLOSED
1. Koper district		
Lazaret	–	
Škofije	–	
Fernetiči	–	
Lipica	–	
Sežana rail station	–	
Kozina	–	

Piran, Izola, Koper		– maritime traffic operating
2. Gorica district:		
Vrtojba	–	
Rožna dolina	–	
Robič	–	
Učeja	–	
Predel	–	
3. Kranj district:		
Jesenice rail border crossing	–	
Jezersko	–	
Korensko sedlo		–
Rateče		–
Karawanken		–
Ljubelj		–
4. Slovenj Gradec district:		
Vič	–	
Radlje	–	
Libeliče	–	
Mežica	–	
Holmec		–
5. Maribor district:		
Šentilj	–	
Jurij	–	
Maribor rail station	–	
Trate		–
6. Murska Sobota district:		
Gederovci	–	
Kuzma	–	
Gornja Radgona		–
Hodoš, Dolga Vas		

On this day the commander of the 5th Army District, Konrad Kolšek was replaced by Života Avramović, who had until then been the commander of the 3rd Army District. When we received the news of the replacement it was understood almost as a new declaration of war. Života Avramović was known as the general who had occupied Kosovo, nick-named the "Kosovo Pacifier". Before that he was called "the iceman", meaning that he was an uncompromising extremist.

The YNA violated the cease-fire every day. Helicopters marked with the red cross were being used to bring in reinforcements. Towards the evening flights by the Yugoslav Air Force became more frequent. The surrender of the guard posts where the soldiers were cut off from information and tired of waiting for assistance from Belgrade were continuing even though no one was attacking them. After each passing hour we were controlling additional tens of kilometres of our border. The stocks of infantry and artillery weapons were also growing larger by the hour. Both of the Štajerska regions faced difficulties regarding prisoners of war whom they could not accommodate in adequate numbers. Many who wished were given civilian clothes and money for the train ticket home.

Towards the evening Belgrade sent a new ultimatum to Ljubljana. The second phase of the army's attempt to subdue Slovenia by force was in preparation. Janez Drnovšek, Milan Kučan, Dimitrij Rupel and Lojze Peterle devoted great efforts towards convincing foreign ministers, prime ministers and other party leaders from the European countries to finally stop giving support to the idea of a unified Yugoslavia since it was their support that was one of the basic motives for the aggression against Slovenia. During this phase Hans-Dietrich Genscher strongly supported our cause. Some of the second-division politicians were already becoming uncertain. A different kind of notion began circulating, namely that the Slovenian leadership was composed of hawks and doves and that Igor Bavčar and I were conducting an extremely tough policy towards the army. Such interpretations were unfavourable to us because they reinforced the propaganda from the Yugoslav DKP and Tanjug which were both aimed in the same direction. Accusations were coming from Europe that we intended to humiliate the army, that some elements in Slovenia did not want an agreement, and so forth. They also began accusing us of illegal arms imports despite the fact that from the time the war began we had not brought in a single gun or bullet or received any other foreign assistance of this type. No one was prepared to sell us anything, not even a helmet or flak jacket. On the Western markets we were not even able to purchase gas masks for the civilian population.

TUESDAY, 2 JULY

We were prepared for the second wave of aggression, and redeployed part of our forces and replaced the commanders of the regional TO headquarters of the Ljubljana and south Primorska regions. Janez Lesjak took over the command of the Ljubljana region and Vojko Štemberger of the south Primorska region. The Republic Headquarters sent reinforcements to the most vulnerable locations. At the beginning of the aggression we formed an analytical group led by Colonel Ivan Kukec. The group provided the Presidency and the operations group with a break-down analysis of the current military and political situation, as well as an assessment after the first phase of the aggression. The following is a summary of the assessment which we had before the start of the second wave.

PRIOR ANALYSIS

1. THE PERIOD BEFORE THE AGGRESSION
1.1. THE OCCUPYING FORCE
With the accord of the Yugoslav state leadership the aggressor prepared aggression against the Republic of Slovenia according to a previously designed plan code-named BEDEM.

189

The troops were intentionally trained for the planned aggression and reinforcements were being moved to Slovenia from other parts of Yugoslavia.

The state of alert was raised and through the use of the air force and troop movements the aggressor made a "gentle" show of force.

KOS and the military intelligence joined forces engaging officers who collaborated in their spare time, civilians employed by the YNA, family members and retired officers. All such efforts did not produce the desired results. The aggressor did not have an objective picture of the readiness of the Republic of Slovenia and underestimated the opponent.

Special units were brought in to supplement the deficient units with conscripts from other parts of Yugoslavia.

All of these measures worried the majority of YNA personnel, especially those officers who were in some way connected with the Republic of Slovenia. The aggressor increased the pressure on the enlisted men and officers through false propaganda within the installations and through the media in the rest of Yugoslavia.

Conclusion:

The aggressor made political, psychological, propaganda and material preparations for the aggression in good time. The federal and military leadership actively cooperated in these preparations. The aggressor's physical readiness for battle was much higher than its psychological readiness.

1.2. REPUBLIC OF SLOVENIA

In accordance with the political decision adopted by the Assembly of the Republic of Slovenia its state leadership and all other authoritative bodies were preparing defence measures. The raising of battle readiness was achieved on the basis of political decisions originating from the free will expressed by the citizens of the Republic of Slovenia. This resulted in a high level of psychological readiness of the Republic of Slovenia as a whole.

The state leadership and authorised bodies of the RS organised material and professional preparations and assured their implementation.

The expressed will of the citizens of the Republic of Slovenia led to an efficient gathering of information about the aggressor's activities. This enabled an effective drafting and adaptation of defence plans. A high level of security for the collected data on the aggressor's preparations and on our defences was achieved.

The citizens of the Republic of Slovenia were regularly and objectively informed about the preparations for aggression, the existing circumstances in Yugoslavia and abroad. A high level of motivation of the population was achieved, in particular the psychological and professional readiness of all those who actively participated in the defence.

We organised the production and the purchase of equipment required by the TO to replace the equipment which the Yugoslav state-military establishment took from the TO of the Republic of Slovenia.

We undertook measures for the protection of infrastructure facilities, the population and the material reserves. Through the media and at their work place the citizens gained the ability for self-protection. Civil defence was at the highest state of alert.

CONCLUSION:

The defence of the Republic of Slovenia was prepared in good time. A high level of readiness of citizens for the defence of an independent Slovenia and an inferiority in armaments were the two main characteristics. The critical shortcomings were the inability to act within our air space and the fact that the TO of the RS only had light infantry weapons and limited quantities of light anti-tank and anti-aircraft guns.

The system of command was organised well and on time.

2. MILITARY ACTIVITY
2.1. THE AGGRESSOR

The aggressor began military activity by moving its armoured units towards the border crossings and from Croatia into the territory of the RS.According to the plan their objective was to take control of the border crossings as fast as possible which is why they did not have appropriate infantry and logistic support. The armoured units were divided into smaller armoured groups and even individual armoured vehicles. This kind of unprofessional deployment of armoured units was based on an incorrect assessment of the opponent. Due to their incomplete intelligence information and particularly because of the misconceptions of some in Yugoslavia who held that only they could be good soldiers, at the same time considering Slovenians as "sissies who do not like the army or fighting a war", the aggressor underestimated the readiness and the ability of his opponent. Based on this kind of logic the air force was deployed as though it was performing at an air show, which resulted in an unexpected loss of helicopters.

Consequently the aggressor suffered immediate losses which quickly broke down the already shaky morale. The lack of essential supplies and the action of the TO forced the crews to remain in their vehicles which, along with high temperatures, quickly brought on physical fatigue. In order to make up for the failures which resulted from their unprofessionalism and low morale the aggressor began to use non-military methods and acted against civilian targets, killing civilians. The use of aircraft was a feature especially at Murska Sobota, Medvedjek and Brnik airport. The destruction of civilian aircraft was most probably a primitive reprisal for the losses suffered on other battlefields. Such behaviour signifies the exceptionally low level of morality exhibited by commanding officers. The explicit vengeance that was exhibited by the air force was most probably related to the activities of the new assistant to the commander of the general staff in charge of RV (Air Force) and PVO (anti-aircraft forces), General Lt-Colonel Ivan Hočevar who had previously been dismissed by the Slovenian authorities. The use of heavy weapons was also unreliable because soldiers lacked appropriate training but particularly because the soldiers, who were too young and mostly conscripted against their will, were not prepared to die for an objective which was unknown to them. It was evident that the units and their commanding officers were not trained to act under siege. This was probably also the decisive reason why the aggressor refrained from landing troops from the air since the forces which were to assist in such landings were blocked.

CONCLUSION:

Despite the indisputable advantage in manpower and military strength in general the aggressor was unable to achieve a single objective. Relatively few casualties immediately demoralised the soldiers and incapacitated them from further fighting. The unprofessional use of forces and in particular the appalling living conditions have to a large extent diminished the trust of soldiers towards their commanding officers at all levels. The aggressor retained an advantage in the air but refrained from conducting low-level operations because he was aware of the types and quantities of anti-aircraft weapons with which the TO was equipped. Consequently the use of the air force and helicopters in particular was substantially reduced.

The aggressor must have concluded that its forces in the Republic of Slovenia were no longer able to act militarily without reinforcements which were being mobilised outside the RS. The aggressor will probably attempt to bring in these reinforcements during a second offensive.

Probable future activities:

Supplement the armed forces within the Republic of Croatia by reinforcements from Serbia.

Deployment:

Deployment of two battle formations and reserves.

Objective:

During the first phase the No. I. battle formation takes control of the line running: Maribor–Celje–Grosuplje–Vrhnika–Postojna–Sežana.

Second phase:

with the assistance of troop landings at Trojane, the Ljubljana basin and Postojna enable the advancement of the no. II battle formation and the occupation of the Republic of Slovenia.

DEPLOYMENT OF MILITARY FORCES:

Battle formation I.

Direction:	
Varaždin–Maribor	32nd Motorised Brigade and part of the 32nd Engineers Regiment
Koprivnica–Čakovec–Murska Sobota	73rd Motorised Brigade and part of the 32nd Engineers Regiment
Zagreb–Novo Mesto–Ljubljana	140th Motorised Brigade from Zagreb
Karlovac–Metlika–Novo Mesto	622nd Motorised Brigade from Petrinja
Delnice–Kočevje–Ribnica	6th br. Brigade
Ilirska Bistrica–Postojna	13th Motorised Brigade from Ilirska Bistrica

A possibility of engaging the navy units from Istria.

Battle formation II.

Composition: 573rd Petrinja, 236th Rijeka and part of the 144th Ljubljana Motorised Brigades, parachute units and forces arriving from deep behind the reserve lines. Strength of parachute forces – two battalions.

Reserves: 4th Armoured Brigade, 257th motorised brigade from Petrinja and the 522nd Engineers Regiment.

2.2. RS DEFENCE FORCES

Mobilisation was conducted successfully and on time. During the military activities the mobilisation was in line with requirements and ensured the growth of strong military forces in accordance with our needs.

The civilian population cooperated with our forces. A characteristic of the first phase was the obstruction of movements of armoured vehicles by relatively passive obstructions which did not have appropriate support from anti-tank weapons or where such weapons were not used. Light vehicles were used on the barricades which when they were not defended, could be overrun easily. This causes unnecessary material damage.

It was understandable that we needed a certain period of time for the TO to get used to direct attacks on the aggressor's troops. However we overcame this crisis successfully which was shown by the second day of the war. The TO units and the civilians of the RS have exhibited great courage and convinced the aggressor that they are ready and willing to defend their independence. The successful blockading of the aggressor's forces has prevented parachute troop landings and forced the aggressor to temporarily stop military actions. At certain locations the attacks against the surrounded YNA forces were intense which made withdrawal to the barracks difficult.

CONCLUSION:
Despite the lack of heavy weapons the RS defence forces defeated the aggressor and temporarily prevented the continuation of the aggression. The system of military command performed well despite the damage caused to the system of communications. The discipline of the civilian population contributed to the defence efforts. All agencies and organisations involved in the provision of essential supplies performed efficiently.

The TO has seized great quantities of military equipment which have increased the strength of the defence mechanisms of the RS. After the end of the first phase it is our estimation that the conditions for defence have improved but are still somewhat hampered due to blocked road communications.

3. SUMMARY:
The defeat of the much stronger aggressor is proof that the Republic of Slovenia is prepared to defend its independence. Based on the military accomplishments we can conclude that the officers and enlisted personnel of the TO as well as the police are professionally and psychologically qualified for military action.

The state and army leadership of the RS is professionally qualified for conducting military operations and trusted by the general population.

The aggressor was wrong to underestimate the opponent. It is evident that its forces are incapable of successful performance of military activities.

The aggressor has temporarily halted the aggression in order to supplement its forces by fresh, single-nationality units. The next deployment will have a radical objective – the total occupation of the Republic of Slovenia. In our estimation this could be prevented by placing barricades on roads and bridges leading from the neighbouring republic. The barricades must prevent the advance of armoured columns.

The reinforcement of the aggressor's forces should be prevented. It may be advisable not to allow the return of the aggressor's units back to their barracks. The slow pace of negotiations on the withdrawal to barracks reduces the aggressor's defence capability and at the same time allows for the appropriate reinforcement of our units maintaining the siege.

Most of the assessments provided by the above analysis proved to be correct, which is why our preparations for the second offensive were logical and appropriate, except in relation to the psychological aspects of the activities of the YNA air force on the civilian population.

A little after midnight the YNA unit defending the Lazaret border crossing surrendered and we thus gained control of yet another window to the outside world. After 2.00 in the morning however, the new Danse Macabre began.

First the LPA column blocked at Krakovo Forest attempted to break through the barricade. Fighting broke out and Major Boško Prodanovič immediately called for air cover. At 6.45 the YNA air force made a rocket attack on the TO units at the barricade. Our units escaped in time but returned after the attack was over. Air attacks were repeated several times during the day. As we lacked radar equipment to warn us of the approaching aircraft we had to rely on listening in to radio communications carried out between the military air command and the aircraft crews. In this way we prevented many more casualties.

On that day a series of intermittent air and ground attacks continued in all parts of Slovenia. Rocket or bomb attacks were meted out on the transmitters on Nanos, Krvavec, Boč, Domžale, Ljubljana Castle and Pohorje (from installations in Maribor), as well as the barricades at Čatež, Krakovo Forest and Dravograd. The YNA air force again attacked Kočevska Reka. The YNA armoured units attempted to advance towards Dobova, Ormož, Ljutomer, Bregana, Šentilj and Postojna. The tanks again attempted a break out of the Vrhnika barracks but on this occasion we succeeded in stopping them quickly.

In the vicinity of the Bivje intersection, southeast of the Moretini guard post, the TO and police units attacked an armoured vehicle at 10.15 with an anti-tank missile and scored a direct hit. The crew members were wounded. When the policemen were rescuing the wounded crew members they were fired on by the YNA guards from the Moretini post.

Slovenia was once again reverberating with the sound of air raid sirens and detonations of aircraft bombs and tank grenades, but our units were prepared. Our response was fierce. Danijel Kuzma said that someone was certain to arrange again for a cease-fire before we were given a chance to complete our work, which is why he pressured his commanders to act quickly. We deployed the national defence reserves in local communities in order to cover as much of the territory as possible.

At first our units put pressure on the border posts. To clear the border area was not only a military but also the most important political objective. The borders were the reason the war started in the first place. It was later proven that such a decision was of great significance. One after another we liberated the border posts at Pokovje near Solkan, and the guard posts of Kuzma, Nikola Hečimovič, Spičnik, Čeršak, Sladki Vrh, Pristava, Miren, Trata, Jožica Flander and many others because the poor morale of the surrounded YNA squads was already at its lowest level. They were even afraid of their own air force because they knew an air strike was usually followed by a TO attack. On this day we also stopped the tank units at Dobova, Prilepi, Vrhnika, Orchek, Štrigova and prevented certain other minor advances.

A different kind of story was developing at Šentilj where the TO was using captured YNA tanks. Soon after the first shots were fired a white flag appeared on the roof of the barracks. This was the biggest individual victory of the day and had great psychological significance both for our citizens and our defence forces. At the same time it meant that another important communication with the outside world was open. There were so many prisoners that the commander of the 7th regional TO headquarters, Colonel Milošević did not know what to do with them. The battle was shown live on TV. We were told later that all of Austria cheered our tank crews. On this day the TO also attacked and took control of an arms depot at Ložnica which provided both of the Štajerska regions with great quantities of arms. The Gorenjska TO captured the army barracks at Rudno Polje, Škofja Loka and Radovljica. They also attacked certain other installations and were preparing attacks on others.

The second of July 1991 felt like it lasted 240 hours, since there was so much happening that day. Immediately after the air strikes began Igor Bavčar called the new commander of the 5th Army District General Života Avramović and asked him what was the meaning of the strikes and how did the YNA explain this cease-fire. He replied: "This is just the beginning". Bavčar went on: "Be my guest! But in the end the consequences will be worse for you!" The short conversation confirmed a generally held opinion that the second offensive had begun. The consequences were really grave, especially for Avramovič who the next day lost control of Slovenia and a few months later, due to his failures in Croatia, had his entire army district disbanded.

During the heaviest fighting Milan Kučan and Dimitrij Rupel participated in talks with Hans-Dietrich Genscher in Austria. Air raids, air strikes and reports on the advancing armoured columns deeply disturbed the remaining members of the Presidency. It took some time for us at the operations group to assess the real strength of the air strikes and the advancing armoured units, which at this stage were no longer moving in advancing formation. It was a real battle formation with infantry detachments protecting tanks from close encounters assisted by air cover. According to the incoming reports we hardly had any casualties, which was surprising in view of the enemy's extensive air operations. We immediately went into a counter-offensive. If we had had the use of more effective anti-aircraft weapons we would have cleared up matters with the YNA much sooner. At mid-morning the session of the presidency was called but due to overwhelming activity and the need to wait for reports from the field, only Igor Bavčar could get away to attend the session. Ciril Zlobec, who on that day was psychologically dejected, was sitting in for Milan Kučan as chairman. If by coincidence the session was broadcast over TV the morale of our troops would have fallen at least a hundred percent. Many sharp words were exchanged but when I arrived with a handful of the latest reports the storm had already abated. Ciril Zlobec insisted that we again offer the army a cease-fire but I was arguing that we already had a cease-fire which the YNA had violated, meaning that it was not interested in a cease-fire and would otherwise not be staging a second offensive. We all agreed however that another offer could not hurt. Belgrade insisted that we could only negotiate with the command of the 5th Army District in Zagreb, which was an obvious attempt to degrade us. The commanding officer of the RŠ TO Janez Slapar nevertheless sent the following proposal to Života Avramović:

A PROPOSAL BY THE REPUBLIC OF SLOVENIA FOR DEFINING THE CONDITIONS FOR A CEASE-FIRE EFFECTIVE ON 27 JULY 1991 FROM 15.OO HOURS

1. From the above date and hour a cease-fire on both sides is in effect.
2. The RS defence forces pledge that at this hour they will:
   - stop firing
   - lift the blockade of the surrounded YNA forces
   - allow the YNA to assist their wounded and collect their dead, which they could have done all along
   - when all the forces have returned to their barracks their supply lines will be assured
3. The YNA units pledge that on this hour they will:
   - stop firing
   - withdraw the units of the 10th and 32nd Corps and other units brought in from elsewhere, sending them back to their barracks outside Slovenia
   - withdraw the blocked armoured units and special units belonging to the 14th and 31st Corps to their permanent barracks, taking away tanks and personnel carriers on transport trucks
   - refrain from bringing into the territory of the Republic of Slovenia new forces and from conducting any kind of military actions

For the Republic of Slovenia
Acting commanding officer of the RHQ TO
Colonel Janez Slapar

The reply to our proposal arrived at 16.30. It was addressed to the President of the Presidency and in it Života Avramović proved firstly that he was not prepared to negotiate, since he demanded little less then our total surrender, and secondly why he was called "iceman".

HEADQUARTERS OF THE 5TH ARMY DISTRICT
OFFICE OF THE COMMANDING OFFICER
Date: 2 July 1991
No: 2/22–162

PRESIDENCY OF THE REPUBLIC OF SLOVENIA
PRESIDENT OF THE PRESIDENCY
MR MILAN KUČAN

The proposal of the Republic of Slovenia regarding the conditions for the cease--fire effective 2 July 1991 is not acceptable to the headquarters of the 5th Army District. The proposed text does not contain essential proposals which were set by the headquarters of the 5th Army District nor does it contain the essential points set down by the Presidency of the SFRY.

We demand that the text of the proposal includes:

– cease-fire and the withdrawal of all units to at least 2 km from routes of communication,

– deblocking of all YNA installations, barracks and units, ensuring free movement of all YNA units,

– release of all YNA soldiers, their family members, members of ZSUP and customs authorities,

– unconditional safe passage of YNA personnel for the collection of wounded and dead soldiers

– immediate deblocking and return of the YNA and ZSUP property and ensuring normal supply of YNA units,

– return of the captured border posts and other military facilities,

– withdrawal of armed units of the RS to their starting positions.

It is unacceptable that the act on the cease-fire conditions is signed by the acting commanding officer of the TO general staff. The act should be signed by the President of the Presidency of the Republic of Slovenia or a member of the Presidency under his authorisation.

The cease-fire should take effect at 17.00 hours on 2 July 1991.

Commanding officer
Života Avramović, Colonel-General

The cabled message came as a cold shower to those who thought that it was our fault that the army had renewed their attacks after the first cease--fire. Meanwhile Milan Kučan and Dimitrij Rupel returned from Austria and then finally elected President of the Federal Presidency, Stipe Mesić, and one of the Presidency members Vasil Tupurkovski also arrived in Ljubljana. Both of them were more agitated then any of our soldiers. During the talks we watched the TV with the two of them and saw women breaking into the Serbian parliament. It was an unusual scene which showed that the war in Slovenia was not the main concern of the majority of Serbs. This act of the Serbian parents was a reaction to the lists of prisoners and casualties which according to international conventions we had sent to the Serbian Red Cross. While the public media informed the people of Serbia that the YNA suffered only a few casualties and had no prisoners taken, the lists containing several thousand names told another story. It turned out that General Svarun, who I talked to that day, was right when he said that we must persist and that Serbian people would start wondering about the actions of their leaders and generals only after their loved ones started coming home in coffins. Fortunately coffins were few but the lists of war prisoners were so long that at first even the representatives of the Red Cross looked at them in disbelief.

Stipe Mesić and Vasil Tupurkovski came to try and convince us not to persist with the plebiscite decisions because Veljko Kadijević was allegedly by now totally irrational and the two did not even want to mention the state Blagoje Ađić was in. Janez Drnovšek, who had had the opportunity to work with the two visitors for a number of years, warned us that their mediation would not be very significant. We emphasised that the federal authorities still had not formed their part of the commission which was agreed with Ante Marković and Čusić. Lojze Peterle spoke with Ante Marković but it was

197

clear from the conversation that while the foreign ministers from the European countries still came to visit him, no one in Belgrade listened to him any longer.

Over the TV we were then able to see the chief of the GHQ, Blagoje Adžić, who first said that the YNA in Slovenia had easily carried out the decisions adopted by the Federal Executive Council but was then attacked by the TO who proclaimed as the aggressor. He concluded with the following words: "We shall take control and bring matters to a conclusion. Shortly the chief of staff of the Supreme Command, army General Veljko Kadijević will speak to the Yugoslav public."

At the same time the first reconnaissance company of the defence brigade took control of the building that housed the former Republic Headquarters of the TO in Ljubljana which the YNA had occupied on the 5th of October 1990. The second section of the same brigade at the same time surrounded the guard at the military surplus depot at Ruski Car. The commanding officer, a Lt-Colonel, was sent a note calling on him to surrender. After reading it he threw it to the ground in contempt, right by the gates. At that moment a TO marksman fired a bullet just next to where he was standing. The Lt-Colonel wet his pants, and quickly raised his hands above his head, followed by his troops.

After consultations and an assessment of the situation, which in military terms was in our favour although some were not so sure, we decided to offer Belgrade a cease-fire, while other conditions for the cease-fire should be settled by the inter-state commission for which the federal authorities should finally name their representatives. If Belgrade refused such a proposal we would nevertheless unilaterally hold our fire at 21.00 where possible. This would give us a diplomatic advantage.

This is what we did. At a press conference Milan Kučan announced a unilateral cease-fire. The news circled the globe. We sent our units precise instructions to which we again received a familiar reply: "But why now, we only needed a few more hours." Belgrade did not agree to the cease-fire but that did not matter since the YNA offensive had already been broken.

The TO forces from eastern Štajerska succeeded in taking control of the large army depot at Zgornja Ložnica and thus acquired a large quantity of arms to replenish their stocks and equip units waiting in reserve. The eastern Štajerska region was most heavily hit during the two offensives. Up to the end of the war the TO and police units in this region performed 44 military operations and captured 28 YNA installations. In the fighting the TO suffered 15 wounded but no dead.

The situation in the field was quieter. It would have been the same even without the cease-fire, since on this day we cleared the border and captured a number of other military installations across our whole territory.

The generals again made a series of mistakes. Although they were not so naive the second time round, they still greatly underestimated our strength. They did not do anything to improve the morale of their troops. Nietzsche wrote: "How convincing do wrong arguments or bad music sound when

198

marching towards the enemy". Despite this old truth the rigid army, which was rapidly loosing its ground, was unable to make use of the simplest propaganda.

Just as the cease-fire was to take effect we received a report that the column blocked in Krakovo Forest was ready to surrender. The commanding officer, Boško Prodanović, escaped on foot with a group of his soldiers. Next day they were captured near Krško by a special police unit. This was the final fate of the unit which on 27 June at 1.15 crossed our newly declared border and began the aggression on Slovenia, and of the commanding officer who fired the first shot against a newly established country. Colonel Albin Gutman and others who negotiated with Major Prodanović later said that he would have probably surrendered at the beginning if he had not been receiving different orders from Zagreb, with which he was in constant communication. The Dolenjska TO seized all of the armoured vehicles and refitted the majority of them for battle. During the previous few days they had kept a close eye on them, not in order to destroy them but in hope that some day they too would possess such effective weaponry. When I visited them ten days later these armoured vehicles already formed an active part of a well-trained unit and remained within our always ready armed forces until the final departure of the YNA from Slovenia. The disarming of the column also had an important psychological effect on the public which continuously followed its fate.

WEDNESDAY, 3 JULY

During the night individual skirmishes continued, particularly in the Štajerska region. In the morning the fighting again intensified at Radenci, Kog and in Gornja Radgona. The YNA Air Force planes were in the air throughout the day. Early in the morning Andrija Rašeta sent us a message that their helicopters would be transporting the wounded and bringing in supplies. Although the helicopters carrying the sign of the Red Cross were bringing in some reinforcements we did not react because we knew that they would immediately accuse us of breaking the cease-fire. The situation in the field was for us much more favourable than before the second offensive. The border was for the most part secured and the remaining border posts were surrendering even after the cease-fire had taken effect. The rest of the armoured columns no longer presented a threat. The negotiations were under way for their departure from the territory of Slovenia back to Varaždin and Rijeka. The federal authorities had finally named their members of the commission. Prior to the meeting of the two commissions General Rašeta agreed on a cease-fire.

Late in the afternoon Miran Bogataj, Dušan Plut and Boris Žnidaršič left for Zagreb and that evening at Pleso airport met with the delegations from the YNA and ZSNZ (Federal Secretariat for Internal Affairs) lead by Andrija Rašeta and Peter Gračanin. The talks were strained and almost futile because the YNA was still attempting to gain through negotiation what it could not seize by force. Nevertheless, the cease-fire was still holding.

We intercepted a message sent from the political administration of the ZSLO by Colonel Jovan Miškov which praised the courage exhibited by many officers and men in the operation against Slovenia and especially the units of the Rijeka Corps under the command of General Marjan Čad. In the message the army's "political scientists" also wrote that "through their propaganda-information activities they also succeeded in revealing to the world the deceitfulness of the leading Slovenian politicians."

THURSDAY, 4 JULY

The withdrawal of the YNA units to their barracks in Croatia continued. Through the ongoing negotiations we also allowed the withdrawal of certain blocked units back to their barracks in Slovenia. Gradually we were returning the infrastructure but still controlled it appropriately.

It was a day of celebration since all of the border crossings were again under our control. When we looked at the crossed out red circles on the maps our strained and tired faces grew softer. The protection of the measures aimed at securing independence by military force was a success. We were in control of the border crossings with authority over customs which we held throughout the war. Border traffic was again open.

The buses carrying Serbian parents who wished to visit their sons at the barracks arrived in Slovenia. The commendable effort by Spomenka Hribar who tried to organise a warm welcome and accommodate them with Slovenian families was unsuccessful. Present on each of the buses was a YNA security officer who supervised the visit.

Marko Kosin from the foreign ministry talked with the Italian Consul--General Mr Cristiani, who was clearly throughout the war rather too well informed of the ongoing events, and had raised unnecessary panic. On this occasion he also said that after the agreement with Marković, Slovenia set too strict conditions for the YNA withdrawal, for which reason the YNA leadership had adopted severe counter-measures. It was obvious that the balance of power between the Slovenian TO and the YNA was unequal and that the YNA had the material capability to destroy the Slovenian armed forces. He enquired as to how Slovenia viewed the three-month moratorium and who would take control at the border crossings. From the conversation it was possible to sense the apprehension of those who still hoped that Slovenian independence would only be a two-day episode. Against such expectations the border was again in Slovenian hands, this time won with blood. They were losing hope that we would simply give it up and return it to the hands of Belgrade.

Our elation over the fact that all of the border crossings were again in Slovenia's hands was soon dashed by the new ultimatums from Belgrade. At this time the new president of the SFRY Presidency, Stipe Mesić, was beginning his term in office. The Federal Presidency had on that day unanimously – by seven votes in favour (Janez Drnovšek was not present at the session) – adopted the decision by which Slovenia was to return the borders to the control of the federal authorities and disarm its forces by noon on 7 July 1991. We were astonished by the vote cast by Stipe Mesić. Only Janez Drnovšek, who knew Mesić better, was not greatly surprised. The ultimatum issued by the seven from the SFRY Presidency again raised anxiety which had eased off somewhat after the cease-fire was established. In order to make our position clear I sent the following message to those who needed and deserved to be told:

REPUBLIC OF SLOVENIA
MINISTRY OF DEFENCE
Zupančičeva 3, Ljubljana
Date: 4 July 1991

TO THE COMMANDING OFFICERS OF THE REGIONAL AND LOCAL T.O. HEADQUARTERS AND OFFICERS OF THE TERRITORIAL DEFENCE OF SLOVENIA

Subject: Ultimatum issued by the Presidency of the SFRY

The ultimatum issued by the Presidency of the SFRY, adopted at its session on 4 July 1991, calls into question the plebiscite decision taken by the Slovenian nation and all the citizens of Slovenia. It is clear that Slovenia cannot accept the ultimatum, even in the event that the US and EC confirm the decisions adopted by the Presidency of the SFRY, because it is impossible to act against a decision adopted by an absolute majority of the electorate.

World public opinion is pressuring its governments and forcing them to officially recognise Slovenia. At this moment there are over 1,100 mostly foreign journalists in the RS. The media can be used to reveal the objectives of the aggression against Slovenia but the opinions of the government representatives of foreign countries are changing slower than the public opinion. The case of the Kurds, to whom the "countries of Western, humane democracies" offered protection only after the refugee problem became acute and when the rampaging of Hussein's forces caused a great many casualties among them, is a case in point.

In view of the above it is reasonable to expect a further increase in tensions and heavy fighting. During the first round the enemy has learned a lesson and will act differently in the future. We expect the enemy to attack first with its air force, striking our positions, infrastructure and communications. Despite the fact that some of the pilots in previous strikes did not hit the appropriate targets, and even attacked their own forces, we may in the future expect greater damage. This will be followed by the deployment of armoured units and infantry, moving at a slower pace but with greater destructive power. Consequently, we are at this time fully reinforcing our southeastern border because if we succeed in stopping the enemy at the outset or at least prevent its advance deeper into our territory we may count on international assistance and quicker recognition, which could result in an immediate halt of the aggression.

The Republic of Croatia is attempting to remain passive as long as possible but will nevertheless not be able to stay out of the conflict, since if the aggression is unsuccessful in Slovenia it will then be aimed at the borders of Greater Serbia. Despite certain assurance from Croatia we should not count on their support during the initial phase.

Special attention should be given to the psychological state of the troops, the adoption of measures against air strikes, mining of the barricades and provision of adequate rest periods for your men.

We shall not succumb to pressure since it would be absurd if in peace we lost what we had gained in war. In all of its history Slovenia has not been so nationally or politically united as it is at this time, which is our great advantage. Similarly, Slovenia has never before deployed a stronger military force in the defence of its independence. Even according to the worst scenario, the enemy will not be able to engage sufficient force to occupy Slovenia. Slovenia will resort to tactics which will prevent unnecessary loss of life but will in no respect give up its basic objective – independence and freedom. The amount of time it will take us to take full and effective control is dependent on our determination.

I congratulate all of the members of the Territorial Defence of Slovenia for their determined defence of our homeland thus far, and particularly those commanding officers whose units have already scored important military victories against the aggressor.

Janez Janša
Minister of Defence

Despite the ultimatum the withdrawal of the YNA units from their battle positions continued, which was very significant at that time. The tanks from Brnik airport were being removed by transport trailers. We did not allow another tracked vehicle convoy over the roads.

It was my daughter Nika's fourth birthday. I had been away from home for more than ten days. I did not manage to get home on this occasion either, and we had to blow out the candles over the phone.

FRIDAY, 5 JULY

During the night our units were provoked on a number of occasions. We did not use any great force in reply so as not to provoke a major conflict. We adopted certain measures for the release of the prisoners of war who were under International Red Cross supervision. I was preparing for the session of the Presidency and made photocopies of the following draft proposal of possible replies to the SFRY ultimatum:

POSITION OF THE REPUBLIC OF SLOVENIA TOWARDS THE ULTIMATUM ISSUED BY THE SFRY PRESIDENCY

Draft dated 5 July 1991

1. The Republic Assembly shall take decisions with respect to the border and customs administration.

2. The YNA units in the territory of Slovenia have returned unobstructed and with UN assistance to their barracks by 15.00 hours on 5 July 19991. On this date their peace-time infrastructure was reinstated along with all necessary supply lines. The RS defence forces are maintaining control over some of those military installations in which the local commanders are still threatening the surrounding area and are, according to the agreement, making sure that no military units move out of their installations. The barricades are placed outside of the perimeter of the military installations.

3. The TO of Slovenia still has not received the return of the armaments, worth US$ 700 million, which were taken from the TO in May of 1990. In addition, the assessment of war damage caused by the aggression on the RS has not been performed. According to the initial evaluation by a government commission the damage amounts to US$ 2.7 billion.

After these issues are resolved an agreement could be considered on the return of some of the YNA installations in the territory of RS.

4. The armed forces of the RS are present in those areas where their members live and work and their withdrawal to barracks is thus impossible since they do not exist.

We must call attention to the 1st mechanised armoured brigade that left Belgrade and is still moving towards Slovenia, posing a permanent and great threat of the aggression continuing against the Republic of Slovenia. We request that this issue be given appropriate consideration.

5. We are making great efforts to ensure a free flow of traffic on the roads but due to the great damage caused by armoured vehicles and shelling, passage on some of the roads is made difficult. The air space is under YNA control. We are in no way obstructing air traffic, provided that it is not being used for the purposes of further aggression on RS.

6. The RS is treating its prisoners of war according to international conventions, on the basis of which most of them have already been released. On the contrary, the YNA is in certain parts of Yugoslavia still holding imprisoned, in isolation or under difficult conditions several hundred soldiers of Slovenian nationality, who have been detained during the aggression of YNA on RS.

7. The armed forces of the RS are strictly abiding by the cease-fire. By their nature their basic objective is to ensure a permanent peace and establishment of normal living conditions for all citizens of the Republic of Slovenia.

At the session I made use of the above draft but no definite decisions were adopted. It looked as though we were going to wait until the end of the third round of talks with the European Troika. The talks were to be held two days later on Brioni. In the meantime the possibility of the return of border control to the federal army, police or customs officials never crossed our minds. Smaller YNA units continued to surrender. At times, when the regime within the barracks slackened, Albanian and Macedonian soldiers escaped in great numbers.

Lojze Peterle and Janez Drnovšek were on missions to Belgium and Switzerland. From their reports we could sense that there was not much support from the EC and other countries for our independence. In the evening talks were held with Bogić Bogićević and Vasil Tupurkovski who arrived in Ljubljana. We were not too pleased to see them because they had signed the ultimatum. After his arrival Tupurkovski went to the YNA Šentvid barracks where he spoke to the YNA officers, saying that the separatist Slovenia was to blame for it all, while at our meeting he spoke out against Veljko Kadijević.

In the evening we received a more detailed description of the events in

Maribor. The report said that the commanding officer of the 31st Corps, General Mićo Delić and his assistant Colonel Alojz Lipnik filed a request to the 5th Army District headquarters, or more precisely to General Rašeta, for authorisation to bomb Dravograd because the TO had not allowed passage to the units of the 31st Corps. On this occasion Lipnik allegedly said that "at least 20,000 Slovenians ought to be burned in order to bring them to their senses". Apart from Delić and Alojz Lipnik an extreme position was adopted in the 31st Corps by Lt-Colonel of KOS Ratko Katalina and Stevilović, Colonels Stojanovski and Ivanović and many of the junior officers. With the exception of Alojz Lipnik, all of the officers of Slovenian nationality who still remained serving in this Corps (7 in all) were under surveillance. Some of them were undecided and unsure of their role.

SATURDAY, 6 JULY

Vasil Tupurkovski and Bogić Bogičević were present at the next session of the Presidency of the Republic of Slovenia. We asked them to mediate the release of the remaining Slovenian soldiers serving in the YNA. Most of our time (the guests were no longer present) was taken up by forming a strategy for the next day's meeting at Brioni with the European Troika. I persisted in the opinion that we must not give way regarding the borders, since I considered them to be of key importance. Milan Kučan first requested that apart from himself and Janez Drnovšek, I or Igor Bavčar should also be present at the Brioni meeting. However, we later concluded that in view of the circumstances it would be best if we stayed at home. We finally decided that Lojze Peterle and France Bučar be part of our Brioni delegation.

On this day all of the tanks left Brnik airport. After the withdrawal we learned about the adventures of this battalion from a YNA subaltern who had previously cooperated with our police. After returning to the barracks he gave the following account of events:

The morning of 27 June 1991! The beginning of what I and many of those serving in the YNA dreaded. The alert was unusual compared to those we had experienced until then in the army. Everything was done quietly and calmly, in short, unusually so. The soldiers collected the necessary equipment, assembled in the hallway and walked to the garages where the tanks were waiting.

Being a general clerk I remained in the building along with a driver and two other soldiers. I was ordered to collect only the essential field equipment and join the others outside. I gathered up only the essentials and around 2.00 joined the others by the tanks which were forming into two columns. I realised that the battalion was really preparing to leave the barracks. I was experiencing some frightful feelings. I recalled what the top officers said many times. If we were to move out with tanks we should never repeat what happened at Liščica in Bosnia. Which was supposed to mean that the tank units must not be obstructed. It later turned out that no obstructions were in our way. I had no other choice but to take up my station. I hooked a field kitchen to the back of my truck. I could not locate the commander of the battalion so I asked the assistant commander of the brigade as to my orders. He told me that the battalion was

204

going on a mission in a two column formation. I was to be in the column led by the battalion commander and wherever it went I should follow.

The two columns left at 2.40 amid great confusion. The battalion commander's tank broke down and was left at the barracks while the commander drove away in a BVP M-80 infantry vehicle. I should have been at the end of the column but the deputy brigade commander sent me forward so that I was driving somewhere in the middle of the tank formation. We proceeded at a rapid pace on the old road towards Ljubljana. The view of the thundering procession in front and to the side of me was horrific. The sound of speeding tanks, sparks flying from under them, screaming women with children on the road side, on the balconies people in their underwear and pyjamas waving their fists and probably yelling things out in disgust which we could not hear above the deafening noise.

We reached Brezovica where we encountered the first road block made out of cars. It was literally crushed under by the passage of the tanks. A tank was stuck in the ditch on the left side of the road. The owners of the vehicles were hiding by the road side looking at their property being crushed. The balconies were filled with people. I had the feeling that they would tear apart with their bare hands the first one they could get hold of. When we went through the barricade the field kitchen in tow turned over. With everything going on at this intersection I was afraid to stop and unhitch the trailer. I drove on pulling the turned over kitchen for another 200 meters. I finally had to stop and release the load, leaving it behind by the road side.

When we turned left at Brezovica I suddenly realised where the battalion was heading. The battalion's permanent task was the defence of Brnik airport. Its assigned route of approach was through Brezovica, turning right under Toško Čelo towards Šentvid and on to Brnik. The vehicles in front of me were heading directly towards Toško Čelo. I knew we were going in the wrong direction and I also knew what kind of a road passes through Toško Čelo. I hoped that the column would get stuck in the forest and remain there at least until morning. We got to the middle of the forest and stopped. We could not go any further. I sat in my vehicle and waited. Half an hour later the battalion commander came behind us on foot. He was red with rage. He began to scream: "Look at the idiots, where have they got to! How will I be able to explain this to my superiors? What will they do to me when I get back?" A thought immediately crossed my mind: if we ever get back... In short, he was totally beside himself. The order was issued for the column to turn back and descend to the intersection and take the main road to Šentvid.

Total confusion ensued. One of the tanks went off the road while another stopped just before going over a cliff. The others managed to get back down to the main road again.

We proceeded towards Šentvid. By then it was daylight. In places buses were blocking the road. The first tank had no difficulty pushing them aside. The column reached Ljubljana. We drove along Celovška street to the intersection leading to the motorway for Kranj. At the intersection a policeman was arranging trucks into a road block but since the barricade was not completely finished the column passed through, scraping only one or two of the trucks. In Ljubljana people were out on the streets.

The column took the motorway towards Kranj, taking the Vodice exit to Brnik. Along the route from Ljubljana we were followed by two policemen on motorcycles.

In a forest on the other side of Vodice we encountered the last barricade. We broke through it with great difficulty. The column then turned left going along the edge of the forest until it reached the air strip, where it took up battle positions. The men were noticeably worried and afraid. No one spoke, the answers were brief.

Everyone was aware that this time it was for real. Everyone performed their tasks hurriedly. The silence was only broken when a tank was being moved into position. Radio receivers were turned on and only then did we finally realise that there was a war in Slovenia.

The column proceeding through Trzin led by deputy battalion commander Rasić had arrived at Brnik an hour earlier. It took up position in the forest at the main entrance to the airport. On its way to Brnik it encountered similar obstacles to those our section faced. On the motorway it lost one tank, another one sometime later and at Trzin three APCs along with their crews. Three of the APCs were later destroyed and five crew members killed.

The battalion commander established a radio link with his deputy on the other side of the airport. The messages were short.

I was ordered to empty my vehicle and drive to the army barracks in Kranj from where we were to get food and other supplies. But after hearing radio reports on the current situation in Slovenia he cancelled the order. My truck contained approximately 200 meals of dried food and 50 litres of water, which was to provide for the 150 men making up the battalion. Throughout the day we were setting up our battle positions.

I parked my vehicle next to the one belonging to the commanding officer. I erected the tent and set up the command post. In the afternoon around 18.00 the duty officer received a message from Rasić saying that his unit was under attack. He reported that he was wounded and that one soldier had lost a leg, another a heel and a third his hand. The duty officer transmitted the message to Radovanović with a trembling voice.

From the other side of the airport we could hear loud gun fire. Radovanović was furious, threatening to flatten everything including the airport buildings. He started walking to his vehicle. I ran after him saying: What will you gain by destroying everything? Haven't we done enough damage on the way to the airport? Just think, afterwards we will have to return to Vrhnika to our families and all the people that know us so well! Radovanović stopped and tried to explain: "So what else am I supposed to do? I was ordered to get to Brnik but no one told me what I was supposed to do here." He showed me his note book where it was written: "Get to Brnik at all costs." There was more but I did not read further. I told him that the battalion had therefore fulfilled the order and must now wait to receive further orders from the higher command. He then told me that all communications with headquarters had been lost at Brezovica. Without thinking I said: "If I was in your place I would pull Rasić out to join us here so you could have better control over the whole battalion." He did not reply. He went to his vehicle and over the radio ordered Rasić to make his way over to our side of the airport and join our section.

Almost at the same time the brigade commander arrived at Brnik in a helicopter in order to establish contact with the battalion. He landed at the moment the wounded soldiers were being provided first aid. Rasić said later that the brigade commander was completely stunned when he saw the wounded soldiers. He first vomited copiously and then took the wounded soldiers by helicopter to Šentvid where he remained until the end of the war. He failed to establish radio links at Brnik and left without giving any further orders. I still cannot understand today why he did not attempt to get in contact with the battalion commander. He only managed to deliver to Brnik an officer who was to direct an air landing of reinforcements that were to assist our battalion in further operations. The reinforcements never arrived.

From the other side of the airport we could still hear intermittent gunfire and the sounds of exploding anti-tank grenades. Towards the evening a part of the battalion did arrive from the other side to join us. It took positions at the edge of the forest facing the air strip.

The night was peaceful. In the morning we distributed all the available food and water. The soldiers were dissatisfied, confused and afraid, but no one spoke out. The officers were divided into two camps, the moderates composed of the older officers and the extremists made up of the younger officers. We could hear them saying: "Come on you Slovenian Johnnies, let us give you hell! We hope to see the airport in ruins", and the like.

Over the radio we listened to the development of events in Slovenia. When the commanding officer heard that the major battles were being fought at the border crossings it dawned on him that in all probability the battalion's task was to take the airport's customs zone. Since the other section had previously been at the main entrance to the airport he was now furious and said: "The customs were already in our hands but when you take advice from a subaltern this is what happens."

The battalion officers met twice that morning. I was not present at these meetings.

In the afternoon, around 15.00, the soldier on watch duty reported that he had spotted a vehicle driving on the air strip with something like "press" written on it. He also noticed tubes sticking out of it. Radovanović immediately commented that these were most probably missile launchers with which the enemy was attempting to attack the battalion, so the vehicle must be destroyed. Second Lieutenant Ignjatović stepped forward volunteering to shoot at it. Radovanović told him to get into firing position. After he fired a burst from an anti-aircraft gun we heard Ignjatović saying that the vehicle was on fire. We all went to have a look. All we saw was a burning vehicle. Radovanović then said: "Good work, Ignjatović." Later one of the officers came and said that according to the radio reports we had shot and killed two Austrian journalists.

As a result of this tension rose within the battalion. An officer came over to the command post saying that we should stop this stupidity and that one of his soldiers was in shock. He had been given tranquilisers. I was totally confused; I was thinking of leaving but on reflection I concluded that if I stayed I could contribute to the resolution of events at Brnik. I tried to think whom of the officers I could trust. I went over to the officer in charge of the mechanised squadron. We talked for a long time and I could see that he was also outraged by what was happening. He also said that he would be willing to cross over to Janša's army if and as soon as it was possible. This could have either meant that he was on the Slovenian side or that he was just testing my reaction. I told him in all honesty that I was staying with the battalion only until the Brnik situation was resolved or until after the first battle. I left him with apprehension because I was unsure of the consequences of our conversation. Nothing ensued and I felt partially relieved.

In the evening it began to rain. I was with the battalion commander near his vehicle. We were talking when I heard a soldier nearby saying: "Halt, what are you doing here?" I saw someone but all the figures were covered in rain gear. Because I felt something unusual I told the commander I was going to my tent. As I set off a blast rang out. I was knocked to one side and felt a pain in my rib cage while the commander was thrown in the other direction. He was wounded in the hand. Next day when we found the remains of a grenade we realised that it had landed very close to where I and the battalion commander were standing the night before. In my opinion the challenge to halt was directed at someone who fired from close range. The grenade missed because it struck a branch on the way. The attacker escaped through the forest and was shot at by the soldiers who kept watch. Later, on the day our battalion was leaving Brnik we found a dead TO soldier, it was the one who had attacked us, he was killed not far from the guard post.

After the explosion I went over to the commander and helped him up. I noticed he was wounded. I bandaged his hand. He was in shock. His deputy arrived. The deputy said that the battalion should get ready to advance to the airport. He argued that the TO were using their grenade launchers and that the first grenade was fired to determine the ranging coordinates. He was adamant that we were going to be incinerated by morning if we did not leave our present position.

Panic spread through the battalion. We reinforced the sentry posts and everyone was at their assigned stations in their vehicles. We waited in complete silence. At about 23.00 hours the commanding officer of the 1st armoured regiment came to tell us that TO soldiers had been spotted moving in the wheat field just in front of our positions. The battalion commander ordered us to shoot. Heavy machine-gun fire began spouting from most of the tanks standing at the edge of the forest. The firing was so intense that one could see glowing lines of fire emanating from the tanks. Fortunately heavy artillery was not used... I did not hear fire being returned from the opposite side, which is why I still doubt there was anybody in the wheat field. The fire-works lasted long into the night and died down by morning. That morning sentry reported that someone was moving towards him on a bicycle. They were trying to stop him but because he was still coming forward shouting and waving his hands the commander gave the order to fire again. Shots were fired from one of the tanks. The cyclist fell but then got up and ran back in the direction he came from. Later we learned that the cyclist was an officer from the Kranj barracks who was sent to establish contact with us. Fortunately he was not hit but his bicycle was unusable. The officer returned to the Kranj barracks in shock.

In the afternoon the battalion commander held a number of meetings with squad leaders. I was not present but the deputy commander told me that they were mostly discussing the present situation and what had occurred during the previous night. We had no food or water left. The troops looked dismal. We began to dig additional trenches but due to the shortage of food and water the commander ordered that work be limited to only the most essential tasks.

We received an offer from the TO with the possibility to negotiate or at least establish contact. The commander accepted the offer only because he required medical aid.

The battalion commander, his deputy and I sat down to decide whom we should send out as our contact. I suggested it be the officer commanding the mechanised squadron. The deputy commander was ready to agree on anyone just as long as it was not himself. We finally agreed it should be the officer in charge of the mechanised squadron, named Lujić. I went to my tent and quickly wrote a short note which said that I was ready to establish initial contact with the TO. I took it to Lujić, revealing my true intentions because I did not want any more killings on either side. He assured me that he would keep it in confidence and that he shared my view. He later proved to be a man of his word.

After the initial contact with the TO everything went as planned. The TO provided medical aid to the commander, myself and a few other soldiers. Radovanović was told that he should be taken to a hospital because he needed professional assistance. He agreed, taking another soldier and an officer along with him. I believe that the departure of Radovanović was a key to the resolving of events at Brnik. With his departure from Brnik all the tension regarding the activities of the armoured battalion was relieved.

Soon afterwards the air force attacked the airport.

We were constantly listening to the radio and knew about everything that was happening, including the cease-fire between the TO and YNA. After the attack all of the officers gathered at the command post. No one could guess what this could mean. Some argued that the attack came to support the battalion in its attack on the airport and that the battalion should be getting ready for the attack in case the Air Force struck again.

I believe that Lujić's actions at that time caused many officers to change their opinion. He said that now that the Presidency had signed a cease-fire any further military activity could only mean that a coup d'etat had taken place. He affirmed that the army could only act on orders issued by the Presidency and that he would not participate in any kind of coup d'etat. He was trained for the defence of his country and not for anything that was happening now. I immediately agreed with him and so did several of the officers. Rasić, who was now in command, stepped in saying that since the battalion had no communication with the outside world and was unable to receive any orders telling them what to do, we would therefore act on the basis of radio reports and on what the Presidency decided. We finally agreed that our battalion would strictly abide by the cease-fire, taking action only if attacked and that any further decisions be made at meetings with everyone present.

At the next meeting it was decided that Lujić would be the battalion's contact with the TO. When he contacted the TO it demanded to be allowed to inspect the area where shooting had occurred on the previous night. On this day Rasić allowed the journalists to come within the perimeter of the battalion for the first time. In answer to the journalist's question he replied that the battalion had not suffered any casualties and as far as the opposing side was concerned they should ask the TO, since they were the ones who drove their men away and could therefore give them a count. This statement caused a rumour about a great number of casualties at Brnik.

Lujić and I agreed that he would enable me to go to the airport.

The TO agreed that we could get water from the airport but under the condition that only one officer came to get it. I was chosen since I had a truck.

When I got to the airport I had to identify myself. The first one I met was a police officer, Bizjak. He took me to the airport building through a side entrance and allowed me to call my family and talk to the police chief.

I explained the circumstances the battalion was in and assured him that we would not be the first to open fire. I also told him that Lujić could be trusted but that he could not make any decisions on his own. I emphasised that I wished to join the TO and that by training was an instructor for anti-tank missile use. We decided that I should stay with the battalion until the end, acting as a contact and informing them of any exceptional occurrences. From then on I made several trips to the airport every day.

The first soldier managed to escape from the battalion.

The TO permitted us to bring in food supplies from the Kranj barracks. We were all in desperate need of food and water but Rasić was nevertheless suspicious and ordered that food and water from each container be first tasted by the officer who brought it in.

After fifteen minutes of testing the food the officer finally gave his permission that it be distributed. Concealed in one of the food canisters was a letter from the commanding officer, Radovanović. He wrote that he was at the Kranj barracks and that his state of health did not permit him to return to the battalion. He included some kind of instructions on what the battalion should do and several telephone numbers on which he could be reached so that he could issue orders directly from the barracks. Lujić again did his job and convinced Rasić not to believe everything Radovanović said and that the letter was perhaps written under duress from the TO. We decided that Radovanović could not give orders until he returned to the battalion. Rasić never even tried to get in touch with Radovanović and the atmosphere remained unperturbed.

We reached an agreement with the TO which allowed us to come to the airport in small groups to wash. On these occasions we were allowed to telephone our families. For the Slovenians among us I made it possible for them to talk to the police, who gave them detailed instructions on how and where they should escape from their units. It would not have been wise to leave some of the soldiers behind at the airport because this would change the interpersonal relations within the battalion and affect the future development of events. For this reason all of us returned together and afterwards each one left the unit on his own. The parents of one of the soldiers came to meet him at the airport building.

After this the situation within the battalion settled down. It was agreed that I leave my unit at the end when the last of the tanks had left Brnik. Half an hour after this event I was supposed to be picked up by the boys from the airport.

Before the first group of tanks left Brnik, brigade commander Matić arrived. He held a meeting with the officers at which I made some strong accusation against him and then left the battalion. The officers thought I was psychologically depressed and ready to commit suicide. They went out searching for me. I reconsidered and went back and laid down beside a tank. I let the crew know I was there and they immediately called off the search.

After this I was sent back to Vrhnika. Two members of the territorial defence tried to take me away from my unit and even offered me their vehicle to escape in but the risk was too great.

I returned to the barracks and kept in contact with the Ministry of Internal Affairs until my final departure from the YNA.

* * *

Air Force reconnaissance was again very intensive. Helicopters carrying the sign of the Red Cross were again bringing in reinforcements, particularly officers, to those units which were ready to fall apart. The EC delegation visited some of the battle fields in Slovenia. Veljko Kadijević finally made his long-awaited TV appearance. Although he was still intimidating he nevertheless made a sober conclusion that forcing oneself into Slovenia was senseless. He announced new proposals that were going to be made to the Presidency of the SFRY. In view of everything we in the operations group evaluated the situation following Kadijević's speech and on the basis of the activities of the last few days concluded that we were in a good military position. We controlled 99 percent of Slovenian territory, except for the army installations which were under strict supervision and represented an advantage (hostages) rather than a danger. For this reason during the next few days we were very disappointed in view of the Brioni agreement, at least until we read the

210

hastily written declaration – drafted by Van den Broek and edited by none other than Ante Marković – between the lines and found enough manoeuvring space to preserve what we have gained in war.

A wise man said that one gets to know people well under exceptional circumstances. On the first day of the war many people whom I knew well and some not so well called me offering their help. They were volunteering for anything since on the first day we were short of weapons. During the total confusion, when events followed one another with lightning speed, Miloš Bukavec, who organised the celebration commemorating the declaration of independence, joined our coordinations group. He took the vital task of purveyor. From the first and to the last day of the war we hardly slept but we never went hungry. We enjoyed the delicacies of the very capable kitchen staff at the Executive Council building, where day or night we were greeted with a warm meal and a friendly smile. Miloš took care of us when times were hardest. While we were busy talking on the telephone he would sometimes force a cup containing vitamins and proteins into our hands and wouldn't leave before the cup was emptied. "You must eat" he kept telling us, "otherwise your reason will fail you. Do you think you are supermen?" During a war when one is faced with a multitude of problems one does not think of food. Sometimes Miloš had to swallow abuse when we thought he was bothering us with food at crucial moments when it was a matter of life or death. On reflection, however, we all appreciated his efforts, especially those members of the coordination group (Bavčar, Bogataj, Slapar, Kuzma) who spent most of their time in the coordination headquarters and who unlike the others were not relieved every twelve hours. Without regular meals we would certainly not have been able to survive the ordeal with only an hour or two of sleep each night.

Bojan Korzika also joined us on that first day. He was prepared to do anything at all just so he could feel useful. We did use him. Day in and day out he typed the incoming reports into the computer and performed a number of other essential tasks. He worked with us almost until the end of the war when he was replaced by professional operators. Many other people came offering their services. Whenever we met, Jože Pučnik tried to strengthen my determination. At the evening party coordination meetings during the first days of the war we were all in unity. Requests to join us also came from some of the members of those parties which had previously opposed the formation of our own defence system. We were receiving letters from other political parties and associations. Some of the leaders from the Party of Democratic Reform visited our units. But we were most pleased to receive a friendly letter from Niko Grafenauer and our friends from Nova Revija magazine, who like many other Slovenian intellectuals, artist, scientists, economists and cultural workers, through their friends abroad, significantly contributed to a favourable world public opinion of Slovenia.

The cease-fire gradually took hold and we thus had more time to talk about the past few days. Despite the short interval, certain assessments could already be made. Many believed that it was significant that our forces had

211

overcome the initial shock. On the first day of the war our men experienced psychological disturbances. Many could not believe that a war had actually begun. For this reason a gradual expansion of military activities was essential. The Territorial Defence forces and the police considered the non-violent obstruction of the opponent with road blocks and returning fire to be appropriate only in self-defence. They were not so enthusiastic about direct attacks on armoured units without effective anti-tank weapons. The opponent's air force also caused substantial anxiety. After the first air attack at Medvedjek a number of our men suffered severe shock and required medical assistance. But the situation slowly improved. A significant contribution was made by the media – the TV in particular – since it informed our troops in the field about our military victories, as well as about the great destruction which the YNA was causing all over Slovenia.

Throughout we were forced to search for original solutions because we were not equipped well enough to counter the opponent's strength; at the beginning we did not possess a single weapon larger than 100 mm-calibre and were in no position to defend ourselves against the enemy's air force. We only had a few anti-aircraft missiles but attempted to disable the enemy by interfering with their navigation systems. Right at the beginning of the war I ordered the officer commanding the 2nd PŠTO to try shelling and neutralizing the Cerklje military airport that was closest and the one most dangerous to us. When after great effort he succeeded in moving in close to the target and fired a few grenades, the aircraft took off in panic heading for Zagreb and Bihać. He then staged an imaginary attack. On the radio frequency which we knew was being monitored by the YNA he issued all the necessary orders as though a missile attack was ready to begin. All the remaining aircraft quickly left the base. After this the airport was not used in any significant way until the end of the war. With the same objective in mind the unit from the 5th PŠTO attacked the radar station on Ljubljanski Vrh but with less success. We disabled or destroyed other navigation equipment which made flights and effective operation of the enemy air force more difficult. In the event that attacks continued we were even planning an attack on the Bihać military airport. We managed to obtain detailed plans of this airport and a special commando unit began training for this risky but, under the circumstances, important operation.

The civil defence system performed well throughout. During the war local defence authorities bore the major burden of making preparations and adopting necessary measures. The local community civil defence headquarters for the most part performed well in sheltering and protecting the general population. Without them resistance would have been impossible.

Not enough time has passed for me to collect all the accounts from the most important protagonists; for now these have not been documented. I know of the Red Cross operations in which medical teams risked their lives rescuing the wounded; I know of operations in which police officers went to Šibenik in the middle of the war to collect escaped Slovenian soldiers; I know of the activities of our emigrants around the world who organised and helped their homeland in its hour of need. We received offers from Argentina, America and Australia from those who were prepared to take up arms in the defence of Slovenia.

13. THE BRIONI
DECLARATION

A ruler may impair his army in three ways:
1. when he does not understand that the army should not attack, but orders action;
2. when the army should not retreat, but he orders a retreat;
3. when he is unfamiliar with military matters but nevertheless engages in them.

Sun Tzu, The Art of War

SUNDAY, 7 JULY

The day began with unannounced flights by YNA Air Force planes and helicopters. Their activities increased during the morning. We sent a warning to Života Avramović and Ljubomir Bajić in Zagreb. At the same time the meeting at Brioni began between the representatives of Slovenia, Croatia, the SFRY and the EC. Our communications links with Brioni were extremely bad. We impatiently awaited the reports from our negotiators. In the meantime the generals were pressuring us to unilaterally release the captured YNA officers.

At 16.32 our informant in Belgrade sent us a transcript of the speech made by Blagoje Adić in which he announced a new advance on Slovenia. Despite the fact that he made the speech on 5 July, which was after Veljko Kadijević made his TV appearance, his words were a cause for concern. We decided it would be useful if we immediately informed the world public of the contents of this speech in order to increase the pressure on the EC Troika and make them more open to the arguments presented by the Slovenian delegation and less susceptible to the generals and Ante Marković. We summarised the transcript and presented it at the press conference:

SPEECH GIVEN BY THE CHIEF OF THE GENERAL STAFF, COLONEL-GENERAL BLAGOJE AĐIĆ, AT THE MILITARY ACADEMY IN BELGRADE ON 5 JULY AT 13.00 HOURS

1. General Ađić gave the speech to 150 high-ranking YNA officers who were mostly of Serbian and Montenegrin nationality. These officers were chosen to command some of the units in Slovenia and Croatia. They were to replace the commanding officers who during the operations in Slovenia had proved incapable and indecisive.
2. General Ađić made the following conclusions:
a) The YNA had been forced into a war by secessionist elements in Slovenia and Croatia which were blatantly destroying the foundations of Yugoslavia, the gains of

214

the socialist development of Yugoslav society and the common interests of all the Yugoslav nations.

b) Due to the unilateral and drastic actions by Slovenia the situation was dramatic and more difficult than in 1941.

c) The multi-party system has caused conflicts among the Yugoslav nations. Extremist elements came into power intending to destroy Yugoslavia and change the existing social order, replacing it with the worst kind of capitalism.

d) Yugoslavia either exists or it does not exist; anything else is a farce and there is no sense in talking about the difference between a secession and dissociation.

e) Macedonia and Bosnia and Herzegovina are moving closer to adopting similar solutions to those of Slovenia and Croatia.

f) The Federal Government and Marković made a secret agreement with the US and the West for the break-up of Yugoslavia, which was confirmed by the statement Marković gave to the press on 4 June 1991 and which is a complete lie. The deployment of YNA forces in Slovenia was the result of the decision adopted by the Federal Executive Council. The YNA forces were deployed in inappropriate numbers which resulted in defeat. We lost a battle but not the war.

g) At this moment our forces in Slovenia have withdrawn to their garrisons where they are being reorganised, supplemented and are preparing for further activities.

Because these units urgently require officers of your calibre we are sending you there immediately. You will have no right of appeal against this decision and are required to follow strictly the orders of your superiors. You are expected to be decisive and get the units ready for military operations and should arrive at your posts by 20.00 hours on 8 July 1991 at the latest. You will be taken to your assigned locations by helicopter, especially as regards Slovenia, where movements are to a large extent restricted.

h) Yesterday the Presidency of the SFRY adopted an eight-point resolution which was proposed by the Supreme Command Headquarters and aimed at forcing Slovenia to implement the previous decisions adopted by ZIS and the SFRY Presidency. If Slovenia refuses to do so we, the military leadership, as it is now popularly called, shall force the Presidency of the SFRY to enforce unconditionally the adopted resolution. If this does not happen, irrespective of the Presidency of the SFRY we shall attack with full force. We cannot wait any longer, there is no going back. We would be able to complete our job in Slovenia in 10 to 15 days. The conscripted units in Serbia and elsewhere are highly motivated and ready.

The betrayal of Yugoslavia is now unequivocal and it has been confirmed by the decisions taken by Slovenia, Croatia and many officers and enlisted men.

i) Many today resent the use of force by the YNA even though its obligations are set down in the constitution of the SFRY; many are turning the people against us even though the YNA represents the only remaining force which can save Yugoslavia against break-up and catastrophic war among the brotherly nations, which under the circumstances is unavoidable.

j) I again emphasise that we must force Slovenia to remain a part of Yugoslavia until such time as we all reach the kind of agreement that would also be acceptable to us in the YNA.

k) The motto "all Serbs are to live in one country" is unrealistic because this would lead to a war of total destruction, while the battle for Yugoslavia would also resolve this issue according to the principles valid to date.

l) A real possibility to reach an agreement between everyone in Yugoslavia still

215

exists, allowing the Serbs to keep their rights which they have had until now, especially if during the negotiations we implement appropriate policies.

m) Macedonia cannot survive without Yugoslavia because it would be quickly taken over by Albania or Bulgaria. The most difficult situation is in Bosnia and Herzegovina where the Serbs are holding unrealistic views since a Greater Serbia is not a realistic option and cannot be realised without a catastrophe. This is why the battle for Yugoslavia is the only solution and the one giving Serbs a chance to preserve their rights.

n) The circumstances within the YNA are unstable. Low morale is prevalent, which was made explicit in Slovenia. This we must rectify with all available means.

o) Intervention from outside is also possible (Germany, Austria, Hungary, Czech and Slovak republics). Intentions are present to form a community of 130 million people which for us represents a great danger because it is a concept of a Greater Germany.

p) All those officers who are not in favour of Yugoslavia and are not mature enough to handle the present situation should leave the YNA. Traitors should be shot on the spot without consideration or pity. The units which you will command must obey all orders strictly even if it means they must all die in the process. Remember the events at Ljubin Grob during the Second World War. We are in a position where all the nations of Yugoslavia will be grateful to us. We will not necessarily suffer many casualties. We are technically superior. A war demands sacrifices. The casualties suffered in Slovenia were minimal and could be equated to a road accident involving only two bus loads of people. From now on the opponent must be forced to surrender in fear, which means that all those that resist us must die.

r) I can assure you that there are no conflicts within the so-called military leadership; we are engaged to our utmost abilities, working together in a planned, organised and unified manner. You can rely on our support.

s) All of you who have publicly expressed that you could have done much better in Slovenia than we did, will now get a chance to prove it on the front lines in Slovenia and Croatia.

t) Your conduct should bring defeat and shame to all the Slovenian generals and officers who have defected to the enemy. In the end I would like to congratulate you on being chosen for this important task and call on you to use your knowledge and skills to the best of your ability in the battle for the survival of Yugoslavia and the gains of its socialist revolution.

We anticipated that Adić's speech would cause concern among our citizens but we could not have imagined that our negotiators at Brioni would not know how to use it to their advantage. Unfortunately that is what happened, and not through lack of knowledge. As they later explained, the Europeans were extremely inflexible and arrogant towards us and Ante Marković, and an argumentative discussion was impossible. The offer "take it (peace) or leave it (war)" did not provide a great choice, although today I am still not so certain that in the event of a renewed attack on Slovenia the pressure of public opinion in the EC countries would not let them remain entirely passive. Even before then the EC countries did not give us much help either. This was also true of Austria which first promised to help in providing protective equipment and radar information that could be used in early warning for the population, but took so much time getting around to doing so that in the end the help did not amount to anything at all.

Throughout the day the defection of soldiers from the YNA barracks and the unannounced flights continued. Occasionally our commanders called in asking about new developments. A kind of apprehension crept in on all of us. We were getting reports of misbehaviour and a fall in military discipline within our units. Accidents involving firearms started to occur and became more common during the next few days. Žarko Hojnik, for whom we did not know then or now whether he was on the payroll of the police or Delo newspaper, diligently chronicled every accidental shot fired by a TO soldier, but nothing bad about the police.

But more than anything else the Brioni negotiations worried us most. We had agreed with our delegation that they would call in often but they did only once or twice to say that it was a hard struggle and to enquire how many YNA officers we were holding captive. A thought crossed my mind whether it would not have been better for me to attend the negotiations after all. At 22.34 a fax message arrived from Brioni with an English version of the declaration but we could not tell if it was already signed or if it only represented a draft. After reading it we considered Annex 1 to the declaration to be entirely unacceptable and hoped that it would never be signed.

A little after 23.00 the commanding officer of the Novo Mesto garrison demanded to be provided with an escort that would accompany him to Dob to collect the captured officers. Because our people told him to go to hell, Andrija Rašeta called a few minutes later with the same demand, saying that it had been decided at Brioni. We did not grant his request either. The declaration that was sent from Brioni stated that the deadline for the release of prisoners expired at 24.00 hours the next day and that it applied to both sides.

MONDAY, 8 JULY

Immediately after midnight Milan Kučan called and informed us of the decision taken during the telephone meeting of the state Presidency that called on us to immediately release all the captive YNA officers (conscripts had already been released). He was not open to our arguments (what about the more than one thousand of our soldiers who were still held in the service of the YNA, as well as those imprisoned officers who would not follow orders that would force them to act against their own people), but the telephone connection was very poor. We took this decision as a bad omen but nevertheless issued the necessary instructions. We did not however agree to release the prisoners at night because we did not want to take any unnecessary risks. In the morning the delegation arrived in Ljubljana and dispelled our uncertainties. At Brioni it had signed a joint declaration which in short defined the following:
– the Slovenian police control the border crossings (which they had

throughout the "untroubled" period of Yugoslavia) but according to Federal regulations,

- customs revenues remain the income of the Federation,
- air traffic control is under Federal authority,
- the border regime as it existed prior to 25 June 1991 should be re-
-established,
- all blockades of the YNA units and installations be lifted,
- the YNA units unconditionally return to their barracks,
- traffic on all roads should be unobstructed,
- all captured equipment and facilities be returned to the YNA,
- all TO units be demobilised and return to their garrisons (obvious unfamiliarity with the nature of the TO as it was then, since all its units were formed out of reservists),
- all prisoners be released by 24.00 hours on 8 July.

A three-month moratorium was declared on the adoption of any kind of political and practical decisions regarding further steps towards independence. EC monitors were appointed to supervise the cease-fire and the moratorium.

According to the accounts of the participants in the negotiations it was evident that our negotiators (Kučan, Peterle, Drnovšek, Bučar and Rupel) held up well against the unrelenting Europeans. It was van den Broek in particular who was most antagonistic towards Slovenia.

MEMO

On the Brioni talks, dated 7 July 1991

1. Morning introductory meeting with the representatives of the European Twelve:

Milan Kučan:

First expressed his gratitude to the Troika for attending this meeting, the basic objective of which was to reach a peaceful settlement through negotiations. There was a pressing need for negotiations into which Slovenia was prepared to enter all along. In order to hold negotiations a number of different options must be provided, otherwise we could only speak of ultimatums. In our case it was a question of an ultimatum since the conditions were being set by the Federation. The documents adopted by the European Community in no way deny the rights of Slovenian self-determination. Peace is the guarantee for negotiations. Slovenia was attacked on its own territory. We have unilaterally halted military operations. The YNA was still not officially ordered to stop firing and incidents were still occurring. The Presidency of the Republic of Slovenia made a proposal to the Federal Executive Council and to President Stipe Mesić regarding the formation of a joint commission for monitoring the cease-fire. It has given its assurance that our side was honouring all the provisions of the ultimatum which is, however, totally unnecessary. We only defended ourselves. Now new circumstances exist. The war intensified through the use of technical means against which Slovenia is unable to defend itself – shelling, rocket attacks, and so forth – and for this reason the conflict needs to be internationalised. Other Yugoslav republics (Croatia, Montenegro, Macedonia) began adopting an attitude which is in no way opposed to Slovenian self-determination and is in support of peaceful negotiations. Prime Minister Marković, however, thinks otherwise. The Yugoslav army did not return to the barracks. A YNA mechanised armoured brigade was sent to Croatia.

President Kučan asked Minister Hans van den Broek the following question: "How should the deferment of the adopted act on national self-determination be understood? What does the three-month moratorium mean?"

1. It is time for talks on the settlement of all issues related to Slovenian independence and to the cooperation between all nations which are to live in this area. This does not exclude the possibility of establishing new relationships with the Yugoslav republics. This should be based on the decisions adopted by individual republics which are already being taken. The gradual establishment of Slovenian independence will not harm anyone else. This also includes the regulation of rights and obligations which were based on the life of mutual coexistence thus far. Who can in this regard offer us any guarantees? We primarily need a guarrantee from the Federal authorities and the European countries that the YNA will not attack again. We will not be the ones to attack first. It is not only the declaration but also war that has taken place within the period between the last and present discussions. The YNA did not merely intend to be in the border belt but also wanted to take control of the border crossings. It wanted to leave open only eight out of the present eighty border crossings and completely change the border regime – away from European standards. Slovenian independence did not cause the border regime to change. We want European borders; borders do not have to be protected by an army, we are not threatened from the outside. The army should leave the border regions and leave it to the authority of the police and customs. We do not want an iron curtain, nor political or ideological barriers. Due to the armed conflicts on our borders with Austria and Italy Ante Marković shares a different opinion. According to him the borders can only be guarded by the YNA. We propose that the borders be free from the army. Slovenian borders should be protected by Slovenian police. The common Yugoslav-Slovenian border should last only three more months after which the conflicting issues should be resolved. These include the customs as they once were; the position of the Slovenian Assembly which I conveyed to you during the night session in Zagreb. We are still prepared to negotiate despite the ongoing war. We need a partner not an ultimatum.

Hans van den Broek:
(Because I do not speak English I could only indirectly discern the thoughts that were expressed, through the help of an interpreter)

He emphasised the following issues:
- the constitutional act of Slovenia is a unilateral step,
- the border issue should be considered from the beginning,
- as regards customs it is necessary to honour the agreement reached with the Federal Executive Council (Mitrović-Ocvirk),
- the supervision of border traffic is not a problem; with regard to the emblems on the border – the state as it existed before Slovenian independence should be observed,
- a three-month period used for negotiations during which the suggestions made by the European Community should be accepted; Federal forces should be deblocked; all the military equipment should be returned,
- customs issues – an interim solution is possible by which revenues from customs duties should be collected on a special joint account held under joint supervision.

Hans van den Broek explained that the ultimatum stating the conditions for the cease-fire could be softened since a number of conditions had already been met. He hoped that in an hour or an hour and a half more constructive solutions could be arrived at in order to formulate a joint agreement.

Milan Kučan:

Apart from the first condition Slovenia has met all others. We call for a joint commission but the other side is unwilling to participate. I ask what is the reason for this? And as regards the second point: There was a war in Slovenia; the war has been halted; great damage has been caused in this impoverished country. We would also like an answer to this question. With respect to the agreement reached with the Troika, Slovenia is holding to the agreement.

(The statements made with reference to the postponement of the moratorium were not entirely clear to me because I am not familiar with the agreement reached in Zagreb to which President Kučan was referring.)

Continuation of the debate: Milan Kučan said they are repeating what has already been said. He believes that the nature of the talks could have been different. Regarding the borders he said that Slovenia did not go to war because of the flag but something could be done about it now, so that there is no army on the borders at all. He agrees that for now the Yugoslav passport should stay in effect. He said that we do not want the army to return to the borders and are prepared to discuss all other issues during the next three months. Lojze Peterle discussed the customs administration with the Deputy Prime Minister of ZIS and he should be the one to say something about that.

Poos:

- The border should be European; if we speak of status quo then the matter should be returned to the original positions. He supports Kučan's proposal – my impression.

– The army is to return to barracks.

– The YNA argues that it is blocked. It should be unblocked because it has to return to barracks which also applies to the TO and the police. If this happened today then we could begin to negotiate.

Milan Kučan:
Demands a cease-fire which is the only way in which all questions could get an answer. Slovenia does not have a regular army. The YNA was resisted by mobile territorial soldiers, who are at home on the land which they cultivate; The YNA units were blocked by the local militia. This is the continuation of guerrilla warfare. The TO did not attack, it only defended its own ground and is at present still closely protecting certain installations. The Slovenian TO is not stationed in garrisons; it is a completely different entity. The borders could be the point of discussion at today's meeting with the SFRY Presidency. There is disagreement regarding the customs revenues. Slovenia did not intend to keep those revenues which were paid for through goods of non-Slovenian origin. We even agreed that the Slovenian customs would administer Yugoslav customs tariffs.

Lojze Peterle:
He explained the situation as it existed prior to the declaration of independence of the Republic of Slovenia:

...It has been clear for a year that Slovenia should venture on its own path. Ante Marković began the discussions with Slovenia and continued them 10 days after it was attacked. The issues related to the borders, border administration, air traffic control, etc., are issues related to the effective authority of the state. In these fields Slovenian authorities will also work according to Yugoslav regulations. A proposal for a special border regime is acceptable if it is being supervised by someone from abroad.

Hans van den Broek:
The presence of the YNA at the borders is related to customs. If this issue is not resolved then a danger remains that the army will return. The customs issue must be resolved. This will return the YNA back to their barracks and the TO back to their homes. The demanded return of the military equipment remains current. The military equipment must be returned to its original owners. Open issues are those related to customs, the deblocking of the YNA and the TO. He asked President Kučan whether he sees a possibility that an agreement could be reached on customs; if not, a stalemate would continue.

Janez Drnovšek:
Slovenian Territorial Defence controls the border posts and protects the borders; the army must not return. The YNA intended to take control of the border crossings.

Lojze Peterle:
Slovenian people will find it unacceptable if we now allow the aggressor to return to the borders, since before we kept him away by force.

Milan Kučan:
Ante Marković keeps repeating that it is a Yugoslav border where the army must be present – the kind of army that shoots at our people. Perhaps this could be possible before when it was still the Yugoslav Peoples Army and hence also ours. This army today does not contain Slovenian nor Croatian nor Macedonian soldiers; it is now a Serbian army; and whom should a Serbian army protect?

Let us accept the proposal made by Mr Poos (customs, police and border administration).

Hans van den Broek:
In the event the YNA agreed not to take the borders would the TO be demobilised?

Milan Kučan:
Yes, of course!

Hans van den Broek:
We have to hurry otherwise we shall run out of time. We should immediately restore the original state, supervise the situation and on Tuesday send a high-ranking group of monitors to the borders that will perform their duty in accordance with the decisions adopted by the CSCE. We could set the following principles:

1. We reach a general agreement today.

2. The Federal Presidency has full authority with the cooperation from all the members and takes full supervision over the Federal forces (YNA).

3. All other issues would then be resolved through outside assistance. Today contact with the opposing side should be made and supervision of the army and passport control be established. The delegation of the Twelve is prepared to talk to the others. A new meeting with Marković, Mesić...

Milan Kučan:
We agree to negotiate but the Yugoslav Army must not return to the borders.

2. Meeting between the members of the Presidency and Federal Institutions at 13.00 hours.

Those present: Stipe Mesić, Ante Marković, Stane Brovet, Petar Grača-nin, Budimir Lončar, Vasil Tupurkovski, Bogić Bogičević, Branko Kostić, Borisav Jović and Janez Drnovšek.

The meeting was opened by Stipe Mesić. Ante Marković led the debate. Within a wider context Marković emphasised the following open issues:
- borders,
- border region and border guard posts,
- customs,
- a demand that the Republic border police work according to federal regulations,
- air traffic control be conducted in a unified manner.

Vasil Tuporkovski:
A cease-fire is accepted and supervised by a special commission. Regarding the borders he supported Peterle's proposal, saying that the border issues should be resolved in cooperation with the EC and the Troika.

Stipe Mesić:
Points out the changed circumstances; during the last talks with the EC representatives the YNA was still Yugoslav but this is no longer the case since it no longer contains Slovenian soldiers.

Branko Kostić:
Within three months the Republic of Slovenia should reinstate everything as it was prior to 26 June 1991. No one within the SFRY wants to force anyone to stay in Yugoslavia, and the separation should be conducted in a peaceful manner.

Ante Marković:
The discussions should be speeded up; there is no time for wider debate; pragmatic decisions have to be adopted in line with the proposition made by the European Troika. We should return to the conditions that existed prior to 26 June 1991 (including the borders); this was the condition under which Stipe Mesić was elected President. The situation now is as it is. Let us not go backwards in our discussions.

Borisav Jović:
Points out that this is not a Presidency session, that the decisions are not binding and that for him the situation is perfectly clear. He agrees however that the talks should continue.

France Bučar:
The Slovenian parliament adopted all the necessary documents for an independent Slovenia...

Ante Marković:
Returns to the issue of the borders.

Borisav Jović:
There is nothing to talk about!

Janez Drnovšek:
What Kostić said is perhaps true; no one wants to prevent Slovenia from leaving the SFRY without casualties. What is therefore the reason for the moratorium lasting only three months?

Branko Kostić:
No ultimatums were issued. The SFRY Presidency debated this on three occasions and the only request it made was, that the conditions be met. The YNA prisoners, namely, the YNA officers are being treated inhumanely.

Milan Kučan:
We proposed a joint commission but no one was for its formation. He agrees on the postponement of the implementation of the constitutional act. Mesić agrees with him. Kučan continues: Slovenia was in a war which is continuing. Negotiations are possible only if all options remain open and no ultimatums are issued. The YNA must not return to the borders.

Ante Marković:
Interrupts the conversation by mentioning the work of the negotiating teams, made up of Dušan Plut, Miran Bogataj and Žnidaršič on our side and Gračanin, Andrija Rašeta and Šarenac on the other side, which he is confusing with the expert commission, saying that Slovenia was the one to refuse participation in the commission.

Borisav Jović:
Tomorrow the session of the SFRY Presidency will be held to verify all that has been said. Because Slovenia is not prepared to give up its borders, only two possibilities remain: we take the borders by force or let them go. The answer is known: we will not let them go.

Milan Kučan:
We will not give up the borders. They will be protected by the Slovenian police. The YNA may remain at the border garrisons.

Ante Marković:
Again raises all the issues:
– border guard posts must be returned to the YNA,
– border crossings – Republic police administers the crossings under Federal regulations,
– the customs are a Federal authority working according to Federal regulations. For ZIS this means the reinstatement of the conditions as they existed prior to 25 June 1991 which means that the police works according to Federal regulations and all customs revenues go to the Federation,
– air traffic control – under Federal authority.

Budimir Lončar:

After a long introduction he comes to the point. Europe is changing. No one intends to dispute the Slovenian declaration of independence but its implementation must be postponed. For a peaceful solution it must be implemented in stages:
- European cooperation,
- moving in the direction of political behaviour that corresponds to new circumstances,
- consideration of legal succession which must be determined within the transition period and which will ensure peaceful separation. It involves a process of peaceful transformation of Yugoslavia after which Slovenia could become a new international legal subject.

Vasil Tupurkovski:

The intention of establishing a new European border during the moratorium period is unrealistic. Let us not be concerned with the banal, such as border signs and emblems. During the moratorium period a border must be established.

Petar Gračanin:

- the essential point is that the state border is the border of the SFRY and thus also the border of Slovenia (he falls back on Federal constitution and Federal laws).
- united customs administration,
- border traffic is controlled by the Republic police according to Federal regulations,
- border belt – 100 m wide belt and the guard post must be returned to the YNA,
- air traffic control under Federal authority.
Opinion: during the day he repeated himself at least four times.

Ante Marković:

In an irritable manner he demands an immediate "yes" or "no" to the following questions:
- acceptance of the agreement signed between Mitrović and Ocvirk on the customs regime,
- border crossings administered by Slovenian police according to Federal regulations,
- the 100 m border belt and guard posts are returned to the YNA,
- air traffic control under Federal authority.

Dimitrij Rupel:

After the occupation of Slovenia new circumstances arose. Mr Poos proposed a new formula in relation to customs administration which we accept. The talks with the EC delegation represent open issues under the condition that a cease-fire is established.

Milan Kučan:
Addresses a question to Marković:
- did they accept the constitutional acts and the Slovenian resolution of 25 June 1991 or not,
- Was or was not Slovenia in a war?

Ante Marković:
I am not going to answer such questions. He persists in the acceptance or otherwise of the Mitrović-Ocvirk agreement but agrees with Rupel's proposal that a special account be opened for the three-month period in which customs revenues would be collected. Authority over air traffic control should be assumed by the Federation. With reference to the border guard posts he demands that the situation as it existed prior to 26 June 1991 be immediately established and that in the three-month period European border standards be instated.

3. Second meeting with the EC representatives at 19.00

Introduction

Hans van den Broek:
Announces that they will deal with the finalisation of a joint declaration formulated according to the positions expressed that morning and an annex on the subsequently agreed ways of implementing the cease-fire and an eight-point plan. He stresses that this is only a draft.

Principles:

- only the Yugoslav nations themselves can decide on their future,
- it is essential that the negotiations on the future of Yugoslavia begin by 1 August 1991 at the latest, without any conditions and in line with European standards related to human rights, minority status and the right of self-determination, which also includes the right of secession,
- the collective presidency shall have complete authority in accordance with its political and constitutional role and especially as concerns the Federal armed forces,
- the nations involved shall refrain from the use of force.

Explanation of Annex 2.

1. Border regime: The Republic of Slovenia agrees to uphold the border regime as it existed prior to 25 June 1991 (Slovenian police administer the borders according to Federal regulations) for a period of three months.
2. Customs: Federal customs are reinstated, working according to Federal regulations; revenues from customs duties are Federal revenues which are supervised by both the Republican and Federal ministers of finance. The

conditions as of 20 June 1991 are reinstated – the Mitrović-Ocvirk agreement.

Milan Kučan proposes in reply that the customs revenues be collected on a joint account and supervised by six monitors from the republics, one from the Federation and two from abroad.

3. Air traffic control: is under Federal authority

4. Border security: van den Broek stresses that this is a very sensitive matter. He says that the YNA is thinking of a gradual withdrawal from the borders but for the time being wishes to return. He also speaks of an emotional reaction and wounded pride that is being expressed by the army. He continues by listing the most urgent tasks:

– deblocking of army installations
– immediate removal of all road blocks
– immediate return of military equipment

He warns that the deadline for the ultimatum runs out this evening and that something must be done. He says that the army was disgraced and that the politicians are calling on Slovenia to refrain from all military action. Slovenia should release all prisoners and remove all road blocks by this evening. The YNA shall not resort to the use of force. If the EC says it will sign the agreement this does not automatically mean that both sides will act in fairness. Tonight we have an opportunity to make our contribution to peace.

Milan Kučan:

The major problem is the relationship between the YNA and the SFRY Presidency. He asks who is to guarantee the safety of those officers who have fled from the YNA. To accept all of the conditions would mean capitulation. The Yugoslav government is setting unreasonable demands. For six years Slovenia has fought for democracy on its own. The threats by the YNA are threats against democracy in Yugoslavia. Ask Mesić whether the Presidency has any power over the YNA. At present the cease-fire is in effect. We do not know what will happen to the Slovenian soldiers who are held locked up at other garrisons which the army will not acknowledge. These soldiers are in chains and are considered to be traitors. Who is to protect the Yugoslav borders since the YNA is no longer the Yugoslav Peoples Army but a Serbian army? We accept all reasonable proposals but this is not enough. They also have to be accepted by others. Would the YNA be able to issue a statement by which it would promise to cease all military activities for three months? How will Slovenians survive? The borders are the key issue. With reference to the prisoners of war held at Dob – Slovenia proposed a joint commission which the other side is unwilling to accept. Asks that an international committee of the Red Cross which is currently in Ljubljana inspects the circumstances in which the war prisoners are being held. Other proposals are acceptable. We are not being confronted with arguments but with a show of force.

Hans van den Broek:
The status quo is only temporary and made to last for the period of three months. Peace should be given a chance. The international monitoring group arrives on Tuesday.

Milan Kučan:
This means much more than just capitulation; what have we gained by it? Some casualties and three billion dollars in damage.

Hans van den Broek:
Reprehends Kučan for his statement.

Lojze Peterle:
– an international committee should inspect the conditions of prisoners of war,

– we who have halted the pillaging by the YNA are now confronted with ultimatums.

In his opinion the aggressor will be rewarded and the victim will be punished. For the past year Slovenia was prepared to talk about all the open issues and is aware of how the talks will progress from now on. Under such circumstances the Federal government should resign and Slovenia will in the future negotiate only with the military authorities.

Hans van den Broek:
Prepare a list of Slovenian war prisoners. The deadline for the release of all war prisoners is 24 hours (24.00 on 8 July 1991).

After this a plenary session followed at which the declaration was signed.

* * *

On this day we held one meeting after another. First with the expanded Presidency, then with the government and in the evening with the members of the parliamentary parties. All those that participated at the Brioni negotiations were tired and nervous. They tried very hard to get others to explain to us that they were not happy with the Declaration but had no other choice in the matter. Europe issued an ultimatum. During the night I attempted to make a reasonable assessment of the document, especially the first annex which was its only significant part. I read each sentence ten times over trying to find the arguments for and against. After the fifth reading I thought I may have found a centimeter of manoeuvring space among some of the loose definitions but my general feelings were still not very good. I wrote down the arguments that were for and against the Declaration. We discussed the text with some of the members of the operations group. The decision was difficult. At the meetings of the Presidency, the government and the parties' coordinating committees I argued the following points:

■ ASSESSMENT OF THE POSSIBLE IMPLEMENTATION OF THE JOINT DECLARATION FROM THE MILITARY AND SECURITY ASPECTS OF THE REPUBLIC OF SLOVENIA:

The defence forces of the Republic of Slovenia resisted the aggressor through their relatively good organisation, incorporation of civil defence measures in obstructing the aggressor, as well as through the unanimous support of the population and political factors in Slovenia. With a few exceptions the media also provided strong support for the general resistance against the aggressor.

On the first day we adopted an appropriate tactic and isolated, blocked, captured, destroyed or at least neutralised the enemy's forces. The situation remained unchanged even after their use of the Air Force. The defence forces of the Republic of Slovenia also prevented the opponent's attempt to take control of the wider area around Brnik airport, the border crossings and certain other strategic locations. From the moment the order was issued for the neutralisation of the opponent's helicopters to the moment the cease-fire was declared (a good two hours), four helicopters were shot down, two of them were damaged and one was captured.

After the first cease-fire which was requested by the aggressor and assisted by the European Troika on 28 June 1991, the Slovenian defence forces were on the offensive and required only a further twelve hours of intensive military efforts with which to capture, destroy or neutralise the majority of the aggressor's forces in the territory of the Republic of Slovenia. After the cease-fire was in effect the enemy used helicopters to bring in reinforcements and necessary supplies to their blocked units.

By exaggerating certain activities in which the Slovenian forces engaged in blocking the aggressor's units, the enemy resorted to intensive propaganda warfare on the political, diplomatic and other fronts. On the basis of such efforts the enemy created psychological circumstances justifying the use of the Air Force, which through fierce attacks against TO positions, road blocks, infrastructure and civilian facilities caused chiefly psychological damage in Slovenia, while most of the casualties of the air strikes were suffered by the aggressor who by mistake fired on his own soldiers.

During the air strikes the Slovenian forces went on the offensive, capturing many military facilities, depots and guard posts, liberating almost all of the border crossings and seizing great quantities of arms. Among the captured military equipment the anti-tank weapons were of greatest significance because this substantially increased the TO ability to defend itself against the heavy armour. During the battle the Slovenian forces captured and destroyed approximately 35 tanks and other armoured vehicles.

On the day the aggression began there were approximately 22,000 of the aggressor's soldiers and officers in the territory of the RS, 2,000 of whom left Slovenia during the fighting while another 8,000 were captured, fled or surrendered to the police.

At this moment there are still approximately 12,000 of the aggressor's soldiers and officers in Slovenian territory.

With reference to the Brioni declaration and its provisions the following should be considered:

1. (Article 4 – border protection) – The reinstatement of the border regime that existed prior to 25 June would mean that the TO would have to give up 50 of the border guard posts which were taken during the fighting. The YNA controls only 10 percent of the facilities within the border belt which are being defended by insignificant strength. This would also mean that the TO would have to retreat from 34 of the border posts on the Croatian border through which it controls the advance of fresh enemy units into the territory of the RS. Because the declaration does not set a time limit for the proposed border regime based on European standards, this article represents a surrender of military gains.

2. (Article 5 – the implementation of the cease-fire) – The aggressor's forces located outside Slovenia represent a danger to the RS because the conscription of reserves is continuing. The YNA units have not returned to their barracks. The return of the installations and equipment to the YNA is an unacceptable condition because it would lower the defence capability of the RS forces 10-fold, without at the same time providing any kind of firm guarrantees for our safety. The demobilisation of the TO forces is possible within limits and only to the extent in which this would not threaten the balance of power and as long as the Territorial Defence soldiers are allowed to retain their personal weapons.

3. (Article 6 – prisoners) – A strong demand must be issued for the release of all Slovenian soldiers still serving in the YNA and especially those soldiers and offices who are held in military prisons. The international Red Cross should have supervision over the military prisons and the RS should within 24 hours draw up a list of all its citizens who are still serving in the YNA.

A great danger still exists that during the next few weeks the aggressor will replace the shortfall in the number of soldiers with reserves from Serbia and Montenegro and thus place along our borders an army composed of single-nationality units. Similarly, there is a danger that next time the aggressor will begin attacking the centres of command and decision making.

Some of the provisions of the declaration could from the defence and security aspects be acceptable only under the following three conditions:

1. For a limited period of three months.

2. With the adoption of strict measures preventing the aggressor from bringing fresh forces into the territory of the RS.

3. With the establishment of an effective anti-aircraft defence system and reinforcement of all other defence and civil defence systems within the Republic of Slovenia. ■

All in all we were facing a great danger, perhaps as great as on the morning of 27 June when we had to decide whether or not to resist by force. Such decisions are valid when adopted by a great majority. If there was a great difference of opinion the consequences for the nation and the state could be fatal. Because I knew that disunity would cause us to lose the battle, we feverishly searched for an acceptable solution.

During the day we released the captured YNA officers held at Dob. Some of them did not want to be returned to the YNA. They were taken to Zagreb where they were given a change of clothing and after being provided with arms were taken by helicopters back to their units. Despite the signed declaration the YNA did not release any of our soldiers. When protests were made the Europeans only shrugged their shoulders saying that according to Federal laws our soldiers were not being held as prisoners of war. For our TO and police units the declaration was a great disappointment. Our comrades from the Koroška region informed us that they would never give up the border post at Holmec for which they had given their blood and that not even a single Yugoslav soldier would ever be allowed to return there.

TUESDAY, 9 JULY

We were still unable to get a good night's sleep. The situation was tense everywhere. We still controlled most Slovenian territory and the borders. On the borders with Croatia we had 34 border posts which were preventing the YNA from bringing new forces into Slovenia. We demanded that all movements of military vehicles be announced in advance. We were still deploying an appropriate numbers of troops (30,000 armed territorials) which in case of new armed conflicts would suffice for defeating the remaining YNA forces in Slovenia. Because we were short of field vehicles we bought up all of the available quantities from Slovenian car dealers. The Nissan Adria company donated two of their civilian field vehicles to the TO and the police. From Austria we received 12 Puch jeeps that were on display at their dealerships since the factory did not have them in stock. They were all of various colours and models which was an advantage since consequently the YNA had a more difficult time surveying the movements of our special units.

The Presidency met again during the morning. We debated the existing circumstances and numerous breaches of the cease-fire by the YNA. Below I summarise the note of protest that was drafted at the meeting and sent to Belgrade, which included the descriptions of some of the more blatant violations.

PRESIDENCY OF THE REPUBLIC OF SLOVENIA
NUMBER: 060-54/91
Ljubljana 9 July 1991

TO THE SFRY PRESIDENCY, BELGRADE

The Presidency of the Republic of Slovenia has during its 54th session considered the existing circumstances in Slovenia following the establishment of the cease-fire and the discontinuation of military activities following the aggression by the Yugoslav

231

Army. The Presidency has concluded that the Republic of Slovenia is actively working on the implementation of its obligations pursuant to articles 5 and 6 of Annex I to the joint Brioni Declaration adopted on 7 July 1991. The Presidency also concluded that some of the demands or the obligations pursuant from these two articles cannot be implemented without a prior, more concrete agreement, for which the RS authorities await professional assistance and explanation of the Annex that should be provided from the EC monitoring mission.

Based on the information and unambiguous data in the possession of the RS authorities, the Presidency concluded that Federal authorities and the YNA are clearly violating their obligations provided by the Brioni declaration.

1. The competent Federal authorities have as yet not allowed or made possible the opening of Slovenian airports to regular traffic.

2. As at this moment not all of the YNA units have returned to their barracks, which includes those units in Slovenia as well as those present in the territory of Croatia and elsewhere in Yugoslavia, from where the aggression on the Republic of Slovenia began:
– the sections of armoured units from the Pivka barracks are still stationed at the Ajševica barracks at Nova Gorica,
– from the Kranj barracks new YNA units were transferred to the Bohinjska Bela barracks and their vicinity,
– on 7 July 1991 the YNA used helicopters carrying the signs of the Red Cross to bring in reinforcements from Belgrade and Zagreb to the barracks in Ljubljana, Vrhnika, Maribor, Novo Mesto and elsewhere.

b. The YNA is not providing full information to the Slovenian authorities on the flights of military helicopters and refuses to implement the provisions of international conventions related to the monitoring and inspection of air transport. The violation of the convention related to the issue of advance warning of military helicopters has endangered the lives of the two members of the SFRY Presidency, Bogić Bogičević and Vasil Tupurkovski, who on two occasions were being flown in a military helicopter to Ljubljana without prior notice.

c. In the event of a new attack, Slovenia will not so much be endangered by the YNA units who are already present in Slovenia but to a much greater extent by the units which are located in other parts of Yugoslavia. During the first phase of the aggression on Slovenia for instance, the units making up the 32nd, 10th and 13th corps were deployed. Consequently, the extensive mobilisation of the reserves which the YNA conscripted in Serbia, Vojvodina, Montenegro and in some other parts of Yugoslavia, represents a threat to the RS and is at the same time a violation of the provisions of the joint Brioni Declaration. According to our information, the mobilisation is continuing and involves approximately 200,000 troops who are for the most part of Serbian nationality. The conscription of such a large number of soldiers from among reserves of Serbian nationality changed the multi-national character of the YNA, which is rapidly losing its character of "the joint armed forces of nations and national groups". Some of the important YNA units have thus been transformed into exclusively Serbian units (the 1st armoured, mechanised guard division which is now at a state of alert and ready to advance towards the west, for instance). Similarly, the mobilisation of the Serbian TO was also undertaken, which according to the YNA battle plan makes up the second wave forces directed towards the west or in this case against the Republic of Slovenia.

d. The YNA has throughout the cease-fire period surveyed the territory of Slovenia from the air. In addition to helicopters, reconnaissance aircraft are also being used.

e. The YNA has not removed or deactivated explosive charges. It is installing new minefields outside the barracks and in the direction of inhabited areas, thus endangering the civilian population.

3. By agreeing to unconditionally release all prisoners of war the Republic of Slovenia fulfilled the stipulations of article 6 of Annex II of the joint declaration. Most of them have already been released while the remaining numbers cannot be released because the YNA refuses to allow mediation by the Red Cross, thus preventing the implementation of the provisions of article 6. As soon as cooperation from the international Red Cross is provided the Slovenian authorities will start releasing the remaining prisoners of war. The Presidency of the RS also emphasises that the YNA is in violation of this article because it has so far not released a single imprisoned Slovenian TO or police member, nor any other officer or soldier from Slovenia whom it is detaining. The Presidency of the RS has in this relation contacted the SFRY Presidency on two prior occasions (on 6 and 8 July 1991) but never received a reply. Furthermore, the Presidency of the RS stresses that the Slovenian authorities are fulfilling their obligations towards the Red Cross while the YNA has as yet not provided any data (the Slovenian Red Cross has thus far only received information about 42 wounded YNA members from the Yugoslav Red Cross). The YNA will not allow the members of the Red Cross to enter and inspect the military installations in order to determine the way in which the Slovenian officers and enlisted soldiers are being treated.

By issuing a warning of the violations of the declaration by the YNA and Yugoslav authorities, the Presidency of the RS expects the SFRY Presidency, in line with its authority and obligations, order the competent bodies to begin implementing their accepted obligations and ensure a peaceful resolution of the existing circumstances.

We are also informing you that the Assembly of the Republic of Slovenia will in its session on 10 July at 12 noon hold a debate on the joint Brioni Declaration.

The Presidency of the Republic of Slovenia will send a copy of this text to the presiding minister of the European Community, Mr Hans van den Broek.

PRESIDENT
Milan Kučan

On this day the newspaper editorial boards were swamped by letters of "support" for our negotiators. Letters were also addressed to numerous government institutions. Some authors clearly stated their belief that Slovenia had capitulated and that their time had come. The mayor of Koper, Italian-speaking Aurelio Juri, for instance, sent a letter to Ljubljana on 8 July in which he protested against some of the replacements that were made within the TO and the police. Mr Juri accused the Slovenian Government of being responsible for the war. The first paragraph of his letter, written in broken Slovenian, began: "The path towards the independence of Slovenia has clearly become much steeper than you led us to expect. It is therefore more than obvious that the Government has miscalculated or wrongly assessed certain of the steps that were to lead to independence and this has resulted in war."

Mr Mayor of Koper did not stop here, however. Two days later he wrote a much kinder letter to the commanding officer of the 13th Corps who two weeks before had occupied his entire region. He wrote:

"Dear General Marjan Čad!

On 29 June 1991 three young lives were lost at Škofije as a result of the cruelty and irrationality of war. Deeply regretting the tragic event and aware of my responsibility I thus entered into negotiation with you and your subordinates in order to prevent similar occurrences and calm down the situation within the province of Koper and contribute to peace in Slovenia and Yugoslavia. I hope that you will agree with me that we all performed our duty well. Allow me on this occasion to express my special gratitude to Colonel Krstić."

As we could later conclude from the letters which General Čad sent to Slovenia, he was entirely in agreement with the assesment that they both performed their role commendably. General Čad also used the agreement which on 29 June 1991 he signed with Juri, who had received no authorisation for the signing, to excuse his conduct.

WEDNESDAY, 10 JULY

In the morning a meeting of Demos was held. The members were not very enthusiastic about the Declaration. The negotiators themselves were at times unsure whether it was better to accept the ultimatum or not. It would have been easy to prevent or at least to postpone the decision accepting the Declaration in parliament. From past experiences it was clear that although it was very much in its favour – since it was to get back all that it had lost during the fighting – the YNA would try to avoid having to abide by the agreement. This would of course be quite irrational behaviour, but that institution could not now change its skin. The protest that was sent to the SFRY Presidency could have provided us with many excuses. If the opposite side violated the agreement, then we could also implement it at a slower pace. This was not, however, the most decisive issue. The issue which convinced me, and many others with whom I later spoke, to ratify the Brioni Declaration was the simple factor of unity. I was aware that being united over such significant issues as independence and sovereignty was much better, even if the unacceptable ultimatum was signed, than breaking up and being divided; in the latter case we would only be working to the advantage of the YNA and all those who had forced the ultimatum on us. This argument I presented at the Demos session and after describing positive and negative aspects of the Declaration I believe I managed to convince most of them to agree with me.

234

The session of the Assembly began at 12.00 and after a short debate parliament ratified the declaration by more than a two-thirds majority. One big step backwards was made. Now we were left with having to make numerous little steps to move two steps forward.

14. THE RETREAT OF THE YUGOSLAV ARMED FORCES

Following the acceptance of the Brioni Declaration we called in the operations group. We went through the agreement inch by inch – particularly annexe 1 – and with the resolutions now passed we made absolutely ultimate use of the manoeuvring space we had discovered in between the provisions of the annexe. Here I was relying on the fact that three months was a long time in which just about anything could happen, while I was almost certain that there would follow a YNA attack on Croatia. We had agreed to stick to an unconditional withdrawal of YNA units to barracks, and we interpreted this provision as meaning that they should remain there without reassembling for offensive readiness. We would allow no re-forming of YNA units what-soever, nor their crossing of the Slovenian-Croatian border. We would reinforce the new guard posts on that border. With the return of occupied facilities, arms and YNA equipment, we could play for time as much as this was possible. We would not return any offensive weapons. The YNA would have no right to inspect destroyed or captured equipment and facilities. We had already emptied the warehouses some time ago. We would not allow the YNA to get to the border and it in anyway would not have enough men to do so, it we will not allow new units to join them.

This is how we proceeded, and it paid off. Some politicians accused us of sharpening tensions and of igniting a new conflict. But the truth was rather different. This was quite simply the only possibility, otherwise the Brioni declaration would have sealed our fate. During the war we had taken over all the bigger military warehouses. Tens of thousands of tons of military equip-ment had provided untold reinforcement for our defensive power. We were also in possession of more than 50 usable tanks and other armoured vehicles. For the first time we had enough ammunition for all the infantry weapons, and we actually had more operational anti-armour systems than we had men called up. The border was cleared. If everything was returned to the state of affairs before 25 June 1991, it would in our opinion have practically speaking disarmed us and handed back everything we had gained in battle to the enemy, who would again have time to prepare an attack. The Europeans who forced the Declaration on us gave us no guarantee that they would defend us in the case of a new offensive from the YNA. All we got were half-hearted promises that they would recognise us in that event. Poor consolation. They also recognised Bosnia, but this didn't put off the aggressors one bit. On the contrary!

The YNA did not withdraw its mechanised guard divisions to barracks. The mobilisation continued in Serbia. There were no clashes yet in Croatia. If we allowed them, they would cram the border and barracks with Serbian reservists and volunteers. Then we would have to dance to a different tune. Some people maintained that Ciril Zlobec and Janez Drnovšek should be with them when they came, if they could not see now how urgent our measures were. We calmed these inflamed spirits, and worked out our tactics to the last detail. All the barracks were reconnected to municipal services and we pulled back the blockades from their immediate vicinity. But everything was under our surveillance, and the officers had to register with our units upon exiting the barracks.

Naturally, such a position did not suit the army. They sent us constant protests, and we sent our own back. There was nowhere where we obviously broke the Declaration, and we tried to establish in those points where the Declaration did not define things whether the provisions were ambiguous. Escapes from the barracks continued. Even with their charade of bringing troops into Slovenia every day in Red Cross-marked helicopters, they could not bring enough in to take the place of those who had fled. The number of YNA members fell significantly each day. We organised some escapes ourselves, particularly if Slovenian soldiers were involved. Crews for tanks and other military vehicles were incomplete, and for this reason the majority of their heavy artillery was inoperable. In some places there were so few soldiers left in the barracks that even NCOs had to do guard duty.

Belgrade protested even more vehemently. Meanwhile the European observers came and somehow we managed to persuade even them sufficiently for them to believe that the Declaration forbade the bringing in of fresh YNA units to Slovenia. At first they were extremely dubious, but in time we proved to them that such reinforcements could only be Serbian reservists, since there was no new number of soldiers entering the YNA worth mentioning. When they realised this, they were immediately more decisive in their support of our position. But they did not want to hear anything about not returning captured equipment or facilities to the army. In this respect the Declaration was quite clear for them. We could merely procrastinate, and here our commanders became real master tacticians. The first point, however, was more significant.

In the meantime, on 12 July the Federal Government unequivocally demanded the money from our customs duties, and a day later we received a letter from the Federal Secretariat for Defence in which, in accordance with a decree from the Presidency of the SFRY they demanded from Slovenia no more and no less than that we resume sending them conscripts. They demanded the immediate sending of nearly 4,000. Yugoslavia, which at least as far as Slovenia was concerned, had been buried on 25 June, had on the basis of the Brioni document began again to rise from the dead.

On 14 July the 14th Corps announced that they would start to move and resume "regular military training" without our permission, and that they would return to the buildings which we had taken from them during the war.

Again we had to blockade some barracks. The command of the Corps desisted when it realised that the balance of force was not favourable for them. Slowly the fact that they were cornered dawned on them, and in spite of sharper discipline the desertion of soldiers from all units continued. Day by day the YNA in Slovenia was fading away.

For the eventuality that Slovenia might not come back into the federal fold, the YNA general HQ had plans for a push through Croatia into Slovenia, but before doing this they wanted to strengthen their units actually in Slovenia to guarantee a bridgehead and provide some insurance for their expensive hardware in the barracks. Since we did not allow this, the YNA was in a serious dilemma. If they just attacked us out of the blue, they would be clearly breaching the Brioni agreement, and apart from that they would run into fierce resistance. They would also have to weigh up the fact that we would immediately clean up the remnants of their units in Slovenia right at the start of any attack, and before they could penetrate the interior of the Republic. In spite of the mobilisation of reservists, they were still far from having enough strength. Just to use the air force was pointless, because the world public would be sure to respond, and in any case the use of aircraft alone gives you no chance of occupying the smallest piece of territory.

So there remained one single possibility for Veljko Kadijević and Blagoje Ađić, and they used it. The only people who could prevent such a stratagem were the Serbian majority in the Presidency of the SFRY, who would formally have to pass a resolution on the withdrawal of the YNA from Slovenia. The general HQ calculated that at that moment it was better to withdraw the units and expensive hardware from Slovenia. Their plans already included a campaign in Croatia. If they succeeded there, then according to their calculations Slovenia would present no great difficulty. If they occupied Croatia only partially, and in this way secured the borders of a greater Serbia, it would be better in the clashes for them to have the greatest number of units, particularly armoured vehicles, which were still in Slovenia. Serbian politicians had made the same calculations, only theirs were probably more concrete. It was clear to Slobodan Milošević and Boris Jović after the defeat in Slovenia that they could no longer use the entire territory of Yugoslavia for their own purposes, not even through force. The minimal plan envisaged the joining up of territories where Serbs lived into territorially as closely linked a community as possible, and naturally the appropriation of certainly the biggest possible portion of the former common federal property. And of course the biggest part of this was in the hands of the YNA. The equipment and arms which the YNA still had in Slovenia were worth several billion US dollars, plus this was material of which the Serbian leaders intended to make further use in the immediate future. They would no longer be able to extricate this material from Slovenia by force, but they might just do it through negotiation.

In the meantime a commission had started to function. This commission was composed of representatives of Slovenia and the YNA, and was supposed to coordinate certain technical matters in connection with the

238

implementation of the Brioni Declaration. Our part of the commission was headed by Miran Bogataj, who very skilfully drew out the negotiations so much that in the end the YNA had to leave a large part of its hardware in Slovenia.

During the negotiations on Brioni, Janez Drnovšek tried to sound out Borisav Jović about Serbian intentions vis-a-vis the proposal to withdraw the YNA from Slovenia. Jović promised nothing final there, but he openly acknowledged that the YNA property meant a great deal to them, although at the actual talks he decisively opposed any kind of compromise favourable to Slovenia. When even the military high command, on seeing the position in which the YNA found itself in Slovenia after the Brioni Declaration, judged that a withdrawal would at least temporarily be the best solution, the Serbs also agreed to it.

On 18 July the SFRY Presidency passed a resolution whereby the YNA would withdraw from Slovenia in three months (of course with all its equipment and weapons), and before this all our soldiers who were still doing national service in the YNA would be released. It also wrote in this decree that with such a resolution it was not prejudicing the future arrangement of relations in Yugoslavia, nor was it in this way bringing into question the territorial integrity of Yugoslavia. By adopting such a position (point 9 of the decree) the YNA and Serbia had left open a door for their return to Slovenia. Our further activities and the extent of clashes in Croatia finally slammed this door shut on them for good.

Slovenia breathed a sigh of relief. As soon as Janez Drnovšek broke the news to Ljubljana, Milan Kučan called to congratulate me. I returned a similar congratulation, since this had been a joint success, and the outcome had been influenced most critically by our actual joint decision on 27 June to defend ourselves with arms, and of course by the collective valour of our fighters and all the others who acted resolutely during the days of war. Another very important factor was our decisive use of absolutely all the manoeuvring space which we could find in between the ultimative demands of the Brioni declaration. I also took the first opportunity to congratulate Janez Drnovšek. Although his services towards a favourable solution were not such as actually appeared to many people, he did complete his share of the job and after the situation was rather more developed, very well.

My first task was to convince all the others in the Presidency and the government that our goal was not simply the withdrawal of the YNA, but also the creation of such conditions as would prevent them ever returning. We were more than a match for the first armoured brigade at Vrhnika most certainly while they did not have complete crews and were demoralised, and while they were entirely dependent for their basic supplies on our goodwill. But the situation would have been completely different for us if they had dispatched their most modern tanks for example to Banja Luka, fitted them up into perfect working order, filled them with complete, specially picked crews, provided them with the necessary infantry and air support and sent them to our borders. In that case the superiority of armoured units would

239

have been paramount, and we did not have enough supplies for an anti-armour battle over greater distances.

Generally speaking, our arguments were well received by everyone. At first only Ciril Zlobec and Dušan Plut had reservations, although in principle we were all united and our goal had become: "Do everything to make the YNA withdraw as soon as possible and never return!"

The resolution by the SFRY Presidency also came as a surprise to the EC and its monitors in Slovenia. Suddenly they became almost redundant. It is true that towards the end of the moratorium they were more of a hindrance than a help, as the situation had changed radically, but the majority of them were very agreeable and wished Slovenia well.

The broken communications in Croatia and organisational incapacity of the YNA drew the withdrawal out. The clashes in Croatia took on increasingly grave dimensions. My prediction had, unfortunately, come true completely. The wounded beast, which had broken some teeth in Slovenia, had chosen as its next target Croatia, which had left it too late for properly effective resistance. It was forced into frontal clashes, where the YNA with its powerful artillery, aircraft and armoured units had a clear advantage. Zagreb has only the great bravery of individuals and some units of the Croatian army to thank for the fact that the city was not simply surrounded and blockaded. Although they dealt with matters differently, we were able to offer significant help to Croatia's defence in the most critical days. In its conflict in Croatia, too, the YNA made some serious mistakes. It persisted in a frontal attack on Vukovar, where the brave defenders completely wiped out its advantage in aircraft and armour. Without any military need it attacked Dubrovnik, and in this way caused an extensive internationalisation of the conflict.

Towards the end, because of the broken communications in Croatia, whose forces had actually captured several transports, the YNA wanted to withdraw the last contingent of its units through Italy. At first the Italians approved this, but then they bowed to public pressure and revoked the permission. Since the deadline for withdrawal was running out, and the initiative for withdrawal through Italy was if nothing else surprising, we also debated the situation in the government. The following problems were stressed:

■ I. On the initiative of the Yugoslav (Serbian) military command, the government of the Republic of Italy accepted the withdrawal of the remainder of the YNA through Italian territory. The remainder of the YNA (some 2500 officers and soldiers and 800 to 1000 wagons carrying for the most part non combat equipment) should in this way be removed by ferry from Trieste harbour to the port of Bar. Certain information we had indicated that the entire EC has approved such a course of action. Preparations for this should start on Monday 7 October 1991.

This initiative opens up a range of questions, among which it is difficult to clarify the following:

1. Why has a similar withdrawal not taken place via the port of Koper, which has remained open all this time, or through Rijeka, where up until very recently the YNA was in complete control of the situation?

2. Why is Italy (and the EC as a whole) still prepared to do favours for the YNA, in spite of the continuation of the war in the Republic of Croatia?

II. The Republic of Slovenia can either accept this initiative or reject it. It has enough real might at its disposal to be able to prevent such a withdrawal without any great risk. If the Republic of Slovenia accepts and permits such a withdrawal, it must consider above all the following facts:

1. The remainder of the YNA is expected to withdraw via Trieste to the port of Bar. In this sector the YNA is facing serious difficulties from decisive resistance by the Croatian forces defending Dubrovnik and southern Dalmatia. In just a matter of days the withdrawn troops and part of the combat equipment could be used in an attack on Dubrovnik.

2. The resolution on the withdrawal of the YNA from Slovenia was passed at a time when the YNA was still not collaborating directly with Serb forces in the aggression on Croatia. Today this link is more than obvious and every military strengthening of Serbia represents direct help in its aggression on Croatia. In the event of a complete military crushing of the Republic of Croatia the danger for the Republic of Slovenia is again seriously increased.

The units of the YNA – and their equipment – that have so far been withdrawn from the territory of Slovenia (90% of the manpower and over 80% of the moveable property) have for the most part already been actively incorporated into the aggression. Since the connection between an unimpeded withdrawal of the YNA across Croatia's hinterland and the creation of conditions for the continuation of aggression on the Republic of Croatia is obvious and understandable to all, such a course of action would of necessity be to the detriment of our relations with the Republic of Croatia, and would above all come up against an extremely negative response in the Croatian public. Given that we have with this state our longest border as well as numerous ties, this will be a very important long-term factor to consider.

3. The YNA has still not returned to the TO of the Republic of Slovenia the majority of the arms and equipment confiscated last year. In the event of a rapid withdrawal of the remainder of the assets and of the regime to date, which does not allow for effective TO control over the assets removed, and given the clearly favourable disposition of the majority of observers towards the Yugoslav Army. There exists a real danger that the YNA will also remove the property of the TO which is still under their control.

4. We have for the most part verified information that partly before the war and partly after it, the YNA removed from Slovenia a portion of the TO equipment, some of which it destroyed (the warehouse at Črni Vrh). We would also have to account for this lost equipment in this conclusive phase of the first transfer of assets, although the YNA has consistently avoided dealing with this question. It is unacceptable for the YNA to remove one single remaining wagon of equipment until this account is drawn up.

5. In view of the strong cooperation of the Italian authorities with the

YNA, the pretensions of certain extremist Italian parties and even liberals towards the Slovenian coast and given the possible continued sharpening of the crisis in Yugoslavia, there also exists the possibility, or danger, that units of the YNA might also come back by the same route, naturally up to strength and reinforced.

III. A rejection of the proposed withdrawal of the remainder of the YNA via Italian territory could trigger other reactions such as:

1. We might be accused of not abiding by the agreement on the withdrawal of the army or rather the resolution of the SFRY Presidency as accepted by Slovenia.

2. Certain states of the Twelve, or the entire EC might accuse us of deliberately creating an environment of conflict and of behaving irrationally.

3. The domestic public might accuse us of risking conflict for the sake of Croatia, while during the June aggression the Croatians were not prepared to help us.

4. In the event of conflict this may be used as an excuse for the delaying of international recognition for Slovenia.

IV. If we take into account the arguments for and against, we see that there is no ideal solution. In view of this we propose that:

1. The Executive Council and Presidency of the Republic of Slovenia, in accordance with the resolution of the RS Assembly insists on the last member of the YNA leaving the territory of the Republic of Slovenia at the latest by 18 October 1991.

2. The Republic of Slovenia is prepared to facilitate the safe withdrawal of the remaining members of theYNA via the port of Koper.

3. Before this withdrawal it will be necessary to draw up a final account of the YNA and TO assets, and to replace those assets of the TO which were destroyed or confiscated from warehouses both before and after the war.

4. Armoured and other equipment in the possession of the YNA in the territory of the Republic of Slovenia should remain in Slovenia until the aggression on the Republic of Croatia stops, or until the drawing up of a final account of the division of assets.

5. On 8 October 1991 Slovenia takes effective authority over its territory, together with control of its air space. For each overflight by military aircraft and helicopters the YNA must obtain prior authorisation from the competent body in the Republic of Slovenia.

6. Members of the YNA who might still be in Slovenia after 8 October 1991 will be treated according to procedures stipulated in the law for the treatment of members of the armed forces of foreign states.■

Nothing came of the proposed withdrawal of the YNA via Trieste. The deadline passed. As a trade-off for an extension of the deadline and permission to withdraw through the port of Koper we managed to get a large part of the military hardware which the army had still not removed. Our technicians and counter-intelligence agents had cracked the YNA coded communications system and listened to conversations between Zagreb and Belgrade or rather between Andrija Rašeta, Stane Brovet, Šljivić and other generals and admirals. We knew precisely where we had to apply pressure to make them yield. Before each round of negotiations we worked out our tactics, and then Miran Bogataj would normally secure everything we planned. We acquired more than 200 tanks and other armoured vehicles and means of transport, which we so urgently needed. We also hung on to the equipment in the military hospital in Ljubljana and around 700 wagons of a wide variety of military equipment. Janez Drnovšek accused us of risking a dispute because of a few tanks. But this was not just a few tanks, since a rough estimate of the value of the military equipment and arms that we had secured in the final phase showed that we had around US$ 500 million worth of equipment, and in any case we were risking no dispute. We were very well acquainted with the position of the supreme command, which due to the unfavourable development of events in the Croatian battlefields had decided that its bottom line in negotiation was the withdrawal of the remaining troops and officers, and then anything else it could get. The Army had signed a document by which it relinquished all the remaining arms and equipment in Slovenia until the division of assets.

The twenty-fifth of October 1991 was a bright sunny day. We flew in a helicopter over the motorway towards Postojna and observed the last column of Yugo-soldiers which was withdrawing from Cerklje and Ljubljana towards Koper. It was a truly beautiful day. The dreams which the President had allowed us to hope for on 26 June had come true. I am sorry that they did not come true for Peter Petrič and others who were struck down for ever. All the same, we paid a fair price. Large or small – it depends on which angle you view it from. For the orphans and widows of the fallen it was the highest price which it is possible to pay. For the country which emerged and for its leadership, most probably a very low price. It could have been far worse.

The column of military trucks was spread out all the way to Koper. From the air we could clearly see that some of the YNA officers in the parking lots had hidden amongst their personal belongings arms, mostly api M-84s, scorpions, which fetch a high price on the black market in the south. In the inspection before their embarkation our special police were very glad to relieve them of such contraband. They could only take with them the most basic personal weapons, as signed in the agreement.

I even noticed a smile on the face of my normally stern deputy Miran Bogataj. Over the last few weeks, as the leader of our negotiating group he had drained the very lifeblood from them. General Rašeta even started smoking at the negotiations – at his age. They left almost naked and barefoot. In this process we acquired, over and above the cache of military hardware, the Vrhnika barracks, in which there remained in our hands until the "division of assets" equipment worth more than US$ 100 million. It was bought, of course, with Slovenian money, as was much of what they took away. But it could have been far worse.

Our dreams had come true. The land underneath us had acquired a new image. In the mountains and hills we suddenly no longer saw lookouts and defensive positions, our flight did not have to avoid barracks and rocket emplacements, and at the crossroads the tank traps remained simply as a reminder. The view spoke of a pleasant autumn environment, vineyards and Karst hollows, our homeland from which the last uninvited guests were making their hasty departure. We could breathe in freedom, we could feel it in the rays of the autumn sun and the October colours of the forests. I was pleased. It had been worth it.

On the following day we organised a celebration in Koper of the final liberation of Slovenia. Apart from President Kučan, who was the guest of honour, both I and Igor Bavčar addressed those present. I tried in a few sentences to go over again the path we had trodden:

■ For a moment let us look back one year. We will see that in the beginning we had almost nothing. On the day of election of the first democratic Slovenian government the Yugoslav generals confiscated the arms of the Territorial Defence. The Yugoslav Assembly then set up a production line of regulations by which they robbed the republics of those remaining meagre areas of jurisdiction in their own defence. They sent our conscripts thousands of kilometres away into foreign parts. The Yugoslav government, Serbian generals and Serbian Presidency on average twice a month issued serious threats to Slovenia.

But we had a vision of our own independent state, we had the will, skill and courage to put the required weight behind our words. In our own defence structures we did not perform any purges on political or national grounds. We depoliticised the Territorial Defence. When parliament took the decision to stop sending our boys abroad to do their military service, we also carried this out in spite of threats.

"Our parliament allocated exactly the same funds to our own defence and the almost empty-handed TO as it did to the very army which later attacked us. The majority of our anti-armour equipment was used up in the first days of the war. Then we were supplied by our opponent. But the war for Slovenia was not just won by weapons. It was won by the high level of united will among the people and the great majority of all those living in Slovenia. This time we did not wish to miss the historic opportunity. We seized it and no one can take it from us.

A few hours ago the last foreign soldier left our territory. Slovenia is a free and practically sovereign state, much more so than certain other countries which might be internationally recognised but which still have foreign armies in their territory. And it is not simply that we are sovereign – from this moment on there is no force which could take a kilometre of its territory from Slovenia.

Perhaps it is most important today that Slovenia has become safe. Security is a fundamental condition of stability and economic flowering. This does not mean simply that with the withdrawal of the foreign army we have fulfilled one of the essential conditions for international recognition, but also that with their departure our economy has obtained the possibility of the influx of foreign capital, since investments in a secure state are much less of a risk.

In the beginning we had almost nothing. Only people and will. Today, after just over a year, Slovenia has behind it a successful defensive war and, for the future, an adequate defence system. We have gained back almost all the arms of the TO and a good deal of those of the aggressor. Today our young lads are doing their military service at home, and it is half the time they were required to serve in Yugoslavia. We recognise the right to conscientious objection. In spite of the war, this year Slovenia has allocated for military means a third of the money we sent last year to the YNA.

We have become the agents of our own defence. For a state which is not capable of defending itself is not a factor of stability and peace. In a situation when the appetite of one or another neighbour can be aroused, this generally becomes the source of instability and potential conflict. The well-intentioned do not desire such neighbours.

We will endeavour not to have to use arms again, in spite of the fact that in our vicinity there is raging a war and that today we dare not set aside all our cares. As before, and also in the future, arms will not represent a means for Slovenia to achieve all her political aims, but simply the instruments of our own defence in extreme situations.

If ever, today is the right time for us to express our gratitude to all those who did most to ensure that we are independent and free. Sadly those who made the ultimate sacrifice are not with us today. We will endeavour to pay our debt to their memory and to their loved ones in the next few days.

Please allow me to express a sincere word of thanks to all members of the Manoeuvring Structure of the National Defence, who with great personal risk and even greater enthusiasm more or less illegally secured the first steps towards independence, all members of the Territorial Defence of Slovenia, who proved that with a strong will and knowledge of one's homeland it is possible to resist a far more powerful aggressor, members of the internal affairs authorities, who took on a substantial burden of the defensive preparations and combat operations, members of the civil defence and staff of the administrative bodies for national defence, who coordinated certain decisive operations of civil defence, companies and citizens who according to the letter of the law and also voluntarily contributed their technical means for the requirements of defence, the media and in particular those journalists, photographers and photo-journalists who at great risk brought the truth from the actual field to the world, members of the fire brigade, hunters and other associations and organisations who cooperated in defence activities, political parties, the leaders of municipal assemblies, executive councils and other bodies for their active cooperation at a time when the war would not allow them to consider normal procedures, and last but not least our Slovenian relatives in Europe, the USA, Canada, Argentina, Australia and elsewhere, who during our most difficult days gave as much as they could of moral and material support.

Special thanks go to those friends of ours, Slovenians, Croatians and others, who in the uniform of the now defeated YNA, in those days and months when the army was still strong and dangerous, at great risk to themselves and their families, worked unselfishly for the interests of their people. Their help, information and advice were priceless. I am sorry that because of their absence or the nature of their work we cannot name them today, but we will soon redress this wrong.

Permit me, finally, on this historic day, to wish all of us together, as we tackle all the problems that await us, the same common will and sincere cooperation that we showed in the defence of our homeland. In this let the free and independent Slovenia be a safe, pleasant and wealthy home – for us and future generations.■

The great story continued, for but the most critical chapter had been written. Slovenia had indeed taken control of all its territory. The key condition for international recognition had been fulfilled.

A few days after the final withdrawal of the YNA we organised an inspection of the barracks in Metelkova street for members of the former collegium of the Committee for the Protection of Human Rights. The bars on the empty cells of the military prison no longer seemed threatening, thanks mainly to the very people who were visiting it that day. The finale of the battle for human rights, which can only be protected by a state based on the rule of law, began with the resistance against the most totalitarian of establishments in the spring of 1988. At that time a critical mass was achieved. Events then simply followed their own inevitable logic.

EXPLANATORY LIST
OF MAIN FIGURES

Blagoje Adjić, lieutenant general in the YNA head of the YNA General Headquarters, issued the basic instructions for the action by which Slovenia should have been forced to close both Territorial Defence training centres (17 May 1991), and threatened the use of all means available for mass destruction. Directly responsible for the use of aircraft and for the destruction of RTV transmitters in Slovenia; later replaced and retired.

Milan Aksentijević, colonel of the YNA delegate in the Slovenian Assembly, representing the YNA according to the socialist constitution of the SFRY, and participant in the aggression on Slovenia.

Igor Bavčar, during the trial of "the four" the president of the Committee for Protection of Human Rights, in the Demos government Minister of Internal Affairs, and leader of the coordination group that prepared and conducted the defence of Slovenia.

Miran Bogataj, in 1991 deputy to Slovenian defence minister Janez Janša, leader of the Slovenian delegation in negotiations with the YNA, member of the coordination group for the defence of Slovenia.

Ivan Borštner, former YNA officer, Slovenian patriot, convicted at the military court in the trial of "the four" (Janša, Borštner, Tasič, Zavrl), later set up the Slovenian intelligence service.

Stane Brovet, admiral of the YNA deputy to the Federal Secretary for People's Defence, one of the extremists at the top of the YNA, although Slovenian by birth.

France Bučar, president of the Slovenian Assembly that proclaimed independence, formerly a dissident.

Janez Drnovšek, in the Yugoslav period, president and member of the presidency of the SFRY, recalled from Belgrade by Slovenia in October 1991, member of the negotiation team on Brioni, later prime minister of the Republic of Slovenia and president of the Liberal Democratic Party.

247

Miran Frumen, senior agent of the State Security Service, interrogator and active in the prosecution of "the four".

Ivan Hočevar, commander of the Republic HQ of the Territorial Defence in Slovenia prior to the passing of the constitutional amendments, when the TO was still under SFRY military command; he disarmed the TO and stayed loyal to Belgrade.

Spomenka Hribar, member of the collegium of the Committee for Protection of Human Rights, delegate of the Democratic Party in the Slovenian Assembly.

Borisav Jović, president and member of the presidency of the SFRY from Serbia, opponent of Slovenian independence, supporter of intervention even with extreme means; one of the main culprits for the collapse of Yugoslavia through the pursuit of the Greater Serbia concept.

Jelko Kacin, during the preparations for independence, deputy to the Slovenian defence minister, later Minister of Information, member of the coordination group for the defence of Slovenia.

Veljko Kadijević, colonel general in the YNA, Federal Secretary for People's Defence (SFRY defence minister). He expected Slovenia to be an easy objective. After defeat, he paid for his mistake by resigning. He wavered between a Greater Serbian and pro-Yugoslav orientation.

Konrad Kolšek, lieutenant general in the YNA, commander of the military district, several days into the war in Slovenia relieved of duty, but stayed loyal to Belgrade.

Tone Krkovič, commander of Slovenia's special MORIS brigade, member of the coordination group for the defence of Slovenia, main organiser of the Manoeuvring Structure of the National Defence after the disarming of the Slovenian TO in May 1991.

Milan Kučan, president of the League of Communists of Slovenia, responsible for the arrest of Borštner, Janša and Tasič, president of the presidency of the Republic of Slovenia, in February 1991 as a member of the supreme command of the TO signed the "Declaration for Peace", in which he opposed the formation of a Slovenian army; later president of the Republic of Slovenia.

Sonja Lokar, member of the Central Committee of the League of Communists of Slovenia, executive Party secretary, at the parliamentary meeting strongly opposed Janša's and Bavčar's candidature for defence and interior minister respectively. Strong opponent of Slovenia's independence and the formation of a Slovenian army.

248

Andrej Lovšin, graduate of the military academy; following a brief stint in the YNA joined the polic force. When Janez Janša took over the defence department, Lovšin took charge of the intelligence section. One of the creators of the Slovenian intelligence service, and a member of the coordination group for the defence of Slovenia.

Emin Malkoć, colonel in the YNA, head of KOS in the Ljubljana Corps of the YNA, later killed in the aggression on Bosnia.

Branko Mamula, admiral in the YNA, on his initiative, bodies of the YNA security service began surveillance of Janez Janša and carried out the arrest and trial; later retired and replaced by Veljko Kadijević.

Ante Marković, president of the Federal Executive Council (Yugoslav prime minster), ordered the armed intervention of the YNA in Slovenia, directly responsible for the armed conflict in Slovenia; later a businessman in Austria.

Živko Mazić, colonel in the YNA, military prosecutor. First instituted proceedings against Janez Janša in 1985 for an article published in Mladina. Member of the command group for the arrests, and prosecutor in the trial against "the four".

Stipe Mesić, Croat, in May 1991 should have taken over as president of the SFRY presidency (to replace Borisav Jović), but the Serbs prevented his election.

Slobodan Milošević, president of Serbia, chief proponent of the Greater Serbia concept, a leading figure in the aggression on Slovenia, Croatia and Bosnia and Herzegovina.

Vladimir Miloševič, (Slovenian) commander of the Regional TO HQ in Styria, and as a member of the Slovenian negotiating group, kidnapped in the incident during negotiations with the YNA in Maribor.

Lojze Peterle, member of the Committee for Protection of Human Rights, leader of the Demos government during the period of independence, president of the Slovenian Christian Democrats, member of the negotiating group on Brioni, later foreign minister.

Jože Pučnik, former dissident under the communist regime, sentenced to 7 years imprisonment, president of the Demos coalition, presidential candidate in the first free elections in 1990. One of the main instigators of Slovenian independence.

Milan Ranić, captain in the YNA, military investigating judge during the trial of "the four".

Andrija Rašeta, lieutenant general in the YNA, deputy commander of the military district, leader of the YNA negotiating delegation, later replaced.

Dimitrij Rupel, doctor of social science, foreign minister in the Demos government; in the efforts towards earliest possible international recognition for Slovenia he led the country's diplomatic offensive.

Janez Slapar, acting head of the RHQ of the TO; major general; in October 1990 replaced Ivan Hočevar; member of the coordination group for the defence of Slovenia, later replaced because he would not observe the constitutional principle of depoliticising the Slovenian army.

Jožef Školč, president of the Slovenian Liberal Democratic Party (LDS), delegate of the Slovenian Assembly, signatory of the so-called "Declaration for Peace", opponent of the formation of Slovenia's own defence system and measures by which Slovenia could become a sovereign state. Later replaced as head of the LDS by Janez Drnovšek.

Martin Špegelj, Croatian defence minister at the time of the war for Slovenia, very soberly assessed the strategic position, and knew that Croatia would not be able to avoid conflict with the YNA and that the most favourable moment for action was being missed; later retired.

David Tasič, journalist of Mladina, convicted in the trial against "the four".

Franjo Tudjman, president of the Republic of Croatia, former YNA general and then dissident, opposed action to help Slovenia during the aggression by the YNA, president of the Croatian Democratic Union (HDZ).

Hans van den Broek, Dutch foreign minister, leader of the EC negotiators on Brioni (Brioni Declaration). At first indisposed to Slovenian independence, later changed his view and helped Slovenia towards international recognition.

Aleksander Vasiljević, colonel in the YNA, appointed as head of the command group for the arrests and prosecution of "the four". At the beginning of the eighties distinguished himself in KOS actions against the Albanians in Kosovo, later promoted to major general and head of KOS at the YNA GHQ, then retired.

Marjan Vidmar, major general in the YNA, commander of the YNA Ljubljana Corps, ordered the occupation of the old TO RHQ building (4 October 1990), later did not participate in the aggression on Slovenia.

Franci Zavrl, editor of Mladina, convicted in the trial of "the four".

Ciril Zlobec, member of the presidency of the Republic of Slovenia, signatory of the "Declaration for Peace", which was a "demand for rapid, unilateral disarmament"; in a telephone conversation with a foreign diplomatic representation gave away the secret date and contents of the constitutional measures for the take-over of effective power on 25 June 1991.

Jaša Zlobec, member of the LDS, Assembly delegate, major opponent of the formation of a Slovenian army, son of Ciril Zlobec; later ambassador to Belgium.

Delo newspaper, daily broadsheet with the largest circulation in Slovenia.

Dnevnik newspaper, daily tabloid with neo-communist orientation.

Mladina, weekly news magazine which wrote critically about all public affairs, primarily the YNA, but later became pro-Yugoslav and partly neo-communist; its chief editor cooperated with the communist State Security Service.

Mikro Ada, small computing company.

Nova Revija, magazine covering cultural and social issues. Around Nova Revija gathered a group of writers who formulated the Slovenian national programme, later realised by the Demos coalition of parties in observance of the plebiscite decision (90% of the inhabitants of Slovenia voted on 23 December 1990 for an independent state of Slovenia).

ABBREVIATIONS

DKP – diplomatic and consular representations
DV – state security
EGS – European Community
KOS – counter intelligence service
LPA – light anti-aircraft artillery
MES – mines and explosives
MTS – material and technical means
NZ – national defence
PDD – anti-commando action
POO – anti-armour defence
PVO – anti-aircraft defence (Serbo-Croat)
PZO – anti-aircraft defence (Slovenian)
RCOU – Republic Centre for Defence Training
RV – air force (Serbo-Croat)
SDV – state security in the communist system
TO – Territorial Defence
UDBA – communist secret police (original Serbo-Croat UDB)
UOLO – administrative body for people's defence
VEM – military unit of the police
ZIS – Federal Executive Council
ZK-GZJ – League of Communists – Movement for Yugoslavia
ZSLO – Federal Secretariat for People's Defence

IN DOCUMENTS:

BOiV – combat training and education (Serbo-Croat)
DEMOS – Slovenian democratic opposition
DS – social self-defence
GO – border section
HDZ – Croatian Democratic Union
MŠTO – City HQ for Territorial Defence
mtč – motorised brigade
OONP – operational engagement body
OOŠTO – operational body of the TO HQ
OS SFRJ – armed forces of the SFR Yugoslavia
OŠTO – Municipal HQ for Territorial Defence
OVO – armament and military equipment
KPR – assistant commander for political work
pmtd – motorised infantry division
ppp – light infantry regiment
PŠTO – Regional HQ for Territorial Defence
RCO – Republic Intelligence Centre
RSUP – Republic Secretariat for Administration and Justice
RŠTO – Republic HQ for Territorial Defence
SLO – General People's Defence (defence secretariat)
SSNO – Federal Secretariat for People's Defence (ZSLO in Slovenian)
VK – military command

Janez Janša

THE MAKING OF THE SLOVENIAN STATE 1988–1992
THE COLLAPSE OF YUGOSLAVIA

Edited by Aleksander Zorn
Translated by AMIDAS d.o.o. Ljubljana
Design by Jure Jančič
Technical editing by Franc Lenaršič
Published by Založba Mladinska Knjiga, Ljubljana 1994
For the publisher: Milan Matos
Chief editor: Irena Trenc Frelih
Printed by Tiskarna Mladinska Knjiga 1994

Original title: Janez Janša, Premiki
Nastajanje in obramba slovenske države 1988–92
© Založba Mladinska Knjiga 1992

CIP – Kataložni zapis o publikaciji
Narodna in univerzitetna knjižnica, Ljubljana

323(497.12)"1988/1992":929 Janša J.

JANŠA, Janez
    The making of the Slovenian state 1988–1992 : the collapse
of Yugoslavia / Janez Janša ; [translated by Amidas]. – Ljubljana :
Mladinska knjiga, 1994

Prevod dela: Premiki
ISBN 86-11-14157-1

40037376

Po mnenju ministrstva za kulturo Republike Slovenije št. 415–79/93 z dne 10. 1. 1994 se šteje ta knjiga po 13. točki tarifne
številke 3 Tarife davka od prometa proizvodov in storitev med proizvode, za katere se plačuje 5-odstotni davek od prometa
proizvodov in storitev.